D1556937

WHO IS JAMES K. POLK?

American Presidential Elections

MICHAEL NELSON

JOHN M. MCCARDELL, JR.

WHO IS JAMES K. POLK?

THE PRESIDENTIAL ELECTION OF 1844

MARK R. CHEATHEM

UNIVERSITY PRESS OF KANSAS

Portions of chapters 1 and 3 appeared as "'It has caused me considerable embarrassment and not a little pain': The Ruptured Relationship of Martin Van Buren and James K. Polk," in *James K. Polk and His Time: Essays at the Conclusion of the Polk Project*, ed. Michael D. Cohen, and are reprinted by permission of Tennessee University Press.

Published by the University Press of Kansas (Lawrence, Kansas 66045), which was organized by the Kansas Board of Regents and is operated and funded by Emporia State University, Fort Hays State University, Kansas State University, Pittsburg State University, the University of Kansas, and Wichita State University

© 2023 by the University Press of Kansas

All rights reserved

Library of Congress Cataloging-in-Publication Data

Names: Cheathem, Mark Renfred, author.

Title: Who is James K. Polk? : the presidential election of 1844 / Mark R. Cheathem.

Other titles: Presidential election of 1844

Description: Lawrence, Kansas : University Press of Kansas, 2023. | Series: American presidential elections | Includes bibliographical references and index.

Identifiers: LCCN 2023004233 (print) | LCCN 2023004234 (ebook) ISBN 9780700635733 (cloth) ISBN 9780700635740 (ebook)

Subjects: LCSH: Presidents—United States—Election—1844. | Presidential candidates—United States—History—19th century. | Political campaigns—United States—History—19th century. | Polk, James K. (James Knox), 1795–1849. | United States—Politics and government—1841–1845.

Classification: LCC E400 .C48 2024 (print) | LCC E400 (ebook) | DDC 324.973/061—dc23/eng/20230313

LC record available at https://lccn.loc.gov/2023004233.

LC ebook record available at https://lccn.loc.gov/2023004234.

British Library Cataloguing-in-Publication Data is available.

For David

CONTENTS

"Who is James K. Polk?" his opponents shouted during the presidential campaign of 1844. The question was more than rhetorical. Though a candidate of both experience and reputation, the Tennessean seemed an improbable nominee. Indeed, the "smart money" and the conventional wisdom in the spring of 1844 anticipated a contest between former president Martin Van Buren, defeated for reelection in 1840, and Henry Clay, beloved and reviled, loser in 1824 and 1832 and seeking what appeared to be his best shot at an office that had so long eluded him. Leaders of the by now reasonably well-established parties planned their strategies accordingly.

Looming over the impending campaign, the question of Texas—and the larger question of territorial expansion—threatened to disrupt an orderly nominating process. Hoping to avoid this issue, the leading candidates appeared to agree that postponement would best maintain both partisan and sectional harmony, since otherwise the slavery question would be revived, to what outcome no one could predict. Better to conduct the election on more familiar, less divisive issues—tariffs for example—and stimulate voter turnout with songs, rallies, marches, and ballyhoo.

In the final days of his presidency, discredited by the Whig Party that had chosen him to be President William Henry Harrison's vice president, John Tyler managed to arrange the annexation of Texas by a joint congressional resolution. This changed everything and turned the presidential contest of 1844 into a far more consequential election than what might originally had been anticipated.

Giving shape and direction to a surprisingly complex narrative, Mark Cheathem brings to bear his deep understanding of the politics of mid-nineteenth century America. The author of several important studies of elections and campaign techniques in the so-called Age of Jackson, as well as the editor of the papers of Martin Van Buren, Cheathem convincingly explains what went as planned (almost nothing), what went wrong, and why. He thus broadens, deepens, and enriches our understanding of this election.

One clear revelation in this rich new study involves the ability of a still primitive party system to manage internal dissent. Texas annexation revealed the fragility of party loyalties when sectional interests arose. Moreover, the difficulty of promoting a front-running candidacy as conditions changed demonstrated that the party system at the time was more a result of shifting coalitions and loyalties than of deep principles or firm personal allegiances. Clay managed nomination by acclamation, though the rifts within his party damaged his candidacy. Polk emerged as the "dark horse" nominee, riding far more than controlling the expansionist wave.

Add to these conditions a small but growing political antislavery movement and the potential spoiler candidacy of James Birney, an improbable but, until his untimely death, a surprisingly appealing campaign by the Mormon leader Joseph Smith, and an incipient nativist movement concerned over the impact of a new immigrant population, and the wisdom that had seemed so conventional early in 1844 turned out to have been fundamentally mistaken. Cheathem guides readers through these roiling waters with a steady hand and insightful eye, paying particular attention to a robust and engaging political culture.

Polk emerged victorious with a plurality of over 40,000 votes in an election when an extraordinary 78.9 percent of the electorate turned out. By mid-November 1845, voting Americans could reasonably claim to know just who it was they voted for or voted against. "The republic is safe," wrote one commentator on the election's outcome. More prescient was a letter to Polk from a supporter in November 1844: "Your troubles," he warned, "now begin."

"Who the hell is James K. Polk?" Decades later, Americans would remember that everyone in 1844 asked this question. Some examples of it circulated during the 1844 presidential campaign, but this profane version appeared more frequently in later decades. However the question was phrased in 1844, Whigs used it to cast doubt on Polk's readiness to assume the presidency; Democrats used it as an opportunity to explain why their candidate was the right choice to lead the nation.[1]

The reality was that anyone paying attention to US politics during the twenty years before 1844 knew who James K. Polk was. He had served fourteen years in the House of Representatives; two of those years were as chair of the powerful Ways and Means Committee, and four were as Speaker of the House. Polk left Congress to run for governor of Tennessee in 1839. His victory in that contest and his reputation as a staunch defender of the principles of former president and Democratic statesman Andrew Jackson led Democrats to consider replacing Vice President Richard M. Johnson with Polk on the party's 1840 ticket. This substitution did not take place, however, and President Martin Van Buren, running alone, lost his reelection bid that year. Polk's political career appeared to be on a similar downward trajectory when he lost the 1841 gubernatorial election and the one two years later.[2]

Polk was not unknown in 1844. He just seemed to be an unlikely presidential candidate given the availability of more recognizable options. The Democrats had a list of notable names from which to select their nominee. Three of the most obvious choices were former president and party cofounder Martin Van Buren; former vice president Richard M. Johnson; and Secretary of State (and former vice president) John C. Calhoun. Others on the list included James Buchanan, a US senator and former minister to Russia; Lewis Cass, a former secretary of war and minister to France; and naval war hero Charles Stewart. Given the assumption that Van Buren would be the party's nominee and with the notoriety of some of the other names available, Polk's dark horse victory at the Democratic national convention served notice that 1844 was not going to follow the traditional campaign narrative many members of his party expected.[3]

The other major political party, the Whigs, considered several candidates also, including Senator Daniel Webster, but Henry Clay was the early favorite to be their standard-bearer. A former House Speaker himself, Clay had built a national reputation not only by serving as secretary of state and senator, but also by using his congressional positions to negotiate crucial sectional compromises during the Missouri crisis of 1819–1821 and the nullification crisis of 1832–1833. The Kentuckian was a perennial presidential contender, running in 1824 and 1832, and narrowly losing the Whig nomination in 1840. Considered the preeminent Whig by many contemporaries, Clay, after a series of near-misses, seemed poised to ascend to the presidency.

Complicating things for both Polk and Clay were three other presidential nominees. None of them possessed a viable chance at winning the election, but each one threatened to peel voters away from Democrats and Whigs alike. President John Tyler was a man without a party, the Whigs having expelled him early in his term, but he still hoped to find enough support among Democrats to stay in office. At the very least, he presented Polk with competition among southern voters. Liberty Party candidate James G. Birney was too radically antislavery to expect an electoral win, but his appeal to northern voters was significant enough that it might swing states against Clay. Finally, the prophet Joseph Smith had built a small but influential voting base among the members of the Church of Jesus Christ of Latter-day Saints (commonly referred to as the Mormons). As with Birney, his candidacy had no chance of succeeding, but the significant Mormon presence in Illinois could potentially affect that state's votes, with consequences for the national election.

The stakes for all the candidates in 1844—experienced, underestimated, and unexpected alike—were high, as the United States was undergoing a political transition. The partisan battles of the past few years, fought over economic issues such as banking and the tariff, political corruption, and personal character, remained important. But debates over slavery, nativism, and Manifest Destiny had gained significance, with the different forms of cultural politics that had increasingly become prominent since the 1824 presidential campaign framing all of these issues for voters.

"Who was James K. Polk?" He was the Democratic Party nominee who offered his full-throated support of Manifest Destiny. He was the Democratic presidential candidate who rode into office on a wave of emotionally charged political issues, such as the annexation of Texas, nativism, and slavery, and who took advantage of refined electioneering techniques. He was also the Democratic president responsible for exacerbating the sectional divide that existed in the mid-1840s, one that eventually led to civil war.

ACKNOWLEDGMENTS

Juggling faculty and administrative responsibilities, a presidential papers project, and family health issues in the middle of a global pandemic meant that this book took longer to write than I expected. I appreciate the patience of David Congdon at the University Press of Kansas as he waited for its completion. Also at UPK, Mike Nelson and Fred Woodward supported the project at its earliest stages, and John McCardell, Amy Greenberg, and an anonymous reader provided close readings that greatly improved the final draft.

The following individuals and institutions assisted me by providing access to necessary documents and by answering important questions: the staff at the Church History Library, The Church of Jesus Christ of Latter-day Saints; Jennie Cole and Hannah Costelle, Filson Historical Society; Mutahara Mobashar, Library of Congress; Kelley Sirko, Nashville Public Library/Metro Archives; Meredith Mann, New York Public Library; McKenzie Lemhouse, South Caroliniana Library, University of South Carolina; Lindsay Hager and Kevin Cason, Tennessee State Library and Archives; Terese Austin, William L. Clements Library, University of Michigan; Matthew E. Guillen, Virginia Historical Society; Carolyn Wilson, William and Mary Libraries; and Jessica Becker, Yale University Library. Thank you all for your commitment to serving the public.

Other scholars were also generous in sharing documents and knowledge about specific topics, specifically Eric Brooks, curator at Ashland, The Henry Clay Estate; Tom Coens, research associate professor and associate editor at the Papers of Andrew Jackson; Matthew Costello, vice president of the David M. Rubenstein National Center for White House History and senior historian for the White House Historical Association; and Amrita Chakrabarti Myers, Ruth N. Halls Associate Professor, Departments of History and Gender Studies, Indiana University.

Several friends and colleagues read the entire manuscript before it made its way to the publisher. Tom Balcerski lent his extensive knowledge of the

Democratic Party to strengthen parts of my argument. Michael Cohen is one of the most talented documentary editors I know, and his attention to detail was invaluable. I took a chance that Chris Leahy, whom I had never met, would be willing to lend me his expert knowledge on John Tyler and his presidency, and I am thankful he was gracious enough to accept my request. I admire Spencer McBride for his personal kindness, scholarly generosity, and accessible writing; his familiarity with the history of Mormonism helped me avoid several embarrassing mistakes. Beth Salerno was an unflinching critic of my tunnel vision and blind spots. Over the years, I have learned to trust her judgment not just because she is a careful scholar but also because she is an intuitive friend. Laura Ellyn Smith is a tremendous historian whose extensive knowledge of the era's politics prevented me from retreating into historiographical stodginess. Mike Trapani lent his expertise in New York politics to help me understand the role of nativism in the Empire State. I also want to thank John Belohlavek, Walter R. Borneman, and Mark A. Johnson for their evaluation of Mark R. Cheathem, "'It has caused me considerable embarrassment and not a little pain': The Ruptured Relationship of Martin Van Buren and James K. Polk," in *Polk and His Time: Essays at the Conclusion of the Correspondence of James K. Polk*, ed. Michael D. Cohen (Knoxville: University of Tennessee Press, 2022), and the press for permission to use portions of the essay in this book.

Cumberland University has been my professional home since 2008. It has undergone many changes over the years, but one constant has been the support I have received. President Paul Stumb, Provost and VPAA Bill McKee, and Deans Laurie Dishman, Eric Cummings, and Jenny Mason have been indefatigable in their commitment to my research agenda. I am especially grateful for the summer research stipends I received from the president's office and for a 2021 C. William McKee Faculty/Staff Research Grant. My history colleagues—Rick Bell, Sean Bortz, Natalie Inman, Sean McDaniel, and Tara Mielnik—have tolerated my many idiosyncrasies. Paige Hrobsky, who helped organize my sources, deserves a Dundie award for "most reliable student research assistant." This book would not have been possible without the editorial staff of the Papers of Martin Van Buren at both Cumberland and the University of Virginia: Katie Blizzard, James Bradley, Erica Cavanaugh, David Gregory, Katie Hatton, Max Matherne, Jennifer Stertzer, and Andrew Wiley; Cumberland graduate assistants Josh Williams, Daniel Barr, Ally Johnson, and Charles Ware; and the student workers at both universities.

I would be remiss if I did not acknowledge the important role that John

Marszalek, the retired executive director of the Ulysses S. Grant Association, and Connie Lester, associate professor of history at the University of Central Florida and director of RICHES of Central Florida, have played in my life. Two decades after they shepherded me through the completion of my dissertation, John and Connie remain my models of professionalism. I would not be the historian I am without their mentorship.

It is all too easy for me to lose myself in my identity as a historian; thankfully, I have friends and family who keep me grounded in what matters most. Thanks to the Bandys, Brassers, Hilperts, Meltons, Nadeaus, Risners, Robinsons, Sharps, and Willises for providing respite from trying times. Mom, Dad, Lisa, and Eric, thank you for your love and support. It has been a rough few years, Amber, but I am glad that we are making the journey together. Laney and Alli, I am so proud of the way you have navigated the challenges of transitioning from childhood to adulthood. Finally, this book is dedicated to you, David. Our walks with Piper, conversations about the MCU, and time spent cheering the Preds are some of my favorite moments. I love you.

Unless noted otherwise, all quotations, including any errors or emphasis, are given as they were represented in the cited source.

ABBREVIATIONS

BDUSC	*Biographical Directory of the United States Congress.* https://bioguide.congress.gov/.
CAJ	*Correspondence of Andrew Jackson.* 7 vols. Edited by John Spencer Bassett and J. Franklin Jameson. Washington, DC: Carnegie Institute of Washington, 1926–1935.
CHL	Church History Library, The Church of Jesus Christ of Latter-day Saints, Salt Lake City, Utah.
CJKP	*Correspondence of James K. Polk.* 14 vols. Edited by Michael David Cohen et al. Knoxville: University of Tennessee Press, 1969–2021.
DLC	Library of Congress, Washington, DC.
HDJEMD	*Historical Dictionary of the Jacksonian Era and Manifest Destiny.* 2nd ed. Edited by Mark R. Cheathem and Terry Corps. New York: Rowman & Littlefield, 2016.
JSP	Joseph Smith Papers. https://www.josephsmithpapers.org/.
JSP:C50	*The Joseph Smith Papers: Administrative Records, Council of Fifty, Minutes, March 1844–January 1846.* Edited by Matthew J. Grow et al. Salt Lake City: The Church Historian's Press, 2016.
JSP:D	*The Joseph Smith Papers: Documents.* 12 vols. Edited by David W. Grua et al. Salt Lake City: The Church Historian's Press, 2013–2021.
JSP:J	*The Joseph Smith Papers: Journals.* 3 vols. Edited by Andrew H. Hedges et al. Salt Lake City: The Church Historian's Press, 2008–2015.
LJGB	*Letters of James Gillespie Birney, 1831–1857.* 2 vols. Edited by Dwight L. Dumond. New York: D. Appleton-Century, 1938.
PAJ	*The Papers of Andrew Jackson.* 11 vols. to date. Edited by Michael E. Woods et al. Knoxville: University of Tennessee Press, 1980–.
PDW:Corr.	*The Papers of Daniel Webster: Correspondence.* 7 vols. Edited by

Charles M. Wiltse et al. Hanover, NH: University Press of New England, 1974–1986.

PDW:Dipl. *The Papers of Daniel Webster: Diplomatic Papers.* 2 vols. Edited by Kenneth E Shoemaker et al. Hanover, NH: University Press of New England, 1983, 1987.

PHC *The Papers of Henry Clay.* 11 vols. Edited by Melba Porter Hay et al. Lexington: University Press of Kentucky, 1959–1992.

PJCC *The Papers of John C. Calhoun.* 28 vols. Edited by Clyde N. Wilson et al. Columbia: University of South Carolina Press, 1959–2003.

PMVB *Papers of Martin Van Buren.* Digital ed. https:// vanburenpapers.org/. Edited by Mark R. Cheathem et al. Cumberland University. Lebanon, TN. (Document numbers are indicated in parentheses.)

WHO IS JAMES K. POLK?

1

"A POLITICAL SATURNALIA"
JACKSONIAN PARTY POLITICS, 1824–1840

Presidential elections in the United States have had the effect of shaping political generations. Franklin D. Roosevelt's 1932 election brought hope to Americans shaken by a global depression, and John F. Kennedy's 1960 election inspired the nation literally to reach for the stars. Ronald Reagan's election in 1980 injected modern-day conservatism into the country's bloodstream, while Barack Obama's election in 2008 revived the long-promised idea of a racially inclusive society.

The 1824 presidential election was one such influential election. That year, five candidates—Secretary of State John Quincy Adams, Secretary of War John C. Calhoun, Speaker of the House Henry Clay, Secretary of the Treasury William H. Crawford, and Senator Andrew Jackson—competed for the honor of serving as chief executive. When the dust settled, the fifty-seven-year-old Jackson, a former army general who had achieved fame by defeating the British at New Orleans in 1815, appeared to be voters' clear choice to become president. He won the most electoral votes, the most popular votes, and the most states in 1824. Unfortunately for Jackson, the US Constitution defines victory as a majority in the electoral college, which he did not possess. The constitutional remedy—sending the election to the House—resulted in Adams, not Jackson, winning the presidency. Jackson might have been willing to settle into retirement at his Tennessee plantation, but for one thing: a few days after Adams was declared the winner, he appointed Clay as his secretary of state. This decision, ostensibly anointing the

Kentuckian as Adams's successor, infuriated Jackson and his supporters. The election outcome, and the resulting backlash, led the political generation that followed to continue refining the meaning of democracy in the young republic.[1]

Jackson's supporters began laying the groundwork for their vision of democracy almost immediately. They called the alleged agreement between Adams and Clay a "corrupt bargain" and slammed the new administration as aristocratic and unrepresentative. Adams's pedigree, his international diplomacy, and his cabinet experience lent credibility to the charges of elitism that Jacksonians lodged against the new president. Born in 1767, he came from a notable Massachusetts lineage, his father, John Adams, having succeeded George Washington as president. The younger Adams had served as minister to four different European countries and had also been a US senator. As President James Monroe's secretary of state, the bald-pated Adams held the position that historically had been a stepping stone to the presidency: Jefferson, Madison, and Monroe had all headed the State Department before becoming president, the latter two going directly from the one position into the other.[2]

Clay presented a different kind of target for administration critics. Almost a decade younger than Adams, he lacked his rival's family connections; nevertheless, Clay had enjoyed a meteoric rise to prominence. He completed the terms of two US senators after they resigned prematurely. Clay then served in the House, becoming Speaker in his first term, the youngest to hold that position to that point. Near the end of the War of 1812, he joined Adams in Ghent, Belgium, as one of the five commissioners tasked with negotiating a peace treaty with Great Britain. Clay returned to the House (and the Speaker position) after the war, where he was instrumental in passing legislation that formed the basis for his "American System," an economic program that included a national bank, a protective tariff, and federally funded internal improvements. The Kentuckian also played a prominent role in bringing about the end of the Missouri crisis of 1819–21, which concerned the legality of slavery in the proposed state of Missouri and the unorganized portions of the Louisiana Territory. Clay's work to quiet sectional tensions earned him the complimentary sobriquet "the Great Compromiser." These successes, along with the Speaker's persuasive rhetoric, delivered with his wide-mouthed smirk and theatrical style, appeared to make him a shoo-in to become president sooner rather than later. But Clay had an Achilles' heel. Adams, who spent several months with the Kentuckian in Ghent, observed several times over the years that

Clay was "proficient" in the ways of the world. "His morals, public and private," Adams wrote on one occasion, "are loose." During the 1824 campaign, fellow House member Willie P. Mangum noted the lack "of Moral confidence" that some had in the Speaker. Clay's reputation as a carousing, immoral gambler, which hounded his entire political career, made "Prince Hal," as he was sometimes known, an especially juicy target for Jacksonians who wanted to highlight the corruption of the Adams administration.[3]

Adams and Clay represented the Washington, DC, establishment; their opponents wanted someone from outside the ruling elite to run in 1828. They chose Jackson. The Tennessean was not a complete outsider, having served briefly in both the House and the Senate, but his political experience paled in comparison to that of Adams and Clay. Jackson's tough and resilient military leadership during the War of 1812 earned him the nickname "Old Hickory," and his January 8, 1815, victory over the British led Americans to refer to him as the "Hero of New Orleans" for the rest of his life. But Jackson was also controversial. His treatment of Native Americans during and after the war and his illegal invasion of Spanish Florida in 1818 caused some political leaders, including Calhoun and Clay, to view him with trepidation. Wracked by the effects of dysentery and two bullets obtained in a duel and a street fight, Jackson, older than Adams by a few months, still made a formidable challenger as the nation prepared for the 1828 election.[4]

Two men helped organize support for Jackson's 1828 campaign. One was Martin Van Buren. Born in 1782 and coming from a modest Dutch background, the New Yorker had worked his way up in state politics without many of the inherited advantages of his opponents, eventually making his way into the US Senate in 1821. In the 1824 election, Van Buren supported William H. Crawford from Georgia, believing him to be the purest representation of Jeffersonian Republican ideology. With Crawford in retirement and no longer viable as a candidate for 1828, Van Buren realized that Jackson made a fitting challenger to Adams, whose administration, he believed, was diverging from true Jeffersonian democracy. To overcome sectionalism, Van Buren proposed a party composed of "the planters of the South and the plain Republicans of the north" and identified Jackson as the best option to serve as its candidate in 1828.[5]

Born the same year as Van Buren, John C. Calhoun joined him in supporting Jackson. The South Carolinian, with dark, tousled hair, long sideburns, and a firm mouth, already possessed the penetrating stare for which he would become famous. He had served nearly seven years in the House before joining Monroe's cabinet in 1817. Adams considered him "above all sectional and factious prejudices more than any other statesman of this Union with whom I have ever acted." A lot would change in the coming decades, but at the time of uniting with Jackson, Calhoun was recognized as a nationalist. Calhoun found himself in an awkward position in the 1828 campaign: having won the vice presidency in 1824, he was serving along-side Clay in the Adams administration.[6]

The Jacksonian coalition that formed in the 1828 campaign followed the ideological lead of the Jeffersonian Republicans by prioritizing states' rights over the national government; a rural, agricultural society over an urban, industrial society; and the liberty of free white men to practice representative democracy over the dictation of an elitist political class. Jacksonians began calling themselves "Democrats," but they often still referred to themselves as Republicans to indicate their Jeffersonian roots. Whatever their name, Jackson and his supporters exacted their revenge in the 1828 presidential election. Old Hickory won a convincing electoral victory, Calhoun earned a second consecutive term as vice president, and Van Buren moved from his newly elected position as New York governor to take charge of the State Department.[7]

Having achieved his goal of winning the White House, Jackson found that governing as president presented a different set of problems. One was simply getting along with his advisors. Early in his administration, Jackson's cabinet split over whether to socialize with John Eaton, his close friend and secretary of war, and his new wife, the recently widowed Margaret O'Neale Timberlake. Washington women questioned Margaret's adherence to gender expectations for women, the propriety of her relationship with John during and after her previous marriage, and her sense of entitlement as a new cabinet wife. Washington men found themselves caught in this "petticoat war," with Jackson and Van Buren backing the Eatons, and Calhoun and most of the other cabinet members, along with their respective wives, opposing them, or at least not actively supporting them. Jackson let his advisors know in no uncertain terms that passivity in this matter was the same as opposition. By the time the controversy ended in 1831, Eaton and Van Buren had voluntarily resigned, and the other cabinet members (save one) had been forced to leave office. Jackson blamed Calhoun for conspiring to undermine his political agenda by ostracizing the Eatons, while Van Buren's support of the couple endeared him to the president. The bond between Jackson and Van Buren was so strong that Old Hickory supported the New Yorker's replacement of Calhoun on the 1832 Democratic ticket. The thin, rigid Jackson and the stout, pragmatic Van Buren made an unlikely pairing, but their political partnership worked. Given the outcome of the Eaton affair, there is little wonder why the rivalry between Calhoun and Van Buren continued for the rest of their political careers.[8]

The Democratic Party suffered from factionalism in other ways too. Southern Democrats, for example, were more full-throated in their defense of slavery than their non-slaveowning northern counterparts, who usually acquiesced to pro-slavery demands in order to maintain partisan power over their political opponents. Southern and western Democrats also tended to favor banks and internal improvements more than northern Democrats. The Locofocos, who supported policies that aided the urban working classes, represented another distinct faction. When it came to carrying out the party's agenda during Jackson's administrations, however, Democrats tended to rally behind the president. Those who did not want to conform, such as Calhoun, found themselves increasingly alienated from the party.[9]

National opposition to the Jacksonian Democrats took a few years to organize into something concrete. The Anti-Masonic Party was a minor opposition group that emerged during this period. It held the nation's first national nominating convention in 1831 and ran a ticket in the 1832 presidential election. The Anti-Masons' conspiratorial focus on opposing Freemasonry and the politicians associated with the fraternal order limited their national influence, especially in an era when many leading politicians were active or former members. Another anti-Jacksonian political faction consisted of adherents to states' rights ideology. By privileging states' rights over nationalism, they followed the example of the Old Republicans, a group of southern conservatives that had splintered from the Republican Party in the early 1800s because they believed it had strayed from its Jeffersonian origins of limited government. Calhoun, once a nationalist, became the face of this movement in the 1830s. His alienation from the Democrats during Jackson's first term came in part because of his public support of nullification, a doctrine positing that the individual states had the obligation to void what they considered unconstitutional national laws. States' rights politicians consistently found success in the southern states during this era, but they were unable to consolidate power nationally.[10]

The task of organizing a formidable opposition party to combat the Democrats fell to the Adams–Clay faction, commonly referred to as the National Republicans between 1828 and 1834. This group challenged the Democrats in the 1832 election by running Clay and former US representative John Sergeant of Pennsylvania against Jackson and Van Buren. The National Repub-

lican ticket went down in defeat, but it helped spur a more organized opposition party in Jackson's second term. During the 1833–34 winter congressional
session, Clay enlisted Calhoun and Adams to help do battle with the president. A reluctant Senator Daniel Webster of Massachusetts shortly joined
them in their efforts to combat "the mad pranks of old Andrew." Members
of this new opposition party took on the name "Whigs" as a direct nod to the
British political party that stood up to the English monarchy. Beyond the uni-
fying principle of opposing Jackson, the Whigs wanted a centralized, powerful national government, and they embraced Clay's American System. They
also saw themselves as the party meant to inject religion into government to
better society.[11]

As did the Democrats, the Whigs struggled to balance the competing
interests their party embodied. They shared many of the Anti-Masons' inclinations toward moral reform and often allied with them in New York and
New England. Someone like Adams, who became a leading Whig voice,
even aligned with the Anti-Masons for a time. But Anti-Masons also held
the Whigs at arm's length, particularly at the state level. They found it difficult to see Whigs as anything other than part of the structural problem
with US politics that privileged power over principle. That some prominent
Democratic and Whig leaders, such as Jackson and Clay, were Masons was
proof enough that the two main parties were not that different from one
another. As with the Democrats, southern states' rightists were another faction that sometimes proved problematic for the Whig Party.[12]

Despite their disparate parts, and despite not agreeing on the nomination of a national ticket, the Whigs mounted a significant challenge to
Van Buren's candidacy in the 1836 presidential election. Three Whig candidates—Webster, War of 1812 hero William Henry Harrison, and Senator
Hugh Lawson White of Tennessee—split the party's votes against the Democrat. Van Buren's electoral college margin of victory was 170 to 113 against
his Whig opponents, but the popular vote was close. (South Carolina, as it
regularly did during these years, gave its thirteen electoral votes to an independent candidate.) Only about 28,000 votes (out of nearly 1.5 million)
separated Van Buren from his combined Whig opposition, and a switch of
just a few thousand votes in either Pennsylvania or Virginia would have led
to a House election like the one in 1824.[13]

"We may anticipate comparative peace & quiet in his day; for nearly all
the exciting questions of the time have been happily settled by the bold &
commanding genius of General Jackson," Pennsylvania Democrat James
Buchanan declared about Van Buren's pending administration. Buchanan

was dead wrong, of course. Many of the issues with which Jackson wrestled during his eight years in the presidency—economics, corruption, personal character, slavery, immigration, and Manifest Destiny—carried over into Van Buren's administration. They varied in degree and importance, but these concerns also proved to be many of the same ones that faced the electorate in the 1844 presidential campaign.[14]

ECONOMICS

Economic issues played a significant role in how parties prioritized policy during the Jacksonian period. Two concerns in particular shaped the politics of the Jackson and Van Buren presidencies. The first was the tariff. In 1828, white southerners had been so enraged by the passage of a tariff bill that they called it the "Tariff of Abominations." The tariff remained a political flashpoint for white southerners once Jackson became president. They believed it unfairly taxed their region, which was dependent on imported goods. They also disliked the idea that the national government might use tariff revenue to fund the colonization movement, which proposed compensating enslavers who freed the African Americans they held in bondage, with the intention of sending them to Africa.[15]

The tariff controversy almost led to civil war during Jackson's first term. Following passage of a new tariff in 1832, South Carolina refused to enforce both the 1828 and the 1832 tariffs within its borders. The president accused Calhoun, who had by this time publicly declared his support of nullification, and other like-minded South Carolinians of bringing their state "to the brink of insurrection and treason," and he admonished them that "disunion by armed force is *treason*." Over the winter of 1832–1833, a congressional coalition, which included Calhoun and Clay (now a senator), put together a compromise that gradually reduced the tariff rates, averted a possible civil war, and kept Van Buren from having to address a similar crisis during his presidency.[16]

A second consequential economic issue was Old Hickory's fight with the Second Bank of the United States (the Bank). During his first term, Jackson repeatedly indicated, privately and publicly, that he was convinced that the institution was part of a corrupt conspiracy intent on taking down both himself and American democracy. Indicative of this mindset was his belief that the Bank's president, Nicholas Biddle, had used the institution's money to try to swing the 1828 election in Adams's favor. Jackson's conflict with the Bank broke out into the open in 1832 when its congressional supporters passed legislation that would give the institution a new twenty-year charter, four years before its current contract expired. Jackson vetoed this recharter bill. In his message accompanying the veto, the president blamed foreign investors in part, but he focused on how the Bank and its supporters pitted "section against section, interest against interest, and man against man, in a fearful commotion which threatens to shake the foundations of our Union." For that reason, citizens needed to oppose "any prostitution of our Government to the advancement of the few at the expense of the many."[17]

Jackson's veto message kicked off the Bank War that consumed his second term. In 1833, he decided to remove the government's deposits from the Bank to starve "the hydra of corruption" of its main source of funds and "preserve the morals of the people, the freedom of the press, and the purity of the elective franchise." The deposits were instead to be placed in "pet banks" selected by Jackson. When Secretary of the Treasury William Duane refused to remove the deposits, the president fired him, replacing him with Marylander Roger B. Taney, who carried out Jackson's orders without trepidation. This decision brought down the wrath of the president's opponents. In the winter of 1833–1834, Biddle called in the Bank's loans, which precipitated an economic recession. Anti-Jacksonian congressmen attacked the president, with Clay leading the charge by introducing censure resolutions against both Jackson and Taney for overstepping their constitutional authority and inaugurating "a revolution" of despotism that would destroy the United States. When the censure resolutions passed along partisan lines, Jackson responded with a "protest" message asserting that the president was the "direct representative" of the people. He received some vindication when the Democratic-controlled Senate expunged his censure right before he left office in early 1837.[18]

The political shockwaves of the Bank War carried over into Van Buren's administration. Shortly after taking office, the United States plunged into an unprecedented economic depression for which neither he nor anyone else had a solution. Often referred to as the singular Panic of 1837, this depression was actually a series of economic crises that began in 1837, abated in 1838, then reemerged in 1839. The origins of the 1837 panic were partly attributable to the Bank War, but other internal and external circumstances, such as overextended credit, surplus government revenue, lower cotton prices, and a reversal of foreign investment, were more consequential. These dire circumstances forced Van Buren to prioritize economic concerns throughout his administration. After years of debate and maneuvering, Congress finally passed an independent Treasury bill in 1840 that created a subtreasury system requiring the payment of specie for all government transactions.[19]

CORRUPTION

Rooting out corruption also consumed Americans in the early decades of the republic. The belief that virtue among the citizenry was disappearing, that political leaders were plotting to take away what belonged to the American people, that the nation's future was in the balance every presidential election cycle—little wonder that Americans embraced an apocalyptic interpretation of political actions that is familiar today. This conspiratorial mindset also explains why many Jacksonians reacted viscerally to the controversial outcome of the 1824 election.[20]

Jackson's personal conspiracism and his experience with the "corrupt bargain" prompted him to enter the presidency determined to fight against corruption in the national government. Previous administrations, he explained, had allowed appointees to waste money and assume that their office was "a vested right" they could pass on to their children as hereditary property. Appointees had also used their positions for "selfish & electioneering purposes" to oppose democratic elections. No more—Jackson was putting a stop to this abuse with a patronage policy he called "rotation in office," that is, making government appointments based on political loyalty.[21]

The president's critics saw things differently. They called his patronage policy a "spoils system" and pronounced him a despot. Jackson's desire to reward loyal supporters with government appointments, Clay pronounced, made him "in fact, if not in form, a monarch." The president's opponents used this accusation of despotic behavior to great effect in Jackson's second term. They produced a political cartoon entitled "King Andrew the First" that depicted him in a monarch's robe and crown, holding a scepter, with the torn Constitution under his feet. One version included descriptions of the ways in which Jackson had acted like a king. He had "placed himself above the laws," sought to "destroy our currency," and ignored "the will of the People" when appointing government officials. "Shall he reign over us," the cartoon's creator asked, "or shall the PEOPLE RULE?"[22]

Ultimately, even though Jackson made significant patronage replacements in certain high-level positions and in non-Democratic geographic areas, his changes were comparable in number to those of his predecessors. Some of his appointments, however, exhibited what the president's critics deemed Jackson's indifference to corruption. Samuel Swartwout, for example, used his position as collector of the port of New York to defraud the government of approximately $1.2 million over nine years in the Jackson and Van Buren administrations. In 1834, Jackson had to replace Postmaster-General William T. Barry, the lone cabinet holdover from the Eaton

Andrew Jackson's actions against the Second Bank of the United States galvanized his political enemies into an organized opposition party called the Whigs. (Courtesy of the Library of Congress)

affair, after congressional investigations found the post office's finances "in a state of utter derangement." Corruption also permeated the removal of Native Americans during Jackson's administration. It was so rampant that relocating the Choctaw Indians west cost the United States $2 million dollars more than the estimate for the entire removal process.[23]

Jackson's critics also pointed to his propensity for favoring personal loyalty over national interest. The most dramatic example was John Eaton, but Van Buren presented an even juicier target. "Mr. Van Buren is the direct representative of the patronage of the General Government," opposition newspaper editor Duff Green wrote during Jackson's second term. "It is to it, and to it alone, that he owes his standing in the party." The same Whig cartoon depicting Jackson as "King Andrew" called Van Buren his *"Prime Minister* and *Heir Apparent."* Whigs nicknamed the bewhiskered New Yorker the "sly fox" and the "Little Magician," allusions to Van Buren's supposed preference for working secretly behind the scenes to further his career. His self-immolation during the Eaton affair, his appointment as minister to Britain, his selection as Jackson's running mate in 1832, and his presidential nomination for the 1836 election—all solidified the Whigs' perception of Van Buren as a man who would sacrifice every principle on the altar of his political ambition.[24]

Van Buren's presidency did not save him from these partisan accusations. If anything, he became a Whig caricature of an elitist fop. By the time Van Buren, who grew up the son of a taverner, ran for reelection in 1840, Whigs had turned him into the epitome of Democratic corruption. The most dramatic rhetorical evisceration of the president came in April 1840. As House members began debating an appropriations bill, Pennsylvania representative Charles Ogle introduced an amendment intended to remove funding for the White House, including repairs, furnishings, landscaping, and upkeep. In his supporting speech, he detailed Van Buren's alleged ostentatiousness. Jacksonians had complained about a $5,000 appropriation during the John Quincy Adams administration, Ogle noted, yet Jackson and Van Buren had requested almost $90,000 in appropriations for extravagant furnishings, renovations, and landscaping, and Van Buren wanted even more to turn the White House into a "Presidential palace," decorated like those of the European monarchs. On and on Ogle went, listing plants, trees, statuary, and other Democratic wastefulness. Van Buren had not only spent "the PEOPLE'S CASH," he had also refused to expend his own, preferring to save it "*with sordid parsimony.*" Van Buren and his fellow Democrats were, in the words of one anonymous Whig, "a party without principles."[25]

PERSONAL CHARACTER

Going hand in hand with political corruption were questions about personal character. The earliest presidential elections had emphasized candidates and their characters over policies. It was not enough for the people themselves to be virtuous; they believed their rulers needed to act virtuously, both privately and publicly. The Jacksonian period witnessed the development of well-organized, active national political parties emphasizing issues and agendas, but candidates for the White House were still expected to be morally upstanding. This type of personal character was defined in various ways, including preserving honor, practicing religious ethics, exhibiting masculinity, and maintaining racial purity.[26]

Democrats and Whigs alike faced questions about their personal character. Both Jackson and Clay came under fire for having fought duels, a ritual increasingly denounced in broader American society but one that remained central to perceptions of masculinity and honor in the South and the West. The two men were also criticized for failing to adhere to contemporary beliefs about Christianity. In addition to Jackson's history of engaging in violence, he faced questions about the adulterous origins of his marriage to his late wife, Rachel. Clay was not as quick to lose his temper as his Democratic rival, but his reputation for gambling and womanizing followed him into the 1830s. In the 1832 election, Democrats revived the old claim that the Kentuckian "spends his days at the gaming table and his nights in a brothel." Whig senator Daniel Webster, who ran for president in 1836, also shared Clay's reputation of liking liquor and ladies too much.[27]

Van Buren was not violent, but he found himself attacked on other questions of character. In addition to accusing the president of being cheap and wasteful in his 1840 speech, Charles Ogle also called him a sexual pervert. Van Buren, "an exquisite with 'sweet sandy whiskers' . . . must have undulations, 'beautiful mounds, and other contrivances,' to ravish his exalted and ethereal soul." What was the Whig representative referring to? The president had authorized White House landscapers to create "a number of clever sized hills, every pair of which, it is said, was designed to resemble and assume the form of AN AMAZON'S BOSOM, with a miniature knoll or hillock on its apex, to denote the n—ple." "These silly fancies," Ogle pronounced, "are better adapted to please the sickly and vicious taste of palace dandies, than to gratify the simple eye of plain, republican freemen." Van Buren was also portrayed as unmasculine. During the 1836 campaign, a critical biography of him stated that it used to be that "anybody could tell by his looks that he was not a woman." Now, however, Van Buren was "what the English call a dandy [i.e., a vain fool]." The vice president attended the Senate "laced up in corsets," and the only thing that identified him as a man was "his large *red* and *gray* whiskers." Democrats countered with the charge that a group of Ohio women had presented William Henry Harrison, "the *Heroine* of Tippecanoe," with a petticoat as a sign of his cowardice for recommending the abandonment of Fort Stephenson during the War of 1812.[28]

Richard M. Johnson was also prominently targeted over questions of personal character. Born into a well-to-do Kentucky family in 1780, the dashing Johnson embodied the martial glory that had been attractive in recent elections. He had fought in the War of 1812; in fact, following the 1813 Battle of the Thames, various people and newspapers had credited him with killing Tecumseh, the Shawnee leader who attempted to unite various Native American groups in a confederacy to oppose the United States. Although there was no reliable evidence for attributing Tecumseh's death to Johnson, he still became a household name and went on to serve in the Senate and the House. An 1833 campaign biography and an 1835 play based on Tecumseh's death helped increase Johnson's visibility and popularity among Democrats and led the party to put him on the ticket with Van Buren in 1836. But the decision was not made without trepidation. They hesitated because for years Johnson had maintained an interracial household back home. It included Julia Chinn, an enslaved woman of mixed race, and their two daughters, Imogene and Adaline, whom Richard and Julia prepared to live as free women in white society. After Julia died in 1833, Johnson attempted a similar arrangement with her niece Parthena Chinn, who was also enslaved. These circumstances became national news when Parthena ran away. Her decision to flee indicated that she was not a willing participant in the Kentucky Democrat's desire to duplicate the household he had created with Julia. Johnson's order to have Parthena whipped once she was captured and to have her and her children sold to one of his creditors conclusively ended the arrangement he had sought.[29]

Johnson's brazenness in living openly with Julia Chinn and acknowledging their offspring as his own elicited sharp public condemnation deeply steeped in the racism of the era. For many white Americans at the time, personal character meant maintaining racial purity, which became clear as this offensive gossip spread widely during the 1836 campaign. "How it would look in the eyes of civilized Europe and the world, to see the Vice President, and his yellow children, and his wooly headed African wife, in the city of Washington, mingling in all the giddy mazes of the most fashionable and respectable society in the country?" one Rhode Island newspaper asked. Washington journalist Duff Green sarcastically pointed out that "mere political automatons" such as Van Buren's supporters did not care whether Johnson was "married to, or has been in connexion with a jet black, thick-lipped, odoriferous negro wench, by whom he has reared a family of children" and whom he was trying to compel white society to accept. Two anonymous *Richmond Whig* correspondents warned that Johnson's flaunting of white southern norms threatened "the purity of our maidens, the chaste dignity of our matrons" and left white women susceptible to being sexually assaulted by Black men.[30]

The questions about Johnson's household may have contributed to his close call in the 1836 vice presidential election, in which he was unable to secure a majority of the votes to win the office in the general election. The constitutional prescription was for the Senate to choose the winner from the top two vote-getters, in this case, Johnson and the Whig candidate Francis Granger. On February 8, 1837, forty-nine of the fifty-two senators cast their votes to decide the vice presidency (three senators abstained). Johnson won 33 to 16, thus ending the first (and, to date, only) vice presidential contest decided in the Senate.[31]

SLAVERY

As the furor over Johnson's interracial relationships revealed, slavery continued to be a divisive political topic, as it had been since the nation's founding. The late 1820s and 1830s witnessed a shift in antislavery strategy as Black abolitionists began emphasizing political violence as a means of ending slavery. David Walker's 1829 pamphlet *Appeal to the Coloured Citizens of the World* argued that enslaved African Americans needed to use education, religion, and violence to free themselves from their white oppressors. In 1831, enslaved Virginians under the leadership of Nat Turner took up arms against the racist system that kept them in bondage. That same year, white reformer William Lloyd Garrison founded the *Liberator*, a national abolitionist newspaper. In 1833, he headed up the formation of the American Anti-Slavery Society. Garrison took a pacifist approach to ending slavery, calling for moral suasion over violence. Whether advocating violence or nonviolence, these abolitionist efforts posed a major threat to slavery's continued existence in the United States.[32]

Slavery's defenders did not back down in the face of this growing resistance. Pro-slavery forces began a more vigorous defense of the institution, drawing on history, contemporary science, white Christianity, and racist stereotypes to present slavery as an abstract social system that derived its good from the moral character of the enslaver. Underlying these philosophical arguments was an economic reality: using the enslaved labor of African Americans was financially lucrative. Cotton production, for example, which depended upon enslaved laborers, had exploded since the end of the War of 1812, rising from just over 200,000 bales produced each year to nearly 750,000 bales in 1830. In addition to cotton, important cash crops—sugar, rice, tobacco, and indigo—also depended on a growing pool of enslaved laborers. Consequently, the number of enslaved people increased by nearly 500,000 in the 1820s. During that decade, between 93,000 and 134,000 enslaved people (at an estimated sale value of $57.3 million) were sold via the domestic slave trade, many of them forced to migrate from the upper South to the lower South. In the 1830s, the domestic slave trade brought approximately 226,000 enslaved people into Alabama, Louisiana, and Mississippi alone. Most of those enslaved individuals who were bought and sold were compelled, often through violence, to work for the white enslavers who were filling the very lands that Andrew Jackson had forcibly and fraudulently seized from Native Americans in the 1810s and again in the 1830s.[33]

In response to the backlash against slavery, hundreds of spontaneous and preplanned antiabolitionist and anti-Black riots took place during Jackson's second term. In 1835 alone, 147 such incidents occurred, with 109 in a four-month period from July to October. The "Snow Riot" of August 1835 led to nearly a week of terror for African Americans living in the nation's capital as whites burned their businesses, homes, and schools. Jackson's administration added fuel to the fire when the president, himself a long-time enslaver, supported Postmaster General Amos Kendall's decision to limit the circulation of abolitionist material in the southern mail system. The "monsters" who were trying "to stir up amongst [sic] the south [sic] the horrors of a servile war . . . ought to be made to attone [sic] for this wicked attempt with their lives," Jackson told Kendall. Those who supported "this wicked plan of exciting the negroes to insurrection and to masacre [sic]," he continued, should "be compelled to desist, or move from the country."[34]

Disagreements over slavery presented Van Buren with challenges throughout his presidency. Early on, Van Buren's actions seemed to soothe the uneasiness of some white southerners who were taking a wait-and-see approach toward his expressed commitment to protecting the institution. He supported pro-slavery resolutions that Calhoun introduced in the 1837–1838 congressional session aiming to stop the introduction of antislavery petitions and calling for the federal government to protect slavery, including in the District of Columbia. When the *Amistad* case presented itself, Van Buren also stood behind slavery. In 1839, a group of enslaved Africans seized control of the Spanish ship carrying them to a Cuban port, but instead of sailing to Africa as intended, they mistakenly landed in New York. The self-emancipated Africans were taken into custody, their fate lying in the hands of the Van Buren administration. In January 1840, Van Buren, with his cabinet's backing, issued an executive order that directed the enslaved men to be turned over to the Spaniards who owned them prior to their successful rebellion. Abolitionists stepped in and sued, eventually taking the *Amistad* case to the US Supreme Court, where John Quincy Adams spoke on their behalf. The Africans won their freedom (although only after Van Buren left office), but white southerners praised the president's support of slavery.[35]

Slavery also hovered in the background of one of Van Buren's first foreign policy decisions. In 1836, Texas declared its independence from Mexico, partly in response to attempts to limit slavery in the north Mexican state that became the Lone Star Republic. After a successful revolution, Texas's representatives pressed the United States for diplomatic recognition or even annexation. Van Buren and other Democrats tried to keep Jackson from taking any decisive action regarding Texas, fearing that it would harm their party's chances in the presidential campaign. The day before Jackson left office, however, he saddled his successors with a long-term problem by recognizing Texas as an independent nation.[36]

Van Buren was displeased, to say the least. Having survived a brutal presidential campaign in which white southerners had questioned his commitment to slavery and northerners his commitment to liberty, he did not want to take a stand on whether Texas should be annexed to the United States. With the onset of the 1837 depression drawing Van Buren's energy, he delayed, then delayed some more, as Texas's leaders and expansion-hungry white southerners, both privately and publicly, called for annexation. Congress proved no more willing to address annexation than Van Buren. Its members not only faced solving the economic depression but also the onslaught of antiannexation petitions that poured into both houses of Congress in the first two years of Van Buren's administration. Finally recognizing the futility of waiting on the United States to make a decision that had little support, Texas tabled the idea in 1838. Southern enslavers, however, kept their eyes on the West.[37]

MANIFEST DESTINY

As the example of Texas showed, territorial expansion was yet another issue prevalent in the nation's political discourse. Although the term "Manifest Destiny" was not formally used to describe the process of empire-building until 1845, the practice was baked into the European colonization of the Western Hemisphere and found fertile ground in the new American republic. White Americans had always believed that God had predestined the North American continent to be conquered by the US government, but the new Jackson–Van Buren administration and its Democratic allies in Congress embraced even more fully the opportunity to carry out territorial expansion.[38]

The main thrust of Manifest Destiny during the 1830s took the form of Indian removal. Jackson came into office with the stated intention of pursuing "a just and liberal policy" regarding Native Americans. This stance, announced in his inaugural address, turned out to be chimerical. Given his history of fighting and killing Native Americans and duplicitously negotiating treaties with them during and after the War of 1812, few people were surprised when Jackson took actions that seemed more intent on seizing Native American land than helping them maintain their society. His appointment of anti-Indian cabinet officers and federal officials indicated his intentions from the start. Any question about the president's ultimate objective disappeared following his first annual message, sent to Congress in December 1829. In it, he outlined his belief that cultural assimilation (i.e., indigenous groups adopting white culture) had failed. Native Americans, Jackson argued, needed to voluntarily remove to territory west of the Mississippi River. Those who wished to stay would have to agree to follow the laws of the states in which they resided. The following May, Congress made Jackson's policy law. The Indian Removal Act promised native groups that if they voluntarily removed, they would receive territory west of the Mississippi River in exchange for their land in the East. The legislation also designated a small appropriation for the government to carry out the removal process. The results of the Indian Removal Act were predictable. Some native groups, such as the Chickasaw and Choctaw, reluctantly agreed to remove. Others, such as the Cherokee, Creek, and Seminole, actively, and sometimes violently, opposed removal. The Cherokee famously took their case to the US Supreme Court on two occasions during Jackson's presidency, but their legal efforts failed to halt the march toward their removal.[39]

The justification for the Trail of Tears, which resulted in an estimated 4,000 Cherokee dying as a result of their forced removal in 1838, may have been provided by Jackson, but Van Buren brought the process to fruition. He and Old Hickory shared the same opinion of cultural cohabitation: it simply was not possible. Once in office, Van Buren continued his predecessor's removal policy, with predictable backlash. Removal opponents blamed the president for capitulating to southern demands for Cherokee land. "The people of the North have so long submitted to Southern dictation, that they will do it again in this instance," one Pennsylvania newspaper angrily noted. Overall, Van Buren's administration contributed significantly to the forced removal of Native Americans that took place between 1830 and 1843, when approximately 90,000 indigenous people (out of about 120,000 living east of the Mississippi River) were compelled to give up their lands.[40]

In addition to continuing the Jackson administration's forced removal of indigenous peoples, Van Buren also persisted in fighting Native Americans in Florida. In late 1835, Seminole Indians opposed to Jackson's removal policy ambushed a contingent of Florida militia. What had been a smoldering ember burst into the flame of warfare, inaugurating the Second Seminole War. Lasting from 1835 until 1842, the conflict depleted US financial resources, exposed deficiencies in the US Army, and weakened national morale. Early in his administration, Van Buren promised the country that he would continue the "philanthropic and enlightened policy" of Indian removal undertaken by Jackson. Instead, his prosecution of the war against the Seminole brought condemnation from his opponents. One Whig newspaper called it an "unholy and desolating war," and another accused Van Buren of inflating the cost of the war in order to fund an "*Army of Office Holders* and contractors" loyal to the president.[41]

Van Buren faced other challenges posed by the nation's commitment to Manifest Destiny. Beginning in late 1837 and lasting more than year, the Canadian Rebellion, an internal dispute among Canadians in both lower and upper Canada, almost embroiled the Van Buren administration in a war with Great Britain. In December 1837, British naval forces sank a privately owned American ship, the *Caroline*, because it was assisting rebel forces. As part of the effort, the British killed an American crew member. Van Buren ordered US troops to the border area to tamp down American anger and calls for war. Despite a retaliatory American burning of a Canadian ship in May 1838, Van Buren reaffirmed his nation's neutrality, and the crisis largely subsided. This conflict was not the only one with Great Britain, however. In 1838, a crisis erupted along the Maine-Canadian border over control of the Aroostook River valley. New Brunswick lumberjacks began cutting timber in this territory, which both nations claimed but which

Mainers had settled. Maine governor John Fairfield responded by calling out his state's militia. Once again, Van Buren directed US troops to the border. Ultimately, Britain and the United States agreed to let a boundary commission settle the dispute, but tensions between the two nations lingered.[42]

IMMIGRATION

A final partisan issue that emerged in the 1830s was nativism, that is, xenophobic opposition to immigrants. In the early years of the republic, Americans had generally accepted foreign immigration to fill up the land to which the United States had laid claim. The French and Haitian Revolutions quickly changed this dynamic: Republicans usually welcomed those fleeing the violence and upheaval; Federalists feared the political and social disruptiveness that opening up the nation's borders might bring. The controversial Alien and Sedition Acts of 1798, enacted by a Federalist president and Congress, placed restrictions on those seeking citizenship and made them susceptible to deportation by presidential fiat. Republicans fought this undemocratic legislation, but its passage and enforcement illustrated the fear of immigrants that overtook the nation during its first decade of existence.[43]

Jackson's presidency produced a similar partisan divide when it came to immigrants. Democrats tended to accept them into their ranks, but Whigs viewed them with trepidation. The respective parties' responses to immigration became politically important because of the explosion in the number of people looking to move to the United States. In the ten years before 1832, annual immigration averaged 15,695 persons; between 1832 and 1836, it jumped to 61,221. It was not just the size but the composition of this immigrant wave that drew the parties' attention. The number of immigrants coming from Great Britain remained relatively stable, but those making the journey from Ireland and Germany did so in increasingly significant numbers. Both groups were motivated in part by worsening living conditions in their home countries, with the Irish in particular facing immense poverty and starvation. Many Irish immigrants came to the United States impoverished and unskilled and found themselves competing with native-born Americans for survival in eastern urban areas.[44]

Most Irish immigrants were also Catholic, which only increased prejudice against them. Catholics found themselves lumped in with Freemasons and Mormons as groups allegedly pledging their loyalty to an un-American cabal of secretive, manipulative leaders and engaging in unmentionable wickedness. Anti-Catholic bigotry bubbled to the surface in the mid-1830s in dramatic fashion. Individuals such as painter and inventor Samuel F. B. Morse, who helped develop the telegraph, accused Irish Catholics of invading the United States for the pope. Rumors also swirled that Catholic priests used the confessional to seduce single and married women, that Catholics committed incest, and that they "cut unborn infants from their mothers' wombs and threw them to the dogs before their parents' eyes." Like many conspiracy theories, the evidence for these alleged Catholic depravities was thin or nonexistent, but the consequences could be dangerous. In 1834, for example, local men burned a Catholic convent in Charlestown, Massachusetts, after unfounded reports circulated of young women being held there against their will. A similar attack against a Baltimore convent occurred the following year.[45]

Jackson largely avoided any suspicion about supporting Catholicism, telling one concerned female correspondent that "our exellent [sic] constitution, gurantees [sic] to every one freedom of religion." Van Buren was not as fortunate. During the 1836 presidential campaign, Whigs dredged up an 1829 letter he wrote to Felix Cicognani, in which he assured the US consul to the Papal States that Catholic Americans "stand upon the same elevated ground which Citizens of all other Religious Denominations occupy, in regard to the Rights of Conscience." Critics turned this letter, intended to serve as a reminder of religious freedom in the United States, into proof of Van Buren's papist leanings, a preposterous allegation in light of the president's Dutch Reformed upbringing. His opponents also accused him of being a secret Catholic conspiring to turn over control of the United States to the pope. The nation's economic depression seemed to divert attention away from these anti-Catholic suspicions, but they still appeared at times, if in a different form. In criticizing the president's excessive use of executive power, for example, one Vermont Whig newspaper compared the very questioning of Van Buren, "the High Priest of democracy," to a Catholic challenging the authority of the pope: it was verboten.[46]

Beyond these personal attacks, the flames of anti-Catholic nativism continued to smolder as nativists organized their movement in more formal ways. The Protestant Reformation Society, founded in 1836, took as its mission the propagation of anti-Catholic material and the conversion of Catholics to Protestantism. It and similar nativist groups employed inflammatory publications, such as *Six Months in a Convent* (1835) by Rebecca Reed and *Awful Disclosures of Maria Monk, as Exhibited in a Narrative of Her Sufferings During a Residence of Five Years as a Novice, and Two Years as a Black Nun, in the Hotel Dieu Nunnery at Montreal* (1836), as part of a cottage industry of anti-Catholic material that circulated and reinforced nativist arguments about the Roman Catholic Church and conspiracy theories about the pope as the biblical Antichrist. By using personal, gendered stories to create sympathy for the nativist cause, these accounts emulated the slave narratives produced by abolitionists. The Protestant Reformation Society also established a speakers bureau, encouraged ministers to preach anti-Catholic sermons, and partnered with the anti-Catholic *American Protestant Vindicator* newspaper in New York.[47]

Along with unfounded personal allegations about Van Buren's Catholicism and the dissemination of anti-Catholic propaganda, nativism lingered in other ways. The annual number of immigrants moving to the United States during his administration averaged 80,097, an increase of nearly 19,000 per year over the last five years of Jackson's presidency. Nativists increasingly spread a conspiracy theory proposed in the 1820s that warned that the pope and European monarchs were plotting to send immigrants to the Mississippi valley, with eventual plans to start a war to destroy the Protestant-majority United States. As a result, Native American Associations—nativist groups that sought to maintain white Protestant domination in American society—began forming. They had two goals in mind. The first was restricting immigrants' access to citizenship and suffrage. Much like in the late 1790s, potential voters for the other party struck fear in some people's minds. The Washington, DC, branch, for example, petitioned Congress to strengthen the naturalization laws to make it more difficult for immigrants to achieve citizenship. The second objective was limiting the number of lower-class immigrants able to enter the country. Nativists argued that this group of people was not only draining resources that belonged to native-born citizens but forcing US citizens to pay for their purported laziness. National lawmakers did not act on either request, but nativists clung to the hope that their warnings about the joint Catholic/immigrant conspiracy at work would eventually be heeded.[48]

CULTURAL POLITICS

Helping frame these issues for voters were the various expressions of cultural politics increasingly used during presidential campaigns. These electioneering techniques and practices took many forms. Auxiliary organizations consisted of political supporters that kept voters engaged between elections and provided electoral energy during campaigns. Often, these auxiliary organizations held public conventions and mass meetings that brought a candidate's message in front of potential supporters. Sometimes candidates undertook campaign tours that took them across states or regions to meet and woo voters. When not speaking in front of voters in person, candidates also used public correspondence to make their case for election. These letters could be private, but even when they were, the expectation increasingly was that they would be published in a newspaper or some other form that could be read by voters across the nation. In a society boasting a high literacy rate, print culture, which included newspapers, pamphlets, and campaign biographies, provided different avenues for crafting a candidate's image and policies. Parties and candidates relied on more than the spoken and written word, however. Material culture—banners, buttons, and the like—offered voters tangible ways of identifying themselves with a party and candidate, while political cartoons and songs gave parties eye- and ear-catching ways to disseminate their message. Women participated actively in these efforts, even though they were unable to vote or hold office.[49]

At the heart of cultural politics was the reality that convincing voters to switch party affiliation was a difficult prospect—most voters stayed with the party they supported in their first election. The relaxation or elimination of suffrage laws helped the voter participation rate jump from 26.9 percent in 1824 to 57.6 percent in 1828, a level to which it stayed close in the 1832 and 1836 elections. These newly eligible voters were up for grabs, and the political parties slowly recognized that issues were not the only way to win or retain their loyalty. Political parties increasingly utilized the various methods of cultural politics to convince voters to support their candidates, while voters used them to express their willingness or unwillingness to endorse presidential tickets and party platforms. By the 1840 presidential election, the Whigs understood that attracting voters required the full-fledged integration of cultural politics into presidential campaigning. Unfortunately for Democrats that year, it was a lesson learned too late.[50]

THE LOG CABIN AND HARD CIDER CAMPAIGN OF 1840

Van Buren faced a tough reelection bid in 1840. Whigs made a prudent decision in selecting someone to challenge him. Instead of making the obvious choice of Henry Clay, the Whigs handed the nomination to William Henry Harrison, one of the three losing Whig candidates in 1836. Harrison held several advantages over Clay. He did not possess the baggage the Kentuckian did from a political career spanning three decades. Harrison was also a war hero and military figure, a combination that Jackson had shown could attract voters. Finally, he had undertaken a campaign tour in 1836, under the guise of commemorating the anniversaries of War of 1812 battles in which he had participated. Even though this style of electioneering was frowned upon, previous presidents, such as Washington, Monroe, and Jackson, had set a precedent for making extended trips to meet the voters. Their efforts had been less blatantly about politicking, but by breaking that mold during an election year, Harrison demonstrated that he understood the future of presidential campaigning.[51]

For vice president, the Whigs nominated former Virginia governor and US congressman John Tyler. Tyler, who turned fifty years old during the election year, was well connected. His father, who served as Virginia's governor three times, roomed with Thomas Jefferson at the College of William & Mary and was friends with Patrick Henry and James Monroe. Tyler's classmates included men who became future leaders, including US Army general Winfield Scott. A reluctant supporter of Jackson in 1828, Tyler broke with Old Hickory over the nullification crisis and resigned his US Senate seat to avoid carrying out the Virginia legislature's order to vote for expunging Jackson's censure from the congressional record. He had appeared as a Whig vice presidential nominee on some ballots in 1836; now, Tyler was the official nominee.[52]

Unsurprisingly, Van Buren's handling of the economy drew the most criticism from Whigs. They accused the president and his party of using the government to line their own pockets at the expense of the people. "Power is always stealing from the many to the few," Harrison told a sympathetic crowd in July 1840. Drawing inspiration from Charles Ogle's speech, Whigs especially enjoyed depicting Van Buren as an out-of-touch elitist. Some of their songs dubbed the president "King Matty," and Virginia governor James Barbour called him "a monarch almost absolute." One New Yorker maintained that Van Buren was a "counterfeit bill" who had "believed and acted upon the principle of Corruption" from his earliest political days in the state. A Whig meeting predicted that the Harrison–Tyler ticket would prevent the Democratic "'Spoils' Crew" from causing "future mischief to the country."[53]

As if the Whig attacks were not enough trouble, Democrats also faced internal division. Questions about Vice President Johnson's interracial relationships again became a campaign issue. Reports circulated among Democrats that he was living openly with "a young Delilah of about the complexion of Shakespears swarthy Othello . . . some eighteen or nineteen years of age and quite handsome." This young woman, whose name may have been Dinah, was Parthena's sister and another of Julia Chinn's nieces.

Democratic operative Amos Kendall pronounced himself "shocked" by Johnson's behavior, having been reassured "that this habit of his younger days had been abandoned." Johnson "openly and shamelessly" appeared to think that becoming vice president provided "the seal of public approbation to his conduct in that respect." Keeping him on the Democratic ticket, Kendall warned, would "be a lasting reproach to our party and our country." Jackson agreed that Johnson's new relationship would make it difficult to win the votes of "the whole religious portion" of Kentucky and Tennessee.[54]

Consequently, several challengers to Johnson emerged, most prominent among them James K. Polk. After fourteen years of service, the forty-three-year-old Speaker of the House had retired from Congress in March 1839 to run for governor of Tennessee. Polk won the gubernatorial race later that year and appeared to be an emerging star within the party. He also had Jackson's endorsement; in fact, Democrats began calling him "Young Hickory" during this campaign, a moniker that stuck. The former president made it clear that Johnson could not be the party's vice presidential choice. If Johnson, "the weakest candidate that is named," became the Democratic nominee, he would "loose [sic] the democracy thousands of votes," Jackson argued. "If he takes the field . . . he will weaken the cause & strengthen Harrison every where [sic]." Jackson's pleas went unheeded. Van Buren and his New York allies remained resolute in their determination not to involve themselves in the vice presidential question, and the Democratic convention delegates ultimately decided on a no-nominee strategy.[55]

Even without this internal dissension, Van Buren's reelection chances were in trouble. The Whig Party deployed cultural politics to great advantage against the Democrats. Jackson's criticism that Whig voters were being "led by hard cider, coons, Log cabins and big balls" identified many of the images associated with the Whig's successful 1840 campaign. Democrats handed their opponents their main rhetorical weapon when, early in the campaign, one of their Baltimore newspapers said that if the party gave Harrison "a barrel of HARD CIDER, and . . . a pension of two thousand a year," he would "sit the remainder of his days in his LOG CABIN." In hindsight, it was an error of massive proportion. Whigs built log cabins of all sizes and distributed hard cider as indicators of Harrison's identity as "a cider-swilling, raccoon-skin-capped man of the people." (This image was manufactured: Harrison was not a lowly Ohio farmer but rather the scion of a wealthy Virginia family.) The use of the raccoon as a party mascot was also intended to identify the Whigs and their candidate as representative of the average American. Often identified with racism against African Americans today, the use of "coon" at the time symbolized the frontier and the characteristics of hard work and independence associated with those living on the edges of American civilization. Finally, the "big balls" that Jackson mocked referred to the Whigs' use of material culture to generate enthusiasm, in this case, large balls, made of leather or paper and bearing political slogans, that were rolled in parades. A model Whig event in 1840 would have had women cheering from the sidelines as party supporters pulled a replica log cabin—with a barrel of hard cider prominently displayed on its porch and coonskins attached to its walls—down a road, a large ball touting Harrison and Tyler rolling along not far behind.[56]

Democrats largely ceded the ground of cultural politics to the Whigs in 1840. Given their use of some of these electioneering techniques in previous presidential campaigns, this failure was inexcusable. It was especially so because Van Buren outlined a successful strategy early in the campaign year. In a seventy-five-page document full of advice on how best to approach the 1840 New York state elections, the president bluntly identified what Democrats were doing wrong and how they could fix it. Whigs were outworking and outorganizing the party of Jackson, and Democrats needed to use the upcoming state elections as a testing ground for the presidential campaign. Van Buren urged Democrats in the New York state legislature to coordinate the party's efforts and called for the creation of auxiliary groups "in each town in the State to be composed of the most active & young friends of the cause." In this way, Democrats could counter the Whigs' enthusiasm and ultimately "preserve & promote the purity & freedom of elections."[57]

Van Buren did not follow his own advice, and neither did most Democrats, but there were exceptions to the largely moribund national party effort. In Tennessee, Democratic stalwarts undertook a vigorous campaign. Jackson used the twenty-fifth anniversary of his victory over the British to energize Democrats. Despite his poor health and faltering finances, he traveled to New Orleans, attracting tens of thousands of people as he made stops along the way. The former president also wrote letters criticizing Harrison's politics and offering encouragement about Van Buren's prospects. Polk was another champion of the party's cause in Tennessee. He organized Democratic speaking engagements and stumped for Van Buren across the state using strong and forceful rhetoric. Jackson complimented him and other Tennesseans for "doing their duty well." Unfortunately for Democrats, these efforts were all too uncommon in 1840.[58]

The Whig ticket ultimately proved victorious. Harrison won 234 of 294 electoral votes, almost 53 percent of the popular vote, and nineteen of

Table 1.1 1840 Presidential Election Results

State	Total votes	WHH Pop.	WHH Pop. %	WHH Electoral	MVB Pop.	MVB Pop. %	MVB Electoral	JGB Pop.	JGB Pop. %	JGB Electoral
Alabama	62,511	28,515	45.6		33,996	54.4	7			
Arkansas	10,682	4,664	43.6		6,018	56.4	3			
Connecticut	56,936	31,597	55.6	8	25,282	44.4		57	0.10	
Delaware	10,839	5,967	55.1	3	4,872	44.9				
Georgia	72,168	40,246	55.8	11	31,922	44.2				
Illinois	93,179	45,576	48.9	9	47,443	50.9	5	160	0.17	
Indiana	117,026	65,305	55.8	9	51,691	44.2		30	0.03	
Kentucky	91,105	58,489	64.2	15	32,616	35.8				
Louisiana	18,914	11,297	59.7	5	7,617	40.3				
Maine	93,007	46,613	50.1	10	46,200	49.7		194	0.21	
Maryland	62,292	33,533	53.8	10	28,759	46.2				
Massachusetts	126,197	72,532	57.5	14	52,047	41.2		1,618	1.28	
Michigan	44,350	22,933	51.7	3	21,096	47.6		321	0.72	
Mississippi	36,525	19,515	53.4	4	17,010	46.6				
Missouri	52,639	22,971	43.6		29,668	56.4	4			
New Hampshire	59,152	26,294	44.5		32,744	55.4	7	114	0.19	
New Jersey	64,454	33,351	51.7	8	31,034	48.1		69	0.11	
New York	441,144	225,817	51.2	42	212,528	48.2		2,799	0.63	
North Carolina	80,155	46,376	57.9	15	33,779	42.1				
Ohio	273,814	148,141	54.1	21	124,770	45.6		903	0.33	
Pennsylvania	288,150	144,023	50.0	30	143,784	49.9		343	0.12	

Rhode Island	8,495	5,213	61.4	4	3,263	38.4	—	19	0.22	—
South Carolina*	—	—	—	—	—	—	11	—	—	—
Tennessee	108,680	60,391	55.6	15	48,289	44.4	—	—	—	—
Vermont	50,766	32,440	63.9	7	18,007	35.5	—	319	0.63	—
Virginia	86,394	42,501	49.2	—	43,893	50.8	23	—	—	—
Totals	2,409,574	1,274,300	52.9	234	1,128,328	46.8	60	6,946	0.29	0

*South Carolina's state legislature cast its eleven electoral votes.

The 1840 US presidential election results for William Henry Harrison (WHH), Martin Van Buren (MVB), and James Gillespie Birney (JGB). Source: Michael J. Dubin, *United States Presidential Elections, 1788–1860: The Official Results by County and State* (Jefferson, NC: McFarland, 2002), 71–82.

twenty-six states. (The antislavery Liberty Party, which ran James G. Birney for president, proved inconsequential to the outcome.) Whigs also seized control of both congressional chambers. Several factors contributed to their victory. One was their effectual employment of cultural politics—the Whigs were simply better at using these electioneering techniques to their advantage. Another was the ineffectiveness of the Democratic ticket. Van Buren's detachment from electioneering did the party no favors and reinforced perceptions that his aptitude for public leadership—as president or as party leader—did not match his abilities as a behind-the-scenes party manager. The Democratic convention's refusal to name a vice presidential nominee allowed regional candidates such as Polk to emerge, indicating dissatisfaction with the party's executive leadership. The main reason for Harrison's victory in 1840, however, came down to Van Buren's handling of the economic depression. Democrats had held the presidency for twelve years, and many voters connected the economic fissures that appeared in 1837 to the Bank War that began in Jackson's first administration. This assessment was too simplistic given the many circumstances that played a role in the nation's economic crisis, but voters held Van Buren responsible.[59]

Despite their loss, Democrats had reason to be optimistic. Results in several states were close, undermining any Whig assertion of a mandate from the people. Much like other presidential elections, small shifts in popular votes across several states would have given the incumbent president a second term. Therefore, it was easy for Van Buren and his supporters to dismiss the election as a political anomaly, as "the instrumentalities and debaucheries of a political Saturnalia, in which reason and justice had been derided." "I trust, still, in the virtue of the great working class," Jackson encouraged Van Buren in the election's aftermath, "that they will rally and check at once this combined corrupt coalition and on their native dunghills set them down." Convinced that voters had been fooled by the Whig spectacle, Democrats looked forward to throwing obstacles in the path of Harrison and his party. Little did they know that the providential design in which many of them believed would help their efforts.[60]

2

"OLL FOR KLAY" THE WHIG NATIONAL CONVENTION

William Henry Harrison had defeated Martin Van Buren in 1840, but not everyone was convinced that he was going to be a successful president. According to John Quincy Adams, now serving in the House, 75 percent of people who voted for Harrison had not wanted him to win. "There is little confidence in his talents or firmness," the former president observed. Acknowledging that the December day's snowfall might be causing his despair, Adams nevertheless concluded, "Harrison comes in upon a hurricane; God grant he may not go out on a wreck!"[1]

Unfortunately, that is exactly what happened, and it did not take long to get there. On March 4, 1841, the throngs watched as, just after 10:00 A.M., the sixty-eight-year-old Harrison headed toward the Capitol. When the president-elect appeared on the portico to give his address and take the oath of office, "a deafening shout went up from the glad hearts and exulting voices of an emancipated People," a crowd estimated at close to 60,000 people. Harrison delivered his inaugural address, the longest in US history, in full despite the cold day. One month later, he was dead. In late March, Harrison took to his bed with what appeared to be a severe cold. The attending physician later described the illness as pneumonia; more likely, it was enteric (or typhoid) fever, a gastrointestinal illness caused by contaminated water. On Sunday, April 4, news began to spread that for the first time in the nation's history, a sitting president had died in office. As Harrison's body lay in state in the East Room of the White House, Americans looking for re-

John Tyler, ca. 1841. (Courtesy of the Library of Congress)

assurance in such trying times could take comfort in reading reports about his last words. According to the doctor who treated the president until he took his final breath, Harrison said, "Sir, I wish you to understand the true principles of the government; I wish them carried out, I ask nothing more." Five members of the grieving cabinet noted in their acknowledgment of Harrison's death that "the last utterance of his lips expressed a fervent desire for the perpetuity of the Constitution, and the preservation of its true principles." Reportedly, this admonition to pursue "the true principles of the government" was intended for Vice President John Tyler, who found himself unexpectedly thrust into power.[2]

Tyler received word of Harrison's death in at his home in Williamsburg, Virginia. He hurried back to Washington, arriving before dawn on April 6. Tyler took up temporary residence at Brown's Indian Queen Hotel, where he was administered the presidential oath of office. As the first vice president to assume office upon the death of a president, Tyler's actual title and powers were open to interpretation. Was he the president, fully vested with the office and authority of the chief executive office, or the "Vice-President acting as President," as Adams argued, assuming "not the office, but the powers and duties of the said office?" Tyler considered "himself qualified to perform the duties and exercise the powers and office of President," but he still thought the ceremony necessary. The following month, both houses of Congress affirmed Tyler's ascension to the presidency. His decisiveness would not prevent critics from calling him "His Accidency," but Tyler's actions set precedents, followed by vice presidents who faced similar circumstances, that were eventually codified in the Twenty-fifth Amendment in 1967.[3]

Tyler's background served as a Rorschach test for politicians of all stripes, who saw in the new president what suited them. Democrats could point positively to Tyler's senatorial career during Andrew Jackson's administration, when he had voted with Old Hickory's supporters to confirm Van Buren as minister to England, to oppose the federally funded internal improvements contained in the Maysville Road bill, and to support the Indian Removal Act of 1830. Whigs liked that, in 1824, Tyler had supported Crawford and opposed Jackson; they loved even more that he had broken with the Democrats over the nullification crisis and the Bank War in the 1830s. Patriots applauded his opposition to Britain and his military service, however minor, during the War of 1812. (His membership in a local militia company that saw no action often led his enemies to refer to him derisively as "Captain Tyler.") Americans in the Jeffersonian tradition found his support of meritocracy, a strict construction of the Constitution, and states' rights reassuring; those with Hamiltonian inclinations appreciated his endorsement of the distribution of land revenue sales from the national government to the individual states, which provided healthy economic growth in the more developed eastern states. At one point before becoming president, Tyler headed up the Virginia Colonization Society, which gave antislavery reformers some comfort, but he thought slavery was a necessary evil and was himself an enslaver, both marks in his favor for white southerners. Whereas Harrison had entered the 1840 campaign as the proverbial blank slate on which Whigs could project any political ideology, Tyler came into the presidency having embraced positions on a relatively wide range of issues that made him theoretically acceptable not just to Whigs but also to Democrats.[4]

The comments that flew during the transition period reflected the variety of opinions about Tyler. "President TYLER is a Whig—a true Whig; and we risk nothing in expressing our entire confidence that he will fulfil, in all their extent, the expectations of the People," the editors of the *Daily National Intelligencer* reassured their readers. Clay predicted Tyler's administration would be like a regency, "very apt to engender faction, intrigue, etc." Adams called the new president "a political sectarian, of the slave-driving, Virginian, Jeffersonian school . . . with all the interests and passions and vices of slavery rooted in his moral and political constitution—with talents not above mediocrity, and a spirit incapable of expansion to the dimensions of the station upon which he has been cast by the hand of Providence." Former navy secretary James K. Paulding deemed Tyler "a common place [*sic*] person, selected by Fortune for a high station for which he has few qualifications." *Washington Globe* editor Francis P. Blair viewed Tyler as a pro-Bank Trojan horse who had cloaked his deceit in "his ultra states rights and Democratic professions" during the campaign. On the one hand, Jackson thought Tyler was "a true States [*sic*] rights man" sent by Providence to save the nation; on the other, he questioned whether the Virginian would "sell himself to Baal . . . [and] take that unprincipled swaggering demagogue, Clay, for his guide and worship him."[5]

Elevated to the presidency in an unprecedented way and facing doubts about his ability to fulfill his role from both Whigs and Democrats, Tyler remained determined to lead a united nation free from partisanship and committed to its constitutional foundations. He had given a brief speech upon taking the vice presidential oath of office that had condemned "the spirit of Faction—that destructive spirit which recklessly walks over prostrate rights, and tramples laws and constitutions in the dust." As he assumed the presidency, Tyler reiterated his belief in those values. "In the administration of the government, I shall act upon the principles which I have all along espoused, and which you and myself have derived from the teachings of Jefferson and Madison, and other of our distinguished countrymen, and my reliance will be placed on the virtue and intelligence of the people," he wrote less than a week after Harrison's death.[6]

On April 9, just three days after arriving back in Washington, Tyler issued what many considered his inaugural address. It repeated much of what he had said upon taking over the vice presidency, but he expanded on his principles and objectives. He began by promising to rely on "the intelligence and patriotism of the people" to combat "the spirit of faction." Tyler said that his foreign policy would focus on justice and honor; key to these goals would be a strengthened and efficient military. He also believed that "a complete separation should take place between the sword and the purse," a reference to the combined control over the nation's military and its money that was considered antithetical to the country's republican roots. Contrasting himself with his Democratic predecessors, Tyler denounced the use of government patronage to create "an army of officeholders" beholden to the president and pledged not to remove any government official "who has faithfully and honestly acquitted himself of the duties of his office." The nation's financial situation also justifiably concerned him. He promised to practice "the most rigid economy," avoid public debt as long as the nation stayed out of war, and distribute any excess revenue in ways that discouraged corruption. Tyler would turn "to the fathers of the great republican school for advice and instruction" on his role as president. Finally, he conveyed his desire to operate a limited national government to avoid "a central system which would inevitably end in a bloody scepter and an iron crown."[7]

Upon entering the White House, Tyler stepped into a maelstrom of oversized egos and presidential ambitions. Two men in particular—Daniel Webster and Henry Clay—had been jousting to control the direction of Harrison's administration. By accepting the secretary of state post, Webster appeared to have gained the upper hand over his former rival. Senator Clay, however, was still the nation's leading Whig, and Harrison had reportedly spoken so glowingly of the Kentuckian following the Whig victory over Van Buren that some, including Clay, considered his remarks an endorsement for the 1844 election. Both men thought the new administration would necessarily focus on the nation's financial depression, and both believed their respective positions gave them the advantage in swaying Harrison's approach to the economy. The president's unexpected death and Tyler's ascension to power provided both Webster and Clay hope that they would be able to exert even more influence over the nation's political agenda.[8]

But Tyler was determined to mark an independent path that rewarded "superior qualifications" as opposed to mere partisanship. He identified several such partisan factions that existed when he took office: "Clay-men, Webstermen, anti-Masons, original Harrisonians, old Whigs and new Whigs,—each jealous of the others, and all struggling for the offices." Determined not to choose sides in the Whigs' intraparty squabbling, Tyler looked "to work in good earnest to reconcile them." "Little did I then dream that I myself was destined to be at so early a day the object of intolerant assault," he remembered later. In visiting with Tyler just a few weeks into his administration, one friend described the president as "very much emaciated," an indication of the stress that he was under.[9]

Tyler acted independently, but he was not an island unto himself. In addition to the advice of his cabinet, the membership of which carried over from Harrison, three men in particular proved influential as his informal advisors: Beverley Tucker, Abel P. Upshur, and Henry A. Wise. All were part of the "Virginia Cabal," which also included former Virginia governor and current US representative Thomas W. Gilmer and US representative Francis Mallory. These Virginians thought that their state was losing power because of an abolitionist conspiracy to harm the influence of slaveholding states like their own. They also believed, to varying degrees, in states' rights. Many of them were former supporters of Jackson and brought to Tyler's administration three lessons they had learned from watching Old Hickory operate as a president: the utility of an informal circle of advisors, the effectiveness of the presidential veto in establishing political power, and the usefulness of populist appeals to enact an agenda.[10]

Tyler trusted this Virginia Cabal, and he needed them as allies, because he found himself embroiled in an immediate conflict with both his cabinet and with Whig Party leaders, especially Clay. This contretemps proceeded from a decision that Harrison had made during his brief time in the White House. He had initially dismissed Clay's advice to call a special congressional session to address the nation's persistently troublesome economic situation, but before his death, Harrison learned from Secretary of the Treasury Thomas Ewing that action to bolster the national economy was imperative. Acknowledging the seriousness of the situation, Harrison called a special session, to convene on May 31, 1841, to discuss "sundry important and weighty matters, principally growing out of the condition of the revenue and finances of the country." Faced with a persistent economic crisis, Tyler had little choice but to continue with Harrison's plan.[11]

Despite the nation's financial turmoil, Tyler was not initially interested in developing economic solutions of his own, but he also did not want Clay to bring up the idea of a national bank. "I design to be perfectly frank with you," he wrote. "I would not have it urg[e]d prematurely—The public mind is still in a state of great disquietude in regard to it." If Clay insisted on raising the issue of the bank, Tyler wanted him "to consider whether you cannot so frame a Bank as to avoid all constitutional objections." "I have no intention to submit any thing to Congress on this subject to be acted on," the president concluded, "but I shall leave it to its own action."[12]

Tyler would not get his wish. Clay wanted a national bank, he believed the people demanded one, and he was determined to use the special session to get it. He may have been emboldened by a letter he received from

Ewing shortly before setting off for Washington. "The president cannot without manifest inconsistency recommend a Bank in his message," the Treasury secretary wrote. Tyler would try "to avoid the question at the special session," something "Congress will not permit." The president, therefore, would be forced to "acquiesce" to the legislature. Ewing also informed Clay that Tyler "speaks of you with the utmost kindness, & you may rely upon it his friendship is strong & unabated."[13]

Congress convened on May 31, and Tyler presented his message to its members the following day. He addressed several topics, but the heart of his message, unsurprisingly, emphasized the nation's economic situation. Tyler recommended the creation of "a suitable fiscal agent" not controlled by the government or private individuals. The three previous attempts at regulating the economy—Biddle's Second Bank of the United States, Jackson's "pet banks," and Van Buren's independent Treasury—had been unsuccessful, and he wanted Congress to come up with a system that worked. Tyler promised to support Congress's solution, with a caveat: he would reject "any measure which may, in my view of it, conflict with the Constitution or otherwise jeopardize the prosperity of the country." Clay and his supporters were thrilled: Tyler appeared to be ceding control of the nation's economic recovery to Congress.[14]

Despite the economic pressures that had precipitated the special session, John Quincy Adams spent the first seventeen days leading an effort to repeal the "gag rule," the procedure that had governed the rejection of antislavery petitions for several previous sessions. Ultimately, his effort failed, and the "gag rule" remained in place. Despite Clay's assurance that Adams's "disturbance" had not prevented "a fine spirit generally prevailing" in Congress, the debate exacerbated the partisan and sectional tensions among legislators. Once discussion of the "gag rule" ended, the Tyler administration and congressional Whigs tried to find common ground on an economic solution. Attention centered on reviving the national bank or creating a new "fiscal agent." Even after Whigs gave Tyler an opening to define his own constitutional remedy, the president, Treasury Secretary Ewing, and other advisors sent Whigs mixed signals about what exactly they wanted. Their one point of emphasis was preserving states' rights. Clay, meanwhile, pursued his personal agenda of bringing back a national bank. When Congress finally passed a bill in early August, it gave Congress more control over the proposed banking system than Tyler had anticipated. He was furious. He believed that he had been clear about what he wanted Whigs to send him, even warning them that he was willing to veto unacceptable legislation. Webster was convinced the president would still sign the bill, but several members of the Virginia Cabal were in Tyler's ear, encouraging him to use the veto to protect southern states' rights and the Constitution.[15]

Against the unanimous opposition of his inherited cabinet, Tyler sent his veto message to the Senate on August 16. In it, he reminded senators that never in his political career had he supported the idea of a national bank, and he criticized the provisions of their bill that he believed trampled on state sovereignty. Gilmer had predicted that if Tyler vetoed the Whig bill, "a dreadful tornado will blow for a time, and then, mark it, a calm sunshine will ensue," exposing true partisan loyalties. He could not have been more wrong. Months of frustration with Tyler came to a boil that night. A crowd of disgruntled Washingtonians gathered at the Log Cabin Hotel and discussed taking their insults to the president's very doorstep. Ignoring the admonitions of the city's Whig mayor to abandon their plans, a segment of the crowd marched up Pennsylvania Avenue, stopping at a tavern on 10th Street to fill up on more liquid courage. They then made their way to the White House, where they broke down the outer gates and gathered "among the pillars of the splendid East Portico." Now about 2:00 A.M., the inebriated crowd "commenced hooting, hissing, drumming, and making" enough noise to wake up some of the residents. Shouts of "Down with John Tyler!!" and "Resign, God d—n you!" mixed with the notes of "the 'Rogue's March' and other insulting airs," played by "a kind of Calathumpian Band." One of Tyler's daughters reportedly was "crying in hysterics 'father, they will kill you.'" After "insulting the dignity" of the president by "daubing the doors, and filling the key-hole of the same with human excrement," the crowd dispersed.[16]

It was a shitty way to treat a president, and things just got worse for Tyler. Other protests sprang up around the country in the following days. Some of the same individuals who protested at the White House burned the president in effigy the next night. Flaming images of Tyler lit up the sky across the nation. Whigs in Tuscumbia, Alabama, hanged the president in effigy "over a chicken house near Hereford's Tavern," but rain kept them from setting their creation ablaze. In Nashville, Tennessee, Whigs tore down one of the log cabins from their 1840 campaign to use for a bonfire, on which they put a likeness of Tyler "clothed in coonskins, and with a bottle of hard cider under his arm." In Paducah, Kentucky, Whigs used "six pounds of gunpowder" to blow up a figure of Tyler sitting on a throne. Whigs in Albany, New York, hung banners calling Tyler "BENEDICT ARNOLD" and

"JUDAS ISCARIOT." A number of people, including Henry Clay's brother Porter, who was a minister and cabinetmaker, reportedly wanted to assassinate Tyler—a president they refused to see as legitimate.[17]

It was not an issue that would seem to warrant such intense reaction, but Americans had from the beginning of the republic responded passionately, and sometimes violently, to real and perceived economic distress. The protestors may have been upset about the ongoing economic depression that had begun during Van Buren's presidency, but, given their rhetoric and partisan identity, they also felt betrayed by Tyler. Whatever motivated the protests, such strong, negative emotions boded poorly for his presidency.[18]

All in all, Tyler's first veto was decidedly unpopular among Whigs and indicated that he was out of step with both his party and the public. Clay compared Tyler's political confidants to Jackson's informal circle of advisors, known as the "Kitchen Cabinet," "a cabal" at work to undermine the traditional workings of government, and a "corporal's guard" "endeavoring to form a third party." The term "corporal's guard" stuck and was primarily used to describe Tyler's Virginia Cabal and his non-Virginia advisors, such as Massachusetts representative Caleb Cushing. Still, Tyler did not learn his lesson. The following month, he vetoed a second bill addressing the nation's financial state. What made this decision particularly repugnant to many of the president's associates was the fact that he had looked over the legislation ahead of time and had given his tacit approval before it was introduced. Embarrassed and angry at being perceived as a puppet of a cabal instead of the master of his domain, the president decided that he would rather risk the backlash from vetoing another bill than accept legislation he did not support.[19]

Democrats applauded Tyler's courage at standing up to Clay and the Whigs, while some of the president's men went to great lengths to defend him. Henry A. Wise, for example, engaged in fisticuffs with Edward Stanly on the floor of the House that required the corpulent Alabama representative Dixon H. Lewis to insert himself "like an elephant among a parcel [of] dogs" until order was restored. Tyler's intransigence and his supporters' behavior thoroughly appalled the Whigs. As a result, rumors of a cabinet dissolution spread like wildfire through Washington. Some compared the early progression of Tyler's presidency to the chaos of the Eaton affair that had marred Jackson's first term. Others welcomed a shake-up to rid Tyler of the millstone of Clay Whiggery. "We are on the eve of a cabinet rupture," Wise reported gleefully.[20]

The following weekend, Tyler's entire cabinet, except Webster, resigned.

Ewing offered the most pointed criticism in his resignation letter. He claimed that the veto had "no origin in conscience, and no reference to the public good" and asserted that he could not "be one of the instruments by which the Executive wields these combined, accumulated, and dangerous powers," namely, the uniting of "the purse with the sword." Webster decided to stay on. He and Tyler appeared to share the same vision of foreign relations; there was no reason to throw that away and potentially harm the country. Having anticipated the resignations, Tyler moved quickly to name replacements. In doing so, he chose those who agreed with him on the bank issue. The two most consequential appointments were South Carolinian Hugh S. Legaré as attorney general and Abel P. Upshur as secretary of the navy. Like Tyler, both Legaré and Upshur supported Manifest Destiny; believed that even though slavery was not the ideal institution, formerly enslaved people could not possibly live in the United States without precipitating a race war; and saw abolitionism as a threat to the nation's future.[21]

The Whigs' initial reaction was surprising. At a party dinner, Clay and other party leaders reportedly "talked freely & jocosely about the cabinet going out & seemed quite unconcerned about it." Whig senators gave Tyler little trouble on his cabinet nominations, approving them the same day they were submitted. Whigs may have been so accommodating because party leaders had already decided to divorce themselves from the president and his administration. A committee of eight Whig congressional members was appointed to prepare a statement to the public on the events of the extra session. Congressional Whigs unanimously adopted this "Whig Manifesto," which placed the blame for the failures of the special session squarely on Tyler's shoulders. Whigs had brought him into office with Harrison, but now they were washing their hands of him. Tyler and his advisors "should be exclusively hereafter deemed accountable," the statement asserted. And though Whigs would respect the president and support his measures when possible, they wanted the people to know that Tyler had "voluntarily separated himself from those by whose exertions and suffrages he was" made president. In other words, the Whigs had not abandoned the president—he had abandoned them. What Clay had predicted earlier in the summer—that Tyler seemed determined to "detach himself from the great body of the Whig party"—was coming true.[22]

The Whigs ordered 20,000 copies of their address printed, looking to distribute them to the public in time to head off any political fallout during the fall elections. Their strategy failed. In the post-veto (mid-August 1841) gubernatorial and state legislative elections, Whigs suffered defeat after de-

ent, is manifested by its leaders," Webster observed during the elections. When the results were known, he told his son, "The recent elections show that the Whig party is broken up, and perhaps can never be reunited." The lame-duck congressional session that followed the elections did nothing to help the Whigs. They accused Tyler of abusing his patronage power and ignoring his own promises to bring reform to government appointments. Criticism of the president increased as Whigs debated yet another impeachment attempt. This one failed too, but Whigs were clearly signaling that Tyler would find no reprieve for the remainder of his term. His assertion of executive privilege over papers related to various executive matters, including his use of patronage, only made matters worse.[25]

As Tyler tussled with the Whigs over the economy and other issues, he began to see foreign relations as a source of possible political strength. His approach to foreign policy relied on several propositions. First, Tyler subscribed to the Jeffersonian perspective that acquiring territory was essential to creating an electorate of yeoman farmers tied to the land and, consequently, committed to the government's success. More territory also meant that the national government was less able to control the people. Second, Tyler believed that slavery should accompany this territorial expansion. Like many elite white Virginia enslavers, he was invested—literally—in perpetuating the racist institution that exploited enslaved laborers. Third, like many Americans, Anglophobia shaped Tyler's view of how the conquest and control of territory provided security for the nation. He perceived abolitionism as an insidious tool the British wanted to use to end slavery in the United States and increase their power in North America. Finally, Tyler followed in the footsteps of fellow Virginians Jefferson, Madison, and Monroe in seeing the republic's expansion as key to alleviating sectional discord and preserving the Union.[26]

All of these factors—support for territorial expansion and slavery, fear of Britain, and a desire for sectional unity—played a significant role in what became Tyler's two key foreign policy objectives, introduced in his first annual message of December 1841 and pursued most aggressively when his political future was in doubt. The United States' successful settlement of competing claims to the Oregon territory in the Pacific Northwest and its strategy to annex Texas would play an important role not only in shaping the latter part of Tyler's presidency but also in influencing how the 1844 presidential campaign unfolded.[27]

THE OREGON QUESTION

The United States first laid claim to the Oregon country in the 1790s. Included in this territory was the present-day Canadian province of British Columbia and the whole of the present-day states of Washington, Oregon, and Idaho, plus parts of Montana and Wyoming. The British also had a vested interest in the nearly 450,000 square miles that constituted the area. By the 1810s, both nations were competing for control of land and the fur trade in this part of the Pacific Northwest. In 1818 and again in 1827, the United States and Great Britain made formal agreements to jointly occupy Oregon. In 1842, the two governments authorized Daniel Webster and Alexander Baring, Lord Ashburton, to reopen discussions. Ashburton offered less territory than previous Britain ministers, and Webster naïvely thought that convincing Mexico to give the United States control of San Francisco would provide it with the Pacific harbor it would otherwise lack if the United States accepted Britain's proposed boundary. Tyler injected himself prominently into these negotiations and into other unsettled diplomatic issues between the United States and Great Britain concerning the US-Canadian border. The Treaty of Washington (later called the Webster–Ashburton Treaty) of 1842 settled the boundary questions, but to Tyler's frustration, it ultimately failed to provide any progress on the Oregon question.[28]

This lack of resolution coincided with Oregon becoming more attractive to American settlers. Beginning in 1837, pro-Oregon politicians, such as Democratic senator Lewis F. Linn of Missouri and Whig representative Caleb Cushing, who John Quincy Adams thought possessed a "ravenous appetite for the occupation of Oregon," urged the United States to move aggressively in claiming possession of the territory. Supporters submitted resolutions and presented petitions showing that the American people wanted Oregon. Americans nevertheless remained a minority there, outnumbered by the British and indigenous populations, until 1843. That year, Americans living in Oregon were guaranteed 640 free acres if certain residency and improvement expectations were met. This promise led to the "Great Migration," when 875 Americans took up residence in the territory. The following year, when voters were deciding on the next president, 1,475 Americans made the decision to settle in Oregon. Many of these settlers came from areas, such as the states of the Old Northwest, where slavery had never existed; others migrated from slave states but were not themselves enslavers. The absence of slavery, which was officially outlawed in Oregon in 1844, "create[d] a white yeomen's haven" and became a bold free-soil experiment for the white Americans, many of them Democrats, who chose to settle there. These expansionist efforts ensured that the Oregon question would be part of the campaign conversation in 1844.[29]

THE REPUBLIC OF TEXAS

Texas was the other geographic area of interest to Tyler. Since the end of annexation efforts during Van Buren's presidency, the Texas government had pursued several opportunities to provide the Lone Star Republic some stability. Its leaders—specifically Presidents Mirabeau B. Lamar and Sam Houston—used both money and the threat of military force to try to convince Mexico to recognize Texas's independence; they also reached out to Britain and France with various diplomatic proposals and trade agreements.[30]

Tyler first broached the topic with Webster in the weeks following the September 1841 cabinet reorganization. "I gave you a hint as to the possibility of acquiring Texas by treaty. I verily believe it could be done," he wrote. Tyler acknowledged that the question of slavery would factor into any annexation discussion, but he believed that he had the answer. Limiting the domestic slave trade would diffuse the enslaved population in the upper South, he argued, gradually ending it in those states. Northerners uncomfortable with slavery could be confident that the subsequent increase in the number of free southern states would offset any slave states that came into the United States because of Texas. Webster was not interested in pursuing Texas, but Tyler was, admiringly mentioning the Lone Star Republic in his first annual message in December 1841.[31]

The annexation issue largely lay dormant throughout the political battles of 1842, as Webster's reluctance to pursue Texas kept Tyler at bay. The secretary of state had opposed annexation while in the Senate, and he continued to do so as the nation's chief diplomatic officer, fearing that pursuing such a course would exacerbate sectionalism and stir up the animosity between enslavers and antislavery forces. By early 1843, however, it had become clear to Tyler that he and the Whigs would never reconcile and that finding a home within the Democratic Party was just as unlikely. Positioning himself for a presidential run in 1844 required Tyler not only to consider forming a third party but also to identify an organizing principle to galvanize supporters into a potent electoral force. Texas annexation offered just the opportunity.[32]

Tyler was encouraged to move forward on the annexation question by Virginia Cabal members Henry A. Wise and Thomas Gilmer. In April 1842, Wise, who later claimed to have planted the idea of making Texas annexation the central issue of Tyler's presidency, gave a speech in the US House that laid the foundation for pro-annexation arguments used in the 1844 presidential campaign. In it, he emphasized the conspiratorial threat of Great Britain against the United States and the benefits of moving slavery geographically westward. Wise also argued that annexing Texas would allow abolitionists "to mitigate those evils of slavery," which they could not do if it remained independent. In January 1843, Gilmer wrote a public letter coming out strongly for bringing Texas into the Union. In it, he argued annexation was an issue of national importance, not just "a Southern or local question." He further contended that annexing Texas would allow non-slaveholding states to sell their goods in a domestic market free from foreign competition; that adding Texas to the Union would not stir up the slavery controversy; and that if the United States did not take control of the Lone Star Republic, Great Britain and its abolitionists would "either possess or control Texas." Uniting in its defense, therefore, was the only path forward. As it turned out, Gilmer's letter would play an influential role in the following year's presidential campaign.[33]

In early 1843, however, what mattered was that both Gilmer and Wise held Tyler's ear and encouraged him to pursue Texas. Antiannexation forces did not stand idly by while the president and his advisors pushed their expansionist agenda. Even before Tyler began seriously pursuing Texas, John Quincy Adams spoke forcefully against the proposition. In a September 1842 speech to his constituents, he described nullification and Texas annexation as part of "the slave-breeding conspiracy against the freedom of the North." It was this Slave Power conspiracy that had controlled the United States for decades and that now had its sights set on taking Texas; it included presidents, cabinet members, Supreme Court justices, Speakers of the House, high-ranking military officers, and others in government, all seeking to use Texas to expand the power of the slaveocracy. It was not a new argument, but it was an effective narrative to propose in an era when conspiracy thinking flourished. As discussion of annexation increased in early 1843, Adams joined twelve other congressmen in issuing an address declaring that by adding Texas to the Union, "*the undue ascendency of the slaveholding power in the Government shall be secured and rivetted beyond all redemption.*" In a heated, private conversation with Webster, he told the secretary of state that he believed Tyler's foreign policy goals, including annexation, "were parts of one great system, looking to a war for conquest and plunder from Mexico, and a war with England and alliance with France." Webster assured Adams that he opposed annexation and that "it could never be effected by him or with his consent." Unconvinced, the former president made numerous trips to the State Department in the ensuing weeks to research the conspiracy that he believed was afoot.[34]

Webster had not been entirely forthcoming with Adams about his effectiveness as a safeguard against annexation. He was, in fact, already thinking about resigning weeks before they met. Webster wrote to Nicholas Biddle, the former Bank president, that although he and Tyler were on good terms personally, the president was pursuing "movements in which I cannot concur." Tyler wanted to run for president in 1844, Webster said, and he was "giving *offices* to hungry applicants" with that singular goal in mind. "I am expecting, every day, measures, which I cannot stand by, & face the Country," he sighed. He officially informed Tyler of his resignation on May 8, 1843. Tyler was not displeased with Webster's decision to step down, and neither was the Texas government. Isaac Van Zandt, Texas's chargé d'affaires to the United States, reported that Webster was "very much in the way" and too "fearful of his abolition constituents in Massachusetts." Van Zandt predicted that if Abel P. Upshur replaced Webster as expected, "it will be one of the best appointments for us. His whole soul is with us. He is an able man, and has the nerve to act."[35]

Tyler did indeed elevate Upshur as Van Zandt had hoped. His appointment opened the door for the Tyler administration to approach annexation more aggressively. Upshur's Anglophobia combined several conspiracy theories prominent among white southerners into one paranoid amalgamation. He believed Great Britain would lure enslaved people to Texas with the promise of freedom. In response, he reasoned, the southern states would go to war with Texas to recover their enslaved human property, with Mexico presumably inserting itself to win back its former territory. When the northern states refused to assist their fellow Americans in their military effort, the United States would divide, allowing Britain to establish economic hegemony in its absence. Only by admitting Texas to the Union as a slave state could the United States avoid this fate.[36]

The pro-Calhoun newspaper editor Duff Green fleshed out this purported British conspiracy while acting as an unofficial agent (or as some called him, "the ambassador of *slavery*") for the Tyler administration in Europe. From his arrival in London in late 1841 through 1843, he reported on, and intervened in, several developments that he deemed important to the United States. Green's interaction with British government officials and exposure to its press convinced him that Great Britain was conspiring to establish its economic supremacy globally, in part by abolishing slavery in the United States. The former editor used European periodicals to spread his conspiracy theories anonymously. So convincing were Green's reports that Tyler and Upshur ignored those of Edward Everett, the US minister to England. Everett, who was marginalized after Webster's resignation, was hesitant to lend credence to some of the rumors that Green was spreading, preferring to take a more measured approach. This was not the trend within the Tyler administration, however. By the summer of 1843, Upshur was dismissing Everett's official reports as naïve and accepting at face value Green's description of Britain's alleged schemes in Texas.[37]

As Green peregrinated around Europe collecting intelligence and spreading disinformation, the Tyler administration continued its campaign to build support for annexation among the American people. From September through November 1843, Upshur wrote anonymous pro-annexation editorials for the *Madisonian*. The earliest of these propaganda pieces attacked Great Britain for its plot to control both Texas and Oregon and downplayed the possibility of slavery's expansion into Texas if it were acquired. Later ones accused Adams of doing everything in his power "to make the annexation of Texas a pretext for the violent disruption of the Union."[38]

The Tyler administration also tried to manage two related concerns. One was dampening Texas's growing interest in Britain's influence. As Tyler shared with Waddy Thompson, US envoy extraordinary and minister plenipotentiary to Texas, he was concerned that Britain was pursuing two goals: "the instant and total abolition of slavery" in the Lone Star Republic and Texas independence. If either supposition proved to be true, Tyler told Thompson, "it is of essential importance that Texas should not yield it." The Houston administration in Texas wanted assurances that the United States was going to pursue annexation soon, but Upshur was limited in what he could promise until Congress reconvened in December. In the meantime, the secretary of state told William S. Murphy, the US chargé to Texas, that he needed to convince Sam Houston, who had "an obvious leaning towards" Britain, that the people of Texas wanted to be annexed. Murphy had to do so, however, without alienating the Texas president. The other concern was maximizing Everett's official position as US minister to Britain. It was one thing to have Green freelancing; influencing Her Majesty's government against interfering in Texas was quite another matter. Upshur tried to convince Everett, who was reluctant to support annexation, that it was a necessary move to protect slavery against British abolitionism. When Everett relayed that Britain was not interested in Texas or in spreading abolitionism, the secretary of state rejected his report, believing that the British government was being deceitful. If he did not know already, Everett must have realized that the die was cast: the Tyler administration was going whole hog for annexation.[39]

Consequently, in September 1843, Upshur approached Isaac Van Zandt several times about opening negotiations. The Texas chargé d'affaires was operating outside of official channels, but both he and Upshur seemed to believe that hammering out the details and presenting the treaty as a fait accompli was the best strategy for success. By early December, the two men appeared to have fleshed out the treaty terms, which were expected to be made public before the end of the year. The two major obstacles were Sam Houston and the US Senate. The Texas president was annoyed at Tyler's dawdling on the issue and indicated publicly that the Lone Star Republic might be more interested in operating under Mexico's influence than in joining the United States.[40]

Convincing two-thirds of the Senate to approve an annexation treaty also seemed unlikely, and Tyler's December 1843 annual message was ambiguous enough that it left many Americans and Texans confused about whether his administration was truly interested in pursuing this objective. As Upshur told Murphy, Tyler had avoided the topic in his message "until he could present the actual treaty of annexation." There was every reason to think that consummating the union between the United States and Texas was inevitable, the secretary of state wrote optimistically, with "*a clear constitutional majority of two thirds*" supporting annexation. Clay was incredulous when news of a possible annexation treaty started leaking in early 1844. "Is this true? Especially that 42 Senators have concurred in the project?" he asked. "If it be true, I shall regret extremely that I have had no hint of it." Whether or not support in the Senate was as high as reported, Upshur and Van Zandt were finalizing the terms of an annexation treaty. These included Texas becoming a US territory, with the possibility of statehood; the protection of slavery within its borders; Texas's relinquishment of its public lands; and the United States' assumption of Texas's public debt.[41]

As representatives of the two nations were hammering out this agreement, Tyler and his advisors continued their pro-annexation efforts. Helping them in this regard was Robert J. Walker. Born in Pennsylvania, the Mississippi senator became the "unofficial spokesman for the administration" during the winter 1843–44 congressional session. One Democratic newspaper editor later described the short, curly-haired, volatile Walker as "the most adroit manipulator then in public life," the "Delilah" who convinced Tyler to embrace Democratic policies such as annexation. Walker had several motivations: popular pressure in Mississippi, where many, but not all, citizens shared his vision of Manifest Destiny; his own landowner-ship in Texas; and his aspirations for becoming the Democrats' vice presidential nominee in 1844. Enhancing Walker's voice was his uncle William Wilkins, who took over for James M. Porter as Tyler's secretary of war in February 1844.[42]

One of Walker's first efforts regarding the Texas issue was writing a pamphlet that articulated the pro-annexation argument. In it, he argued that slavery was a ruinous institution that was destroying the United States by depleting southern soil. Yet slavery was so profitable that getting rid of it was unthinkable. A tipping point was fast approaching, he believed, when the supply of cash crops would begin to diminish. When that day came, Walker predicted, the United States would face disaster. Southern enslavers would not only lose their profits, but they would also be faced with the prospect of having to emancipate those they held in bondage. Now free, these formerly enslaved people would remain within the confines of the United States, competing for northern jobs and threatening racial violence. The solution, Walker offered, was making Texas a "safety-valve" for slavery. As Texas became saturated with slavery, the institution, and the people enslaved by it, would naturally move southward into Mexico and Latin America. Annexation, Walker concluded, was "essential to the security of the South, the defence of the West, and highly conducive to the welfare and perpetuity of the whole Union." Walker's treatise appeared in national newspapers and set the tone for discussion of the annexation issue.[43]

In addition to producing this pro-annexation pamphlet, Walker also wrote Andrew Jackson a confidential letter urging him to reach out to Houston and encourage his old friend to support the effort. He flattered Old Hickory by telling him "this would be the crowning act" of his many contributions to the nation. Jackson did not need convincing to support annexation. In December 1843, he had asserted confidently that "if made at washington [DC]," Houston would "cheerfully enter into the treaty." The following month, however, Jackson aide William B. Lewis expressed some concern to Old Hickory that "all is not *right*" in Texas. He reported that Upshur and Van Zandt had been waiting six weeks for the Houston administration to approve official negotiations, but none were forthcoming. "I think you had better write to Houston," Lewis urged his longtime mentor. Jackson doubted that the Texas president was waffling, especially with "a large majority" of the Texas Congress supporting annexation. Opposing it would put Houston "in a perilous situation & destroy him forever." Nevertheless, Jackson wrote his friend that he hoped that he would "throw no impediment" in the way of Texas being annexed.[44]

Houston was not sitting by idly. In December 1843, he sent Texas chargé James Pinckney Henderson to Washington to pursue three objectives: an annexation treaty, an offensive and defensive alliance, or a defensive treaty, in that order. The Texas president also sent his private secretary Washington D. Miller as a personal envoy to the Hermitage, where he presented Jackson with a letter that pronounced Houston "determined upon immediate annexation to the United States." Jackson instructed Miller to take Houston's letter to Washington and give it to Walker "to use confidentially to promote" an annexation treaty.[45]

The stars seemed to be aligning for a successful annexation treaty, but a tragic event changed everything. On Wednesday, February 28, 1844, just one day after former Second Bank of the United States president Nicholas Biddle passed away at his Philadelphia estate, Captain Robert F. Stockton invited various political and diplomatic dignitaries from the nation's capital aboard the USS *Princeton* to witness a demonstration of the ship's new weaponry. "A humbug sort of fellow, a speculator, intriguer, politician & popularity hunter," according to one observer, Stockton was looking to convince Congress to appropriate funds that would allow him to build more ships like the *Princeton*. Among those aboard Stockton's ship that fateful Wednesday were several notable politicians and diplomats, including President Tyler, Secretary of State Upshur, Secretary of the Navy Gilmer, Texas chargé Van Zandt, Senator Thomas Hart Benton, and Mexican minister plenipotentiary to the United States Juan N. Almonte. Julia Gardiner, the president's love interest, was also there, dressed in "a white tarleton" and "a crimson Greek cap." Others joining the excursion were Julia's father, former New York state senator David Gardiner, and Dolley Madison, the seventy-five-year-old former first lady. The *Princeton* left dock at noon, traveling down the icy Potomac River. The original demonstration ended at 2:00 P.M. Shortly after 4:00 P.M., as the ship traveled back up the river past George Washington's Mount Vernon home, Gilmer insisted on another demonstration in honor of the first president.[46]

About 100 of the estimated 300 to 400 people aboard the *Princeton* gathered on deck for the demonstration, while the rest stayed below as the band played "Home Sweet Home." To the left of the "Peacemaker," one of the ship's massive twin guns, stood Gilmer, Upshur, Senator Gardiner, Commodore Beverley Kennon, and Virgil Maxcy, former US chargé to Belgium. To the right stood Stockton and Benton, with Senator Samuel

AWFUL EXPLOSION OF THE "PEACE-MAKER" ON BOARD THE U.S. STEAM FRIGATE, *PRINCETON*, ON WEDNESDAY, 28th FEB^Y 1844.

The USS Princeton *explosion killed six people, including Secretary of State Abel P. Upshur and Secretary of the Navy Thomas W. Gilmer. The loss of these two cabinet members altered the Tyler administration's approach to Texas annexation. (Courtesy of the Library of Congress)*

Phelps farther back and to the rear. John C. Calhoun's son Patrick was walking away from the "Peacemaker" when it was fired at approximately 4:30 P.M. The breech exploded to the left, leaving six people "killed and shockingly mutilated." "The blood was running in crimson streams down the deck," one man on board reported, the faces of the dead "so blackened by the smoke of the powder and distorted in the agonies of death" that they were unrecognizable. Five of the six died instantly. Gardiner, Gilmer, Kennon, Maxcy, and Upshur were the names that everyone read about in the news reports that circulated in the days to come. Maxcy's right arm was severed at the elbow, "yet retained in the sleeve of his coat." Both of Gardiner's legs were "broken above the knee," and both of Kennon's arms "were broken in several places and one of his feet came off in attempting to get his boot off." The gruesome aftermath revealed that all five men had also suffered significant head injuries. Gilmer's wife, Anna, mother of their eight children, "became frantic" at the sight of her husband's body, and many other women on board reportedly fainted, including Julia Gardiner. The sixth fatality was "a stout black man about 23 or 24 years old" named Armistead (sometimes referred to as Henry). Often absent from contemporary reports or simply referred to as Tyler's valet, the enslaved man was leaning on another cannon when shrapnel from the "Peacemaker" struck him.[47]

Tyler was below deck when the accident occurred and remained unharmed. As he carried Julia off the boat, she recovered her senses and, in her recollection decades later, "struggled so that I almost knocked us both off the gang-plank." The president suffered no physical injuries from the accident, but the consequences of the *Princeton* explosion weighed heavily on him as he attended the funeral ceremonies of the five white victims whose lives ended that Wednesday afternoon. "What a loss I have sustained in Upshur and Gilmer," Tyler wrote one of his daughters. Not only were two of his closest advisors and staunchest supporters now dead, but their absence also came at a crucial moment in his administration and left him in a precarious political position. The Senate was considering an annexation treaty with Texas that Upshur had carefully crafted and that Gilmer had supported. Tyler was counting on this treaty to help him stay in the White House; what would happen now was anyone's guess.[48]

Upshur's work of the past few months, putting together both a draft treaty and a coalition of senators who would support it, now appeared to be in jeopardy. Recognizing that his administration faced a critical turning point, Tyler moved swiftly to replace his deceased cabinet officers. On March 5, three days after their funerals, Tyler nominated John Y. Mason, a Democrat and a federal judge from Virginia, as Gilmer's replacement. Filling the absence at the top of the State Department was a more monumental decision, especially given the circumstances. Just one day after nominating Mason, Tyler submitted John C. Calhoun's name to the Senate as Upshur's replacement. Calhoun's southern allies were especially adamant that he had to accept the post and make his way to Washington as quickly as possible to conclude the treaty negotiations. Henry Wise appeared to be the central figure who persuaded Tyler to select Calhoun, and the president likely needed some convincing. He did not fully trust the South Carolinian to treat annexation as a national, not a sectional, issue. Van Zandt reported the day before Calhoun's nomination that Tyler wanted annexation completed before "the gentleman to whom he intended to offer the permanent appointment" as Upshur's replacement took over. This hardly spoke of confidence in Calhoun. What may have swayed Tyler to choose Calhoun was a rumored quid pro quo: a cabinet post for the South Carolinian and his accompanying support for the annexation of Texas, in exchange for the

South's backing of Tyler, either as the Democratic nominee for president or the choice of a third party.[49]

Calhoun accepted the cabinet appointment and set off for Washington with the stated intent, he told both his family members and the president, to resolve the Texas and Oregon questions, then retire. Calhoun was sworn in on March 30, 1844, and went to work immediately. Within two weeks of his arrival in Washington, the new secretary of state had made an agreement with Texas's emissaries, based on Upshur's previous negotiations. Along with this understanding was Tyler's promise to provide Texas with US military support against "all foreign invasion" during the treaty process. Things appeared set to head to a Senate largely favorable to annexation. Before his unexpected death, Upshur had calculated that he had more than enough votes to ratify the treaty. But before sending the proposed treaty to the Senate, Calhoun made a decision that confirmed Tyler's suspicions of his aggressive sectionalism and threatened to undo all the work that his administration had undertaken to successfully conclude annexation.[50]

While going through the mail that had piled up in the State Department office since Upshur's death, Calhoun found a letter from Richard Pakenham, the British minister to the United States. Two days before the *Princeton* tragedy, Pakenham forwarded correspondence from Lord Aberdeen, the British foreign secretary, clarifying Britain's policy toward Texas. The December 26, 1843, dispatch denied that Her Majesty's government was pursuing a secretive abolitionist agenda regarding Texas. The British government did indeed support the spread of abolitionism around the globe, but, the foreign secretary remarked, it was not going to "interfere unduly" in Texas to end slavery. Aberdeen added that Britain would "neither openly nor secretly resort to any measures" that would "stir up disaffection or excitement of any kind in the slave-holding States of the American Union."[51]

Aberdeen's comments should not have been surprising given the official information Everett was sending from Europe. Pakenham undoubtedly intended the correspondence to put to rest any concerns Tyler or the Senate had about Britain's intentions regarding Texas or the United States. But the Tyler administration interpreted the situation through the conspiratorial lens fashioned by Duff Green and others. Instead of acknowledging the reality of British abolitionism and accepting Aberdeen's reassurances that it was not intended to target US slavery, Calhoun wrote a reply indicating Tyler's disapproval of Britain's desire to "procure the general abolition of slavery throughout the world." The secretary of state framed the annexation of Texas as a defensive move by the United States to protect its domestic slavery. Calhoun then appealed to the US census to argue that the differences between African Americans in the North and South were palpable. Free African Americans in the antislavery states, he argued, had "invariably sunk into vice and pauperism, accompanied by the bodily and mental afflictions incident thereto—deafness, blindness, insanity and idiocy, to a degree without example." Enslaved people in the South, on the other hand, "enjoy[ed] a degree a health and comfort" comparable to other working-class populations "in Christendom." They had never "attained so high an elevation in morals, intelligence, or civilization" as in the South, Calhoun asserted. Pakenham's reply reiterated Britain's stance toward abolitionism and Texas, to which Calhoun responded with a further defense of slavery as the best condition for enslaved people and the need for Texas's annexation to preserve the institution.[52]

Calhoun included his April 18, 1844, letter to Pakenham in the documents accompanying the annexation treaty, which arrived in the Senate on April 22. The treaty and the additional documents were meant to be kept secret, but no one could realistically have expected confidentiality with such an explosive issue. Senator Benjamin Tappan of Ohio sent copies of the treaty and the significant accompanying documents to New York, where they were published on April 27. Newspapers across the United States subsequently reprinted them, allowing people to read for themselves the administration's pro-slavery justifications for annexation. Reaction to Calhoun's correspondence with Pakenham was swift and condemnatory. Some argued that the secretary of state had intentionally emphasized slavery to divide the nation, create "a Southern confederacy," and "make himself the great man of the fragment which he expects to tear" from the Union. Others thought the South Carolinian was positioning himself for the Democratic presidential nomination. Even if they did not smell a conspiracy, others criticized the sectionalism of Calhoun's letters. "This shows a great want of tact, as well as judgement," William B. Lewis complained to Jackson. "He should have placed the measure upon broad *national* principles." Webster pronounced himself "utterly astonished" at Calhoun. The annexation treaty and the evidence the current secretary of state had put forward supporting it "make sensible people ashamed of their Country. Never did I see such reprehensible sentiment, & unsurpassed nonsense." Philadelphia diarist Sidney George Fisher called Calhoun's arguments about slavery's benefits "laughably absurd. . . . On the subject of slavery & the South he has long been a mono-maniac."[53]

Calhoun did not hide his rationale for writing Pakenham as he did or for including the correspondence with the annexation treaty. Prior to assuming his cabinet post, he had argued that "we must show, as fixed a determination to defend our property & our safety, as the friends of the tariff & the abolitionists do to assail them." His Pakenham letter put that strategy in motion. The annexation treaty was "a question of life and death," Calhoun wrote South Carolina governor James Henry Hammond as the Senate debate took place in May. The secretary of state expected that his letter would be "the foundation" for any discussion about annexation, and he wanted the South to rally to his standard. "Now is the time to vindicate & save our institutions," he implored. It was time to learn if northerners were as willing to defend the South as white southerners had been to help their northern neighbors. During the Jackson administration, Sidney George Fisher had described Calhoun as "no plotting politician but a chivalrous enthusiastic champion of the peculiar and unfortunate doctrines which he has undertaken to defend." In reality, there is no reason the South Carolinian could not have been both strategic and principled. Despite Tyler's later denial, Calhoun also had the president's approval.[54]

The Pakenham letter set the narrative that dominated the Senate discussion. On May 10, the treaty moved from the Committee on Foreign Relations to the full chamber for debate. Benton led the Democratic opposition to ratification. His speeches and resolutions painted a conspiratorial picture of the Tyler administration secretly manipulating circumstances and producing propaganda to hoodwink the people into supporting annexation, an effort that portended war. Other senators were also concerned about the possibility of military conflict, along with the treaty's lack of specificity about Texas's boundary with Mexico. Annexation supporters among the Democratic senators included Walker, James Buchanan, and Levi Woodbury, all of whose names were under consideration for the Democratic Party ticket in 1844.[55]

As the Senate debated annexation, Whig and Democratic delegates prepared to gather in Baltimore to select their respective party's tickets, and Tyler supporters planned their own independent convention to compete with that of the Democrats. The main contenders—men such as Calhoun, Clay, and Webster, among others—had spent the last few months, and in some cases years, making their case for nomination. The old party divisions over issues such as the tariff and banking were on the delegates' minds, but recent events made it clear that annexation was going to play a major role in determining not only the party candidates but also the contours of the subsequent presidential campaign.

THE WHIG FIELD

Following Tyler's expulsion from the Whig Party, it appeared obvious to most people that the Whigs would run Clay for president in 1844. As the man many party members considered their leading statesman and greatest champion, he was the logical choice. They could count on Clay taking the fight to the enemy, whether it was Tyler or the Democrats. But not all Whigs agreed. Clay's prominent role in heading the opposition to the Tyler administration led some to question whether his loyalty was to party or personal ambition. Antislavery Whigs were not happy with Clay being an enslaver, which caused them to look elsewhere. Other Whigs, as they had in 1839, simply wanted a fresh face, someone untainted by the political battles of the last two decades, someone who could win. Having made a serious error in placing Tyler on the ticket with Harrison, they believed they could not afford another mistake.

Consequently, three other names besides Clay's emerged before the party's national convention as possible candidates for the 1844 presidential nomination: John McLean, Winfield Scott, and Daniel Webster. For some Whigs, McLean's experience made him an attractive alternative to Clay. Born in 1785, the New Jersey native had been a newspaper editor, a lawyer, and a supreme court judge in his adopted state of Ohio. His national experience included two stints in the US House and a brief appointment as commissioner of the General Land Office before President James Monroe named him postmaster general in 1823. Jackson considered rewarding McLean's loyalty in the 1828 election by keeping him in the cabinet but decided that moving him to the US Supreme Court might quell some of his obvious presidential aspirations.[56]

McLean's ambition to become president percolated in the next two elections, but it came to naught. By 1840, he appeared satisfied to remain on the Supreme Court. McLean was not mentioned as a candidate that year, and he turned down an appointment as secretary of war early in Tyler's administration to stay on the bench. Whig losses in the fall 1842 elections, however, rekindled interest in McLean. Some Whigs believed that as a former Jacksonian, he could lure Democrats to their party if Van Buren was nominated. McLean had been a supporter of internal improvements and a protective tariff, but he had also taken a moderate approach to the Bank question, which allowed both sides to find something positive about his candidacy. A devout Methodist, he also interested more religious-minded Whigs, a constituency that Clay, the rumored gambler and womanizer, might find difficult to energize.[57]

Henry Clay, 1844. (Courtesy of the Library of Congress)

Accordingly, McLean supporters in Ohio, Michigan, and Pennsylvania began organizing on his behalf. McLean responded to the interest by providing analysis as to why his potential opponents were unfit for the presidency. But by mid-1843, he had gotten cold feet and had decided to stay on the bench. McLean reportedly proclaimed that "any Whig who would allow himself to be taken up against [Clay] must be a fool," which suggests that he thought his odds were too poor to chance. Publicly, McLean's reasons were more virtuous. The presidency, he wrote a correspondent, "sinks below the ambition of an honorable mind, when it is attainable only by a sacrifice of the loftiest patriotism." Therefore, he concluded, "I do not desire and would not receive the Presidency, if within my reach, as the instrument of a party." This private letter, which made it into the newspapers, did not entirely quash speculation that Whigs might choose McLean, but it ended any realistic chance that he would be their presidential nominee.[58]

Winfield Scott, who had been a contender for the Whigs' 1840 presidential nomination, represented some party members' idea of the perfect candidate. Scott had joined the US Army in 1808 at the age of twenty-one and had taken part in every major US military conflict since then except the First Seminole War. He also possessed diplomatic skills, which had proven extremely valuable when Van Buren had called on him to help quell the rising tensions along the Canadian border. Some Whigs were just looking for someone, anyone, to keep Clay off the ticket. When Whigs and Democrats alike had approached Scott about running for the presidency in 1840, he balked, in part because he thought he was everyone's "*second* choice" and also because he "was absolutely indifferent whether I ever reached the office of President." Scott's nomination never gained momentum at the 1839 Whig national convention, where he came in a distant third to Harrison and Clay. Scott may have lost the nomination, but he gained a promotion when Tyler appointed him the US Army's commanding general.[59]

Before the 1839 nominating convention, Scott had reassured Whigs that if their party lost in 1840 and needed "a leader of the forlorn hope," then they could "reckon upon me for that service." As their party descended into chaos during the Tyler administration, some Whigs believed they should take him up on his offer. In addition to his military experience and organizational skills, Scott's love of socializing, which earned him the nickname "Old Fuss and Feathers," endeared him to some Whigs. But he could also be arrogant and aloof, and his views were not always aligned with mainstream Whigs. For example, Scott spoke favorably of Thomas Jefferson, considered the Democrats' philosophical forefather. He also believed that a strong, competent leader—someone like himself perhaps—could serve as president for life. Another deficiency was his supervision of Cherokee removal during Van Buren's presidency, which had resulted in the Trail of Tears. For many Whigs, this was unforgiveable. Yet another issue was Scott's equivocal views on slavery, which one newspaper observed would "probably, not give entire satisfaction to the *ultras* of either side of the question." He believed that Congress could not regulate slavery within an individual state but that it did have the authority to decide on the institution's continued existence in the nation's capital. He also supported gradual, compensated emancipation, which won him no friends among many southern Whigs. Taken together, Scott was not a candidate on whom Whigs could depend to turn out the vote in their favor. Some Whig political leaders thought nominating him was a necessary compromise to follow the winning formula of selecting a military hero—this time a younger, hopefully healthier, version—but many party members remained leery of a Scott candidacy.[60]

Daniel Webster was a third possible challenger to Clay. Continuing his diplomatic career in another capacity after resigning his cabinet post in May 1843 seemed a logical next step. But some supporters had other plans for Webster. A group of New Hampshire Whigs, for example, distributed circulars nominating him for president. The "hundreds if not thousands" of signers endorsed Webster as "Defender of the Constitution" and lauded his diplomatic skill as preparatory for assuming the presidency. Webster graciously declined, informing his supporters that "the tendency of opinion among those to be represented in the Convention is generally and strongly set in another direction." Reports that Tyler endorsed his former secretary of state over Clay likely did little to encourage some Whigs to pursue Webster's nomination. Indeed, one Whig senator criticized him for "playing second fiddle to such a scoundrelly ninkompoop [sic] as" the president. Webster, who would be sixty-three when the new presidential administration began in March 1845, decided that practicing law to earn money was more imperative than pursuing what appeared to be a doomed attempt at winning the Whig Party's nomination. Even though there was an absence of substantial enthusiasm for Webster, some Whig newspapers speculated that he was the mastermind behind the push to nominate McLean or even that he wanted to put Calhoun in the White House.[61]

CLAY FOR PRESIDENT

These efforts to find an alternative to Clay largely fell by the wayside as the Kentuckian's candidacy gained momentum in 1842. For several weeks after retiring from Congress in March, Clay stayed in Washington, recovering from a likely heart attack. During that time, Whigs in North Carolina, New York, and Georgia endorsed him as their choice in 1844. When Clay returned to his home in Lexington, residents there met him with great fanfare. At a June 9, 1842, barbecue held in his honor, he gave what amounted to a campaign kickoff speech. It was part autobiography, part attack on his enemies, and part rallying cry for the Whigs. Clay concluded with a snarky remark about Tyler being but "a mere snap—a flash in the pan." This final comment reminded Clay's friends of one of his weaknesses: he sometimes let his words get away from him. "He must hereafter remain a little quiet and hold his jaw," Kentucky governor Robert P. Letcher advised fellow Whig John J. Crittenden. "In fact, he must be *caged*,—that's the point, *cage him!*" Crittenden knew better: like it or not, his friend was "going ahead like a *locomotive*."[62]

Clay assured Letcher he would "keep cool and stay at home," but he soon broke his promise, setting out on a cross-country trip to court voters. In September, he traveled to Dayton, Ohio, to address the state's Whig convention. One newspaper estimated 200,000 people in attendance, which did not count the tens of thousands who reportedly heard Clay speak on his way to the convention. He next visited Indiana, where he gave an address while "laboring under a severe cold." At the end of Clay's speech in Richmond, a Quaker named Hiram Mendenhall, representing "a committee of Abolitionists," presented him with a petition asking him to "let the oppressed under your control, who call you 'master' go free." The Whig press dismissed the petition as being signed not by a majority of true abolitionists but by Democrats and "Ladies and Gentlemen of Color" who had been attending "a Negro Camp Meeting" in a neighboring county. Only a third of the signers were abolitionists, according to one newspaper, which noted that "many of them [were] Females," as if their opinion, like that of the African American signers, did not matter.[63]

After Mendenhall presented the petition, Clay responded at length. But it was not an extemporaneous speech. The petition had been printed in a local newspaper the previous month, and Clay indicated in his speech that he had some prior knowledge of its content and of the signers. He chastised Mendenhall for confronting "a total stranger" whom he could have met at any other time. Clay pointed out that the laws of the land allowed slavery to exist and that the United States itself was founded on slavery. And even as he proclaimed that he believed slavery "a great evil," there were "far greater evils" in his opinion, namely, "a sudden, general, and indiscriminate emancipation" of enslaved people. Instead of the gradual emancipation and colonization of formerly enslaved people, Clay warned, what Mendenhall was asking for would lead to "civil war, carnage, pillage, conflagration, devastation, and the ultimate extermination or expulsion of the blacks." Far better, he argued, to maintain "the mild and continually improving state of slavery" that existed. Clay pointed to Charles Dupuy, one of the enslaved men who labored at Ashland and who was accompanying him on his trip, as an example of his treatment of African Americans. In Clay's telling, Dupuy had traveled across the continent with him and had never run away, even though he "had a thousand opportunities, if he had chosen." The Kentuckian concluded his diatribe with a challenge and an insult. Clay asked Mendenhall and the abolitionists he represented if they were willing to raise the $15,000 (about $565,000 in 2022) needed to free the nearly fifty enslaved people working at Ashland. He ended by telling Mendenhall to "go home, and mind your own business, and leave other people to take care of theirs."[64]

Clay's argument showed his attempt to thread the needle on the slavery issue. As an original member of the American Colonization Society, founded in 1816 to remove formerly enslaved African Americans to Africa, and as a member of Congress, he had tried to avoid condemning outright the institution of bonded labor that helped support his lifestyle. To some degree, all four prospective Whig nominees accepted the legality of slavery, but only Clay was an enslaver who had a vested interest in continuing the institution for his personal benefit. It remained to be seen if his identity as an enslaver would help or hurt him if he became the party's nominee.[65]

The rest of Clay's tour produced mixed results. In Indianapolis, he outlined his platform: a uniform currency; a protective tariff; restrictions on executive power, especially the use of the veto; the distribution of proceeds from land sales; and a limited program of internal improvements. Democratic critics called "the Clay Barbecue" in Indianapolis "a decided failure" and reveled in describing the chaotic scene of a steer running loose during the speech and the sight of Clay supporters shoving food into their "*great greasy holes.*" Clay's final stop—in Columbus, Indiana—was by many accounts a disaster. He arrived in an irritable mood, which he blamed on his travels, and tried to beg off speaking, but the crowd demanded his presence. Crittenden, who accompanied his friend on the tour, spoke first. His speech reportedly "descended to the vilest and most scurrilous billingsgate," but his delivery was called "quite pleasing, very deliberate, distinct and forcible." When it was Clay's turn, "an old soldier of the last war . . . not exactly understanding the order of the day" shouted, "*Hurra for Jackson.*" Clay responded with "a tone of sarcasm, resembling the growl of a tiger—"'Hurra for General Jackson!' . . . And where is your hurrah for your country?" According to the same report, he ranted "for several minutes, boiling with rage," before apologizing and giving "a set speech on the Tariff." "It was all a most pitiful failure," the paper concluded. With that dismal conclusion, Clay headed home.[66]

But not for long. In late November 1842, Clay set out for New Orleans on a visit "purely of business and of health." Well-wishers gathered to see Clay as he made his way down the Mississippi River, but the crowds failed to excite him. To some correspondents, Clay gave a muted response to prevent his "tour being given a political aspect." The explanation he gave his wife, Lucretia, was more honest: "an indiscribable [sic] state of feeling prevented my having any agreeable excitement by these demonstrations." Clay's lack of interest in political activities may have been a sign that he was still stinging from his last public appearance in Indiana. More likely, he was thinking about his debts, which were considerable ($19,391, or about $731,000 in 2022). His correspondence with Lucretia and their son Thomas while in New Orleans was full of concerns about the nation's economy and his own personal financial "embarrassments." As Clay's visit to the Crescent City drew to a close, he informed Thomas that his health was better, but "I cannot regain my spirits entirely." But the rest had apparently been good for him, so much so that he gave a speech in Memphis on his way back to Ashland. It was standard Clay fare—the currency, banking, executive overreach, the American System. His financial situation continued to worry him, but by the time he returned home in early March 1843, Clay's focus was on winning the Whig nomination and positioning himself to beat the Democratic nominee in the general campaign.[67]

To help secure the Whig nomination, Clay chose to attack Tyler. In a speech given in Lexington in April, he accused the president of using executive patronage to gain the support of the Democratic Party and thereby win himself a second term, not as a Whig, but as a Democrat. Clay also argued that when it came to important issues, such as the tariff and the distribution of revenue generated by the sale of public lands, congressional Whigs (including himself) "had done every thing that could be expected of them," but Tyler's use of the veto had "thwarted" their efforts. He continued these themes in speeches and correspondence, sometimes tailoring his message to address the specific interest of a group. For example, when speaking at an agricultural fair in Bourbon County, Kentucky, his theme was American-made products. Clay's messaging was clear: unlike Tyler, he was a tried-and-true Whig on whom party members could depend to fight for their principles if he became president.[68]

Clay also attempted to undermine potential challenges from within the mainstream Whig Party. He declared his intention "to remain perfectly passive until the nomination is made" and to support the eventual nominee "as I can consistently with honor, delicacy and propriety," but he was

THE GREAT AMERICAN STEEPLE CHASE FOR 1844.

Americans of all political persuasions expected Henry Clay to win the Whig presidential nomination. His presumed challengers included John C. Calhoun, John Tyler, and Martin Van Buren. (Courtesy of the Library of Congress)

determined not to be cast aside as he had been in 1839. To weaken his opposition, Clay made it clear that he would not make deals with anyone to be his running mate. When word reached him that some New York Whigs were attempting to galvanize support for McLean, Clay acted quickly. "Measures have been adopted there to counteract these machinations," he assured a friend. He believed that Webster presented the most formidable obstacle to the presidential nomination, and he worked especially hard to convince party leaders that the Massachusetts politician was unelectable. "Mr. Webster cannot control a solitary Electoral vote in" New England, Clay proclaimed to one correspondent. To another, he wrote, "Mr. Webster is now powerless" in Massachusetts. Clay pulled no punches when it came to undermining his rival. "I always regret that any great man (for such he is in some respects) should be wanting in self respect and dignity," he told one ally. Clay was determined to do everything in his power to win the presidential nomination, and putting Webster on the ticket was not part of his plan.[69]

Identifying someone compatible to join Clay on the ticket was something Whigs had to consider carefully. Webster seemed out of the question, but other options existed. Native sons were popular: Massachusetts Whigs wanted Governor John Davis, and Georgia Whigs endorsed Senator John M. Berrien. Other possibilities included McLean; Scott; former senator John M. Clayton of Delaware; former representative Millard Fillmore; Representative Francis Granger (a Whig vice presidential candidate in 1836); and John Sergeant (Clay's running mate in 1832). Privately, Clay remarked that he "like[d] Clayton better than any who have been talked of." Generally, however, he stuck to his principle of not "indicat[ing] any preference." He acknowledged that given the sectionalism of the nation, the Whig ticket would likely need to be regionally balanced with one candidate from a free state and one from a slave state. Since the party, not the presidential nominee, chose the running mate, Clay ultimately followed precedent and left it up to the national convention delegates to sift through the contenders.[70]

Even though the Democrats had yet to choose their nominee, Clay began laying the groundwork for his campaign against the man he thought they would pick: Martin Van Buren. By mid-1843, Clay observed that other Democratic contenders were attempting to sabotage Van Buren's chances much like the Whigs had done to him in 1839. The lack of Democratic unity encouraged Clay: "I believe we shall beat them, and more signally than we did in 1840." Of the other possible Democratic choices for president and vice president, he was especially critical of fellow Kentuckian Richard M. Johnson, whom he deemed "extremely needy" and possessing "an insatiable thirst for office." He expressed surprise that Lewis Cass "should ever have been thought formidable." Clay also had little use for James K. Polk, whom he accused of reviving the "corrupt bargain" charge of the 1824 presidential election.[71]

As winter approached, Clay decided once again to undertake a trip to New Orleans. Earlier in the year, he had turned down John Clayton's suggestion to commence a campaign tour, telling him "it would kill me." In the summer of 1843, Clay changed his mind, informing one group of North Carolina supporters that he intended to visit them the following spring. By December, Clay had decided to turn what normally would have been a trip to New Orleans on plantation business into a journey that would include campaign stops in six southern states: Alabama, Georgia, Louisiana, North Carolina, South Carolina, and Virginia. The trip would take place "on ground which I never trod before," he told one correspondent. Clay arrived in New Orleans just before Christmas and departed in late February 1844. While there, he received numerous invitations to visit and speak at future stops. Some he accepted; others he declined, either because the location was not on his itinerary, or because he was concerned about his health. Clay's desire "to avoid public entertainments with their train of excitements" was understandable given his history of heart problems.[72]

But a campaign tour required public appearances and addresses, and as Clay left New Orleans on his trip, he did what Americans had come to expect of presidential candidates. In Mobile, Alabama, Clay discussed his work on the 1833 compromise tariff that had ended the nullification crisis, proposing that a "reasonable" tariff policy was best for all Americans. He struck a nonpartisan tone in Georgia's capital city of Milledgeville, telling crowds there that the battle over the nation's political future was not being fought between "enemies of the country, but between two great parties aiming at the good of the country but differing in the means of accomplishing so great an object." Clay used the presence of Georgia governor George W. Crawford to reminisce about his initial support of the governor's cousin, William H. Crawford, in the 1824 election and his eventual decision to back Adams over Jackson in the controversial House vote that followed. Clay mentioned other events in which he had played a crucial role, such as the Missouri Compromise and the Compromise of 1833. Some onlookers might have wondered why the Kentuckian thought it prudent to bring up his vote against the Treaty of New Echota, which had given Cherokee land to the state, but he made it clear that he blamed the Jackson administration for the "corruption" that had produced the treaty. In Savannah, Clay continued along similar lines, but he introduced banking policy as another point of departure from the Democrats. "I am now as hoarse as a circuit rider" from giving so many speeches, he wrote at one point. By the time he reached Raleigh, North Carolina, in mid-April, he had made at least ten speeches of varying lengths.[73]

In Raleigh, Clay gave a speech—on his sixty-seventh birthday, no less—considered his major preconvention address. In it, he hit on the usual themes, paying particular attention to the economic trifecta of the tariff, the national currency, and banking. He referred listeners to his past record on the abolition of slavery, deeming it "not necessary" to discuss at that time. Clay dismissed Democratic claims that the Whigs had won in 1840 because of "the display of banners, the use of log cabins, the Whig songs, and the exhibition of coons." In reality, he argued, the Harrison–Tyler campaign "was a great and irresistible movement of the people," symbolized by those forms of cultural politics. And, Clay reminded the crowd, the Democrats had initiated the use of "symbols and devices to operate upon the passions of the people," a reference to the Old Hickory clubs, hickory poles, and hickory twigs twice used to elect Jackson president. Democrats were just sore at being beaten at their own game.[74]

Texas annexation, however, threatened to derail Clay's desire to focus on the recent Whig versus Democratic battleground of economic issues. Before he left for New Orleans in December 1843, he had received a letter from Crittenden informing him that Tyler was expected to raise the topic in the annual message he sent to Congress. Clay believed that the president was attracted to the idea "for his own selfish purposes," that is, to find an issue that would salvage his presidency. As for himself, Clay was not interested in "present[ing] new questions to the public. Those which are already before it are sufficiently important and numerous, without adding fresh ones." He recommended that his friends "pass it over, if it can be done, in absolute silence." If they found themselves forced to respond, Clay advised voting against it, a position he had previously made public. His opposition was based on several factors: the United States was already too large, annexing Texas was "impracticable" and likely unconstitutional, it would produce sectional division within the nation, it "would be utterly destructive" of the Whig Party, and it would lead to war with Mexico. Despite his opposition, Clay predicted that "Texas is destined to be settled by our race"—just not now and not under Tyler's watch.[75]

By his own account, Clay did not encounter crowds who were clamoring for Texas annexation. "Of one thing you may be certain," he told Crittenden in late March, "there is no such anxiety for the annexation here at the South as you might have been disposed to imagine." Three weeks later, Clay reported that during his entire tour, he had "found a degree of indifference or opposition to the measure of annexation which quite surprized me." He did not believe reports coming out of Washington suggesting the strength of the annexation movement in the Senate. It seems that he dismissed the "great excitement at Washington" over annexation as simply a political gambit by Tyler, supported by rabid pro-slavery southerners. It was nothing to worry about, Clay decided, because voters were more concerned about real issues, such as the tariff. This turned out to be wishful thinking.[76]

Clay originally intended to wait until he reached Washington to address annexation publicly. After consulting with several allies in North Carolina, however, he decided to write a letter from Raleigh. Why he chose this moment to issue a public statement on annexation is unclear. Was it as simple as Clay having time to sit down and write it out? Was he afraid that Van Buren would beat him to the punch and get his message out first? Both are potential explanations. Another possibility is that several of the friends

Clay consulted with, including former navy secretary George E. Badger, told him that Texas annexation had become a national issue that he needed to address. Senator Willie P. Mangum and other Whigs in Congress kept their North Carolina friends apprised of the annexation treaty proceedings. As someone who was not only living in Washington but who was receiving letters from Memucan Hunt, the former Texas minister to the United States who had worked on the 1837 annexation proposal, Mangum was an especially crucial conduit for information on the Texas government's perspective. Former Virginia senator Benjamin W. Leigh also may have played a role in convincing Clay that a timely statement was necessary. Leigh, who attended Clay's April 13 speech in Raleigh, wrote Mangum in late March that "*present action* is not adviseable" on Texas. Leigh may have added to the pressure on Clay to make a statement about annexation while in Raleigh.[77]

Whatever Clay's reasoning, he decided that now was the time to make his views known to the public. He drafted a public letter and sent it to Crittenden. He asked his friend to consult with Mangum, Senator John M. Berrien of Georgia, and other Whig allies in Washington about the proper timing of its publication. "I feel perfectly confident in the ground which I have taken, and feel moreover that it is proper and politic to present to the public that ground," Clay told Crittenden. He thought that congressional members were overestimating public support for annexation. Clay also calculated that Van Buren would oppose annexation. "We shall therefore occupy common ground," he stated. "His present attitude, [sic] renders it necessary that I should break silence." If the former president publicly supported annexation, Clay believed it would damage the Little Magician's campaign. Then Clay made a prediction, one that he would quickly come to rue: "The public mind is too fixed on the Presidential question, the current is running too strong and impetuous to be now affected by Texas."[78]

Clay's "Raleigh letter," as it came to be called, appeared in the Whig-controlled *Daily National Intelligencer* (Washington, DC) on the morning of Saturday, April 27, 1844. In it, he said publicly what he had communicated privately to Crittenden. "Annexation and war with Mexico are identical," Clay asserted. "What the United States most need are union, peace, and patience." Going to war with Mexico would also be unjust, given its weakness compared to the United States, and might lead European nations, such as Britain or France, to become involved. Even if Mexico were willing to give up Texas voluntarily through a treaty, Clay argued, there were other issues. "A considerable and respectable portion" of Americans opposed the idea; for that reason, it would be far better not to pursue annexation in order to avoid "introduc[ing] a new element of discord and distraction" to the people. He also highlighted the sectional nature of annexation, and he told white southerners that their plan to add Texas to protect slavery would backfire. He predicted an incoming Texas would be divided into five states, three of which would be antislavery. These new additions would endanger the future of slavery and weaken pro-slavery political support. Finally, Clay pointed out that the United Stated would have to assume Texas's debts, which he considered ill-advised. In concluding his letter, he added that annexation was "not called for by any general expression of public opinion."[79]

Partisan reaction to Clay's letter went as expected. Supporters thought it was "immeasurably superior to all other papers which have yet been published on the subject." Whigs in Washington were reportedly "in a perfect state of exultation and scarcely knew how to contain themselves." "He has met the question *plump!*" the *Richmond (VA) Whig* crowed. Clay's critics were less enthusiastic. The pro-Tyler *Madisonian* reminded readers in the nation's capital that Clay and John Quincy Adams had tried to secure Texas in the 1810s and 1820s. Thomas Ritchie's *Richmond (VA) Enquirer* called the Raleigh letter unoriginal and pedestrian, "an inferior production." Jackson observed that in Nashville the letter had "prostrated Clay with the Whiggs," some of them saying they were "abandon[ing] Clay forever." Whether it affected Clay's standing with Whigs would quickly become clear, as party delegates were already headed to their national convention.[80]

THE WHIG NATIONAL CONVENTION

Across the nation in April 1844, Whigs set out for Baltimore, where three party conventions were scheduled to begin later that month. Maryland Whigs would choose a gubernatorial candidate, national Whig delegates would nominate presidential and vice presidential candidates, and a group of young Whig men would ratify the national ticket. Getting to Baltimore took many forms. Colonel John Johnston, a former Indian agent, rode "616 miles on horseback." A group of young Whig men from New York built an ark, made "in good log-cabin style," that they used to float to Baltimore; they brought with them "a splendid 'brass band.'" Those wanting to travel by train or steamboat could purchase a round-trip ticket from Philadelphia to Baltimore for five dollars. As they made their journey to the conventions, some Whigs took time to stop at Mount Vernon to visit George Washington's tomb before continuing on.[81]

Whig visitors found a city full of electioneering excitement, a veritable beehive of activity. Baltimore's streets and squares were "jammed with crowds." One Philadelphian noted the presence of large numbers of Whig women in the city. He expected them to "fill the windows" of buildings as delegations marched by, "beaming upon us with their sweetest smiles, and strewing our way with Spring flowers." "No city in the Union has ever witnessed so beautiful a display," he pronounced. Hotels and boarding houses began filling up two weeks in advance of the conventions, but delegates were assured that private homes would "be thrown open" if needed to accommodate everyone. A "full-rigged" ship, named the *Tariff*, had been built to take part in the Young Men's Convention procession. Baltimoreans who lived immediately north of the city's harbor and who wanted to avoid the political spectacle found it difficult to do so. "Triumphal arches" had been erected at Calvert and Hanover Streets, close to the convention site, and nearby Monument Square was set to be illuminated once the conventions began.[82]

Every street corner and storefront seemed to be occupied by merchants who understood how to use the political pomp and circumstance to appeal to the delegates' wallets. One business had "a full supply of Coon Walking CANES." Another offered "Oll for Klay" convention badges for those fully committed to the Kentuckian, while the "Whig Banner Songster" included "a choice collection of popular WHIG MELODIES" and a brief sketch of Clay's life, "illustrated with WOOD CUTS." The proprietors of the Fountain Hotel brought in "seventy-five baskets" of "Clay Champagne" so that Whigs would not go thirsty. Convention attendees could also win a $50,000 prize if their ticket was chosen as part of a lottery drawing advertised as "one of the grandest schemes ever offered to the public." Isaac Cruse was nonpartisan in his sale of hams, noting that they were "suitable for the Democratic or Whig Convention." The convention crowds, estimated to reach 100,000, were also predicted to attract pickpockets, so visitors were warned to carry only the money they needed. Instead of buying books, trinkets, and symbols, some delegates found other ways of demonstrating their partisan allegiance. "In boxes are live coons from Missouri," one newspaper correspondent wrote, "and walking about are two-legged Western coons in fringed rifle shirts." All of this pageantry was primarily focused on helping Whigs move past the disappointments of the doomed Harrison–Tyler administration and toward a brighter political future.[83]

On Wednesday morning, May 1, four days after Clay's Raleigh letter was published, Whig delegates gathered in the Universalist Church located on the corner of Calvert and Pleasant Streets in downtown Baltimore. According to one report, this building was chosen because "its flat ceiling and rectangular walls reverberate sound well, so that speakers are heard with ease and distinctness." The convention opened with prayer and the selection of officers. Seventy-eight-year-old Ambrose Spencer, a former US representative from New York chosen to fill the role of convention president, read an address that asserted that there was only "one name that thrills our bosoms, and arouses and fixes our hopes as the saviour of our country." Spencer noted that there were several vice presidential aspirants and that support for the various contenders was likely to divide along sectional lines, but he asked the delegates to "give place to compromise and conciliation." Spencer briefly mentioned the party's platform as something they would address as the convention developed and also acknowledged the party's prior bad luck, with Harrison's unexpected death and the ascension of Tyler to the presidency. (Perhaps in an effort not to curse the party's proceedings, he refused to mention Tyler by name.)[84]

After Spencer concluded, Benjamin Leigh stood and proposed that the delegates move to the nomination of president and vice president. In advance of the convention, Clay had sent a letter indicating that he was choosing not to attend out of a "sense of delicacy and propriety," which met with the delegates' approbation. After giving a grandiloquent description of the Kentuckian as the man who, among other things, "would be the President, not of a party, but of this entire and blessed Union," Leigh presented Clay's name to the convention. According to a reporter, at that moment, "there was a burst which shook the church to its foundations, and must have been heard to a great distance round. The sound was deafening, and the cheers long continued and repeated again and again," with older delegates "waving their streaming handkerchiefs in the air, and calling out to their younger associates, 'give him one more.'" By their response, the delegates unanimously agreed to Clay's nomination.[85]

Now came the difficult part of the convention: the Whigs had to decide on Clay's running mate. They had a choice of several candidates, some of whom had been mentioned prominently before the convention, others less frequently. One New York Whig's preconvention reaction to the idea of Webster's name accompanying Clay's on the ticket probably spoke for many of the convention delegates: "What besotted folly! What delirious madness! What hideous treason!" Given his friendship with Clay, John Clayton seemed a good choice. Clayton, however, squashed the idea before it could gain momentum. Having been told that Delaware Whigs intended to nominate him at their state convention in 1843, he had written a public letter declining the nomination in advance; he sent a similar letter to the

1844 nominating convention. When Clay had emerged as the solid Whig choice in 1843, some of John McLean's friends urged him to consider setting his sights on the vice presidency. The Supreme Court justice, however, was not interested in settling for second billing. Like Clayton, he sent a letter to the national convention declining the vice presidential nomination.[86]

Less prominent names also appeared in Whig correspondence and newspapers. One was that of Senator George Evans of Maine. According to one Maine newspaper, Evans's nomination would not produce "any provocations or disappointments" among Whigs. But neither did it produce excitement. Other names floated beforehand included former US representative Abbott Lawrence and Senator Nathaniel Tallmadge. Lawrence was a strong Whig leader in Massachusetts, and his status as a textile magnate made him a potentially attractive candidate to southern Whigs. National discussion of Lawrence's nomination, however, appeared to have started too late to warrant serious consideration. He and Webster were also openly at war, and the Whigs could not afford party disunity of such magnitude. Tallmadge was a former New York Democrat who had broken with Van Buren because of the president's hands-off approach to the Panic of 1837. Because of this stance, some Whigs had seriously considered making Tallmadge their vice presidential preference for the 1840 ticket. During Tyler's administration, Tallmadge had "given to all the leading Whig measures a manly and liberal support." Despite those Whigs urging his nomination to help Clay secure New York in the general election, the fact that Tallmadge was not an "original Whig" seemed to end any chances he had to join the ticket.[87]

After a brief "scene of confusion and terror" resulting from some structural instability in one of the church's support pillars, Whig convention delegates undertook the serious consideration of four vice presidential candidates: John Davis, Millard Fillmore, John Sergeant, and Theodore Frelinghuysen. Given the alleged corruption of the Tyler administration, fifty-seven-year-old John Davis of Massachusetts seemed a good option. Known as "Honest John" because "a more honest man or politician does not exist," he had proven to be a formidable Whig in Massachusetts. After Davis won a plurality of the vote in the 1833 gubernatorial race, the state legislature selected him to fill the office when his main opponent John Quincy Adams withdrew in his favor. The state legislature also chose him over Adams when a Senate seat came open in 1835. In 1840, Massachusetts Whigs turned to Davis when they needed to win back the governorship, a task in which he succeeded. These victories seemed to portend well for his future political prospects statewide and nationally. Not only was Davis a winner, he was loyal to the party. In September 1842, Massachusetts Whigs expressed their confidence in Davis by endorsing him as Clay's running mate in 1844. Davis's chances for the vice presidential nomination hinged on Webster. The two men had once been friends and allies; they had even bought land together. Their relationship soured in the fall of 1842, however. Upset with his fellow Massachusetts Whigs for nominating Clay for president, Webster gave a blistering speech in Faneuil Hall lambasting their choice and defending his decision to remain in Tyler's cabinet. When Democrats won both the governor and lieutenant governor offices a few weeks later, largely because of Whigs who voted for the Liberty Party candidates, Davis and other Whigs blamed Webster. Given Davis's record of success, this should not have been a fatal blow, but like with Lawrence's candidacy, the fear of party disunity ended any realistic chance that he would appear on the Whig ticket in 1844.[88]

Millard Fillmore also emerged as a potential vice presidential candidate. The former US representative from Buffalo first became involved in politics as a John Quincy Adams supporter before joining the Anti-Masonic Party. Fillmore entered Congress clinging to Anti-Masonry, but he eventually became a Whig. During his last term in the House, he placed second in the Speaker race and chaired the powerful Ways and Means Committee. Clay recognized Fillmore's strong standing with congressional Whigs and considered "him able, faithful, and with uncommon business habits." Fillmore fulfilled the purpose of geographically balancing the ticket, and he was also antislavery, an important consideration in reaching out to northern party members. The New Yorker, however, was not fond of Clay's views on banking and his rejection of Anti-Masonry in 1832. Privately, the forty-four-year-old Fillmore expressed doubt that Whigs would nominate him. Thurlow Weed, one of the strongest Whig leaders in New York and a delegate in Baltimore, proved him right, undermining his chances for the vice presidency by telling fellow convention attendees that the New York Whigs needed Fillmore to run for their state's governorship, a position he did not want. Not only did Fillmore miss a chance to become Clay's running mate in 1844, but he also wound up losing the gubernatorial race later that year. He would make it onto the Whig ticket as vice president in 1848, however, taking over the presidency when Zachary Taylor unexpectedly died in July 1850.[89]

Pennsylvanian John Sergeant had a strong case for the second spot. He had originally entered Congress as a Federalist shortly after the War of

1812, but by the mid-1820s, he was an Adams supporter. After serving one term in the House, Sergeant found himself unanimously nominated as Clay's running mate at the 1831 National Republican convention. The Clay–Sergeant ticket went down in defeat to Jackson and Van Buren the next year. Sergeant returned to Congress as a Whig in 1837, eventually resigning in 1841. His attraction to Whigs, especially longtime party members, was evident. Sergeant was a known quantity, and his place on the 1832 ticket had not been the reason for Clay's loss to Jackson. As a supporter of Clay's American System, there would not be any ideological disagreements between the two men. Perhaps most significantly, Pennsylvania, with its concerns about the tariff, was a critical state to keep in the Whig column. Unfortunately, even before Sergeant's retirement from Congress in 1841, he had never possessed significant popularity. His public inactivity since then rendered him even more irrelevant in a critical state and made nominating the sixty-four-year-old politician a difficult proposition.[90]

Finally, there was Theodore Frelinghuysen. The New Jerseyite spent twelve years as his state's attorney general before serving a term in the US Senate, where he opposed Jackson's Indian removal policy and supported the Bank. After leaving the Senate, he served as mayor of Newark and as chancellor of New York University. Cut from a different cloth than the other three vice presidential hopefuls, Frelinghuysen possessed several advantages for the Whigs. Like Clay, during the Bank War he criticized Jackson for violating the constitutional separation of powers between the executive and legislative branches. Another factor in Frelinghuysen's favor was his support of several benevolent societies during this period, including the American Bible Society, the American Colonization Society, and the American Temperance Union. His membership in these and other organizations, many of them Protestant, reflected Frelinghuysen's religious conversion in 1820, following the death of his younger brother, Frederick. Frelinghuysen's Christian perspective had a political component too. In his anonymous work, *An Inquiry into the Moral and Religious Character of the American Government* (1838), he outlined his belief that the nation was engaged in a Manichean spiritual battle, which was manifest in the political sphere. He blamed Jefferson, Jackson, congressional leaders, and politicians in general for allowing Christianity to be "regarded as an outlaw to the institutions of the country." For the Whigs, who had emphasized their religious morality in the 1840 presidential campaign, Frelinghuysen's Christian worldview was a major mark in his favor. That he was also anti-Catholic was helpful, given the Whigs' nativist leanings, although they did not intend to make

Theodore Frelinghuysen, ca. 1844. (Courtesy of the Library of Congress)

the issue a campaign priority. Finally, Frelinghuysen's stance on slavery was moderate enough to appeal to voters from all regions of the country. He clearly thought slavery was wrong, but he also believed that abolition of the institution would cause too much pain for everyone involved. Frelinghuysen opposed immediate emancipation as too dangerous and disagreed that southern society was evil because of slavery (or the corollary—that the North was good because it had abolished slavery). Instead, colonization was the answer. This approach to ending slavery gradually fit Frelinghuysen's conception of the United States as a Christian nation.[91]

After the names of these four men—Davis, Fillmore, Sergeant, and Frelinghuysen—were placed before the delegates, voting began. Each delegate was asked to vote aloud for their preference, with a simple majority of 138 votes necessary to decide the question. On the first ballot, Frelinghuysen received the most votes, 101, with Davis winning 83, Fillmore 53, and Sergeant 38. The order remained the same on the second ballot, but Frelinghuysen's total increased to 118. Seeing no path forward to a nomination, Sergeant's supporters withdrew his name. The third ballot was decisive. Frelinghuysen won with a solid majority of 155 votes, a victory met with "loud and reiterated cheering." As was customary, the delegates agreed to a resolution declaring the fifty-seven-year-old Frelinghuysen their unanimous choice for vice president.[92]

The Whig delegates likely chose Frelinghuysen for two reasons. First was his Christian identity. As New Jersey's Henry W. Green, who nominated Frelinghuysen, noted, the vice presidential nominee was "a man of high and lofty character, a man upon whose name there was no stain— upon whose escutcheon there was no dishonor." Given Clay's reputation, a ticket containing a "saint" to balance the "sinner" was a prudent choice. Southern Whigs also may have deemed Frelinghuysen a less dangerous alternative than Davis or Fillmore when it came to slavery. Achieving sectional balance on the ticket was necessary, but adding someone with polarizing views on a critical issue on top of Clay's political baggage would have been imprudent.[93]

Postconvention Whig reaction to Frelinghuysen's nomination was positive. Clay expressed surprise at the choice. Frelinghuysen's nomination "was no doubt unexpected by you as it certainly was by me," he told Thurlow Weed. "Nevertheless it is a most judicious selection, and if he does not add any strength which however I think he will do he will take away none from the ticket." One North Carolina lawyer reported that "the nomination of Mr. Frelingheysen is received by the Whigs in this & all other parts of the State as far as I have heard from with general & entire approbation." "He is emphatically a man without guile, politically, morally and socially," a Whig newspaper editor commented. Democrats "will be puzzled in all attempts to get up falsehoods to detract from his reputation or talents." Another newspaper reassured Whigs that unlike Tyler, Frelinghuysen was "worthy of the station for which he has been nominated."[94]

The convention ended with the delegates adopting resolutions articulating the party's platform. As expected, it focused on economic issues. The Whigs sought "a well-regulated national currency" and a revenue tariff that offered protection of the domestic labor of the country." Additionally, they wanted to ensure that revenue from public land sales was distributed to the states to help fund internal improvement projects. The delegates also pledged support for a one-term limit for Clay. Harrison had made that promise in the 1840 campaign, and Clay had reiterated the "one-term principle" just weeks before the Whigs convened in Baltimore, calling it "important to the happiness and integrity of the whole country." Having in mind the perceived excesses of Tyler's administration, the resolutions also called for "a reform of Executive usurpations." If the Whigs were victorious in the fall, the resolutions concluded, they would pursue policies that guaranteed that the government would work with "the greatest practicable efficiency, controlled by a well-regulated and wise economy."[95]

Missing from the Whig platform was any mention of Texas annexation. How the delegates could fail to address what was exciting debate in the halls of Congress and consuming conversations in the boardinghouses and taverns of Washington almost beggars belief. To be a delegate meant one was politically active, or at least cognizant, so they must have been keenly aware of the treaty debate as they began arriving for the convention. The delegates seemed to believe two things: the treaty would not pass the Senate, and the Democrats, by nominating Van Buren, would not choose to make annexation an issue. Under these circumstances, Texas annexation would likely remain part of the political conversation, but the campaign itself would follow familiar paths. The Whig platform also did not mention immigration. Despite party members' nativist sympathies, some Whig leaders had come to believe the nativist movement would peel away their voters, something they could not afford. If they had known that nativist violence would explode in Philadelphia that summer, they likely would have made a different choice.[96]

Democrats took immediate satisfaction in the outcome of the Whig convention. "This coon Convention excelled all former ones in drunken debauchery and Bacchanalian revelry," one partisan Ohio newspaper crowed. Tennessee editor Samuel H. Laughlin reported that most Whigs had never heard of Frelinghuysen and could not even pronounce his name. His antislavery sentiments presented an obvious line of attack to pursue during the general campaign. Democrats even welcomed Frelinghuysen's reputation as "a moral and religious man," since it gave them an opportunity to highlight Clay's "immoral character." All in all, many Democrats must have felt confident that the Clay–Frelinghuysen ticket posed little threat to their party's chances in the race. Van Buren was their obvious choice to run as president, and whomever convention delegates chose as his running mate at the end of May, victory was not going to elude them as it had four years before. Two well-known statesmen, who embodied their respective party's principles, would compete on well-trodden political ground, and Van Buren would gain his revenge for 1840. There would be no surprises this time. Or so they thought.[97]

3

"AN ENTIRELY NEW MAN" THE
DEMOCRATIC CONVENTION

Democrats faced a hard choice as they looked ahead to 1844. One path they could take involved sticking with Martin Van Buren. Despite his loss in 1840, his supporters could argue that an unprecedented economic depression had made it impossible for him to succeed. They could also point to what Andrew Jackson descriptively called the "Logg cabin hard cider and Coon humbugery" campaign tactics of the Whigs as the cause for their defeat. Having seen the effectiveness of the Whigs' approach, Van Burenites could claim that they were better prepared for the next presidential campaign. But Democrats also had reason to cast the New Yorker aside and find someone new to run. The 1837 economic crisis had originated under Jackson, but Van Buren's plans for pulling the nation out of its financial depression had done little to address the pain people felt. His unwillingness and inability to address their concerns allowed Whigs to paint him and his fellow Democrats as elitist snobs during the 1840 campaign. The nation's continued economic distress under John Tyler seemed to ensure that Whigs would welcome a Van Buren candidacy in 1844.[1]

The men expected to challenge Van Buren for the nomination illustrated the vast well of experience from which the party could draw. Included in their number were former and future presidents and vice presidents, diplomats, war heroes—men whom voters could trust to lead them into the future. These aspiring nominees—Charles Stewart, James Buchanan, John C. Calhoun, Lewis Cass, and Richard M. Johnson—had their eyes set on unseating Van Buren. Of the five, Calhoun and Johnson—two former vice presidents—had the strongest résumés, but the other three were not inconsequential. An additional factor was James K. Polk, in the conversation to become the vice presidential nominee. Some Democrats were beginning to think the Tennessean might be the answer to a divided party. Defeating Van Buren's built-in advantages and overcoming their own personal and political weaknesses was not going to be easy for any challenger, however. These contenders and their supporters reassured voters that even if Democratic convention delegates chose someone besides Van Buren as their nominee, the nation would be safer in their hands than in those of the Whigs.

MARTIN VAN BUREN

When Van Buren's presidency ended in March 1841, he headed home to Kinderhook, New York. Along the way, crowds of well-wishers feted him, while critics took their jabs. New York lawyer George Templeton Strong, never one to pull observational punches, described Van Buren's procession in his usual acerbic manner. "A disgusting assemblage of the unwashed democracy they were, generally speaking, a more rowdy, draggletailed, jailbird-resembling gang of truculent loafers than the majority of them I never witnessed before," he recorded. "The rain . . . was a blessing to some of them, for the ablution was badly needed." As for "Matty himself," he rode in "a shabby barouche" and appeared "older than I supposed."[2]

Once he reached his home, called Lindenwald, Van Buren took up "the life of a leisured country gentleman," meaning that he hired other people to do the work of transforming what had been a "modest farm into a model country gentleman's estate." But for all his concern about picking out wallpaper, bragging about eating fish from his own pond for breakfast, and growing cabbages, Van Buren's mind never strayed far from politics. He blamed "*both* the State & Federal institutions arrayed agt. me" for the failures of his presidency, and he complained that it was "impossible to retain the respect of mankind if we can be influenced by Log-Cabins, & coon Skins." Having once reached the political mountaintop, Van Buren was unwilling to walk through the valley of the shadow of political death for long. The correspondence he received from fellow Democrats in the months after his departure from office convinced him that he might be able to resurrect his truncated political career. As one group of Philadelphia Democrats told him after Thomas Hart Benton rebuffed their solicitation to be the Democratic nominee in 1844, "we have come to the conclusion, that you are the man, upon whom the *true* Democracy of the Country can

Martin Van Buren near the end of his presidency. (Courtesy of the Library of Congress)

and will unite." In response to rumors about his availability as a candidate in 1844, Van Buren took the traditional stance of political humility wrapped in obvious interest, but he was being disingenuous. He still had the political fire in his belly, and he was already looking to reclaim his place in the White House.[3]

But how could Van Buren get there? He landed on the plan of making an extended political tour. The idea was not new to him. In 1839, he had proposed visiting the southern and western states to understand their perspective for the upcoming election. Polk, however, convinced him to alter his trip to focus on the mid-Atlantic and New England states. Now, nearly three years later, Van Buren determined to embark on a more substantial journey, one that would take him throughout the South, the West, and the Midwest under the pretext of visiting his daughter-in-law Angelica's family in South Carolina and Andrew Jackson in Nashville. In reality, he once again would be taking the political temperature of voters and testing his own popularity.[4]

In early February 1842, Van Buren left Lindenwald and headed south. His former navy secretary, James K. Paulding, joined him in Philadelphia and together they arrived in Charleston, South Carolina, in late February. Van Buren spent more than a month in South Carolina, visiting with his former secretary of war, Joel R. Poinsett, and with Angelica's family, the Singletons. From there, Van Buren and Paulding followed Jackson's advice and took the southern route across Georgia to Alabama, then to New Orleans. After enjoying the hospitality of the Crescent City for about a week, they headed up the Mississippi River on their way to Nashville, arriving in late April. Van Buren stayed in Middle Tennessee for more than three weeks. Most of this time was with Jackson at the Hermitage, but he also made a trip down to Columbia to meet with Polk. After leaving Nashville, Van Buren's next major stop was Henry Clay's Ashland estate in Lexington, Kentucky. As he headed toward Indiana in late May, Van Buren also spent time at the home of his former vice president, Richard M. Johnson. The month of June involved brief visits at several towns and cities in Ohio, Indiana, Illinois, and Missouri. Van Buren spent the last two weeks of his tour in the Great Lakes region, which included stops in Chicago, Milwaukee, Detroit, Cleveland, and Buffalo. He arrived back at Lindenwald in mid-July, having spent far more time away than he originally intended.[5]

From the start, Van Buren denied that he was undertaking a political tour. He informed Poinsett that his desire was "to pass among as quietly as any other private Gentleman would do, willing to see any body that wants to see me, but without parade or ostentation." This statement rang false, as Van Buren began making political commentary—sometime brief, sometimes longer—once he reached Tennessee. His denials of an electioneering tour also fell flat because of his meetings with Jackson, Polk, Clay, and Johnson. What he and these four politicians discussed privately is unknown. Polk denied that he and Van Buren talked about the political future "either verbaly [sic] or in writing" and said he had not heard of any such conversations having occurred during the Tennessee leg of Van Buren's trip. Clay simply recorded that they "had a great deal of agreeable conversation, but not much on politics." Neither Jackson nor Johnson left a record of their time with Van Buren.[6]

Van Buren's visits with these four men were clearly not just focused on reminiscing about past political battles. He was a pragmatic politician who understood several things. First, he wanted to ensure that Jackson still believed in him. Without his blessing, seeking the Democratic presidential nomination would be futile. Second, Van Buren needed to feel out both Polk and Johnson for a couple of reasons. It was important to determine if either one would be willing to run with him or, more importantly, if they were interested in challenging him for the nomination. Last, Van Buren had to size up Clay. Had Harry of the West resigned from the Senate to enjoy retirement, or was he giving himself more time to prepare for 1844? It seems plausible that some discussions about the next presidential campaign took place during each visit.

Ultimately, Van Buren's five-month tour across twenty (out of twenty-six) states achieved its purpose. He spent at least two days in fourteen of those states, allowing time to meet with potential voters and converse with local, state, and national politicians. He came away impressed by "the invariable & great kindness with which I was every where treated by the mass of the people, & the Democracy in particular." Van Buren also received reinforcement that his defeat in 1840 had been "the result of the most criminal practices agt. the purity of the elective franchize." His sentiment was clear: when the people were allowed to vote free from interference, they chose the party of Jackson and Van Buren. The results of the 1842 elections seemed to indicate that voters had indeed regretted 1840: Democrats convincingly won control of the US House, retained control of key legislatures in states such as New York, won the majority in the critical legislature of Virginia, and seized power in traditional Whig bastions, including the Massachusetts state senate. These victories helped redeem Van Buren. Jackson predicted that the party would choose him as its presidential nominee in the next election. Democrats "are a Just and gratefull [sic] people," he told Blair, and Van Buren "is the strongest man that can be presented." Amos Kendall assured Van Buren that "there are few of our western and southwestern friends who do not look to you as our candidate."[7]

The official launch of Van Buren's candidacy came in January 1843, when a group of Pennsylvania Democrats endorsed the former president with so much enthusiasm that the final cheers given at the end of the meeting "shook the very foundations of the immense building" in which they met. The Philadelphia meeting elicited letters of endorsement from Jackson, Benton, and fellow New Yorker Silas Wright Jr. Two days later, Indiana Democrats also nominated Van Buren and asked for his opinions on what they deemed the important topics of the day: banking, the distribution of the surplus revenue, the tariff, the executive veto, and his support for whomever the Democratic national convention nominated for president. Van Buren responded with detailed positions on each question. He opposed the surplus distribution and "a National Bank in any form, or under any disguise, both on constitutional grounds and grounds of expediency." He endorsed the executive veto "as it exists by the constitution" and favored a revenue-generating, protective tariff that discriminated among the various products to which it would be applied. As for supporting the party's presidential nominee, Van Buren responded "unhesitatingly" in the affirmative.[8]

The question of when to hold the Democratic national convention loomed large as Van Buren's campaign took off. Silas Wright preferred a date eighteen months before the election, arguing that an earlier convention would unite the party and keep the presidential nomination question from consuming the Democrats' political agenda when Congress convened in December. Van Buren's former attorney general, Henry D. Gilpin, agreed with Wright: waiting until the spring of 1844 to make nominations would be "most unwise." Other Democrats, especially Calhoun, wanted the date pushed to May 1844 to give themselves more time to organize an effective campaign against Old Kinderhook. Van Buren ultimately agreed to follow the lead of the states in setting the convention date. George Bancroft was optimistic about the later date. "As a general question November or an earlier day is best," he wrote Van Buren, but "for you, May is best, because the longer the question of preference is discussed, the stronger will be the expression of that preference."[9]

Momentum for the New Yorker's candidacy continued to build throughout 1843, and by January 1844, Van Buren appeared to be firmly in control of the nomination. He was so confident that he approached Bancroft to write a campaign biography. He directed his friend to produce "a full statement of my course & character sufficiently comprehensive & accurate to serve as a text Book for our orators, & at the same sufficiently eloquent to impress the multitude." Van Buren emphasized that he wanted a New York publisher "to enlist public attention more effectually" and that Bancroft's name "should be informally, at least, communicated to the public before it appears" in print. There was hardly a need to go through such trouble if one anticipated failure in Baltimore, which Van Buren clearly did not.[10]

CHARLES STEWART

As Van Buren prepared for the result he and others considered inevitable, other contenders lurked. Charles Stewart was the most surprising name to emerge as a possible challenger to Van Buren. Born in 1778, Stewart had joined the US Navy as a lieutenant at age nineteen and had quickly risen through the ranks. Within six years, he had commanded three separate ships and had fought in the First Barbary War (1801–1805), earning the rank of captain. Stewart's service in the War of 1812 garnered him a Congressional Gold Medal; his command of the USS *Constitution* during the conflict also won him the nickname "Old Ironsides." Over the next three decades, Stewart served in the Mediterranean and the Pacific, held a position on the Board of Naval Commissioners, and oversaw the Philadelphia Navy Yard.[11]

Stewart's career was not without controversy, however. He faced several court-martial charges in 1825 for allegedly transporting a Spanish spy on his ship during a three-week trek in the Pacific. During the trial, testimony revealed that Stewart's wife, Delia, had known about the spy but had not reported it to her husband. She refused to testify on his behalf, an indication of how strained their marital relationship had become. The court found Stewart not guilty, but the trial ended the Stewarts' tumultuous ten-year marriage; the divorce took years to settle. Shortly after his marital separation, the commodore began a lifelong relationship with a woman named Margaret, who bore them a son. Stewart's court-martial, household arrangement, and divorce attracted virtually no press attention during his time in the national limelight as a potential presidential candidate. This disinterest, in an era when other politicians' lives were scrutinized, may have been a testimony to his naval career or simply the perception that he was not a viable candidate for the White House.[12]

Stewart's name was briefly mentioned as a possible presidential candidate for both the Whigs and the Democrats in 1840, but nothing serious developed. Some Democrats remained interested in him as they looked ahead to 1844. The members of the "Old Ironsides Club" of Philadelphia asked if they could nominate him, an honor he did not decline. An 1843 political lithograph included Stewart as one of several possible contenders. His name also appeared in newspapers and even in straw polls that year. Interest in Stewart's future picked up when the sixty-five-year-old commodore, his hair no longer chestnut, thinning on top and grown long else-where on his head, relinquished command of the Home Squadron naval patrol unit in late 1843. Reports had Tyler appointing Stewart the acting secretary of the navy; this rumor quickly proved unfounded. Increasingly, however, some people wondered if he would emerge as a strong contender for the Democratic presidential nomination. One correspondent saw him as a possible compromise candidate because he was "free from the family quarrels" that divided the Democrats "and could therefore be received as a pacificator" by all of the party's factions.[13]

When Texas annexation emerged as a key campaign issue, Stewart be-gan to attract more attention. In response to an April 1844 query from a Mississippi congressman, the commodore wrote that there were "numer-ous, cogent, powerful, and urgent" reasons in favor of annexing Texas immediately. By early May, some newspapers were predicting that Stew-art had become the Democratic frontrunner. He had worked his way up from a "humble station" to lead the US Navy, having been "a consistent and firm Democrat from early youth." White southerners would like his tariff views, and Stewart was also solidly anti-bank and pro-annexation. He had "many friends," and, perhaps most importantly, he was "not a politi-cian" and would "have no party debts to pay, and no personal wrongs to redress." According to these organs, Stewart was the only Democrat who could maintain the loyalty of the Calhounites, attract Tylerites, and capture Whig voters. As late as May 26, one newspaper reported that if Van Buren did not win the nomination on the first ballot, Stewart was likely to be the Democrats' choice. The possibility of Stewart's nomination troubled those outside of the Democratic Party. Tyler's supporters were quick to point out that the commodore's embrace of Texas annexation had come late. Whigs respected and trusted his naval experience, but they could not identify "what peculiar civil qualifications" made him ready to be president; there were "ten thousand other men in the nation" who were better prepared to move into the White House than Stewart. Undoubtedly, Whigs were not interested in seeing the strategy they had used to good effect in 1840—nominating a military hero with little to no political experience—employed against them in 1844.[14]

JAMES BUCHANAN

For a brief time, James Buchanan was also in the running for the nom-ination. The Pennsylvanian, who would turn fifty-three before the nom-inating convention met, enjoyed several qualities that marked him as a contender. First, he had demonstrated his fidelity to Jacksonian principles while a member of Congress, supporting Jackson's approach to foreign policy and voting to expunge his 1834 Senate censure. More recently, he had favored the repayment of the $1,000 fine (plus interest) levied against Old Hickory for contempt of court when he placed New Orleans under martial law near the end of the War of 1812, an insult that the General had resented for decades. Buchanan's congressional allies also included the staunch Jacksonian senators Benton, Wright, and Lewis F. Linn. Second, Buchanan possessed his own foreign policy experience that positioned him well for the nation's current situation in the global community. Jackson had appointed him as the US minister to Russia in 1832. Buchanan also served as chair of the Senate Committee on Foreign Relations for five years and was decidedly Anglophobic too. Last, Buchanan had early in his congressional career "messed," or boarded, with southern politicians who exposed him to the region's political beliefs and cultural practices. Consequently, Buchanan became a strong supporter of slavery, which pleased white southerners. He was what contemporaries called a "'doughface,' or a northern man with southern principles." Along with his connections to the West, his friendliness with New England Democrats, and his residence in the mid-Atlantic state of Pennsylvania, Buchanan's southern connections boded well for his potential as the Democratic presidential nominee. A convention of Keystone State Democrats met in January 1843 and nominated him as their choice to head the party's ticket in 1844. The convention delegates proclaimed Buchanan "a preeminent and dazzling luminary" and endorsed a biographical sketch that asserted he had never cast "a *single vote* against Democratic principles."[15]

But a Buchanan candidacy also faced some formidable obstacles. First, Jackson did not trust him. As the nation waited for the House members to cast their votes for either Jackson, Adams, or Crawford following the inconclusive 1824 election, Buchanan seemed to offer Old Hickory a bribe: if he promised to retain Adams in the State Department, then Buchanan would guarantee Jackson Pennsylvania's vote in the upcoming House election. Although it is unclear whether Buchanan was acting slyly or naïvely, Jackson never got over his perception of the encounter, especially when the alleged "corrupt bargain" between Adams and Clay took place. Buchanan also faced questions about his personal life. He had never married, despite several courtships. Buchanan had taken advantage of his bachelorhood by boarding with other unmarried congressmen and forming significant partisan voting blocs. Being an unmarried president was not a disqualifier—Democratic stalwarts Jefferson, Jackson, and Van Buren had all been widowers when they assumed office—but there had never been a bachelor president. Adding to the weight of Buchanan's bachelorhood was the widely discussed nature of his relationship with Senator William R. King of Alabama, an experienced legislator and diplomat who was well known enough that he was mentioned as the Democrats' possible vice presidential nominee in 1844. Buchanan and King had first become messmates and political allies in 1834, but some people believed that their relationship went deeper. For years, newspapers and colleagues had referred to King as "Aunt Nancy" or "Miss Nancy," terms that could refer to one's effeminate fashion choices but also to someone who participated in same-sex relations. Gossip about Buchanan and King's relationship reached Polk's household in January 1844, when Tennessee representative Aaron V. Brown sent Sarah Polk a letter calling King "her" and "she" and describing him as a "prude," "*Mrs. B.,*" and Buchanan's "*wife*" and "*better half.*" Brown also wrote about King that "*aunt Nancy* may be now seen every day, triged [tricked] out in her best clothes & smirking about in hopes of seeing better times than with her former companion." It is not clear whether Buchanan and King were in a same-sex relationship, but the public perception of both men at the time may have harmed their chances of getting on the ticket in 1844.[16]

Buchanan's campaign never gained significant momentum, partly because he was ill for several months. Consequently, in late 1843, he decided to step aside. As he announced to Pennsylvanians in his withdrawal address, he wanted "to drive discord from the ranks of the party" and allow Democrats to choose "among the candidates whose prospects are more promising." Twelve years later, Buchanan's deferred gratification paid off when he defeated two candidates, one of whom was Millard Fillmore, for the presidency.[17]

JOHN C. CALHOUN

The ever-recalcitrant John C. Calhoun emerged as another possible presidential nominee for the Democrats. Despite his assessment of William Henry Harrison as an elderly, naïve child, Calhoun had voted in favor of all of his cabinet appointments in 1841. Once Tyler took over after Harrison's death, Calhoun questioned many of the new president's policies and principles. He viewed Tyler as inconsistent and under Clay's control. During the tumultuous congressional sessions of 1841, Calhoun began articulating his platform for the 1844 Democratic nomination. It was one that reflected his proslavery, states' rights ideology. He supported the subtreasury system and slavery and opposed the national debt, the spoils system, the recharter of a national bank, the revenue distribution, and changes to the tariff of 1833.[18]

By the end of 1841, friends began urging Calhoun to come out for the nomination, a wish he was happy to accommodate. Over the next year, Calhoun positioned himself for the Democratic nomination by denouncing the growth of executive power under Tyler and championing, as he had a decade earlier, the need for a lower tariff. Outside of his home state of South Carolina, Virginia represented Calhoun's strongest base of support, but he had two problems there. First, influential Democratic newspaper editor Thomas Ritchie and his Richmond Junto supported Van Buren. Second, some of Calhoun's influential friends were part of Tyler's inner circle. The South Carolinian hoped he could count on two members of the Virginia Cabal—Secretary of State Abel P. Upshur and Secretary of Navy Thomas Gilmer—but they appeared more inclined to remain loyal to the president than to jump ship.[19]

Among northerners, Calhoun's political philosophy made it unlikely that he would be able to attract many voters in the region. Some New Englanders might appreciate his Yale connection; those living along the northern seacoast might find his commitment to free trade appealing. Beyond that, it was difficult to see a way forward north of the Mason–Dixon Line. Pennsylvania, once considered a Calhoun stronghold, was so far gone that supporters barely organized there. Calhoun's opposition to the Dorr War also hurt him. The reasoning behind this political revolution against the duly elected state government of Rhode Island—support for voting rights and opposition to labor exploitation—too closely resembled that of enslaved people who periodically rose up against the white majorities in southern states. Calhoun's unwillingness to support the Dorrites in their fight against the state government clearly indicated that his conception of democracy, for both Black and white Americans, was circumscribed. Despite his possessing some northern support, southern voters constituted Calhoun's base. He knew both their needs and their fears. Mississippi congressman William M. Gwin said what many white southern voters likely thought as they looked ahead to 1844. "I want a slaveholder for President next time regardless of the man," he wrote Andrew Jackson, "believing as I solemnly do that in the next Presidential term the abolitionists must be put down or blood will be spilt." Southern voters like Gwin wanted someone wholly committed to defending the institution—someone like Calhoun.[20]

Like many politicians, then and now, Calhoun failed to recognize the deficiencies in his candidacy. For one, his arrogance won him no friends

THE MOUNTAIN IN LABOR.

Martin Van Buren and John C. Calhoun were widely considered two frontrunners for the Democratic presidential nomination in 1843. Depicted here as mice emerging from a Locofoco (Democratic) volcano, they face John Tyler's thought of beheading them and Clay's plan to trap them. (Courtesy of the Library of Congress)

among potential political allies. Centering his tariff opposition might have won him votes in his native region, but it also served to remind the electorate that Calhoun and like-minded southerners had almost dismembered the Union just a decade ago. His supporters, though more ideologically united than those of some other possible nominees, also lacked the patronage that would have helped him raise more money, sway influential allies, and build widespread national support.[21]

In February 1843, Calhoun followed Clay's example and announced that he would resign his Senate seat to appear available for a presidential nomination. His supporters spent the rest of the year attempting to generate enthusiasm for their candidate. In March, the Virginia state convention rejected Calhoun's plea to elect national convention delegates by district. Calhoun blamed Silas Wright and other Van Burenites in New York for a decision "establish[ing] the most intolerable despotism," by which "the great central non slave holding States will control the election, to the exclusion of the rest of the Union, & especially the South." In August, Calhoun's supporters attempted to take control of the New York City convention to select delegates to the statewide convention, but they lost by one vote. This allowed the New York state convention to select Van Buren delegates to the national convention. These delegates rejected Calhoun's district plan and endorsed the protective tariff. One concession made to the Calhounites was an agreement to support a May 1844 meeting of the Democratic national convention. In a final push to demonstrate Calhoun's viability as the party's nominee, his congressional allies attempted to wrest control of the appointment of US House officers away from the Van Burenites. This effort failed when not one Van Buren ally lost their election to an officer post.[22]

This final setback led Calhoun to pause his campaign for the convention nomination. In December 1843, he sent supporters an address to that effect. He focused his decision on the convention "constituted as it must now be," which he deemed "repugnant to all the principles, on which, in my opinion, such a Convention should be founded." He also spent considerable space on the importance of the tariff issue. The following month, Calhoun sent out an amended address. Much of it repeated the first version, but he added two paragraphs at the end that addressed abolitionism. He denounced "any candidate" who supported abolitionism or associated with those who did. For Calhoun, the tariff and abolition/antislavery were inextricably intertwined. "The one robs us of our income," he argued, "while the other aims at destroying the source from which that income is derived." Close friends probably understood that Calhoun was not simply referring to Clay—he was also warning southern voters about Van Buren. Calhoun told his brother-in-law that he expected the Democrats to split along sectional lines unless northern party members "should reverse their course on the Tariff & slave questions, which I do not expect." He also predicted that Van Buren's nomination would lead to an easy victory for Clay.[23]

LEWIS CASS

Another possible Democratic nominee was Lewis Cass. The War of 1812 general had served as territorial governor of Michigan for nearly two decades before replacing John Eaton as secretary of war when he resigned from Jackson's cabinet in 1831. Before leaving the presidency, Jackson appointed Cass US minister to France. His absence from the United States during Van Buren's administration and the 1840 election kept Cass from being associated with the party's weaknesses, but it also left potential voters unfamiliar with him. During these years, when asked for his views on political issues or his interest in running for office, Cass gave cagey answers.

This led some to question his loyalty to the Democratic Party and his commitment to its principles.[24]

Nevertheless, Cass returned from France in late 1842 and gained the early support of some prominent Democrats, including Virginian William C. Rives and Pennsylvanian George M. Dallas. As he traveled home to Ohio, Cass stopped in Boston, New York, Philadelphia, and Washington, attempting to convince Democratic leaders of his viability. He made a serious misstep, however, when he visited a Cincinnati Masonic lodge in early 1843. The stop made sense given his past position as a Masonic grandmaster in Ohio and Michigan, but Cass alienated his fraternal brothers by refusing to address them if they wore "their masonic paraphernalia." This decision showed some recognition of Freemasonry's unpopularity in Ohio, but by agreeing to meet with them at all, Cass showed poor political judgment.[25]

To combat criticism that he possessed no true political principles, in December 1842, Cass exchanged public letters with Mahlon Dickerson, a fellow cabinet member under Jackson. In a brief response to Dickerson's questions about his Democratic fidelity, Cass asserted that he supported Jeffersonian principles, opposed a national bank, and favored a national currency based on specie. A couple of months later, he provided a more detailed overview of his views at the request of Indiana Democrats. He reiterated his opposition to a trio of Whig policies—a national bank, the distribution to states of revenue from the sale of public lands, and a constitutional amendment to limit the executive veto power—and his support for a moderate tariff. He also stated that holding the party's nominating convention at "the last reasonable moment" would best capture the people's will and avoid interparty division. Cass also came out in favor of territorial expansion. He wrote a group of Cincinnatians in 1843 that he "would take and hold possession of the Territory upon the Pacific [i.e., Oregon], come what might." Shortly after writing this letter, Cass spoke at a July 4th ceremony in Fort Wayne, Indiana, that celebrated the opening of the Wabash and Erie Canal. In describing the importance of the new canal, he remarked that the nation's institutions were in no better hands than in those of westerners. These public statements, in one biographer's estimation, "portrayed Cass as a moderate Democrat in the spirit of Jefferson and Jackson"; he was also clearly positioning himself as the candidate best embodying Manifest Destiny for Democrats.[26]

As 1843 progressed, Cass tried to maximize his connection to Jackson to draw in other Democratic constituencies. His efforts were assisted by William B. Lewis, a sycophant whose longtime loyalty to Old Hickory was surpassed only by his ambition for political rewards. Lewis had a contentious relationship with Van Buren, which led him to throw in his lot with Cass for 1844. In early 1843, Lewis sent Jackson a flattering letter about Cass, praising his "great *tact* and *skill*, as well as *ability* and *moderation*" in handling "difficult, *delicate*, and *inciting* subjects"—just as Jackson had. Lewis also forwarded a copy of a recently published pamphlet about Cass's life, the first campaign biography of the former minister. Several months later, Cass followed up with a letter to Jackson that smacked of obsequiousness. Lewis urged Jackson to respond to Cass's letter. To soften up the former president, Lewis told him that Cass intended to write his memoirs; "obtaining correct information" would not only be important for accurately capturing Jackson's life but also would "have great weight" in how the era was remembered. Old Hickory could not fail to understand the implication for his own legacy; however, he did not seem aware that his former aide had made up the story. Lewis drafted a response, which Jackson used as the basis for a letter in which he thanked Cass for his service as secretary of war and praised him for his recent work as minister to France.[27]

But the major obstacle in Cass's campaign was the candidate himself. Cass embraced some forms of the cultural politics that had taken hold of the nation during the 1840 campaign, writing letters that were published in newspapers and periodically giving speeches. In other areas, he fell short. He had just turned sixty years old, and he was already beginning to show the physical decline that would become fodder for the press in later years. Cass possessed a "stilted public demeanor" and was "a colorless extemporaneous speaker." He also took no active part in building "the machinery of party," such as securing campaign financing or in creating a newspaper network, and he turned down far more speaking invitations than he accepted. Much of the work to help Cass win the nomination fell to others. It remained to be seen whether Cass's hands-off approach would pay political dividends.[28]

RICHARD M. JOHNSON

Richard M. Johnson, whom Thomas Hart Benton called "the damnedest political wh[or]e in the Country," also campaigned for the 1844 Democratic presidential nomination. By this time well known to party members, Johnson's bona fides were not simply his alleged killing of Tecumseh or his stint as Van Buren's vice president. His principles also aligned with mainstream Democratic ideology. First and foremost, as a member of the House in 1819, he had defended Jackson's actions during the First Seminole War. Instead of the House censuring the general, Johnson argued that it should thank him for protecting the American people by following "in the footsteps of the immortal Washington." Johnson also endorsed Indian removal, a major policy initiative of the Democratic Party in the 1830s. He opposed a national bank and supported a protective tariff, issues on which Democrats were less united. Johnson also endeared himself to some Democratic voters by standing up to Jackson. For example, he consistently supported internal improvement projects, such as the 1830 Maysville Road bill, which the president eventually vetoed. He and Jackson also did not see eye to eye on the location of a federal armory in the West. Johnson likewise went beyond the president's instructions in attempting to bring about a peaceful resolution to the Eaton affair. In conversations with several of Jackson's cabinet members, Johnson indicated that they could keep their posts if they simply socialized with the Eatons. This was not what Jackson had authorized him to say, and it led to speculation that the Kentuckian was angling to put himself into the cabinet following its implosion, a charge that Johnson denied. Taken together, his actions demonstrated that Johnson was loyal to Jackson but he also possessed independence.[29]

But there were also reservations—some political, some personal—about Johnson's competency. Following the War of 1812, he had bungled an attempt to raise the compensation for congressional members, sponsoring a bill to increase their salaries before backtracking after popular outcry arose. He and his brother, James, also found themselves accused of wasting government money when their attempts to help establish new military forts in the West resulted in unfulfilled contracts and excessive spending. Once he became vice president, anti-Johnson sentiment remained high among some of the Democratic faithful. In Virginia, for example, Democrats argued that he could not be trusted: he was "a bank man, an internal improvement man, and a tariff man!" As vice president, Johnson exercised little power. His most consequential action came from a change in the Senate rules, which gave the vice president, as president of the upper chamber, the power to appoint committee members. Johnson made sure that all the Senate committees had a Democratic chair and a safe Democratic majority. He actively supported the Senate "gag rule," engaging in correspondence with Lewis Tappan in which he lectured the abolitionist leader on the importance of maintaining each state's right to protect slavery. He also commented on the proper role of women in society, which, in his view, did not include signing antislavery petitions, such as those presented in the Senate. Johnson was not the reason why the Democrats lost to Harrison, but in some Democrats' eyes, he bore part of the blame for not inspiring voters to support a second Van Buren presidential term. And, of course, there was his open practice of interracial relationships in Kentucky.[30]

Despite his weaknesses and his place on the losing Democratic ticket in 1840, Johnson still seemed presidential timber to some Democrats. He was, after all, a war hero who had suffered permanent physical impairment from multiple wounds he received during the Battle of the Thames. Unlike Calhoun, he had been a loyal, yet independent, Democratic soldier in the party battles of the 1830s. Johnson's Anglophobia before and during the War of 1812 also fit the tenor of the Democratic Party in the early 1840s. Nevertheless, his well-known flaws and his status as the second-oldest Democratic contender (Johnson would be sixty-four at the time of the 1844 election) may have prompted sober second thoughts among some supporters given what had happened with Harrison.[31]

Johnson showed no desire to retire from his political career after leaving the vice presidency. When voters sent him to the Kentucky legislature in August 1841, he went. The following year, Johnson began publicly commenting on national issues, indicating his support for the Dorrites in their fight to more fully democratize Rhode Island, the effort to refund Andrew Jackson the fine that he had paid following the War of 1812, and a bankruptcy law. He also commented on the ongoing tension with Great Britain over Oregon, telling attendees at a July 4th event that he personally would lead troops into battle if needed. To gauge interest in his candidacy among voters, Johnson decided to undertake a campaign tour. He spent three months in the late summer and fall traversing Pennsylvania, New York, and Washington, DC. By his own estimate, he gave one hundred speeches of varying lengths. Johnson's efforts garnered him a presidential nomination from Democrats in Kentucky, Ohio, and Pennsylvania over the winter of 1842–1843.[32]

Bolstered by his successful tour, Johnson spent the next year electioneering. A campaign biography preceded Johnson's setting out on the campaign trail in the spring of 1843. He first visited the South and the West, picking up endorsements from Democrats in Arkansas and St. Louis and from German-born citizens in Natchez, Mississippi. During his tour, Johnson focused his rhetoric on the Oregon territory. For example, in Springfield, Illinois, he reportedly gave as his motto: "Take possession of Oregon, peaceably, if we can; forcibly, if we must." While on the trip, Johnson also agreed to attend a July meeting of the Oregon General Committee of Ohio in Cincinnati, telling them that he supported "the immediate occupation of Oregon by the arms and the laws of the Republic." His campaign jaunt was so successful that he announced that he would visit New York and New England later that summer. Between September and December, Johnson made his way from Virginia north to New Hampshire, making stops along the way in several cities along the East Coast.[33]

These efforts could not overcome significant obstacles. Johnson's decision to turn down an opportunity to establish a newspaper under his campaign's direct control and instead to wait for established organs to throw him their support proved foolish. Not having a loyal newspaper at his disposal made it difficult to combat insinuations about his interracial relationships and rumors that he had openly declared that if he could not be president, then he wanted Clay to win. By early 1844, he was publicly stating that his nomination was "in the hands of the people," but privately he believed he would not be nominated for either position on the ticket.[34]

THE VICE PRESIDENTIAL QUESTION

Along with deciding on their presidential nominee, Democrats also had to choose who would run with him. Any of the men vying for the presidency would make a suitable running mate, of course. Old guard Jacksonians who viewed the 1840 defeat as an anomaly thought reuniting Van Buren with Johnson was the logical choice. After all, they believed their ticket had only lost that year because of the Whigs' "doggerel rhymes and vulgar pictures." Other contenders were US senator Silas Wright Jr. of New York and Levi Woodbury of New Hampshire, who had served as head of both the Navy and the Treasury Departments under Jackson. Both men were prominent, longtime Jacksonian Democrats who could be counted on to further the party's interests. Anti-Van Buren Democrats were rightfully skeptical of both men, however, since both Wright and Woodbury had strong ties to the eighth president. Woodbury had the added weight of having overseen the Panic of 1837 as Van Buren's secretary of the Treasury. Other names mentioned for the vice presidency included Van Buren's former secretary of war Joel R. Poinsett, former US representative William R. King, and former US minister to Great Britain Andrew Stevenson, but efforts on their behalf quickly fell apart.[35]

Polk's name also appeared in discussions about the vice presidential nomination. Despite Van Buren's loss to Harrison in 1840, the Tennessean's friends thought Young Hickory was well positioned to win reelection as the state's governor in 1841 and possibly place himself in position for bigger things. "I shall be disappointed, if your success in this contest does not lead on certainly to your elevation to the Presidency," one friend told him. James C. Jones had a different idea, however. Polk's Whig opponent in

HANDICAP RACE PRESIDENTIAL STAKES 1844.

Prior to the Democratic nominating convention, Martin Van Buren was viewed as the leading challenger to Henry Clay, but there were others in the Democratic field of contenders. Lewis Cass was catching up to Van Buren, the slavery issue was weighing down John C. Calhoun's chances, and Richard M. Johnson was happy to "hook on" as the nominee's running mate. John Tyler, meanwhile, was trying to ride two horses, a sign of his willingness to choose whichever party would win him the White House. (Courtesy of the Library Company of Philadelphia)

the 1841 gubernatorial race emulated his party's approach in the previous year's Log Cabin and Hard Cider campaign. "Lean Jimmy" Jones's humor and wit made it difficult for Polk, who tried to counter his opponent's electioneering with logical arguments against the Whigs' national program. Polk would have been outmatched, except that he was a good storyteller ("the Napoleon of stump speakers," by one account) with his own humorous streak. Unfortunately, he was also in poor health, which required him to rely heavily on his wife, Sarah, "to coordinate a writing campaign among his political allies." Ultimately, even Sarah's adept management of her husband's communications was unable to prevent his loss to Jones by around 3,000 votes. Jackson told Van Buren that it was the Democrats', not Polk's, fault for his loss: "Govr, [*sic*] Polk deserves the thanks of the Democracy of the whole union he fought the battle well & fought it alone."[36]

The 1841 gubernatorial election was Polk's first political defeat in Tennessee and his first loss in a political contest since he had failed to win the Speaker of the House election in 1834. Given his success at both the state and national levels, he could have retired or returned to full-time law practice. Polk had no plans to do either. His survey of the political landscape told him that his loss was an aberration. "We had the power to succeed," he assured one friend. "I have fought a good fight, and in many parts of the State, as you know, almost single-handed unaided and alone." Polk believed Tennessee still leaned Democratic and, for that reason, he told one associate, the party needed to "continue to do battle in the cause of sound principles." Supported by Tennessee Democrats, Polk set his sights on winning back the governorship from Jones. He outlined the arguments he planned to use in an October 1841 speech given in front of a friendly audience of Nashvillians and Democratic legislators. Polk painted a picture of Whigs as hypocritical, self-serving Federalists-in-disguise, intent on acquiring and keeping power at the expense of the people. They had won the presidency in 1840 by resorting to "rediculous [sic], unmeaning and disgusting pageants" instead of relying on "argument and sober reasoning." The Whigs had not fulfilled their promises since taking charge; instead, the economy remained in shambles, and abolitionists were being allowed to gain the ear of white Americans. Whigs were so morally degenerate that they had even turned on their own choice for vice president, resulting in Tyler being "hung and burned in effigy, . . . [and] denounced as a traitor to his party." Polk assured his audience that Tennessee voters had not fully grasped the issues when they voted him out of office in August. "If I shall ever rise again," he told the audience, "I expect to *rise from the people.*"[37]

Polk was focusing on the governorship, but others were looking to bring him onto the national stage. Calhoun's camp began making indirect overtures to convince him to join the South Carolinian on the 1844 Democratic ticket. Yet Polk's support for a late 1843 convention date helped solidify him with Van Buren's allies. Fellow Tennessean Robert Armstrong even suggested that his friend might turn out to be the compromise presidential candidate when Van Buren and Calhoun failed to secure the nomination. During the summer of 1842, Polk made a trip north, hoping to suss out his political prospects and to secure a personal loan from Democratic friends. He succeeded at the former but failed at the latter. This interest in Polk prompted opposition from some influential party leaders, such as Robert J. Walker, who had their own ambitions for the 1844 ticket.[38]

The 1843 gubernatorial election, then, was an important test for Polk's standing in the Democratic Party. The choices seemed clear: win and possibly cement the second spot on the 1844 ticket; lose and be consigned to the political graveyard. After announcing his candidacy in the spring of 1843, Polk scheduled more than eighty speaking engagements from March to election day in August. The campaign would take "four months of unceasing riding and speaking," Polk told Van Buren, covering more than 2,300 miles and requiring speeches of five to six hours on many days. Despite engaging in his own vigorous form of electioneering, Polk criticized the Whigs' "flags and fiddling" campaigning, arguing that "this election was to be decided by an appeal to reason." Although he sometimes allowed his dry humor to peek through, Polk largely stuck to reason and argument in his speeches. The 1843 gubernatorial campaign mirrored the national debate taking place. Polk argued that the Whigs were consolidating the national government's power through their advocacy for an unconstitutional bank and a protective tariff that would harm Tennessee voters. Jones pointed out that the Democrats were to blame for the weak national economy and that his opponent had been in Washington when the most damage had been done. The state's own partisan issues also played an important role. Democratic legislators refused to fill Tennessee's two empty US Senate seats in conformity with prior tradition, arguing that the process was unconstitutional. Whigs used the issue to paint their opponents as demagogues denying voters a voice in the Senate. When the nearly 110,000 votes were counted, Jones won by 3,833 votes.[39]

Devastated that his faith in the people's virtue had proven unfounded, this period was "the darkest hour of Polk's political life." His defeat prompted Van Buren and other leading Democrats to move him down, or even off, their vice presidential short list. Even Jackson briefly wavered in his support of Polk's vice presidential chances. But all was not lost for the Tennessean. Some anti-Van Buren Democrats still wanted a Cass–Polk ticket in 1844, and Richard M. Johnson predicted that Polk would win the nomination for vice president. Polk also worked to keep himself relevant to the discussion. He assured Van Buren that Tennessee could still be counted on to vote Democratic in 1844. When the state legislature met later that fall, Polk personally pressured allies and acquaintances to support his vice presidential shot. His strategy was to have Tennessee endorse him for vice president but not to issue a preference for the top of the ticket. The implicit warning was that if Van Buren wanted Tennessee's support, then he needed to reward the state by selecting Polk as his running mate. His strategy worked: out of the thirteen nominating convention delegates appointed by the state Democratic convention that met in November 1843, twelve of them were pro-Polk. By actively backing Van Buren, Polk kept his name in front of party leaders and ensured that any convention discussion included him.[40]

"A FATAL LETTER"

As Democrats looked toward their convention, events shook up the prevailing wisdom of what its outcome would be. On March 20, 1844, Francis P. Blair's *Globe* published a letter from Andrew Jackson that laid out a clear argument for the immediate annexation of Texas. Jackson's letter, written thirteen months earlier in February 1843, explicitly engaged with Thomas W. Gilmer's January 1843 pro-annexation letter. Tennessean Aaron V. Brown, who was serving in the House, had sent Jackson a copy of Gilmer's letter when it was published and had asked for his thoughts on it. Jackson's reply was an overt endorsement of annexation. He faulted John Quincy Adams for failing to obtain Texas while he was president because it allowed Britain to extend its geographical influence in North America. If Britain allied with Texas, Jackson argued, it could invade the United States at any moment. War was not the only menace he foresaw. The British could also use Texas as a base to stir up slave rebellions, producing "a servile war" across the South. It was a dystopian vision that Jackson had indulged since his second term as president, when he had censored the US mail because he feared that abolitionist pamphlets would produce similar "insurrection and . . . massacre."[41]

With Jackson's letter in hand, Brown approached Blair in March 1843 and asked him to publish it in the *Globe*. The Democratic editor refused, saying that he "thought it unwise to make new issues pending the present presidential canvass." Pro-annexationists bided their time, waiting for just the right moment to use it. That time came one year later. With the Texas issue now an important part of the political conversation in early 1844, Blair decided that his reasoning no longer applied. Several days before placing Jackson's letter in the *Globe*'s pages, he forwarded it to Van Buren. With the annexation question gaining prominence, Blair told him, "it will do no harm to have it in your power to scan a paper which will have mighty weight with our party & which is looked to by Tyler as a great support to his prospects."[42]

Jackson's letter undoubtedly gave Van Buren pause when he read it. Texas had not been a topic of their regular correspondence and, despite the circumstances behind the letter's publication, for Old Hickory to have taken such a strong stance without mentioning it to his former vice president left Van Buren not a little perturbed. His replies to Jackson the rest of the month were uncharacteristically short. As he contemplated Jackson's communication and its ramifications, another letter crossed his desk in the early days of the spring that changed the course of Van Buren's career and the Democratic Party's future.[43]

In a letter dated March 27, 1844, Democratic representative William Henry Hammett of Mississippi, a former Methodist minister who had once served as chaplain of the US House, wrote Van Buren asking for his "opinions as to the Constitutionality & expediency of immediately annexing Texas to the United States." Silas Wright questioned Hammett's motives in sending Van Buren his query and warned his friend not to tip his hand on Texas. It would only allow the Whigs to "take advantage of that Knowledge to Keep in the dark as to their position and that of their candidate, until they had seen your Course." "I give you this detail," he told Van Buren, "because I have not been able to make up my own mind perfectly satisfactorily, as to the man and his *bona fides*, since these conversations." Wright considered Hammett "rash, impetuous, and not a little influenced by the Calhoun influences" and perhaps more interested in the notoriety he might gain from Van Buren responding to his query than in the answer itself.[44]

Before drafting a reply, Van Buren asked several close friends for their advice. His former law partner Benjamin F. Butler conveyed to Van Buren conversations he had had while in the nation's capital, as well as his own thoughts. He believed that Texas could only be admitted as a territory and that any annexation treaty "*should not* contain any stipulation or guaranty for the protection of *slaves* or *slavery*." Butler's visit to Washington was necessarily brief, he reported, because he was on his way to the Hermitage to consult with Jackson about the annexation issue. New York ally Jabez D. Hammond was even blunter. "I could not vote for a Candidate for the Presidency who I believed would under any circumstances favor annexation," he told Van Buren. "It is not a question on which I can be influenced by personal considerations or by political expedience. It affects a principle, with me too sacred to be violated for such considerations." He continued with a frank warning about New York: "I may be mistaken, but I believe there are thousands of Democrats in this state who on this subject think & feel as I do."[45]

Van Buren took his friends' counsel under advisement and decided that whatever Hammett's motives, the Mississippian was going to serve as his conduit to the people. Over a seventy-three-page draft, Van Buren scrawled, in his usual meandering and ponderous way, a historically grounded and clearly stated explanation of his opposition to the immediate annexation of

Texas. After providing a survey of US territorial acquisition, he pronounced annexation constitutional. Next, Van Buren argued that because Texas and Mexico were ostensibly still at war, Mexico would "regard the fact of annexation as an act of war on the part of the United States" and would "prosecute her attempts to regain Texas, regardless of consequences." He continued by warning that immediate annexation would cause more harm than good. Van Buren also took the opportunity to criticize white southerners who had moved to Texas in the 1820s and 1830s and had participated in the Texas Revolution, actions undertaken against the government's wishes. He also punctured the rumors that white southerners were floating about Britain's interest in making Texas part of its global empire. Van Buren avoided mentioning slavery here (indeed, he did not mention it explicitly once in the entire letter), but he dismissed the idea that Britain or any European nation would try to take control of Texas. If his prediction proved wrong, then he was confident that "the great principle of self-defence" would unite Americans against such a threat. Van Buren concluded his lengthy response by promising Hammett that if he became president, and if Congress and a majority of the people deemed annexation necessary for the nation's safety, then he would consider it his executive responsibility "to carry into full and fair effect the wishes of a majority of the people of the existing States."[46]

Van Buren completed the final draft of the letter on Saturday, April 20. Satisfied that he had explained himself plainly and convincingly, and confident that the people, or at least Democratic voters, would see the logic of his argument, Van Buren dispatched his son Abraham to Washington with the letter. He wanted allies there to vet it before passing it on to Hammett. Abraham arrived in the capital on the evening of Friday, April 26, and made his delivery to Mrs. Scott's boardinghouse on South Pennsylvania Avenue, where Silas Wright and his wife, Clarissa, were staying. Wright read the letter quickly, slept on it that night, then read it more closely the next morning. Satisfied with its contents, he showed it to his messmates, a group that included John Fairfield of Maine, at breakfast. "They pronounced very favorably, and urged instant publication," Wright wrote Martin Van Buren. He and Abraham then consulted with Ohio representative William Allen and with Thomas Hart Benton, both of whom thought the letter needed to be published that evening. Wright concurred. He and Abraham made one more stop. They found Hammett a little after 3:00 P.M., presented him with Van Buren's reply, and asked for his permission to publish it, even though he had not yet read it. Wright reported that the Mississippian "was frightened" but consented to their request. They then rushed to the *Globe* office, making it by the 4:00 P.M. deadline that ensured that the letter went into the evening edition.[47]

On Sunday morning, Wright attended church. He reported that "the Illinois, Indiana, and Ohio uneasy men" were complaining the loudest about Van Buren's letter. He attributed their grumbling to "the panic agents [that] were active behind the curtain," including Calhoun, President Tyler, and his son Robert. Their interference was not unexpected. Wright reported that other Democratic congressmen were "perfectly satisfied with the letter." "I cannot attempt to say what the effect of all this may be upon the Convention, or the election," Wright concluded, "but I feel clear that our principles and our character are safe."[48]

Van Buren had given Wright the authority to use the letter as he deemed best, publishing it when it would be most fortuitous to his convention chances. The same Saturday morning that Wright and other Democrats were reading and assessing Van Buren's letter, Clay's "Raleigh letter" appeared in the *Daily National Intelligencer*. Instead of waiting to gauge the public reaction to the Kentuckian's letter, Wright pushed to get Van Buren's views in print. Unfortunately for Van Buren, this was a strategic mistake. The public now had in hand both presumptive candidates' letters, and they did not appear to be dramatically different. The coincidental timing of the two letters' publication even led some to speculate erroneously that Van Buren and Clay had conspired to make an agreement during the New Yorker's 1842 visit to Clay's Ashland estate. No evidence of such an agreement exists, and it would have required both men to predict that Texas annexation, not the tariff or the banking system, would become the prominent issue it did two years after their meeting. Nevertheless, the appearance of the letters, both of which opposed immediate annexation, on the same day posed a problem for those who believed in Manifest Destiny. Who would be their champion?[49]

Jackson was especially disappointed in Van Buren. Old Hickory received news of the Hammett letter in an environment that reinforced his personal support of immediate annexation. A pro-annexation meeting met in Nashville on Saturday, May 4, the day that Clay's letter against bringing Texas into the Union became public knowledge in the city. Van Buren's letter arrived that same evening, landing "like a thunderbolt from a clear sky" among Democrats, according to one Whig editor. Both letters were published in Nashville on Monday, May 6. Jackson reacted to Van Buren's letter with frustration and disappointment, undoubtedly exacerbated by the vertigo and "great pain in head and body" from which he was suffering.

Clay's letter had made him "a dead political Duck" until the Hammett letter appeared, Jackson told Blair. During his recent visit to the Hermitage, Butler had led Old Hickory to believe that Van Buren supported immediate annexation. Now there was no difference between the two presumptive candidates on what Jackson considered the most important issue. Van Buren's decision to oppose immediate annexation left Jackson "truly filled with regret" and "mortified" and stoked his conspiratorial fears about Britain's interest in Texas.[50]

Now that Jackson had a clear view of where things stood, he had a decision to make. He could stand by his longtime ally despite their differences over annexation, or he could throw his support to someone else. He consulted with local Democrats, who reportedly were so distraught they were discussing the need for a third-party candidate, such as Calhoun or even Tyler. Neither of those men were options for Jackson. As he told Blair, "however we may be attached to men, we cannot abandon principle." Jackson thought the Democratic Party needed a leader loyal to its values, someone who would stand steadfastly in favor of annexation. An avid newspaper reader, Jackson had undoubtedly seen the April 30 issue of a Nashville newspaper, in which Polk unequivocally told a group of Cincinnatians, led by future US Supreme Court justice Salmon P. Chase, that he had "no hesitation in declaring that I am in favor of the immediate re-annexation of Texas." (A common argument in 1844, the use of "re-annexation" indicated the belief of annexation advocates that Texas rightfully belonged to the United States via the Adams–Onís Treaty, ratified in 1821.) Polk could not have written a clearer endorsement of Manifest Destiny that matched Old Hickory's. Polk had recently returned from his Mississippi plantation, and he had been giving the upcoming Democratic convention much thought. If Van Buren supported annexation and the convention delegates chose the correct running mate for him, then Polk believed the Democratic Party would be in a strong position to win. The Hammett letter only served to convince Polk that his chances for second place on the ticket had "decidedly improved."[51]

But others were already envisioning bigger things for Polk. Tennessee representative Cave Johnson described the Democratic reaction to the Hammett letter as chaotic: "We are broke up *here* & I see *no hope* of mending matters." If the party dumped Van Buren, he announced, then Democrats needed to start over with "an *entirely new man*." His preferred replacement was Wright, who had told Johnson that he was not available. In their conversation, however, Wright had made an interesting statement about Polk's prospects. "[He] s[ai]d. that you was the only man he thought the No[r]thern democrats would support if Van B. was set aside because you was known to be firm & true to the cause," Johnson reported. He noted that Polk's letter in favor of immediate annexation "gives great satisfaction to the Texas men" in Washington.[52]

Jackson was thinking along similar lines as Wright. On the night of Friday, May 10, longtime Jackson friend Robert Armstrong sent Polk a letter urging him to leave for the Hermitage immediately. Enclosed in this letter was a note from Andrew J. Donelson. "It is important that you should see us here without delay," Jackson's nephew told Polk. "I am particularly anxious that the ground occupied by the Genl should be thoroughly understood by you. What he may now say if not modified by disclosures recently made will produce important results." Armstrong wanted Polk at the Hermitage by Sunday night. Polk made it to Nashville on Sunday but waited until Monday, May 13, to finish the journey to Jackson's plantation with Armstrong. On the way, the two men encountered Donelson. He was riding into Nashville with a letter from his uncle, which Jackson wanted published in the pro-Democratic *Nashville Union*, "reiterating and reaffirming his views upon the sub[j]ect of the annexation of Texas." Instead of continuing on to Nashville, Donelson returned with Polk and Armstrong to the Hermitage. As Polk sat in the room with Jackson, Donelson, and Armstrong, the general pronounced "immediate annexation as not only important but indispensible." Van Buren, in his estimation, had written "a fatal letter," had lost the faith of the Democrats, and was no longer a viable nominee. But Jackson believed that the Democrats had an opportunity to steal Whig voters from Clay if they nominated a solid annexation man from the South, and Polk was "the most available man." Although Jackson privately waffled on whether Polk should be first or second on the ticket, it was clear that the Tennessean, not Van Buren, had his trust moving forward.[53]

Polk reacted to Jackson's proclamation with astonishment and denial. He told Cave Johnson that "I have never aspired so high" and it was likely that "the attempt to place me in the first position would be utterly abortive." After a night's rest, Polk still expressed some doubt about Jackson's idea. He did not see how securing the presidential nomination for himself could reasonably occur without destroying the party's unity. Van Burenites would make up the majority of the convention delegates, Polk predicted, and they expected to control both nominations. As he wrote, he seemed to hit upon a plan (or maybe it had been brewing in his mind overnight) that would prevent the convention from "break[ing] up in confusion or without

James K. Polk, 1844. (Courtesy of the Library of Congress)

a nomination." Polk advised Johnson to find a way to get one delegate from each state to meet once they reached Washington and come up "with a plan to save the party." If these delegates could agree on a candidate beforehand, it would avoid a contentious nomination process and prevent party leaders in Washington from interjecting themselves into the nominations. Polk recommended several other delegates that Johnson could trust with the plan.[54]

Like Polk, Jackson took a night to contemplate his next step. On Tuesday, May 14, he sent Donelson to the offices of the *Nashville Union* with his public statement on the annexation issue. Portraying himself as a dispassionate observer called on by friends to respond to Van Buren's letter, Jackson briefly outlined his thoughts on the development of Mexico–Texas relations and the role that the United States had played in them both during and after his administration. Then he drove home his point: if Texas did not join the United States, then "New Orleans and the whole valley of the Mississippi would be endangered. The numerous herds of savages within the limits of Texas, and on her borders, would be easily excited to make war upon our defenceless frontier." Texas, in his view, was "the key to our safety in the south-west and west." Only in closing did Jackson directly address Van Buren's arguments against immediate annexation. In dismissive language that must have stung Van Buren and his supporters, Jackson said that his former vice president had "evidently prepared his letter from a knowledge only of the circumstances bearing on the subject as they existed at the close of his administration without a view of the disclosures since made." It was a searing indictment that marked Van Buren as out of step with the party that he had helped create. Within a week of Jackson's letter being published in the *Nashville Union*, the newspaper was predicting that Van Buren would withdraw and a compromise candidate would be selected. Heading the list of possible successors, which included Calhoun, Cass, Stewart, Tyler, and Buchanan, was James K. Polk.[55]

With two weeks until Democratic delegates converged on Baltimore to decide their nominations and platform, things had shifted dramatically. Van Buren had equivocated enough on annexation that some Democrats, already uncertain about his chances to exact revenge for his loss four years earlier, became convinced that the convention had to choose someone besides him to lead the party to victory. Van Buren was aware that the political ground had shifted, yet he remained confident that writing his letter to Hammett had been the right decision. "I did it with my eyes fully open to the possible outbreak in the quarter where it has occurred," he told Bancroft, "but I am sincerely as well satisfied with my course now as when it was adopted." It remained to be seen if Democrats were just as pleased.[56]

As the Democratic convention drew near, the party faced a dilemma: Should its delegates nominate Van Buren or turn to someone else? The

Texas annexation proved fatal to Martin Van Buren's chances at the Democratic presidential nomination. Other Democratic leaders confront him on his reluctance to face the issue, as Andrew Jackson tries to force him to engage. (Courtesy of the Library of Congress)

Little Magician still had his supporters. Benjamin F. Butler had outlined the logic of a Van Buren candidacy to Jackson shortly after departing the Hermitage in late April. First, many of the convention delegates had been instructed to vote for Van Buren and needed to honor their pledges. Second, Van Buren's approach to annexation was the best option for southern Democrats to gain Texas. Third, Democrats who rejected Van Buren's nomination were simply clearing the way for a Clay administration. "Mr. Van Buren is the only man who stands the least chance of being elected," Butler concluded. In a public letter that echoed Butler's in content, if not in tone, Benton lambasted the immediate annexationists for injecting the Texas question into the election and threatening the nation's future. Virginian George C. Dromgoole echoed Benton's sentiments about the threat to the nation and, reminiscent of Butler's letter to Jackson, declared himself unable to be a single-issue voter on annexation when a Whig victory would allow multiple unwelcome policies that would affect white southerners. Members of the Ohio congressional delegation warned of a conspiracy "to set aside the will of the American democracy" by having the delegates ignore their instructions to vote for Van Buren. Some northern Democrats also emphasized that the party's wing in their region had compromised with southern members on many past issues, and they expected southern Democrats to reciprocate on Van Buren's nomination.[57]

Two weeks before the convention opened, Amos Kendall sent Van Buren an extensive analysis of how the annexation debate was affecting Democratic unity in Washington. Congressional Democrats were upset with Van Buren's letter, a discontent he blamed on "the continual ding-dong rung in their ears by a few members, the public officers in the City and the letters sent in through the influence of Tyler office-holders abroad." "Many of them profess to prefer you to any man living," Kendall told Van Buren, but "they have caught the parrot note—'*he cannot be elected.*'" In his estimation, Cass and Richard M. Johnson posed the only real challenge to Van Buren's nomination, with Johnson having the edge. Kendall warned Van Buren that if the Baltimore convention did not produce a candidate in favor of immediate annexation, the southern delegates were going to secede and nominate their own candidate. "Such recklessness, such selfishness, such disregard of principle and justice, I did not expect to see in the Democracy of my time," Kendall lamented.[58]

PRECONVENTION MANEUVERING

As delegates prepared to meet in Baltimore, the foundation was being laid to find a viable alternative to the former president. The first steps in this direction came from Mississippi. The state's Democratic leaders had lined up strongly behind Van Buren before publication of the Hammett letter, but once he came out against immediate annexation, they moved quickly to distance themselves from his candidacy. Leading the charge was Robert J. Walker. Two days after the Hammett letter was published, he assembled approximately twenty-five Democratic congressmen in an anti-Van Buren meeting. It produced "a general & set[t]led hostility to Van Buren" and sparked a coordinated newspaper campaign against his nomination. Walker and six other Mississippi delegates to the Democratic national convention, including Hammett, sent the *Globe* a letter that was unequivocal in its stance. The people of Mississippi wanted immediate annexation, and the state's representatives to the Baltimore convention were going to support a candidate who agreed with them. Members of the Indiana congressional delegation described their reluctant disavowal of Van Buren as being the product of months of constituent correspondence and "a feeling of distrust" shared by the New Yorker's "ardent and uniform supporters." By the time Walker was done, Van Buren had lost the support of every Mississippian, as well as all but one of the Indiana delegation. Clay gloated at reports of the dissension: "I do not think I ever witnessed such a state of utter disorder, confusion and decomposition as that which the Democratic Party now presents."[59]

Van Buren also found himself in trouble in Virginia, another crucial southern state. Following the party's state convention earlier in the year, Thomas Ritchie's *Richmond Enquirer* had proclaimed that the Democrats in the state, who were divided between Calhoun and Van Buren, were "firmly and indissolubly re-united." These assurances were ill-founded, as "demon discord" threatened to tear the state party apart. Even before the Hammett letter was published, Virginians alerted Ritchie that if Van Buren was nominated, the "Slang Mummeries, Songs &c" of the 1840 election would be repeated, and "we will be defeated." Ritchie himself forwarded to Silas Wright correspondence warning that if Van Buren "goes against Texas . . . *all is gone.*" Democratic losses in the 1844 spring elections that followed on the heels of the Hammett letter's publication only increased the demands that someone besides Van Buren, someone "sound on the *Texas question*," head the party's ticket. Ultimately, Virginia Democrats rescinded their obligation to support the former president, passing resolutions to that effect at the May 3 meeting of the Shockoe Hill Democratic Association in Richmond. They called for the "re-annexation of Texas" and argued that its acquisition was necessary to protect slavery. They also recommended that Virginia delegates to the Democratic national convention be allowed to vote for someone other than Van Buren, who received word prior to the convention that his standing in Virginia had fallen. "You are *deserted.* Ritchie, [William H.] Roane, & [Andrew] Stevenson are *all* out *against you* on the Texas question; *positively, openly,* and *unequivocally against you,*" one correspondent told Van Buren. Ritchie also wrote his longtime ally, enclosing a packet of letters from leading Virginians calling for another nominee, and telling him, "We cannot carry Virginia for you." Momentum in Virginia appeared to be moving toward Cass, who had come out in favor of immediate annexation in the aftermath of Van Buren's letter. Just days before the convention, Ritchie was all but certain that if Van Buren were nominated, his chances to carry Virginia were nil.[60]

Van Buren was aware of the furor that his letter had set off among Democrats, but he was convinced that he had made the right choice. He told Ritchie that the reports from Virginia had not changed his determination to pursue "the correctly ascertained, and well understood wishes of the Democracy of the United States" regarding his political positions, including that toward Texas. To a group of Mississippi Democrats, Van Buren proclaimed that he "would wholly fail in securing either their respect or esteem, where [*sic*] I to sustain any other course in regard to this very important subject." "Having reference only to the election, there was certainly room for doubt" about expressing himself so fully and transparently about Texas, Van Buren wrote Bancroft, but he was willing to take the chance. Van Buren told Wright that his approach to Texas annexation "will in the end be amply justified by a vast majority of our Countrymen, and in my confirmed conviction, is also the only one by which the country can be carried in Safety through present & future difficulties." He was determined to "pursue steadily and undismayed the path of duty," believing that voters would support his convictions in the end.[61]

The preconvention politicking for the top nominees began in earnest once the delegates started arriving in Baltimore. On Wednesday evening, May 22, 1844, Ohio editor Samuel Medary brought together leading Van Burenites in Washington to discuss the expected delegate support. They calculated that the former president could receive a majority, but that the anti-Van Buren delegates might be able to pass the two-thirds rule, which would require a nominee to obtain not a simple majority, but two-thirds, of the votes cast by convention delegates. The following day, the New York delegates met and determined to prevent anyone else from the nomination if the two-thirds rule passed. Wright informed Van Buren that he thought "the result altogether uncertain." "You have witnessed the disgusting flood of Texas letters, and therefore can immagine [*sic*] the effects and course of individuals, who are weak enough to suppose that question is to make Presidents of them," he commented.[62]

The two-thirds rule was going to play an important role in how the convention developed. Democrats had adopted it at their first national nominating convention in 1832 to signal strong party support for Van Buren's place on the ticket with Jackson, but not without dissent—some party members considered the two-thirds rule undemocratic. Now, in 1844, its use was being threatened as an obstacle to the New Yorker's nomination. If this rule was adopted, "we are water-logged at once," Bancroft wrote Van Buren, and if a majority vote was enacted instead, "secession is menaced." Some Democrats rightly believed that the two-thirds rule was a deliberate strategy to eliminate Van Buren from contention. If no candidate was able to obtain the necessary votes under the rule, delegates would feel free to abandon their preconvention pledges to vote as instructed for certain candidates. There was even speculation that once Van Buren's name had been dropped, the delegates might do an about-face and return to the majority vote to select another candidate.[63]

Whether or not the two-thirds rule passed, the Tennessee delegation seemed destined to play a critical role in shaping the ticket. Following Wednesday's Van Buren caucus, the delegates from Polk's state (excepting Aaron V. Brown and Andrew J. Donelson, who had not yet arrived) held their own meeting. A majority of the delegates opposed Van Buren's nomination and supported the two-thirds rule. Cave Johnson, who was Polk's point person at the convention, realized that his friend's association with Van Buren was jeopardizing his shot at the vice presidency. With this realization in mind, Johnson approached Massachusetts delegates George Bancroft and Marcus Morton with a proposal. The plan that ultimately unfolded was straightforward and predicated on the assumption that the convention would adopt the two-thirds rule. First, Van Buren's supporters would push his nomination on the first ballot. If, as expected, he did not receive a two-thirds majority, then the New Yorker's supporters would call on anti-Van Burenites to put forward their choice, presumably Cass. When he also failed to secure the required votes, southern delegates would then suggest Wright as a compromise presidential candidate. Because the names of other vice presidential candidates were prominently attached to Van Buren or Cass, the delegates would be looking for a compromise candidate for second place on the ticket. Polk's considerable southern support, with additional backing in Illinois, Massachusetts, and New York, would put him in a good position to gain that nomination.[64]

Here was the brilliance of Johnson's plan. Wright had already made it abundantly clear that he did not want the presidency. If he declined, then perhaps, just perhaps, the delegates would put Polk at the top of the ticket, since he could not be held responsible for Van Buren's and Cass's rejection and Wright's declination. It was a tricky proposition, but such an outcome seemed plausible to Polk's Tennessee friends. "You have more friends here than any man in the field & if your name had been brought before the country for the first place, we would have had far more unanimity," Gideon J. Pillow assured him. "I am satisfied you are the choice of 2/3 of the convention for the Vice, & almost every one of your friends say they would prefer you for the Presidency. Things may take that turn yet." But they had to tread carefully, he told Polk: "We of the south cannot bring that matter up. If it should be done by the north it will all work right, but if we were to make such a move it would in all probability injure your prospect for the Vice."[65]

THE CONVENTION

On the eve of the Democratic convention's opening on Monday, May 27, one sympathetic newspaper contrasted the two parties' approaches. The Whigs were "trying to tickle the fancy of all classes, by speeches, addresses, and resolutions" and by using "songs, Clay clubs, processions, and carousals . . . to make the election of our chief magistrate an occasion of festivity and frolic." Democrats, meanwhile, "looked passively on," satisfied "that because our principles are right, they must succeed." "This course is entirely wrong," the article continued. "If we are to be beaten again by such ridiculous means and appliances, it will be our *own* fault."[66]

The Democratic delegates who gathered in Baltimore did not match the revelry recorded in the accounts of the Whigs' meeting earlier in the month, but they were still in a festive mood. One Van Buren correspondent described "the City overflowing with Company" and "the Publikc [sic] Houses all full of great crowds of people discussing the possible presidential candidates." "The streets, and the house at Barnum's, night and day are crowded full of people, and talking, laughing, porting, &c., continue all the time," another eyewitness remarked, "and there is no such thing as eating, sleeping, thinking, or resting, in any decent form whatever." Observers commented on the ways in which the Democratic delegates interacted with the local citizens. "The Watirs [sic] at the Hotels say the demacrats [sic] are all Gentlemen," one New Yorker reported, while a local newspaper noted that Baltimoreans treated their visitors with "kindness and respect."[67]

But all was obviously not well beneath the surface of public merriment. As many delegates were arriving by train and coach and settling in their rooms (or going to the bars), Democrats were clearly divided, and finding common ground seemed impossible. "I confess myself much surprised at the extent of the *distraction* and the bitterness of feeling" among the various factions of the party, Pillow told Polk. Everything "is chaos and darkness," reported one Tennessee delegate. Another pronounced, "We are in a most deplorable condition." "We are in the midst of the most reckless and desperate system of political intrigue that I have ever witnessed," Henry D. Gilpin told Van Buren. One Whig observer said it well when he sneered, "Discord, suspicion, doubt, and apprehension prevail in their ranks."[68]

DAY I OF THE CONVENTION (MONDAY, MAY 27)

As noon approached on Monday, Democrats began streaming into the Egyptian Saloon, located on the top floor of Odd Fellows Hall on Gay Street. "As far as I can judge, there is a greater collection of talents & character than we have had at any time before," Cave Johnson observed. Not every-one was as enthusiastic as the Tennessean, however. The venue was small, poorly ventilated, and "as hot as Belshazzar's furnace," according to one delegate. The aesthetic of the main convention room, which one newspaper account described as "look[ing] very like a miniature edition of the Egyptian Tombs," matched the somber mood of some delegates entering the convention. "The very atmosphere is burthened with the putrid odor of the corruption so rotten & rife in men's hearts," *Democratic Review* editor John L. O'Sullivan told Van Buren.[69]

As an on-site reporter, O'Sullivan was positioned to observe some chicanery that took place at the start of the convention. Van Buren supporters had wanted to make New Hampshire governor (and Van Buren friend) Henry Hubbard the convention president. But the anti-Van Buren delegates executed a preemptory procedural strike. According to multiple accounts, North Carolina's Romulus M. Saunders, a former House Speaker, current US representative, and the "leader of the opposition," called the convention to order a few minutes early. This gave anti-Van Buren delegates the opportunity to elect Hendrick B. Wright of Pennsylvania, a pro-Buchanan delegate, as convention president. Newspaper accounts reported that the convention started "precisely" at noon or even "a few minutes after" and that Wright was elected with unanimous consent "amid the liveliest greetings of satisfaction and approbation." These reports undercut O'Sullivan's version of events, which was admittedly biased—he was writing to Van Buren after all. Nevertheless, Van Burenites were caught off guard by the move, which suggests they possessed a "lack of tactical planning and aggressive leadership" reminiscent of their work during the 1840 presidential campaign.[70]

It was an inauspicious start for Van Buren supporters, and things quickly turned worse. Saunders introduced a resolution asking the convention to adopt the 1832 and 1835 convention rules. The intent was to require the delegates to agree to the two-thirds rule. Cave Johnson quickly asked for the certification of the delegates by a committee made up of one representative from each state, under the guise of ensuring that no unauthorized delegates had slipped in. Everyone understood what Johnson was trying to do, however—he was trying to buy more time for pro-Van Buren supporters to shore up votes against the two-thirds rule. The convention was at an impasse. Neither side wanted to concede ground on which should come first—the vote on the two-thirds rule or the certification of the delegates. In stepped Robert J. Walker. One Democrat later described him as the "great intriguer" at the 1844 convention. "Walker is a man of the mole policy," they wrote, "*he works underground and in the dark.*" He asked Saunders to withdraw his resolution, which he did. Then Walker submitted a resolution asking that each state delegation appoint one representative to report the names and credentials of each member. This resolution was approved, and members were appointed. The delegates continued wrangling over procedural issues until the afternoon session was adjourned, a relief to all inside the cramped, poorly ventilated hall.[71]

At 4:00 P.M., the convention was gaveled back to order. Complaints about the small size of the Egyptian Saloon continued, as did discussion about the certification of the state delegations. Early in the evening session, the credentialing committee certified each state's delegates and confirmed that the number of votes each state would receive would equal their electoral votes. (The only exception was South Carolina, which did not send official delegates because of internal disagreement with the way in which the party had made its selections earlier in the year.) Some delegates wanted to continue discussing the convention's organization, but others were ready to deal with the main issue at hand. Saunders once again moved for the adoption of the 1832 and 1835 rules. Remember, Saunders told his colleagues, "we go for principles, not men." His motion set off a furious debate. New York delegate Daniel S. Dickinson wrote his wife that he was having difficulty finishing his letter to her because of the noise level of the convention. "A Mississippi roarer, whose voice is as harsh as the rough edge of thunder, is speaking right behind me, nearly deafening me," he complained, and "there are two roarers speaking on the stairs."[72]

Benjamin F. Butler responded to Saunders's motion by offering an amendment setting aside the two-thirds rule. In an impassioned speech, he warned his colleagues that if they adopted the two-thirds rule, they ran the risk of not being able to make a presidential nomination. None of them truly believed any of the candidates could obtain the required support under the rule, he argued. The climax of the speech came when Butler declared that the 1840 election was not "a proper expression of the will of the American people." The *Globe* noted that his comment was met with "thunders of applause." O'Sullivan described a more dramatic scene. In denouncing the 1840 election as representative of neither the Democratic Party nor the nation, Butler "stamped with indignant reprobation upon it &c. &c. He became white with excitement and actually in his process of stamping on it, jumped up three or four times from the floor two or three feet high." Because of the late hour, Butler withdrew his amendment, and the convention adjourned. As the day's proceedings ended, the delegates poured out into the street where they were greeted by the large crowd that had been standing outside all day. "I never saw such excitement in my life," South Carolinian Francis W. Pickens reported to Calhoun. "Immense crowds every night & addresses in the streets &c—of the most vulgar demagoguism."[73]

The first day of the convention closed without any clarity on the two-thirds rule. O'Sullivan reported to Van Buren that "we feel that we have the best of the day." Butler had made "the strongest point of our position—the popular enthusiasm for the reversal of 1840 and the atonement of its disgrace." In a postscript, however, the reporter shared that "the news this evening are not so favorable." Some of the delegates who opposed the two-thirds rule were wavering. "Intrigue is so active and treachery so corrupt, that nothing can be relied on, and you must be prepared for the worst," O'Sullivan warned. "I see & hear a great deal that almost literally turns my stomach." He was not the only one pessimistic about Van Buren's chances. A fellow New Yorker told Van Buren that the supporters of Cass and Richard M. Johnson were conspiring to deny him the nomination. Cave Johnson, meanwhile, sent Polk word that the Tennessee delegation had determined to go for Silas Wright as president, believing that "public opinion will not justify us in giving our vote to Van."[74]

DAY 2 OF THE CONVENTION (TUESDAY, MAY 28)

Delegates returned to the convention hall on Tuesday morning, where the proceedings started at 9:00. Convention president Hendrick Wright began by reminding delegates that they needed to prioritize "the welfare of our beloved country, abandon men, and go for measures." Only in that way could they avoid handing the election to the Whigs and their "contemptible exhibitions of buffoonery and mummery unworthy of an enlightened and reflecting age." After speeches by several delegates, including Walker, the delegates proceeded to vote on whether to adopt the two-thirds rule. At Wright's instruction, each state delegation decided internally on its mode of voting, either as a unit or individually, with passage requiring only a majority vote. When the votes were tallied, the two-thirds rule had been approved easily, 148 to 116. The sectionalism of the vote was apparent. Of the free-state delegates, 64 percent (102 out of 160) rejected the two-thirds rule. If the free states showed a clear preference for deciding nominations based on a majority vote, the slave states expressed an even stronger desire in the opposite direction. A majority of 87 percent (90 out of 104) of their delegates voted in favor of the rule.[75]

With the debate over the two-thirds rule finally settled, the delegates took

a recess. They returned at 3:30 P.M. to begin selecting a presidential candidate. Winning the nomination now required 177 of 266 votes instead of
the 134 that would have produced a victory under the majority rule. When
the first ballot was counted, Van Buren held a sixty-three-vote lead over
Cass, with Johnson the only other candidate winning votes in double digits.
Buchanan, Calhoun, Stewart, and Woodbury split the remaining thirteen
votes. A request that Van Buren, having secured a majority, become the
nominee was "objected to by several" and ruled out of order. On the second
ballot, Van Buren's lead over Cass shrank by thirty votes. More concerning was that he only held a plurality over his five opponents. (Woodbury
did not win any votes on the second ballot.) Over the next two ballots, the
New Yorker continued to win a plurality, but his lead diminished each time.
Stewart dropped off after the second ballot, leading one newspaper to comment that the commodore had "been conquered as easily as the forlorn alli-
gator that recently ventured away from his own element into the streets of
New Orleans." Woodbury disappeared after the third ballot, with Calhoun
barely hanging on. This left three viable candidates besides Van Buren. Buchanan's vote rose slightly each ballot, while Johnson's tally peaked on the
third ballot and began a slow decline. Most concerning for Van Buren's
supporters was Cass. The Michigander was within six votes of the lead by
the end of the fourth ballot. The fifth, sixth, and seventh ballots saw him
overtake Van Buren. Johnson's support was petering out, while Buchanan
had reached his unimpressive peak on the fifth ballot and was beginning to
decline. It had clearly become a two-person race: Van Buren versus Cass.[76]

With voting trending toward Cass, Ohio Van Burenites tried to stop
the momentum. US representative John K. Miller argued that Van Buren

Table 3.1. First through Seventh Ballots for Presidential Nomination at 1844
Democratic National Convention

Ballot	Van Buren	Cass	Johnson	Buchanan	Calhoun	Woodbury	Stewart	Total
1st	146	83	24	4	6	2	1	266
2nd	127	94	33	9	1	0	1	265*
3rd	121	92	38	11	2	2	0	266
4th	111	105	32	17	1	0	0	266
5th	103	107	29	26	1	0	0	266
6th	101	116	23	25	1	0	0	266
7th	99	123	21	22	1	0	0	266

* One North Carolina delegate did not vote on this ballot.
Source: *Washington (DC) Daily Globe*, 6 June 1844.

should be the presidential nominee based on the first ballot; at one point, he "jump[ed] up on the table and the whole house was thrown into the most violent commition [*sic*]." "Above the confusion suddenly" one Pennsylvania delegate called for Andrew Jackson to be the party's nominee. The "mingled applause and good-humored laughter" that accompanied this proposed resolution quickly dissipated into chaos again. "The whole convention had well-nigh got into a general pel-mell fight," according to Pillow. Ohio newspaper editor Samuel Medary reportedly "acted a most disgraceful part," and another Ohioan "threw off his coat as if determined to go into a regular fight." With the delegates still in an uproar, at 7:00 P.M., the convention adjourned until the next morning.[77]

A pattern had become apparent during Tuesday's balloting. Maine, Missouri, New York, and Ohio voted for Van Buren each time; collectively, they represented seventy-five votes. Cass had eight states that voted for him each time (Alabama, Delaware, Georgia, Indiana, Michigan, Mississippi, Tennessee, and Virginia), also totaling seventy-five votes. By the end of the day, six other states (Connecticut, Illinois, Maryland, New Jersey, North Carolina, and Vermont), representing forty-seven votes, had also moved solidly into the Cass's column. Johnson had consistent support from Kentucky and Arkansas (fifteen votes total) in the first seven ballots, while Louisiana (six votes) had settled on supporting Buchanan. The other four states (Massachusetts, New Hampshire, Pennsylvania, and Rhode Island) split on the seventh ballot; they represented forty-eight votes. Most concerning of these latter four delegations for Van Buren was Pennsylvania, which had voted for him on the first six ballots but had split its votes among him, Cass, Buchanan, and Johnson on the seventh. Keeping Cass from moving the Keystone State's twenty-six votes solidly into his column appeared crucial to Van Buren's chances of survival. It seemed likely that unless something dramatic occurred, however, it was only a matter of time before Cass emerged as the party's nominee.[78]

As the delegates dispersed into the night following Tuesday's session, there were still other possibilities in play besides a Cass nomination. Louisiana and New Hampshire had been the only delegations to vote consistently for Buchanan, but he had started gaining some ground during the day. Johnson was trending in the other direction, but there was no reason that he could not stage a comeback on Wednesday given the six states that had voted for him throughout the day. Despite the shake-up that was taking place, Calhoun's chances seemed as dim as when the convention began. One South Carolinian took satisfaction in his estimate that Van Buren was "dead forever," but he expressed frustration that the "lifeless" southern delegations were not championing Calhoun.[79]

Then there was Silas Wright Jr. Two days before the convention began, Cave Johnson wrote Polk that if the delegates reached an impasse on Van Buren and could not agree on any of the other leading candidates, then "a majority will probably fall on" Wright. He "is right on the Tariff & will be right on Texas, agt. *the treaty* but for immediate annexation by law." For those reasons, southerners would find him acceptable, and northerners would consider him the next best thing to Old Kinderhook. Johnson even argued that they "must force" Wright to accept if Van Buren were rejected. There was one major problem: Wright was dead set against being the nominee. Prior to the convention, he gave New York delegate John Fine a letter stating his denial of a nomination, to be presented to the delegates if it became clear that they saw him as a substitute for Van Buren. If Democrats did not want Van Buren, Wright wrote, then they would not want him, either. In case he had not been clear, Wright reiterated in his closing paragraphs, "I am not, and cannot, under any circumstances, be a candidate before your convention for that office." Part of Wright's resolve came from his own self-awareness that he was not cut out for the office, but he also was unwilling to betray Van Buren. Wright believed that pro-annexationists would use him to torpedo his friend's chances, then toss him aside to select someone more amenable to their influence. Van Buren was not oblivious to his decision. Nevertheless, he sent Butler a letter authorizing him to bring forward Wright's name, with his endorsement, if it became clear that he, Van Buren, would not gain the nomination. "Should the affair take that direction, I hope you will immediately make it your business to see Mr. Wright, and prevent him by all means in your power from declining the nomination," Van Buren wrote, instructing Butler to speak in his name. "Nothing could occur that would give me more pain than his refusal under such circumstances."[80]

The Tennessee delegation had another plan in mind, but executing it required some finessing to ensure Polk made it onto the ticket. George Bancroft saved them the trouble of making the first move. He approached Pillow with the idea of abandoning Van Buren for Polk. This proposal was surprising given Bancroft's closeness to Van Buren. The Boston Brahmin had not only started writing a campaign biography for his friend, but he had also ensured that eleven of the twelve Massachusetts delegates to the 1844 Democratic national convention were pro-Van Buren. Bancroft's decision to move on from Van Buren was a bad sign for the former president.

Table 3.2. Eighth and Ninth Ballots for Presidential Nomination at 1844 Democratic National Convention

Ballot	Van Buren	Cass	Buchanan	Calhoun	Polk	Total
8th	104	114	2	2	44	266
9th**	2	29	0	0	233	264*

* One Georgia delegate did not vote. Ohio cast one of its votes for Marcus Morton.
** Before unanimous consent.
Source: *Washington (DC) Daily Globe*, 6 June 1844.

Bancroft had also come to the convention intending to do everything in his power to support Polk as Van Buren's running mate. Newspaper editor Jeremiah George Harris, one of Bancroft's political operatives in Massachusetts, had spent four years as editor of the *Nashville Union*. Harris knew Polk from his time in Middle Tennessee, and he periodically shared his "zeal" for the Tennessean with Bancroft in their correspondence. Bancroft had a personal relationship with Van Buren, then, but he was also acquainted with Polk, albeit from a distance. As the Bostonian later told Polk, when it became clear that Van Buren was not going to be able to win the nomination, "it flashed in my mind, that it would be alone safe to rally on you." Bancroft convinced the New Hampshire delegation to go along with his plan and gained the support of Governor Marcus Morton in his own state's delegation. At that point, Bancroft talked about his idea to Pillow, who responded that the best strategy was for the northern delegations to raise Polk's name as a compromise candidate. The next several hours, extending past midnight, witnessed political maneuvering the Sly Fox of Kinderhook undoubtedly would have appreciated if it had not sunk his nomination.[81]

While Bancroft and the Tennesseans were working the delegates, Butler was setting in motion another plan. The day's proceedings had made it clear to him that Van Buren's chance at the nomination was lost. Butler had also heard that Richard M. Johnson was going to withdraw, allowing his supporters to move to Cass. This prospect was unacceptable to Butler. He was determined to salvage the convention for New York and for the principles Van Buren represented. To that end, he also visited delegates late into the night. Butler concluded that there was sufficient support in several delegations to bring Wright forward as a nominee. The one insurmountable obstacle to his plan was Wright's clear aversion to the nomination. Butler decided to move forward anyway, citing *"new* circumstances" that would convince Wright to change his mind.[82]

As Polk's supporters worked to win over the frustrated delegates, Benton wrote Jackson from Washington. "We are in a bad way here—about as we were in 1824–25" when Adams and Clay had stolen the election. "A nest of members of congress" was now trying "to nullify the will of the people" by robbing Van Buren of the nomination. Benton blamed corruption, in the form of "offices, 100 millions of Texas lands, 10 millions of Texas stock," for "making fearful havoc among our public men." Benton's employment of conspiratorial rhetoric indicated how deeply he believed that the events transpiring in Baltimore were part of a long history of antidemocratic corruption. Given his perspective, he likely would have viewed the late-night maneuvers by Polk's supporters in the same light if he had known about them.[83]

DAY 3 OF THE CONVENTION (WEDNESDAY, MAY 29)

After a night of scheming and politicking, the delegates were set to reconvene at 9:00 A.M. With that deadline looming, Butler called together the New York delegation an hour earlier to discuss his plan to nominate Silas Wright. His strategy proved unsuccessful. The New Yorkers were divided over whether to pursue his nomination; without a unified front, there was no way to convince other state delegations to fall in line with them. When the convention was gaveled into order, the Democratic delegates moved ahead with the eighth ballot. The votes revealed that it was now a three-person race. Two of the contenders—Cass and Van Buren—were expected, but a new name emerged: James K. Polk. As it had previously, voting proceeded geographically, starting in New England. Maine voted for Van Buren, but New Hampshire cast its six votes for Polk. Massachusetts followed suit, giving a majority of its vote to the Tennessean. By now, delegates caught unawares knew something was brewing. Alabama, Louisiana, and Tennessee voted unanimously for Polk, with Pennsylvania and Maryland also throwing votes his way. By the end of the eighth ballot, the vote stood 114 for Cass, 104 for Van Buren, and 44 for Polk.[84]

Polk's appearance on the ballot for the first time signaled that something had shaken loose within the delegations. Reah Frazer of Pennsylvania made the case for switching his vote to Polk, an argument with which many delegates likely identified. "The Lancaster War Horse," as Frazer was known, indicated that he had followed his constituents' instructions by voting for Van Buren, then Buchanan. Now, he and other Pennsylvania delegates were supporting Polk, "the bosom friend of Old Hickory . . . the pure, whole hog, locofoco democrat . . . a man who goes against the ring-streaked and speckled whig party, with all its odious, abominable measures." New

Yorkers were not willing to cede the nomination just yet. New York's Samuel Young resurrected the argument against the two thirds-rule, causing a furor when he blamed "the political Nero of this country" for conspiring "to enkindle the flame now raging in the democratic citadel" and implied that Tyler headed a "mongrel administration." A Georgia delegate demanded to know the identity of this "political Nero"; several delegates shouted "John Tyler." Young may have meant to insult the president, but some southern delegates, especially those from Georgia, inferred that his use of "mongrel administration" was attacking Calhoun and other white southerners. They may have interpreted "mongrel" as a term suggesting racial mixing, a verboten concept for many white southerners steeped in the racism of the era. That kind of insult often prompted a violent response from elite white southern men who deemed it essential to protect their honor. Hammett, whom Van Burenites could rightfully have blamed for their candidate's fatal problems at the convention, called on southern delegates to abstain from saying anything "harsh or intemperate." Other delegates chimed in with admonishments not to let the heated rhetoric distract them from their purpose. Instead of answering demands to identify the object of his ridicule, Young and the rest of the New York delegation walked out to consult about their next move.[85]

The New York delegation's absence did not halt the movement toward a final resolution of the presidential nomination. The ninth ballot began without the Empire State, and it became clear with each passing vote that Polk had the momentum. As Virginia indicated its support for the Tennessean, the New Yorkers returned. Butler rose and announced that he was voting for Polk. He spoke only for himself, but everyone understood that the New York delegation was conceding Van Buren's nomination and putting its support behind the former Speaker. States that had already cast their votes for another candidate switched to Polk; states that had not yet voted came out in enthusiastic support of him. At one point, Maryland delegate John Kettlewell asked about South Carolina: "Who knows anything of our lost sister?" Francis W. Pickens and Franklin H. Elmore were present as unofficial representatives of South Carolina, and the delegates responded to their introduction "with the waving of hats and handkerchiefs." After both men promised the Palmetto State's support for Polk in the coming campaign, Hendrick Wright announced the Tennessean's unanimous selection to cheers.[86]

The ninth ballot finally brought the most contentious part of the convention to a close. An "indescribable" enthusiasm filled the convention hall, bolstered by congratulations from the Democratic members of Congress. Pillow spoke at length about Polk's qualifications, taking care to observe that his friend had "no political sins to answer for to the country." He also noted that Polk "occupie[d] the only ground truly American" on Oregon and Texas—the Democratic nominee was "in favor of resisting British aggression at every step." When Pillow concluded, the delegates, much to their relief, took a recess. News of Polk's nomination was conveyed via the newly installed electromagnetic telegraph line between Washington and Baltimore, over which Samuel F. B. Morse had sent the first message—"WHAT HATH GOD WROUGHT"—just five days before. "The dark sky of yesterday has been succeeded by the brightest day democracy has witnessed since your election," Donelson reported to his uncle. "We feel relieved. No one entertains a doubt of the vigorous and united action of the whole party." Shortly after the convention, Jackson provided a succinct analysis of why Van Buren's candidacy had collapsed in Baltimore. "The moment I saw Mr. V. Burens letter and heard the effect it had produced on his friends at the great Texas meeting at Nashville, I was fearfull he would be dropped by the democracy of the south & west in favour of the immediate reannexation of Texas," he told Blair. If Van Buren had simply come out "for immediate annexation," Old Hickory sighed, "he would have carried the south & west by acclamation."[87]

Two Democrats in particular congratulated themselves for orchestrating Polk's nomination. "I was up nearly all night last night in bringing about this result," Pillow crowed triumphantly to Polk. "Some *true men* in the North" quickly saw the brilliance of his plan, but "I got no help on the work which was done last night from our home people." Not known for his humility, Pillow continued, "Some of our own *faithful* delegation, to whom I have referred several times in my letters—who have done all they could in their secret, assassin-like manner to destroy your prospects & sacrifice you, are overwhelmed with astonishment at this strange result." Several days later, he was still reveling in how luminously he was espousing Polk's cause. As Donelson sarcastically told Polk, "Pillow is admirably suited to the task of responding to the applause which every where welcomes your nomination." Bancroft held similar views of his own work. Decades later, he claimed that "Polk owed his nomination by the Democratic Convention to me." According to his self-promoting account, Bancroft went to Baltimore knowing that Van Buren could not be nominated because of the annexation issue. By the Tuesday evening adjournment, he also realized that Cass could not win. That was when Bancroft decided on Polk and single-handedly brought his plan, and the votes of Massachusetts and New York, to the Tennessee delegates. He recalled that "they naturally accepted the name of Polk joyfully and distributed among themselves that part of the work which I thought they could best do."[88]

Two other Democrats abstained from self-congratulation but were essential in helping Polk's cause in Baltimore. Cave Johnson had been one of Polk's biggest champions in the run-up to the convention, and his calm, steady work in Baltimore likely put more delegates at ease than did Pillow's vainglorious approach. After the convention, Tennessee delegate Williamson Smith told Polk that he could not single out the most important person in securing his nomination, but he recommended that the Democratic nominee give Johnson "a post of honour." (Polk followed Smith's advice, appointing Johnson to his cabinet the following year, as he also did Bancroft.) In the months after the convention, both Bancroft and Ohio journalist Ellwood Fisher credited Donelson with the idea of having the New England states bring Polk forward as a compromise candidate. In response to Bancroft's 1887 claim that he had been the main influence behind Polk's nomination, Jeremiah George Harris painted a different picture. He reminded Bancroft "that Donelson was Polk's confidential manager" at the 1844 convention and that Jackson's nephew "did a good deal of private management for Polk at Baltimore, at his *own* instance no doubt." Whether Bancroft, Donelson, Johnson, or Pillow deserved the most credit, the outcome was the same: Polk was the Democratic nominee.[89]

The delegates had overcome their most formidable obstacle, but they still had work to do. When they returned at 4:00 P.M. for the afternoon session, their task was to select a vice presidential nominee. Walker immediately nominated Silas Wright. A Kentucky delegate withdrew Richard M. Johnson's name, which cleared the way for Wright's selection. He received 258 votes. Georgia cast eight votes for Woodbury for the stated purpose of "expressing their approbation of that pure and able statesman." That may have been the case, but some of its delegates were probably still miffed at New York's Samuel Young and wanted to make a symbolic gesture of defiance. John Fine noted that Wright had asked that his name not appear before the convention "in any event," but he "hoped that Mr. W. would consent to serve." "The idea of running Silas Wright subordinate to General Jackson's chief cook and bottle-washer, Colonel Polk!" laughed diarist Philip Hone.[90]

Having apparently settled the vice presidential nomination, the delegates moved on to other business. They organized a committee to produce a platform that would articulate the party's principles in the upcoming campaign and discussed publishing campaign material. To "shouts of laughter," one Ohioan sarcastically suggested that the Democrats raise money to help the Whigs defray the costs of the campaign material they had produced in anticipation of Van Buren being Clay's competitor. A fellow delegate chimed in that the Whigs could get reimbursement "from the funds of the defunct Bank of the United States." After a hearty set of congratulations to the convention officers and others, the delegates adjourned for the day at 7:30 P.M.[91]

The jocularity that accompanied the latter half of the day's proceedings overshadowed a serious problem: Silas Wright sincerely did not want to be on the ticket. When telegraphed news of his vice presidential nomination, he declined twice, noting that he would "support Mr. Polk cheerfully" at the top of the ticket. Some of the New York delegates asked Wright to reconsider. The reply: "Under no circumstances" would he accept. Frazzled by his friend's intransigence, Fine asked him what he should tell the convention. The answer was concise and pointed: "What Mr. Wright has already said." Wright was informed that a committee of five was being dispatched to Washington to try to change his mind. Undoubtedly perturbed at being put in the position of making multiple statements on something he had been clear about, Wright wrote a final, definitive declination. He asked two New York congressmen, Preston King and Orville Robinson, to take his letter to the convention. Since train service had stopped for the night, the two men set out for Baltimore by wagon.[92]

DAY 4 OF THE CONVENTION (THURSDAY, MAY 30)

The delegates had agreed to reconvene at 7:30 A.M. on Thursday. When they arrived, they were informed that "it was doubtful" that their work on the vice presidential nomination was complete. Setting aside that news, the delegates moved to adopting the principles on which their ticket would run. As chair of the resolutions committee, Butler reported the platform to the convention. It began with a rejection of the "factitious symbols" and "displays and appeals insulting to the judgments and subversive of the intellect of the people" employed by the Whigs. Instead of this expression of cultural politics, the Democrats placed "a clear reliance upon the intelligence, the patriotism, and the discriminating justice of the American masses." "We regard this as a distinctive feature of our political creed," the second resolution declared.[93]

Having differentiated themselves generally from their opponents, Democrats now outlined their specific principles. They supported a limited gov-

George M. Dallas, ca. 1844. (Courtesy of the Library of Congress)

ernment, which included opposition to internal improvements. Its members believed the national government should protect all facets of the nation's economy equally and should act with fiscal responsibility. Democrats also opposed a national bank and wanted the government's money kept separate from banks. Another important position concerned slavery. "Congress has no power, under the constitution, to interfere with or control the domestic institutions of the several States," the platform read; that power belonged solely to the states. Abolitionist attempts to interfere with slavery "are calcu-lated to lead to the most alarming and dangerous consequences; . . . have an inevitable tendency to diminish the happiness of the people, and endanger the stability and permanency of the Union." Accompanying these resolutions was a statement supporting the citizenship rights of immigrants. To these traditional positions were added some more recently adopted by the Democrats in response to the actions of the Tyler administration. The platform proclaimed the party's opposition to the distribution of land revenue to the states as "repugnant to the constitution." Another resolution expressed the Democrats' support for the executive veto as limited by the Constitution, noting that a presidential veto had "thrice saved the American people from the corrupt and tyrannical domination of the Bank of the United States." The platform also staked out the party's unequivocal support for territorial expansion in Oregon and Texas. An additional resolution acknowledged Van Buren's service to the party and to the nation. The delegates unanimously approved these resolutions and agreed to form a publications committee to coordinate the party's media campaign.[94]

At some point during the early morning discussion of the resolutions, King and Robinson arrived from Washington with Wright's letter in hand. Its contents confirmed what many delegates dreaded. "Present my profound thanks to the convention for this mark of confidence and favor," Wright had written, but it was "impossible" for him to accept the offer. He told Butler a few days later that part of his decision stemmed from the fear that "the Calhoun Clique" would use his nomination "to strike a fatal blow at the ticket." Wright's definitive handwritten statement forced the delegates to reopen the balloting for the vice presidential nomination. Marcus Morton of the Massachusetts delegation refused to allow himself to be nominated, and Buchanan's friends also declined on his behalf. On the second ballot, seven individuals received votes: Cass, Woodbury, Richard M. Johnson, former senator and US minister to Russia George M. Dallas of Pennsylvania, Senator John Fairfield of Maine, former New York governor William L. Marcy, and Charles Stewart, with Fairfield the overwhelming vote-getter. "What the deuce has got into people!" Fairfield wrote his wife, Anna. "They seem to be determined to consider me a very clever fellow to thrust honors upon me 'whether I will or no.'" He need not have worried, because one delegate had plans for someone else to occupy the second spot on the ticket. After the results of the vote were announced, Robert Walker "expressed a hope" that Dallas, his uncle by marriage, would receive the nomination "by acclamation" on the next ballot. After initially supporting Van Buren early in his campaign for the nomination, Dallas had broken with him after the New Yorker had come out against immediate annexation. Before the convention, Dallas had preferred Cass, but he seemed satisfied with Polk's selection.[95]

Table 3.3. Vice Presidential Balloting at 1844 Democratic National Convention

Candidate	1st Ballot	2nd Ballot	3rd Ballot
Lewis Cass	—	39	—
George M. Dallas	—	19	219
John Fairfield	—	93	31
Richard M. Johnson	—	26	—
William L. Marcy	—	5	—
Charles Stewart	—	23	—
Levi Woodbury	8	44	6
Silas Wright Jr.	258	—	—
Total	266	249*	256**

* The Delaware, Mississippi, and New Jersey delegations and one Indiana delegate did not vote.

** The Delaware and New Jersey delegations did not vote.

Source: *Washington (DC) Daily Globe*, 6 June 1844.

The delegates took time after the second ballot to inquire about the political stances of the candidates, with particular focus on Fairfield and Dallas. A Kentucky delegate asked if Fairfield favored the annexation of Texas; other delegates affirmed that he did. Another delegate questioned Dallas's support of the Bank's recharter in 1832. Walker remarked that his uncle-in-law had only been acting under the instructions of the Pennsylvania legislature; at the time, and ever since, the Mississippian assured his colleagues, Dallas had opposed the idea of a national bank. Walker also added that the Pennsylvanian had been one of the first politicians to state publicly his support for Texas annexation and had done so "long before the excitement on this subject" had become a national issue. With these questions answered, the third ballot proceeded, with Dallas winning easily over Fairfield and Woodbury.[96]

"At the first meeting of this *august* assembly," the acerbic Philip Hone commented, Dallas "was no more dreamed of than John Tyler." That may have been true, but the convention's ultimate choice to go with Dallas made strategic sense given the circumstances that had unfolded. His home state of Pennsylvania was more electorally significant than Fairfield's Maine. Just as importantly, the tariff issue was critical to any candidate's chances of winning the presidency, and Dallas's ability to sway Pennsylvania and other states in Polk's favor on that topic could prove to be decisive. But Democrats had to be concerned that nominating Dallas would alienate Van Burenites. Not only had supporters of the former president been unable to secure his selection, but their efforts to salvage the ticket by putting Wright on it had also failed. Whether they would fall in line and help bring New York into the Democratic column come the general election was one of the big questions the party faced.[97]

Having settled the vice presidential question, the delegates moved to adjourn. Convention president Hendrick Wright offered a final charge that the delegates "enter into the approaching contest with vigor, with energy, and with a determination to triumph." But convention attendee Arthur L. Magenis, the "Missouri Earthquake," had the last say. "You have sacrificed Mr. Van Buren by a bargain!" he screamed at the delegates as they streamed out of the convention hall, some of them laughing, while others just ignored his outburst. "You've killed Van by your damned two-third [sic] rule!" The convention "has committed a gross fraud—a fraud upon the democratic party—a fraud upon the country," he declared. "I denounce it. I know that it is useless to spend more breath upon the subject here, but the people will see it, and treat it as it deserves to be treated." Magenis's passionate remarks, shouted at the backs of the departing delegates, highlighted the intraparty wounds that Polk and Dallas would have to heal over the next few months.[98]

REACTION TO THE CONVENTION

As news of the nominations spread, many Democrats celebrated their party's decisions. Portraits and biographies of Polk went on sale within two weeks. The week after the convention closed, a party meeting in Washington reportedly witnessed "an enthusiasm not even second to that displayed at Baltimore" when Polk's nomination had been announced. Politicians such as Stephen A. Douglas of Illinois, Andrew Kennedy of Indiana, and Andrew Johnson of Tennessee spoke to the Democratic faithful until 1:00 A.M. Kennedy delivered one of the night's best zingers, when he informed listeners that "a handful of *Polk*-berries was enough to kill *any Coon!*" Several dozen Whigs interrupted Johnson's speech with heckling, then built a bonfire to draw fire engines and their accompanying bells in an effort to drown him out. When these attempts at shutting down the meeting failed, they brandished "brick-bats" (i.e., a piece of brick or rock) in an act of intimidation. Democrats finally chased them off by warning them "they would be punished as they deserved if they did not cease disturbing the meeting."[99]

In Philadelphia, the fifty-one-year-old Dallas learned that he had been nominated when a group of sixty delegates, including Walker, took the train to his home. Hearing voices at 3:00 A.M., and fearing that something might have happened to one of his daughters, Dallas "rushed down in his night cloths [sic]," his luxurious white hair undoubtedly unkempt, where he was given the good news. Later that night, approximately 12,000 Democrats gathered in Independence Square, where a banner inscribed "Polk, Dallas, Texas, and Oregon" was displayed. The celebrants eventually made their way to Dallas's home, where he spoke "in favor of James K. Polk, Texas, and Oregon."[100]

News of the ticket began trickling into Nashville on Monday, June 3. Confirmation came when convention delegate William G. Childress arrived in the city on Wednesday night. The *Nashville Union* placed the Polk–Dallas banner in its paper the following morning, leading to an all-day Democratic celebration. They fired cannon salutes to Polk, Dallas, and Texas, and displayed a "lone star" banner made by local women. In a jab at Clay, a band played "Get out of the way Ole Kentucky" in the city streets. That evening, a large crowd gathered to hear Democratic stalwarts revel in Tennessee's place on the ticket and expound on their prospects for victory over the Whigs. Fireworks capped the evening. In Vicksburg, Mississippi, William M. Gwin reported that the "astonishment" with which Polk's nomination was received quickly changed into "one of the happiest days of my life." Vicksburg citizens shot off hundreds of rounds in celebration, and "men who have been enemies for months met shook hands & pledged themselves to fight shoulder to shoulder through this contest."[101]

Polk's immediate response to his nomination is not extant. He began writing letters to associates on Saturday, June 8, correspondence in which he expressed surprise that he had received the presidential nomination and denied that he had sought the honor. "But if it be conferred by the voluntary voice of my countrymen," he told one correspondent, "I will not decline it." Polk expressed his hope that his nomination would be able "to restore harmony to the action of the Democratic party." Acknowledging the need to soothe ruffled feathers, Polk wrote Silas Wright to reassure him of his innocence in the efforts to maneuver Van Buren out of the top spot on the Democratic ticket. "Certainly nothing was further from my thoughts" than winning the nomination over Van Buren, he stated disingenuously. Although Wright was particularly incensed at Tennessee's role at the convention, he did not appear to blame Polk. And although Polk and Van Buren did not correspond directly following the convention or even during the campaign, the Tennessean's effort to ensure that Wright did not hold a grudge was an essential step to take.[102]

Van Buren was uncharacteristically quiet about the turn of events that

Democrats and Whigs alike expected a tough campaign battle between James K. Polk and Henry Clay. Clay beats Polk in a cockfight. Martin Van Buren, standing outside the ring, comments, "They rejected me, let them look to their Champion!" (Courtesy of the Library of Congress)

had taken place at Baltimore. He had known that taking a principled stance might cost him the nomination, but he preferred losing on principle than stooping to pandering. The letters of commiseration that crossed Van Buren's desk on a regular basis in the weeks following the Baltimore convention undoubtedly affirmed that he had made the right decision. Despite not corresponding with Polk during the campaign, Van Buren played the dutiful, noble statesman for the party ticket. He received several addresses and speaking invitations from Democratic groups, and his response was consistent. Polk and Dallas "are both gentlemen possessed of high character," he wrote one group of New York Democrats. Van Buren also convinced Silas Wright to throw his hat in the ring for the governor's chair in New York, which promised to help not only Democrats in the crucial swing state but also nationally.[103]

As for the Whigs, they were thrilled with the prospect of taking on the unexpected Democratic ticket. "*Polk!* Great God, what a nomination! I do really think the Democratic Convention ought to be damned to all eternity for this villanous business," Kentucky governor Robert P. Letcher exclaimed. Senator Willie P. Mangum of North Carolina described a crowd of an estimated 800 people, out of which "the feeblest wail of some twenty or thirty voices" celebrated Polk's nomination when it came over the telegraph in Washington. "We will literally crush the ticket," he predicted. "They feel it. They know it." One Virginian called Polk "the tool & sycophant of Andrew Jackson & Martin Van Buren," while Horace Greeley's *New-York Daily Tribune* dubbed Polk an unoriginal "buffoon" and Dallas a low-energy "lawyer of fair talents." Though not a Whig proper, Sidney George Fisher echoed the sentiments of many party members. "Polk is a fourth-rate partizan [*sic*] politician, of ordinary abilities, no eminence or reputation & chiefly distinguished for being a successful stump orator in Tennessee," he observed. Dallas was "very bland & courteous in manner, . . . a reckless partizan [*sic*] totally devoid of principle & capable of upholding or relinquishing any opinions whenever his own or his party's interest require it." Fisher predicted that the Democratic ticket was "doomed to disappointment."[104]

The response of some Americans to the presidential nomination of the former Speaker and governor, the man who had lost his last two gubernatorial elections and whose career appeared to be in decline before the Baltimore convention, was, "Who the devil is Polk?" For the voters who did not know him already, they would soon find out.[105]

"IN THE HANDS OF THE SLAVE POWER" THE CAMPAIGNS OF JOSEPH SMITH, JOHN TYLER, AND JAMES G. BIRNEY

Although mostly overlooked now, three other contenders for the presidency emerged in 1844. By all accounts, Joseph Smith, John Tyler, and James G. Birney each believed that they possessed the principled vision that the United States needed to navigate the treacherous political waters the country faced. None of the three stood a serious chance of coming out on top, but neither could they be dismissed out of hand. Each campaign threatened to alter the delicate political balance just enough to make the election's outcome uncertain. By the time the polls opened in November 1844, only Birney's campaign was still active, the other two having ended in concession in one case and murder in the other.

PREPARING A PROPHET FOR THE PRESIDENCY

On the face of it, Joseph Smith's entry into the 1844 presidential race appeared odd. Born in 1805 in Sharon, Vermont, Smith moved with his family to Palmyra, New York, in 1817. Palmyra was located in the "Burned-over District" of western New York, named for the numerous religious revivals that spread like wildfire in the area. As an adolescent, Smith struggled with his spirituality. He received some clarity in 1820, when he said that God the Father and Jesus the Son visited him, gave him salvation, and told him not to join any church. Three years later, according to Smith, an angel named Moroni appeared to him and directed him to find and translate a book, written on gold plates, that was buried near his home. Smith began his translation in 1827, and in 1830, the Book of Mormon was published. This text recounted an alternate (or complementary, depending on one's beliefs) history of North America and Jesus's interaction with the people living there. That same year, Smith founded what came to be called the Church of Jesus Christ of Latter-day Saints, or Mormonism.[1]

As did many communities of the era that existed outside of mainstream American religion, Mormons encountered significant opposition for their beliefs as the church grew. Smith received new revelations that told him to establish a "New Jerusalem," which would serve as "a gathering place for his followers, a refuge from the calamities of the last days, and the place for a temple." In 1831, he chose Independence, Missouri, located in the northwestern corner of the state, as the site of the "City of Zion." Two years later, local non-Mormon residents forced Smith and his followers to relocate to nearby Far West, Missouri. Once again, Mormons experienced tension with local residents, but this time, it escalated significantly. For several months in 1838, the Mormons faced persecution as Missourians used violence first to prevent them from exercising their right to vote, then to force them out of the state. The violence received official state sanction when Governor Lilburn Boggs issued Executive Order 44, which stipulated that "the Mormons must be treated as enemies, and must be exterminated or driven from the state if necessary for the public peace." This violent response indicated how politically threating others found the Mormons at this early stage. Mormons had little choice but to flee Missouri, eventually settling in Hancock County, Illinois. Their land included the village of Commerce, located on a peninsula jutting into the Mississippi River. Smith eventually renamed the town Nauvoo, which he said meant "a beautiful situation" in Hebrew.[2]

Smith and his followers were politicized not only by the violence they experienced in Missouri but also by the lack of relief they obtained from the national government. Smith was particularly incensed by Martin Van Buren's lack of interest in helping the Mormons. In 1839, Mormons gathered evidence of Missouri's ill treatment of them to present to the president, and a Mormon delegation that included Smith delivered their grievances to Van Buren in Washington. The Prophet, as his followers called him, was unimpressed with the president, both physically and intellectually. "His Majesty" possessed a "frowning brow and considerable body but not well proportioned," Smith reported. "To use his own words [he] is quite fat." He also called Van Buren "a fop or a fool." Van Buren's indifference to the

Mormons' plight prompted Smith's embittered description. The president reportedly told Smith, "I can do nothing for you." Van Buren, who was running for a second term, probably calculated the ramifications for his reelection campaign if he lost Missouri's support by helping the Mormons. A memorial introduced in the Senate in support of the Mormons' efforts to obtain relief also failed to gain traction. This response confirmed Smith's impression of Congress as more interested in style over substance.[3]

Smith's visit to Washington marked a turning point in his political maturation. He came away with two lessons. One was that the purpose of the federal government had been corrupted. Instead of protecting the people, including members of minority groups, it was intent on benefiting those in power. Any hope for the nation's future would require significant government reform, something Smith came to believe more and more in the next few years. The second was that Van Buren could not be trusted. Smith's disgust for the president was obvious to two outsiders who visited Commerce in April 1840. One of the visitors recalled that when asked about Van Buren, Smith replied that the president was "*not as fit . . . as my dog, for the chair of state*; for my dog will make an effort to protect his abused and insulted master, while the present chief magistrate, will not so much as lift his finger to relieve an oppressed and persecuted community of free-men." Smith added that the Mormons "intend[ed] to use" their electoral power to support William Henry Harrison over Van Buren in the presidential contest. The incumbent president narrowly won Illinois in 1840, but Smith undoubtedly took delight in the national Mormon vote overwhelmingly going to the Whig ticket.[4]

Smith increasingly viewed the Mormons' political votes as a collective act that should go to the politicians who could best serve the church's interests. He declared about the 1842 Illinois gubernatorial election, "We care not a fig for *Whig* or *Democrat*: they are both alike to us; but we shall go for our *friends*, OUR TRIED FRIENDS, and the cause of *human liberty* which is the cause of God." Ironically, given Smith's antipathy toward Van Buren, Democrats within the state were often the beneficiaries of the Mormon vote, and some Illinois Democrats, including Stephen A. Douglas and Thomas Ford, appealed to Mormon voters by demonstrating sympathy for the church's several conflicts within the state. Smith's political malleability won him no friends in Illinois, however, and residents of the state increasingly labeled the Mormon's bloc voting a violation of the separation of church and state.[5]

Between 1840 and 1844, Smith continued to experience a political evolution as Nauvoo grew into an independent theocratic city-state. It had its own militia, the Nauvoo Legion, which was under the Prophet's control, and its own laws, which were intended to shield Smith and the Mormons from the unfair treatment they believed they had experienced in Missouri. Smith would use these laws to protect himself from arrest several times during these years, leading non-Mormons increasingly to see Nauvoo as a city whose leaders believed themselves above and outside of the nation's judicial system.[6]

Smith also began teaching religious practices that were out of step with contemporary US norms. For example, he told Mormons that they could be baptized by proxy for deceased relatives (a practice known as baptism for the dead) and that humans had the potential to become gods. But by far the most controversial religious practice that Smith introduced was polygamy. In a series of revelations from 1840 to 1844, the Mormon prophet privately convinced select church leaders that God wanted them to institute plural marriage—the celestial wedding of multiple women to Mormon men—in order to realize his "vision of a multilayered patriarchal hierarchy that governed the cosmos." By the time of his death, Smith had undertaken the spiritual practice of plural marriage with approximately thirty-five women. Polygamy in particular caused Smith the most headaches, both outside and inside Nauvoo. Non-Mormons considered the practice immoral, and even some of the few Mormons who learned of the practice at the time found it disturbing and hypocritical.[7]

By the end of 1843, developments in Nauvoo had created an uncomfortable situation for Smith. His political pragmatism, his flaunting of the law, his introduction of controversial religious practices—all had created distrust among not only non-Mormons but also among church members. Circumstances clearly were outrunning Smith's ability to control them, and it was only a matter of time before some conflict seemed certain to unravel all that he had built.[8]

But the upcoming presidential election gave Smith and his followers a new vision and purpose. In November 1843, church leaders decided to send an interrogatory (or survey) to the five men they considered the leading presidential candidates—John C. Calhoun, Lewis Cass, Henry Clay, Richard M. Johnson, and Van Buren—asking "what their course would be towards the sai[n]ts if they were elected." The letters, which went out under Smith's name, explained the Mormons' conflict with Missouri and their attempts to find relief from the executive and legislative branches of the US government. Each candidate was asked to answer the following question: "*What will be your rule of action* relative to *us, as a people*, should fortune favor your ascension to the Chief Magisterey?" To Van Buren's letter were added several lines, asking the former president whether he had changed his mind since he had "treated [Smith] with a coldness, indeferece [indifference] and neglect boding [bordering] on contempt" during their 1839 meeting in Washington.[9]

This type of interaction between voters and presidential candidates had grown increasingly common in the Jacksonian period. Candidates had to think carefully before responding, knowing that their answers would likely be disseminated publicly and would certainly be scrutinized. Three of the five candidates—Cass, Calhoun, and Clay—responded to Smith's letter. Cass's reply echoed the one he had sent in response to an 1834 Mormon petition for redress. He believed "the Mormonites should be treated as all other persons are treated in this Country. . . . they should be protected in their rights, and punished when they violate the laws." Cass also stated that if Missouri and Congress had rejected the Mormons' entreaties, he did not know what remedy the president could provide. Calhoun gave a similar reply, saying that he would follow the Constitution and the nation's laws in "mak[ing] no distinction between citizens of different religion [sic] creeds." He reiterated to Smith, however, what he had told him when they met in Washington in the winter of 1839–40: the Mormon "case does not come within the Jurisdiction of the Federal Government." Clay declined to make any commitments to the Mormons, but he said he had taken "a lively interest" in their situation, thought they had suffered "injustice," and believed they should be protected like any other religious group. The responses left Smith frustrated and angry. According to "the noble Senator of South Carolina," Smith wrote with dripping sarcasm, "a 'Sovereign State' . . . can exile you at pleasure, mob you with impunity; confiscate your lands and property: have the Legislature sanction it; yea, even murder you, as an edict of an Emperor, *and it does no wrong*." Smith warned that if the Mormons did not receive financial compensation for their suffering at the hands of Missourians, then "the consuming wrath of an offended God shall smoke through the nation." Neither Van Buren nor Johnson replied to the Mormon questionnaire, which likely did nothing to improve Smith's respect for the Democratic leadership.[10]

As the calendar turned from 1843 to 1844, Smith contemplated a better alternative than trusting the Mormons' future to those jostling for the Democratic presidential nomination. The solution came on a cold late January morning in Nauvoo, Illinois. After experiencing years of persecution, followers of the Prophet inaugurated a new phase of their church's existence.

Joseph Smith, the Mormon prophet and presidential candidate. (Courtesy of the Library of Congress)

At a meeting of the Quorum of the Twelve Apostles, Willard Richards made a three-part motion: that the Church of Jesus Christ of Latter-day Saints select "indepindent [sic] electors" for the upcoming presidential campaign; that the Prophet—Joseph Smith—"be a candidate"; and that the church "use all honorable means to se[c]ure his election." The Quorum unanimously approved the motion.[11]

Smith responded to his nomination that morning by proposing an unprecedented amalgamation of religion and politics. He told his inner circle of advisors that it would take the church's concerted effort to help him win and gave orders for where members of the Quorum themselves would campaign. Although Smith pledged that he would "not electione[e]r for myself," he was not going to sit on the sidelines while his closest advisors fanned out across the United States. Instead of staying in Nauvoo, he would attend church conferences "all over the nation" following its main conference in early April. God wanted the Prophet to run for the presidency of the United States, but for what purpose? Not to select a partisan president like the Democrats and the Whigs but to choose a president who would "protect the people in their rights & liberties." He reserved specific condemnation for the Whigs, who were "striving for a king under the garb of Democracy." Singling out the Whigs was surprising given the Mormon leader's serious grudge against Van Buren, the "huckstering politician, who would sacrifice any and every thing to promote his re-election."[12]

News of Smith's nomination spread rapidly and thrilled his supporters. The day after the Quorum made its decision, Smith recorded in his journal the comments made by one Captain White, a visitor from nearby Quincy, Illinois. After spending Monday night at Smith's home, the captain toasted at breakfast on Tuesday: "May all your enemies be skin[n]ned. their skins made into drum. heads. for you[r] fri[e]nds to beat upon—also may Nauvoo become the empire seat of govern[men]t." In a column entitled "Who Shall Be Our Next President?," the Nauvoo *Times & Seasons* declared, "There is not a man in the United States more competent for the task" of serving as chief executive than the Prophet. "Under the circumstances we have no other alternative" than to support him, the newspaper continued. "If we have to throw away our votes, we had better do so upon a worthy, rather than upon an unworthy individual, who might make use of the weapon we put in his hand to destroy us with."[13]

Smith and his advisors moved quickly to put together a campaign platform. One appeared in print just nine days after his nomination. Drafted by former newspaper editor William W. Phelps, *General Smith's Views of the Powers and Policy of the Government of the United States* described Jackson's presidency as "the *acme* of American glory, liberty and prosperity." Van Buren's ascendancy to the presidency marked the nation's slide into depression and decay under his "withering touch." Harrison's election seemed to hold the promise of better days, but his death had ushered in Tyler's "three years of perplexity and pseudo whig democrat reign," which had done little "to heal the breeches." "Now, oh! people! people! turn unto the Lord and live; and reform this nation," the document proclaimed. "Frustrate the designs of wicked men." With this admonition given, Smith began outlining his platform. He advised reducing both Congress's size and the compensation paid to its members. He recommended eliminating the court-martial-

ing of military deserters, pardoning all convicts, and focusing laws on reha-
bilitation, not punishment. In tackling the divisive issue of slavery, Smith
advocated for the compensated emancipation of enslaved people, funded
by the surplus revenue from public land sales and the savings from reducing congressional compensation. He also proposed that Congress establish
a new national bank, "with branches in each state and territory." Drawing
on the Mormon experience in Missouri, Smith called for the president to
be given "full power to send an army to suppress mobs," even if a state's
governor did not request the assistance. Finally, he endorsed the nation's
geographic expansion into Oregon and Texas, but he added that it required
"the red man's consent."[14]

Church leaders made sure that *Views* was disseminated to Mormons and
non-Mormons alike in hopes of "spread[ing] far & wide" Smith's platform.
Copies were sent to President Tyler, his cabinet, members of the US Supreme Court and Congress, state governors, prominent newspapers, and
"many postmasters & Individuals." At a March 7 meeting to raise money
to complete the church's temple in Nauvoo, Smith offered an extended explanation of his "unpopular" perspective on Texas annexation. He believed
bringing Texas into the Union was necessary for two reasons: it would keep
the British from controlling the territory, and it would lessen the South's
"evil" political power. Smith also expounded on his proposal to get rid of
slavery. Abolishing the institution would add free African Americans to the
US military, who could then be used in conjunction with Native Americans
to fight against the British in Texas. Anticipating objections to allowing
emancipated African Americans an equal place in US society, Smith echoed
the general idea, if not the motivation, found in Robert J. Walker's "safety
valve thesis." The Mormon prophet proposed sending African Americans
first to Texas, then to Mexico, "where all colors are alike." "If that was not
sufficient," he concluded, "I would call upon Canada, and annex it."[15]

Smith put forward a platform highlighting issues that appealed to multiple constituencies: Democrats and Whigs, northerners and southerners,
enslavers and abolitionists. Smith's hope was that he could draw together
Americans who recognized, as he did, that the nation was headed down
the path of perdition, and staying the course was not an option. It was a
platform born not just out of political calculation but also out of Smith's
personal experiences. He had experienced debt and the inside of a jail cell,
he knew the importance of westward expansion to the survival of his religious community, and, most significantly, he realized that a government
that protected its vulnerable (white) citizens was essential.[16]

Avoiding persecution was a common theme in Smith's reasoning for seeking the presidency. "As to politics, I care but little about the Presidential Chair," he told the March 7 gathering at the temple construction site, but Mormons had just as much a right to form a political party "to defend ourselves, as for demagogues to make use of our religion to get power to destroy us." Smith continued, "As the world has used the power of Government to oppress and persecute us, it is right for us to use it for the protection of our rights." He would not be running for president "if I & my friends could have had the privilege of enjoying our religious & civel [sic] rights as American Citizen," he told another small group of fellow Mormons. Instead, the church had experienced persecution "like peels of thunder." "If I loose [sic] my life in a good Cause," Smith declared, "I am willing to be sacrificed on the alter [sic] of virtue rightousness [sic] & truth, in maintaining the laws & constitution of the United States if need be for the general good of mankind." Little did the Mormon prophet and his followers know how prescient these words were.[17]

Giving shape and bringing order to Smith's presidential campaign was the Council of Fifty, a group originally established in support of a Mormon view of Manifest Destiny that proposed sending missionaries throughout the Western Hemisphere, but especially to Native Americans, and finding a place in Texas for southern Mormons to settle. On March 10, Smith called together the leading church officials in Nauvoo to discuss proposals received from western Mormons. The following day, the council was officially organized. Its meetings over the next few months focused on three subjects: Mormon settlements in other parts of the United States, the development of what Smith called "theodemocracy," and Smith's presidential campaign. All three were interrelated. The concept of theodemocracy emerged as a priority because Smith believed that the United States was not upholding its promises to protect its citizens. The Mormon experience was illustrative of a broken political system, relying on violence, that needed a supernatural remedy. Smith believed he could solve this problem by becoming president, which would allow him to fulfill God's plan for humanity in the United States. As a result, the American political system would become just and righteous; this work, embodied in Mormonism, would eventually cover not just the United States but the entire globe.[18]

The Council of Fifty was the vehicle by which this process would take place. Consisting of approximately fifty church leaders, including the First Presidency and the Quorum of the Twelve Apostles, the council acted primarily in establishing the church's political identity. Its official name, given via revelation on March 14, 1844, was "The Kingdom of God and his Laws, with the keys and power thereof, and judgement in the hands of his servants." Council members often referred to it as the "Kingdom of God," a hint at how they conceived their purpose. Smith personally understood this "Kingdom of God" to be a literal, not just a spiritual, force. Three meetings in April transformed the council's vision and gave a distinct purpose to Smith's presidential campaign. On April 11, Sidney Rigdon, a member of the First Presidency, told council members that their purpose "was to form a Theocracy according to the will of Heaven, planted without any intention to interfere with any government of the world." When asked to contribute to the conversation about the new constitution being written, Smith responded that he thought the council would not be successful. Only he could fulfill the task, the Mormon prophet declared, and his vision, more democratic in focus than Rigdon's, was "*Vox populi, Vox Dei.* The voice of the people assenting to the voice of God." The council named Smith its "Prophet, Priest & King" and adopted the political slogan, "*Jeffersonianism, Jeffersonian Democracy, free trade and Sailors rights, protection of person & property.*" During this meeting, Smith also identified what he considered two deficiencies in the US Constitution. One was the lack of language, such as that included in the Declaration of Independence, that spoke to the equality, rights, and freedom of Americans. The second was the absence of a guarantee that the president and state governors would use their power to "to enforce those principles of liberty." In Smith's judgment, a president or governor "who does not enforce those principles he shall lose his head" or, at the very least, "he ought to be put away from his office." Given the church's experiences with persecution and the lack of sympathy displayed by many political leaders, Smith's concerns were understandable.[19]

One week later, the council met to discuss early work on a new national constitution that rectified the failings of the US Constitution, a process it had initiated on March 19. The committee tasked with writing the new constitution submitted a partial draft for discussion. It opened with a long explanation that no past or present government was adequate because they did not acknowledge God or govern according to his principles. The United States was one example; its constitution did not include any reference to God. The draft then moved to three articles, written as a direct revelation from God. The first article declared that only God "was the rightful lawgiver to man." The second article identified one man (unnamed but obviously meant to be Joseph Smith) as the sole recipient of God's will for his "kingdom on earth." The last article designated God's "Servant and Prophet" (again, Smith) as possessing the authority "to appoint Judges and officers," who would "execute, [sic] justice and judgement in righteousness, and punish transgressors throughout all my kingdom on the earth." The people, according to this article, would have the choice of accepting or rejecting these government officials "by common consent," and they could also be "punished according to my laws" if they "transgress[ed]." The new constitution indicated that, as one historian of Mormonism noted, "sovereignty was based in God's law, authority was vested in God's prophet, and citizens' rights were tethered to following God's will."[20]

The third meeting—on April 25—proved to be the culmination of the council's preparatory work for Smith's presidential campaign. The Mormon prophet made three recommendations that day: instead of continuing their regular meetings together, council members should join other church members in electioneering across the nation; Mormons should follow the lead of Democrats and Whigs and hold a national nominating convention in Baltimore; and the church should work to appoint electors across the nation who could vote for the Mormon ticket. Then Smith told the council members that they were to stop work on the new constitution. God had given him a revelation, which was that the council was the constitution. This pronouncement allowed the constitution to be a living, breathing embodiment of God's will, capable of adapting to new political circumstances as they arose.[21]

As the Council of Fifty was deliberating about its purpose, the church's conference in early April provided an inflection point for both the church's theology and its politics. The talk that drew many people's attention was Smith's funeral sermon for King Follett, a Mormon constable in Hancock County, who had died on March 9 when a bucket of rocks fell on him as he worked in a well. Smith had delivered a sermon for Follett on March 10, but when the church member's family asked the Prophet to make further remarks about its deceased patriarch, he agreed to deliver them at the church's general conference the following month. On Sunday, April 7, Smith took advantage of the beautiful spring weather to speak for more than two hours on a radical reenvisioning of Christianity that included a redefining of God's eternal essence and humanity's access to divinity itself.[22]

But politics, very much on the minds of Smith and others that spring, also suffused the April conference. In a statement about Nauvoo as the spiritual center of the nation, the Mormon prophet declared, "The whole of America is Zion itself, from North to South." Smith was almost certainly thinking of a political, not just a spiritual, Zion with this statement.

Quorum member John Taylor, a British-born newspaper editor, invoked the names of Washington, Jefferson, and John Adams to make the point that "they were engaged in founding empires and establishing kingdoms" doomed to collapse. Mormons, however, "were laying the foundation of a kingdom that shall last forever;—that shall bloom in time and blossom in eternity." Smith's brother, Hyrum, took this opportunity to announce the council's plan to send approximately 1,000 missionaries to "raise a hell on Earth." "Lift up your voices like Thunder," he told attendees, "there is power & influence enough to put in a President." Quorum president Brigham Young reinforced Hyrum's message. "It is now time to have a President of the United States," he pronounced. "The Government belongs to God." When Young asked who would support the Prophet's election as president, an estimated 1,100 began "clapping their hands and gave many loud cheers." At the end of the conference, 244 men assembled to volunteer their services as electioneering missionaries. Young admonished them to "go humbly and prayerfully trusting and believing in God; and what you desire to do, you will accomplish."[23]

Between 400 and 600 Mormons eventually answered the electioneering call. The majority made the decision to campaign at the April general conference or shortly thereafter. Some missionaries serving elsewhere in the United States also switched their primary focus from proselytizing for the church to helping the Mormon prophet win the White House. In the process of spreading the word about Smith's campaign, electioneer missionaries enlisted the help of other Mormons in the cause. The typical electioneer missionary was a married, thirty-five-year-old man who was a loyal church member and possessed no political experience. Many motivations may have driven their commitment to campaign for Smith, but they all likely would have agreed with Council of Fifty member Amasa M. Lyman's assessment: whether they were working for the kingdom of God in Heaven, on earth, or both, God did "not think any sacrifice to [sic] great to make for the glories of this kingdom."[24]

The church had a presidential candidate, a platform, a plan to spread the word, representatives to do the work, and, most importantly in its eyes, divine sanction. The only thing left to do before the national nominating convention, set for July, was to select a running mate for Smith. The council's first choice was newspaper editor and publisher James Arlington Bennet of New York. He was just the sort of man, living in just the sort of state, whose influence could cultivate legitimacy for Smith's presidential campaign. But there was one major problem: Bennet was at best a nominal church member. The New Yorker's association with Mormonism—his receipt of an honorary law degree from the University of Nauvoo and his appointment as inspector general of the Nauvoo Legion—had all occurred without Bennet stepping foot in Nauvoo. He had never even met Smith. During a visit to New York in August 1843, Brigham Young baptized him into the church, but Bennet admitted to Smith that his "glorious frolick in the clear blue ocean" was "most assuredly a frolic . . . without a moments reflection or Consideration. Nothing of this kind would in the least attach me to your person or cause." There is no evidence that Bennet participated in Mormon religious practices, or that he even wanted to, after joining. His motivation in becoming a Mormon appears to have been advancing his own political ambitions: Bennet wanted to move to Illinois and use the church to enhance his chances of becoming the state's governor.[25]

Nevertheless, Smith still chose Bennet as his running mate. In early March, he instructed his secretary and amanuensis Willard Richards to inform the New Yorker of his nomination. Acting under Smith's authority, Richards directed Bennet to undertake an electioneering campaign, starting with writing to newspapers, then "preach[ing] Mormonism" across the nation on his way to Nauvoo. Anticipating that Van Buren would be the Democratic nominee, and still harboring resentment against him, Smith instructed Bennet "at every stage, tavern, Boat and Company, [to] expose the wickedness of Martinism, in saying if 'he is elected President he will annihilate the Mormons.'" Unfortunately for Smith, there were questions about Bennet's birthplace, which jeopardized his eligibility for the office. To more easily obtain a British copyright for an accounting reference book he had authored, Bennet had in the past misled people into believing that Ireland was his birthplace, when he had actually been born in the United States about six months after his parents arrived in New York. Initially unaware of this deception, when questions about Bennet's birthplace arose, Richards wrote the New Yorker assuring him that he was "the man of our choice." But he also asked him to clarify his origins. Bennet explained his birth story as requested, but he also indicated that he believed Smith's campaign was "a wild goose chase." "I can see no natural means by which he has the slightest chance of receiving the vote even of one state," Bennet declared.[26]

By the time Bennet received Richards's letter, church leaders had decided to move on to someone else. Given Bennet's lack of commitment to Mormon religious practices and politics, that was the right decision. But the choice of replacement was unexpected. Church leadership offered the vice presidential position to Solomon Copeland, an obscure Tennessean who had held minor local political offices and had served one term as a Democrat in the state's legislature. The Tennessean was not a Mormon, but his wife and two of the African American men they enslaved were. Nor was Copeland a prominent figure in an electorally important state. Council of Fifty member Wilford Woodruff had met him while on a church mission in Tennessee in the mid-1830s, when Copeland had assisted him and fellow church members as they faced persecution in Tennessee. This help and the "deep interest" Copeland evinced in the Mormon teachings he had heard nearly a decade earlier were enough to qualify him for the second-highest political office in the church's eyes. Woodruff wrote in mid-March asking him to serve as Smith's running mate, but there is no evidence Copeland ever responded.[27]

As the time for the church's national nominating convention drew near, Smith and his advisors decided to turn to someone they knew intimately for the vice presidential slot: Sidney Rigdon. In many ways, he was the natural choice. Born in 1793, Rigdon had been a Baptist minister before being baptized into the Mormon Church in November 1830. He quickly rose to become part of Smith's inner circle, joining the First Presidency in 1832. In May 1839, Mormons designated Rigdon as their representative to the federal government. As part of that role, he helped initiate the collection of the petitions presented to Van Buren in November 1839. Although he was one of Smith's closest advisors during the church's early years, Rigdon did not always see eye to eye with the Mormon prophet. Over the years, the two had clashed on several occasions, especially in the years immediately before 1844. In April 1842, for example, Smith allegedly approached Rigdon's daughter Nancy about becoming one of his plural wives. Nancy indignantly refused his proposition, and her father, even though seriously ill, admonished Smith for making the proposal. This incident, coming as rumors of polygamy among the church's leaders were spreading inside and outside of Nauvoo, would have created tension between Rigdon and Smith. If true, it undoubtedly contributed to Smith's suspicions about Rigdon's loyalty in the fall of 1843, when the Mormon prophet accused his advisor of plotting to have him extradited to Missouri for the attempted murder of Lilburn Boggs, the governor who had issued the "extermination order" against the Mormons in 1838. These clashes may have convinced Smith initially to look elsewhere for a running mate instead of making the obvious choice.[28]

Despite these squabbles, Rigdon had been a valuable advisor to Smith, and, unlike Bennet and Copeland, he was a practicing church member and willing to join the ticket. At the May 6 meeting of the Council of Fifty,

Smith informed Rigdon that he wanted him "to go to Pennsylvania and run for vice President." Rigdon's move to Pennsylvania made sense for two reasons: he would be able to electioneer in his home state, and the Constitution requires electors to cast one of their two votes for a candidate (either presidential or vice presidential) who does not reside in their state. In practical terms, this meant that since Smith lived in Illinois, his running mate had to be a resident of another state for Illinois's electors to be able to vote for both of them. Rigdon agreed to the arrangement, with the council's unanimous agreement. As one council member commented, an early church prophecy had said that "the Lord promised to vex the nations and the nation could not be vexed worse than for Joseph to be president and brother Rigdon as vice President."[29]

Throughout his campaign, Smith exuded confidence in his election prospects. During one early May council meeting, he mentioned sending out "ministers plenipotentiary" once he was in office. These diplomatic officers would "secure to themselves such influence that when their office shall cease they may be received into everlasting habitations." Two Massachusetts Whigs who visited Nauvoo a couple of weeks later—Charles Francis Adams and Josiah Quincy, the son and nephew, respectively, of John Quincy Adams—found the Prophet full of humor and conviction. Quincy recorded that Smith, "a hearty, athletic fellow, with blue eyes . . . light complexion, a long nose, and a retreating forehead," prophesied that Tyler would not retain the presidency, and he also told them that "he [Smith] might one day so hold the balance between parties as to render his election to that office by no means unlikely." Decades later, Chicago physician Ephraim Ingals remembered spending two weeks with Smith during the spring of 1844. Ingals, then a young schoolteacher, told the Prophet "no one out of Nauvoo expected to vote for him" and asked him why he thought he would become president. Smith's response: "The Lord will turn the hearts of the people."[30]

Divine intervention was not the only tool available to Smith. To further his campaign, Mormons adopted many of the electioneering techniques used by Whigs and Democrats. In Nauvoo, the center of Smith's campaign, John Taylor's two newspapers, *Times and Seasons* and the *Nauvoo Neighbor*, were successful in solidifying local Mormon support. Reaching beyond Nauvoo was also essential, of course. Mormon lobbyists visited Washington, and newspapers were asked to print Smith's platform. Given its electoral importance and national significance, New York received much of the campaign's attention. In the New York City neighborhood of the Democrats'

Tammany Hall and other party establishments, Mormons established the Society for the Diffusion of Truth. This pro-Mormon political association published *The Prophet*, edited by William Smith, Joseph's brother. William also coordinated campaign activities throughout the state, which involved a plurality of the electioneering missionaries sent from Nauvoo. In New York and across the United States, the electioneering missionaries who were "storming the nation" for the Prophet met publicly and privately, in large public events and individual meetings. They seemed to have the greatest success in the West and Midwest. Familiarity with the church there also bred hostility, however, with some voters telling electioneering missionaries that they preferred murdering Smith over voting for him. In the South, missionaries met resistance both to their religious message and Smith's views on slavery. Non-Mormon New Englanders also responded tepidly to electioneering efforts in that region. The mid-Atlantic states proved to be the area where Smith's campaign received the most enthusiastic support outside of Nauvoo. In New York, especially, electioneering missionaries attracted larger and more enthusiastic crowds for meetings, which drew the attention of mainstream newspapers, such as James G. Bennett's *New York Herald*. All this activity led some Mormons to predict that their candidate would be able to bring out 200,000 to 500,000 voters.[31]

The Council of Fifty also designated several church members to attend the Whig and Democratic national conventions held in Baltimore. David S. Hollister traveled from Nauvoo to meet up with Orson Hyde and Orson Pratt, who were in Washington presenting Mormon memorials to the president and Congress. Quorum member John E. Page, who was serving on a mission in Washington, was to join them. The exact meaning of the four men's mission—"to make overtures"—was unclear. They may have expected to lure voters away from the two main parties, strike bargains with them that would benefit the church, or even convince Whig or Democratic delegates to circulate Smith's name as their party's presidential candidate. Whatever the case, things did not go well. Even though Hollister bragged that he "was quite a lion among the passengers" as he made his way east, he also described an incident in which a man pull a Bowie knife on him for saying those who believed Smith had "discarded his wife were *liars!*" Hollister arrived too late to attend the Whig convention, but he reported "all in Joy and enthusiam [sic] among the whigs, while doubt and consternation is manifest among the democrats" who were scheduled to meet at the end of the month. All Hollister wrote about his experience with the Democrats was that though he was not "disheartend [sic]" by the "rather unpleasent [*sic*] feelings produced by a Series of disappointments," he "was not a little chagrined at the little sucess [*sic*] we met with."[32]

While Hollister was in Baltimore attempting to influence Whigs and Democrats, the campaign was proceeding back home. On May 17, the Mormon state convention had met, with delegates representing every state and most Illinois counties. They nominated the ticket of Smith and Rigdon and passed nine resolutions. One pointed out that "much imbecility and fraud is practiced by the officers of government," which required "that a virtuous people . . . correct these abuses, by electing wise and honorable men." Another invited the "good men among all parties in whose bosoms burn the fire of pure patriotism" to join Mormon voters in "reform[ing] the government." A third proposed that "to redress all wrongs," the US government, led by its president, was "as powerful in its sphere as Jehovah is in his." Several speakers, including Smith and Rigdon, then addressed the delegates. The festivities concluded that evening with supporters carrying Smith on their shoulders around a burning barrel of tar and giving three cheers for him and Rigdon at the Prophet's home.[33]

Reaction to the political machinations of Smith and his followers was a mix of dismissal and fear. One New England correspondent called Smith a "false prophet" and contrasted his "worldly ambition" with "the meek and lowly Jesus, who held no political—military office" and who "rejected the proffered crown." Fears that Mormon martial strength might accompany the church's political influence were not far from some people's minds. Smith's unsuccessful petition for congressional authorization to raise 100,000 soldiers to assert US control over Oregon, Texas, and other territories elicited some concern. More alarming was Smith's unorthodox approach to traditional societal norms of all types. Part of this apprehension proceeded from the Prophet's place at the head of the Nauvoo Legion. Already seen as a private army, it held the potential to become a private outfit useful for paramilitary activities beyond Nauvoo's borders, capable of "organiz[ing] from 15 to 20,000 fighting men." Another norm that Smith violated involved the judiciary. By the spring of 1844, the Prophet had made Nauvoo a judicial power unto itself, answerable to no other authority, state or federal. "A criminal has but to seek refuge in Nauvoo, become a Saint and he is safe from the hands of justice," one critic noted. Smith appeared to consider himself above the law, and he seemed to possess the means to ensure that he stayed that way.[34]

Before concluding their May 17 meeting, the Illinois state convention delegates agreed to hold a national convention in Baltimore on July 13, but circumstances in the weeks after the May meeting permanently derailed those plans. On June 7, the inaugural issue of the *Nauvoo Expositor* appeared in print. This newspaper exposed Smith's private practice and encouragement of plural marriage, blasted his hunger for power, and criticized his mixing of religion and politics. The men behind the publication were former Mormons who had fallen out with Smith over these and other issues. From their perspective, they were putting into practice the transparency required of a democracy, something they believed the hypocritical Mormon prophet only talked about. Smith used his power to convince the city council, over which he presided as mayor, to authorize the destruction of the *Expositor*, an order that the Nauvoo Legion, of which Smith was the lieutenant general, carried out on June 10. When the Hancock County justice of the peace issued a warrant for Smith's arrest, the Prophet used the Nauvoo city court to obtain a writ of habeas corpus. Then he declared martial law in Nauvoo. Essentially, Smith was placing himself above the law; at least, that is how Illinois governor Thomas Ford viewed it when he threatened to send in the state militia. Worried that he would be murdered if he did not turn himself in, Smith agreed to surrender. He, along with several other Mormon leaders, were arrested on June 24. Joseph Smith and his brother Hyrum were charged with rioting and treason and held without bail in Carthage, the Hancock County seat. Three days later, a vigilante "committee of safety," motivated by religious bigotry and economic and political fear, took advantage of a small protective detail of state militia to break into the jail and kill the Smith brothers.[35]

Joseph Smith's death elicited numerous reactions. Rarely did these remembrances follow the lead of an Indiana newspaper, which noted that he was the first assassinated presidential candidate. In almost every case, the focus was on Smith's role as a religious leader. "He was killed out of jealousy for the Protestant, evangelical religion," one New Hampshire newspaper observed. "He was killed because he was a Mormon, and had got up a new Bible." The Prophet's murder ended the Mormons' venture into the 1844 presidential race. Even after he learned of Smith's death, David Hollister still "hope[d] the delegates will come one and all and send forth to world such a proclamation as will make the nations tremble and the dark caverns of Hell echo with the wail of devils." Several delegates did meet in Baltimore on July 13 as scheduled, but they decided "to make no movement on the Presidential question." The man who might have stepped into the gap left by Smith's death was Sidney Rigdon, who had left for Pittsburgh on June 18. Three weeks later, he learned about the Prophet's assassination from a newspaper and set out immediately for Nauvoo. At a public meeting in early August, Rigdon gave a sermon emphasizing a prophecy that he was to be Smith's spiritual successor as leader of the church. Brigham Young convinced Mormons that the Quorum, not Rigdon or any other single individual, should serve in the Prophet's place. Rigdon's attempts to assume leadership of the church failed, and neither he nor Young attempted to continue the Mormon presidential campaign that had ended in tragedy. Not until George Romney in 1968 would another Mormon run for the presidency.[36]

JOHN TYLER

John Tyler's candidacy posed a problem for election prognosticators. The first two years of his administration had revealed several things about the president. First, Tyler was determined to chart his own course. If that meant attempting to form a fusion party made up of malcontents, then so be it. Once he was read out of the Whig Party, Tyler's decisions as president were focused on constructing this coalition. Second, he was a man for whom personal honor was foundational to his political decisions. As did many male members of the southern gentry, Tyler took umbrage at affronts to his public reputation. The criticisms of Tyler's actions and the questioning of his motives made him understandably prickly, but it went beyond wounded pride—these attacks struck at the very core of how he saw himself and how he wanted society to perceive him. Saving face required Tyler to react strongly, which he often did. He had been a disastrous president in many ways, had been drummed out of the Whig Party, and lacked strong support among Democrats, but the altered political landscape of the campaign year provided Tyler with an opportunity for redemption. Winning the election still seemed far-fetched, but even if he lost as expected, Tyler's attempt to form a fusion party of the disgruntled held the potential to critically weaken both the Democrats and the Whigs.[37]

During the trying months of 1842 and early 1843, Tyler worked to burnish his image. He gave the New York *Knickerbocker* magazine access to the White House to paint a more positive portrait of himself. The article on Tyler and his family that appeared in the popular periodical attempted to humanize the president. As relayed in one anecdote, a Pennsylvania farmer who visited Tyler told him that he was "a very different man from what I took you to be." Instead of Tyler being "as proud as Lucifer," the man told him he was "as plain as a pike-staff, and as free-spoken as if you had no secrets in the world." Another anecdote recalled the time when Tyler ordered the reinstatement of fired government clerks because he could not "bear to have their wives and children coming to me with accounts of their sufferings, when I can prevent it." In these stories and in the physical description of Tyler—his "prominent and very intellectual" forehead, his "frank and open eye," his "plastic and expressive" face—was a president unrecognizable in Whig attacks. Tyler also used his daughter-in-law Priscilla, who was married to Robert Tyler, to his advantage. The president's wife, Letitia, suffered from chronic illnesses that kept her confined to her room until her death in September 1842. In her absence, Priscilla stepped into the role of first lady to help grease Tyler's social wheels. She followed in the footsteps of her mentor Dolley Madison in holding public social events at the White House, where she used her background as an actress to entertain and charm Washington politicians.[38]

But not everyone was convinced that Tyler had any clue about what he was doing. The president "is a poor, weak, vacillating fellow, heartily despised by everyone, and so completely in a minority in Congress that he has no influence at all," Sidney Fisher observed from Philadelphia. Tyler's efforts to organize a third party to continue his presidential career were transparent. "All his measures have that object alone" in mind, Fisher recorded, and "he courts the mob and low politicians of all kinds" as part of his party-building strategy. Tyler's machinations produced "in every part of the country confusion, alarm, distress, violence and fraud," he continued. "The people discontented and turbulent, & property insecure, the government corrupt, ignorant, imbecile & impotent, debt, taxation, infamy." For people like Fisher, Tyler was a disaster, and winning them over would require strong leadership of the sort they had not yet seen from him.[39]

Winning the presidency on his own terms in 1844 was one way for Tyler to shed the label of "His Accidency." But he had boxed himself into a position that left him with few political friends and a bevy of political enemies. Shortly after leaving the State Department, Daniel Webster tried to paint a picture of the political landscape for the president. Half of his cabinet members were Democrats, but instead of placating the party of Jackson and Van Buren, these appointments had let the enemy inside the gates, and they were "more abusive than ever." Meanwhile, Tyler's "real friends" felt betrayed by his replacement of Whigs with Democrats in other parts of government. The president risked leaving a legacy of "having sacrificed friends, of known worth & fidelity, in the hope of securing the favor of opponents." Tyler's only viable path forward, Webster argued, was returning to what he had pledged to do: implement the principled policies in which he believed, practice integrity in making nonpartisan patronage decisions, stay "above the reach of carping & selfish political partizans [sic]," and, above all, "act for the whole country."[40]

Webster's analysis was gentle, incisive, and correct—and Tyler ignored it. Instead, he pressed ahead with his plans to earn his own four-year term. Despite having burned bridges with the Whigs, Tyler still believed he had two possible paths to achieve this goal. One was convincing Democrats that he was their party's best chance at defeating Clay. To better his odds, Tyler attempted to head off three potential challengers by appointing them to other positions. His first target was Van Buren. When US Supreme Court justice Smith Thompson died in mid-December 1843, newspapers reported that the president was considering several New Yorkers, including Benjamin F. Butler and William L. Marcy, as his replacement. Tyler ultimately offered Van Buren the seat indirectly. As Silas Wright Jr. recounted to Van Buren in early January 1844, Texas land agent and former Jackson appointee John Thomson Mason informed him of the possibility on a visit one stormy day. Wright "met the suggestion with a most immediate fit of laughter," but sobered up when he saw his visitor was serious. Mason slyly mentioned that if Van Buren was placed on the Supreme Court, then that left open the possibility of Wright being nominated for president "with the certainty of an election." When Mason asked him what he thought about the proposal, "I laughed myself almost sick," Wright told Van Buren. It was a preposterous, comical solicitation, made worse because Tyler thought his manipulation was clever, even though Mason denied being sent to test the waters. Wright's response told the president everything he needed to know about how Van Buren would react; Tyler quickly nominated Treasury Secretary John C. Spencer instead.[41]

Spencer's nomination died on the vine later that month, which led Tyler to approach Wright about the open Supreme Court seat. The president sent his son Robert to summon the senator to the White House. When Wright arrived, Tyler used flattery and made "protestations of his genuine democracy" to convince the New Yorker to accept the offer. "I was really embarrassed" to turn him down, Wright acknowledged, but he had let the president know several times that he was not interested in the position. Tyler admitted that he had approached him informally via back channels, which confirmed the New Yorker's suspicions about Mason's January visit. Tyler's overtures to Wright, attempting to remove both him and Van Buren from the presidential field, indicated that he saw not just the former president but the New York senator as possible rivals in the upcoming campaign.[42]

Tyler also tried to curtail Polk's chances in Baltimore. In the aftermath of the February 1844 USS *Princeton* explosion, Tyler offered him the newly vacant navy secretary post. Following a familiar pattern, the president made the overture through a proxy, Virginia newspaper editor Theophilus Fisk. Acceptance of the cabinet position, according to Fisk, would be "an act of patriotism." "Texas and Oregon need such a champion as yourself at this emergency," he told Polk. After consultation with advisors, Polk decided to decline the cabinet appointment in part because all of his political posts had come "directly from the hands of the people," and he wanted future positions to originate from the same source. He also turned down Tyler because he thought accepting the post would indicate his lack of faith in Van Buren's chances for the presidential nomination and might signal Polk's belief that he himself could not win the vice presidential nomination at the convention. Although Tyler continued to use Fisk to float possible appointments to Polk, specifically the posts of secretary of the Treasury and minister to England, the Tennessean had higher aspirations.[43]

Tyler's inability to eliminate Van Buren, Wright, and Polk from contention illustrated his weakness with Democrats. Although some party leaders, particularly in Virginia, saw Tyler as a viable option, most simply did not trust him. He had spent more years in politics fighting Democrats than supporting them. The *Princeton* explosion had also deprived Tyler of two significant cheerleaders in Thomas W. Gilmer and Abel P. Upshur. That Calhoun was so supportive of Tyler and his pursuit of Texas annexation did not help those who remembered the South Carolinian's tumultuous relationship with Jackson, Van Buren, and other orthodox Democratic leaders.[44]

Democratic opposition left Tyler no choice but to pursue his second option, which was running as an independent candidate. The publication of Clay's and Van Buren's letters on annexation in April 1844 renewed hopes that the Democratic national convention would descend into chaos, leaving the door open for Tyler. To generate support for the president, supporters called for a convention to meet in Baltimore at the same time as the Democrats were making their nominations. Tyler described his approach to the convention in the years following his presidency. According to these later accounts, he rejected his friends' advice to take a wait-and-see approach to the Democratic convention in hopes that they would turn to him. Instead, just a few weeks before the Democrats met, he decided "to raise the banner of Texas, and convoke my friends to sustain it." "Many called on me on their way to Baltimore to receive my views," Tyler remembered. "My instructions were, 'Go to Baltimore, make your nomination, and then go home, and leave the thing to work its own results.' I said no more, and was obeyed." His purpose went deeper than simply defeating the Democratic candidate, whoever it turned out to be. Organizing an independent party centered on his pro-annexation candidacy, "the great scheme that occupied me," would kill "those who make politics a trade."[45]

Located on Saratoga Street a couple of miles from where Democratic delegates were meeting, Calvert Hall served as the site of the Tyler convention. "All hell is let loose upon Baltimore, just at this time, and these Tyler delegates are riding the whirlwind," one Democrat observed, "representing themselves as delegates to the regular convention, and scattering distrust of each other among the latter." One newspaper described the Tyler convention as "a farce"; another called it "a kind of mongrel, irregular thing, 'got up' by Northern office holders and Southern 'Chivalry.'" The president's supporters saw things differently, arguing that the convention more closely represented the will of the people because the delegates had been recently selected and "sent directly from the bosom of the People." Entering their convention, many Tylerites were confident that the president was in a strong position to win the election. Some were convinced that his campaign would lead Polk to decline the Democratic nomination. How could the Tennessean, who "ha[d] done nothing towards the acquisition of Texas, but simply write a brief letter in favor of annexation," hope to compete with Tyler, who was ushering annexation to completion? The *Daily Madisonian* predicted that Polk would withdraw from the race, and Democrats would turn to Van Buren in desperation as their nominee. This turn of events would only improve Tyler's chances.[46]

The convention opened at 9:00 A.M. on Monday, May 27, the same day that the Democratic meeting began. As the Tyler delegates were registering, several banners, with inscriptions like "Re-annexation of Texas, Postponement Is Rejection—Tyler and Texas," lined the convention hall as decorations. "A very excellent band" provided music during breaks in the meeting. At 11:45 A.M., the convention came to order. Despite the delegates showing their solidarity by wearing ribbons with Tyler's image, almost immediately there was trouble. One of the delegates objected to Tyler's "*immediate* nomination" and proposed waiting until the Democrats made their nominations before the Tyler convention decided on its own. Cries of "Traitor!" rang out in response. Another dispute broke out over the credentialing process, with some delegates objecting to a resolution that they produce their credentials by arguing that "they were sent there by the people—they came as the people—and as the people, they were above question in the matter of credentials!" A proposed resolution to follow the congressional rules of debate produced yet another vociferous disagreement, with accusations that some delegates were trying "to infringe the freedom of debate" by instituting a one-hour limit on speeches. These outbursts led the convention to appoint four sergeants at arms to maintain decorum.[47]

After this inauspicious start, the convention went into recess. When the delegates returned, the real business of the meeting began. They selected Connecticut businessman Joel W. White as convention president, who reminded the attendees that their responsibility was to nominate "an *honest* man." Tyler, who had "saved the democratic party" from the wreckage of the 1840 election, was "the *only* man" they could choose. The absurdity of calling Tyler—who had reluctantly joined the Democrats in the 1820s, had abandoned them in the 1830s, and had been made the Whigs' vice presidential candidate in 1840—the Democrats' savior seemed to escape the delegates. After the Rev. Dr. M. Z. Kreider of Ohio "address[ed] the Throne of Grace in behalf of their deliberations," he proposed that the convention unanimously support Tyler's nomination. With the exception of two New York delegates, who were identified as "friends of General Cass" (possibly convention vice president Edmund S. Derry and Lathrop S. Eddy), the estimated 1,000 delegates adopted Kreider's resolution. Twenty-nine-year-old Eddy, "a real fighting chicken of a man," renewed the call for the delegates to present their credentials. "The pot was in a stew instantly," one reporter commented. "Stamping and bellowing and shaking of fists at each other" accompanied cries of "turn him out." One elderly delegate stood on a chair and "brandished a huge stick," threatening those around him with violence if they continued the disruption. New York's J. F. Hutton, who earlier in the year had supported Calhoun for the Democratic nomination, stirred the pot by introducing a resolution, seconded by Eddy, calling for a joint Democratic-Tylerite effort to hold a new convention to select nominees in August. His proposal produced a "thunder storm of indignation" and was voted down. After appointing committees to inform Tyler of his nomination, "prepare an address" to the American people, and discuss the vice presidential nomination, the convention adjourned what had been a tumultuous first day. Tylerites announced their nomination of the president by firing "twenty-eight guns: twenty-six for the States, one for Texas, and one for TYLER." Robert Tyler reportedly stopped "smoking long nines in Baltimore street" long enough to use the telegraph to inform his father of his nomination.[48]

The following morning, the Tyler delegates reconvened at 9:00 A.M. After announcing the members of the various committees formed at the end of the previous day's session, the Tylerites turned to the only real question they faced: Who would run with the president? This decision was particularly difficult because Tyler was serving without a vice president. (The constitutional oversight that allowed the vice presidency to remain vacant in the case of death, resignation, or elevation to the presidency was not rectified until passage of the Twenty-fifth Amendment in 1967). The committee charged with making a recommendation on a running mate reported a resolution calling for the formation of a national committee to make the decision. Another delegate proposed a resolution, which was adopted, that the states form their own electoral tickets, with July 4 designated as the target date for announcing them. Much like the Democratic Party's decision not to nominate a vice presidential nominee in 1840 spoke of its division, this decision not to unify around a full ticket highlighted the disunity that pervaded the Tyler convention. In an ironic conclusion to the meeting, White thanked the delegates for "their gentlemanly deportment to preserve order" throughout the event. The convention adjourned with "nine of the loudest cheers . . . for 'TYLER and TEXAS.'"[49]

A five-person committee went to the White House to deliver the official news of Tyler's nomination. He responded with a lengthy defense of his actions as president. Tyler pronounced himself a defender of the Constitution in the face of the Whig Party that had elected him and called himself a victim of both parties' "vindictive assaults." His allies in both the Whig Party and the Democratic Party had nominated him, he continued, and he was obliged to serve. This was especially true because his "name ha[d] become inseparably connected with the great question of the annexation of Texas to the Union." If the presumptive candidates of the two parties (Clay and Van Buren) had indicated their support of immediate annexation in their letters, Tyler claimed, he would have withdrawn his name from the campaign, "but such was not the case." For that reason, he was accepting the nomination and would proceed to annex Texas as soon as feasible.[50]

Others did not share Tyler's optimism. Lathrop Eddy came away from the convention disappointed. He blamed "the secret friends of Henry Clay" for controlling the meeting. All they accomplished was "gagging" Calhoun's supporters and "humbuging" the president. "Poor Tyler is dead. He feels so. They have stolen his *theme*," Willie P. Mangum remarked about the Democrats' embrace of immediate annexation with Polk's nomination. Even as the Tyler convention was nominating the president, John Quincy Adams was meeting with Whigs to quash their effort to remove Tyler from office. A simmering impeachment movement seemed to portend an ignominious political denouement rather than a glorious political rebirth. Andrew Jackson told Francis P. Blair that if the president did not remove his name from contention, "he prostrates himself forever." He also mocked Tyler: "Can he get any one to become vice president with him of any standing?"[51]

Tyler appeared to be a long shot to win the election, but in an already strange campaign that had seen one favorite candidate fail to secure his party's nomination (and would see another nominee assassinated in the coming weeks), there was no reason to think that an unpopular incumbent president might not be able to overcome seemingly insurmountable odds to claim an electoral victory. One Tylerite remarked that though they were "not sufficiently accomplished in grammar and sophistry to sing doggerel songs on the public streets," they possessed "a gift from heaven" that the Democrats and Whigs lacked: "common sense." Rumors that Commodore Charles Stewart, whom the Democrats had considered as a presidential nominee, might become Tyler's running mate undoubtedly caused some concern among both major parties, neither of which had a military man on their ticket.[52]

In the middle of the campaign, Tyler took an unprecedented step for a sitting president: he got married. He had been courting Julia Gardner since just a few months after his first wife, Letitia, died. Julia turned down his first two proposals, possibly because of the thirty-year age difference between them. The death of her father, David, in the *Princeton* explosion seemed to clarify her feelings for the president. After a shorter-than-normal mourning period, John and Julia's wedding took place in New York City on June 26. George Templeton Strong called Tyler a "poor, unfortunate, deluded old jackass" for marrying "one of those large, fleshy Miss Gardiners." Whatever snide remarks the New York diarist made, the newlyweds were so happy with one another that Julia's family chastised her for distracting her husband to the point that he was unable to carry out his presidential duties. "You spend *so much* time in kissing," Julia's sister Margaret told her, "things of more importance are left undone." The first lady's mother also lectured her: "Let your husband work during all business hours—business should take the precedence of caressing—reserve your caressing for private leisure hours & be *sure* you let no one see it unless you wish to be laughed at."[53]

Marital bliss may have convinced Tyler to change his mind and consider exiting the race; more likely, though, two other reasons led him in that direction over the summer. First, Tyler must have realized that an outright victory was impossible. In the unlikely event that he was able to throw the election into the House, as in 1824, winning a majority of state delegations was just as far-fetched. Second, he may have begun thinking ahead to 1848. If Polk won, he had pledged to serve only one term, so Democrats could conceivably turn to Tyler four years later, especially if he could demonstrate that the strength of his support was what carried the day for Young Hickory. If Polk lost, all the better to make a case for Tyler's return to the White House, since he would not bear the scarlet letter of defeat like Van Buren had at the Democratic national convention. Either way, stepping down before the campaign heated up too much would make Tyler look magnanimous and leave open the opportunity to run again in 1848.[54]

While Tyler was considering his options, his supporters attempted to flood the government with administration loyalists who could help him campaign. Given his new brother-in-law's lack of a political party, Alexander Gardiner wrote his sister Julia, the president would be wise to appoint a "careful selection of men, having such weight of character as will enlist the moral influence of the community." Tylerites also began organizing electoral tickets at all levels of government, especially in the critical states of New York and Pennsylvania, putting even more pressure on Polk to bring about some sort of reconciliation with the president's supporters. "Make these men feel the great necessity of my co-operation," Tyler told his son, Robert. The strategy worked. Democrats in New Jersey, New York, and Pennsylvania contacted Robert J. Walker "in great alarm" about the attempted weakening of the Polk–Dallas ticket.[55]

Faced with a dangerous threat to the Democratic Party's chances to regain the presidency, Walker went to the White House to talk to Tyler. In a discussion lasting "several hours," the president laid out his grievances and demands. He complained that he knew his time in the White House was coming to an end the following March, but he could not withdraw because "his friends were so exasperated" by the newspaper attacks on him, particularly those by Blair's *Globe*, that "they would either remain neutral" or vote for Clay. When Walker responded that Polk and Dallas could not control what a few editors published about him, Tyler asserted that he had approximately 150,000 supporters—all former Democrats—who were going to vote in the fall. "If a different course were pursued towards them," he told Walker, and they were welcomed into the Democratic Party and "treated as Brethren & equals," then he would drop out "*at once*" and his supporters would rally to the party standard to elect the Polk–Dallas ticket.[56]

John Tyler's insistence on running as an independent candidate drew ridicule. John C. Calhoun, Henry Clay, Andrew Jackson, and James K. Polk are pushing through the door of the White House, while "Uncle Sam" is kicking Tyler out. (Courtesy of the Library of Congress)

It was political blackmail, based on spurious data, and it worked. "This union & cooperation *cannot be overated* [*sic*]," Walker advised Polk. "In my judgment it would be *decisive* in our favour." News from Pennsylvania reinforced his belief that the Tyler situation needed to be resolved before the campaign heated up. Acknowledging that it was "a delicate matter," the Mississippian suggested that Polk "write a private letter to a friend" extolling Tyler's importance to the Democratic cause and "welcoming his friends . . . back into our ranks." To further minimize the damage that Tyler could do to the ticket, Walker recommended that Jackson come out with a public letter saying something similar and write privately to Blair telling him to fall in line. Jackson agreed to write the kind of private letter that Walker wanted, with one exception: in it, he called Benton "*crazy.*" "Mr Tyler can be praised as to the Bank, Texas &c without assailing any member of our party," Walker sighed. Polk asked Robert Armstrong, Andrew J. Donelson, and Gideon Pillow to sit down with Jackson at the Hermitage and convince him to compose a letter that met the stipulations of wooing Tyler without insulting another important Democratic leader. Jackson's goal, Polk reminded Donelson, was to "reach the President's ego" and convince him to withdraw from the campaign. He also wrote Old Hickory directly, asking him to implore Blair "to cease his war" on Tyler. "These two measures are at this moment of greater importance, than any that have arisen or [are] likely to arise," Polk emphasized.[57]

Jackson was not one to follow advice unquestioningly, and he let Polk know that he disagreed with his recommendation. Walker's suggestion of a public letter showed "great want of common sense." "Such a letter from any of your friends would damn you & destroy your election," Jackson exclaimed. "Tylers [sic] friends are a mere drop in the buckett [sic], & they nor nothing but such [an] imprudent letter as suggested can prevent your election." Despite his obstinacy, Jackson fulfilled Polk's wishes—just in his own way. On the same day he wrote Polk, Jackson sent Blair a private letter. After spending several pages complaining about Benton and explaining in detail why Texas should be annexed, Jackson, citing his poor health, made one short statement on the topic near the end: "Support the course of polk & Dallas, & let Tiler [sic] alone." This sentence lacked the urgency and explanation that Polk had requested, but it was something at least. To Secretary of the Navy John Y. Mason, Jackson listed three reasons why Tyler needed to step aside. First, he could not win. Staying in the contest, Jackson said, would also confirm charges that he was using Texas only to remain president. Finally, Tyler risked validating accusations that he was helping Clay to spite the Democrats. "*He ought to withdraw from the canvass,*" Jackson pronounced. He wrote William B. Lewis the same day as Mason, telling him not to bring up withdrawal to Tyler. If the president raised the topic, however, then Jackson gave his longtime advisor similar advice, but with one addition. He added that Tyler needed to withdraw to preserve his honor. This point was undoubtedly intended to appeal directly to the president's identity as a southern gentleman, something both he and Jackson understood well.[58]

On August 18, Tyler wrote Jackson that his letter to Lewis had convinced him to withdraw from the race. The president claimed that he had wanted to do so "at an early period of my administration," but he had been "overuled [sic] by the advice of others." He believed that the Democrats would succeed if Benton and Blair stopped attacking him. It was a strange letter that revealed Tyler at his worst: insecure and self-absorbed. The president publicly announced the decision to end his campaign two days later. His letter to the American people was self-pitying and defensive, blaming his withdrawal partly on the impeachment efforts, unsuccessful as they were, that had plagued his presidency. Tyler congratulated himself for pursuing Texas annexation in the face of opposition and for improving "the condition of the country" in a variety of ways. In later years, he claimed that he had orchestrated his nomination and withdrawal "to ensure the success of a great measure [i.e., annexation] at a decisive moment." He may have allowed hindsight to convince him that the real goal of his 1844 campaign was only to secure Texas annexation, but the evidence suggests that for a time at least, Tyler truly believed that he could win the presidency.[59]

Reaction to Tyler's announcement was predictable. Julia Tyler deemed his withdrawal letter "dignified, and eloquent, maintaining the principles he has carried through in his administration—full, clear, concise." Whigs described him as having been taken advantage of by "the lying pack of office-hunters and 'buzzards' . . . who infest the White House to impose the most futile falsehoods upon him." The *New York Daily Herald* called Tyler's campaign "nothing but a farce," which had benefited neither the president nor the Democrats. Privately, many Democrats breathed a sigh of relief. From Philadelphia, Joel B. Sutherland conveyed to Jackson his confidence that Tyler's decision would energize Democrats in Virginia, Pennsylvania, and the New England states. Upon receiving this letter, Jackson forwarded it to Polk, adding his own observation that this news would help the Democratic ticket in Ohio. A Tennessee congressman reported to Polk that Tyler's withdrawal letter "will do us great good." Democrats in the nation's capital were "in high spirits" unseen since Jackson's presidency, he wrote.[60]

JAMES G. BIRNEY

As with the campaigns of Joseph Smith and John Tyler, James G. Birney's nomination by the antislavery Liberty Party had little realistic chance of putting him in the White House. There was no reason to think that he posed a serious threat to either Polk or Clay, but the growing sentiment against slavery since the 1840 presidential election presented Birney with an opportunity to peel off voters from the Whigs, potentially altering the results in crucial antislavery states, such as New York.

Those who knew Birney as a young man would have thought him an unlikely candidate to run on an antislavery ticket. He was born into a slave-holding Kentucky family in 1792 and was educated at Transylvania University and Princeton University. After studying with Philadelphia lawyer Alexander J. Dallas, who served in James Madison's cabinet and was George

Dallas's father, Birney returned to his hometown of Danville, Kentucky, where he worked as an attorney for his father's bank. In 1816, Birney married Agatha MacDowell, the daughter of a US circuit judge and a distant relative of James Madison. Birney absorbed the politics of his father, James Sr., who was a staunch Federalist in favor of the party's traditional policies: a high protective tariff, internal improvements, and a national bank.[61]

In February 1818, Birney moved his family to a 235-acre plantation two hours southwest of Huntsville, Alabama. He brought with him at least six enslaved African Americans; by 1824, Birney counted forty enslaved workers under his ownership. His life appeared to be on the same trajectory as thousands of other white southern enslavers who poured into the Deep South following Andrew Jackson's territorial acquisitions during and after the War of 1812. Birney speculated in land, and like many who made that gamble, when the Panic of 1819 set in, he found himself in debt. Birney also emulated the extravagant lifestyle of many enslavers, spending money on unnecessary and expensive accoutrements that marked him as an elite. Adding to his dire financial straits was his propensity for gambling. As Birney's financial situation worsened, he turned to alcohol as a coping mechanism. The death of his seventeen-month-old daughter, Margaret, in 1822 only worsened his emotional state. As Birney remembered later, he "was rapidly pursuing the road to Hell." In 1823, he moved his family to Huntsville and began practicing law. The following year, Birney started serving as solicitor of the Alabama Fifth Circuit Court, which provided a much more stable source of income. That same year, he sold his plantation and most of the enslaved workers living there, retaining ownership of a family of five enslaved people.[62]

Birney's life changed dramatically in 1826. He had resisted his wife's Presbyterianism throughout their marriage, but the turmoil of the past few years finally convinced him to begin attending services with Agatha. As a result, he saw the "folly and the wrong" of his life and became "a follower of Christ." This religious conversion transformed Birney's thinking on many issues. During a stint as Huntsville's mayor a few years later, Birney helped pass a temperance ordinance within the city. He also became involved in the Madison County Bible Society and the Huntsville Tract Society. Birney's views of slavery changed too. Shortly after his religious conversion, he picked up a copy of a journal published by the American Colonization Society (ACS) and sent the organization a small donation that he had collected. Two years later, while visiting his father, Birney convinced his fellow Freemasons in Danville, Kentucky, "to adopt a resolution condemning the interstate slave trade into Kentucky." In December 1829, Birney coordinated a local speaking engagement for ACS agent Josiah F. Polk. Shortly thereafter, he helped found the Madison County (Alabama) Colonization Society. Birney was no longer a man enthralled with the traditional slaveholding paternalism of his region.[63]

In June 1832, Birney met the person who helped move him toward abolitionism. Theodore Weld was traveling the Southeast as an agent of the Society for Promoting Manual Labor in Literary Institutions, and he chose to come to Huntsville in part to meet Birney. According to Weld's later recollections, Tennessee professor Benjamin Larrabee told him that "though a slave-holder," Birney possessed *"nothing of the slave-holding spirit."* Over several days, Birney and Weld discussed a number of issues, social and political. At this point in his life, Birney was looking to "engage in some calling more directly religious or benevolent." His time with Weld began charting the path he would take. Shortly after his meeting with Weld, Birney accepted an invitation to serve as the ACS's southwestern representative, covering a territory that included Alabama, the Arkansas Territory, Louisiana, Mississippi, and Tennessee. His main job was touring and lecturing on colonization. Birney's embrace of colonization revealed his growing discomfort with the institution of slavery. "I cannot, nor do I believe any honest mind, can reconcile the precept 'love thy neighbor as thyself' with the purchase of the body of that neighbor," he wrote. From May to August 1833, Birney penned a series of fifteen letters on colonization that were published in the *Huntsville (AL) Democrat*. The letters attempted to differentiate between colonization and abolition, criticized the influence of free Blacks over enslaved people, and posited that colonization was the right course of action to ensure that southern whites could preserve their society. In essence, Birney thought that a South devoid of African Americans, free or enslaved, was better than a society of white enslavers built on slavery.[64]

In September 1833, Birney resigned his ACS position and moved back to Danville, Kentucky. As he made this transition, his views were changing once again. Birney became convinced that colonization would not bring about slavery's demise quickly enough. The origins of this change stemmed partly from his religious beliefs, which made it impossible for him to reconcile Christian charity with the enslavement of human beings. Birney was also influenced by numerous antislavery writings during this period. In December, Birney helped found the Kentucky Society for the Gradual Relief of the State from Slavery, an organization focused on gradual emancipation. "The subject of Colonization is most favorably received in this State," he wrote, "but there are many, who like myself look upon it as impracticable to arouse the South sufficiently to make it the means of ridding us of *Slavery*." "I am pleased to see all engines at work for the extirpation of slavery from our land," he continued. "I believe the condition of Slavery to be altogether unchristian, and, *therefore*, that its tendency is, to the ruin of us as a people." The address that Birney wrote for this new organization marked his public divorce from colonization. It called for "*the total abolition of slavery*" in his home state. Birney also changed tactics when it came to appealing to white southerners. As a proponent of colonization, he had taken a moderate tone toward southern enslavers. Now, instead of trying to appeal to their better nature, Birney began ridiculing them.[65]

In October 1834, the American Anti-Slavery Society (AAS) encouraged Birney to establish an antislavery newspaper. By the following summer, he was ready to begin publication, but his effort faced vocal opposition. A US postmaster in Clinton, Mississippi, pleaded with Birney to abort his planned launch. "How can you, being both a Christian and philanthropist, publish a journal that will lead both to the butchery of our wives and in[n]ocent children, and to the severing of our Union!" he shouted. The opposition Birney faced in Danville convinced him to move to Cincinnati. Threats of violence there, however, led him to set up shop in nearby New Richmond, Ohio, instead. Birney wanted his newspaper to show that both northerners and southerners were responsible for perpetuating the institution. The first issue of *The Philanthropist* appeared on January 1, 1836, and it prompted an immediate negative response among prominent Cincinnati residents. Hostility against Birney and his newspaper festered, finally exploding in the summer of 1836, as it had in Boston the previous year against abolitionist newspaper editor William Lloyd Garrison. On July 12, the *Philanthropist*'s office was vandalized. A few days later, a handbill appeared on street corners across Cincinnati promising $100 "for the delivery of one James G. Birney, a fugitive from justice. . . . Said Birney in all his associations and feelings is *black*; although his external appearance is white." On July 30, the newspaper office was vandalized again. The mob also went looking for Birney, tar and feathers in hand, to mete out the same type of vigilante justice Illinois abolitionist Elijah Lovejoy would receive at the hands of a murderous mob the following year. Fortuitously, Birney was out of town when they visited his home. These attacks elicited support for Birney from prominent Cincinnatians, such as newspaper editor Charles Henry Hammond, who were concerned about freedom of the press, and about Birney's life as well.[66]

The following year, Birney moved to New York City, where he assumed the position of AAS corresponding secretary. In this capacity, he oversaw publication of Theodore Weld's influential *American Slavery as It Is* (1839). Birney also corresponded with Henry Clay about congressional debates centered on abolitionism. He had visited the Kentucky politician in September 1834 with the goal of convincing him to support abolitionism. Birney's hopes had been dashed then—Clay was "altogether wrong" on the subject of slavery, "had *no conscience* about the matter," and "would swim with the popular current." But Birney was willing to reach out to the Whig leader again. In December 1837, he sent Clay a copy of the AAS's most recent annual report to acquaint him with the growth of antislavery societies across the nation. "I do not think our politicians . . . are at all aware of the impregnation of nearly all the free States, with the abolitionist-principles," Birney wrote. The following year, he mailed Clay a copy of two abolitionist pamphlets. Clay replied to Birney that abolitionism in Kentucky "had been thrown back fifty years" by northern abolitionist "agitation." He also corrected Birney's impression of his views on slavery. He had never supported immediate emancipation, Clay remarked, only gradual emancipation. The latter he could justify in a state where whites outnumbered enslaved people but not in a state "where there might be danger of the Blacks acquiring the ascendancy." He reminded Birney that his abolitionist stance would have prohibited several members of the first generation of American political leaders, including Jefferson, Madison, Monroe, and Washington, from holding public office. Clay also informed Birney that he was not offended by his "opinion that the election of a Slave holder to the Presidency would be a public calamity, so far as it may be supposed to affect me," because he did not anticipate being a candidate in the 1840 election.[67]

Clay was right—he would not appear on a ticket in 1840, but Birney did. Antislavery supporters began seriously discussing the formation of a third party in 1839. Some suggested that such a move would sacrifice moral arguments on the altar of political practice. Others argued that only a separate antislavery party could maintain the ideological purity needed to change the hearts and minds of voters about their duty to their enslaved brothers and sisters. In November of that year, a group of New York antislaveryites nominated Birney and Francis J. LeMoyne, a Pennsylvania doctor and active member of multiple abolitionist societies, for president and vice president, respectively. Both men declined the honor, however, and the project appeared dead.[68]

The Whig Party's nomination of the Harrison–Tyler ticket changed the conversation among some antislavery supporters. Neither man inspired hope that a Whig administration would try to restrain or roll back slavery. Key figures in the antislavery movement, such as Joshua Leavitt, editor of the AAS newspaper *The Emancipator*, considered reviving the idea of a third party. In early April 1840, a group of antislaveryites, representing six states, met in Albany, New York, to discuss the possibility. Although disagreement persisted among the delegates, they eventually decided to nominate Birney for president. Pennsylvanian Thomas Earle, a Quaker, former Democrat, and staunch antislaveryite, received the nod for vice president. The nominating resolution called Birney and Earle "enlightened and virtuous men, firmly devoted to the principles of HUMAN RIGHTS, and capable of applying them discreetly and efficaciously for the abolition of slavery."[69]

Birney's acceptance letter, written shortly before he and fellow abolitionists Henry Stanton and Elizabeth Cady Stanton departed for the World Anti-Slavery Convention in London, criticized Van Buren and Harrison as candidates willing to use their veto power to hinder Congress from limiting slavery and called Richard M. Johnson and John Tyler "*de facto* mocker[s] at the principles of the Declaration of Independence . . . actual insulter[s] of the doctrine of Human Rights . . . [and] practical violater[s] of all the claims of natural justice." "The truth is," Birney observed, "the government of the country is in the hands of the slave power." Replacing Van Buren with Harrison would not solve the problem of slavery; all it would do was put in the White House "another administration equally subservient, to say the least, to the same Power!" With this reality in mind, Birney agreed to serve as the Liberty candidate "as a means of concentrating the votes of abolitionists" against both Democratic and Whig nominees.[70]

The "slave power" trope was increasingly familiar by 1840. Americans had invoked it from the establishment of the nation, and the growth of slavery had only increased its usage, as John Quincy Adams had demonstrated in his opposition to Texas annexation. The Three-fifths Compromise, the Missouri Crisis, Andrew Jackson's election, the gag rule—all provided proof of its existence. The Slave Power was also bipartisan and national: Democrats and white southerners might have been the ones most closely identified with the evils of slavery, but they were assisted by their northern and Whig counterparts. Birney and others like him wanted to expose the Slave Power, believing that voters would join the antislavery cause if only they knew how they were being manipulated by those who chose profit over humanity. Much like Democrats had used the term "money power" to talk about elitist Whigs and their use of the national bank to exploit the average person, the Liberty Party employed the ever-present specter of the Slave Power to focus its members on eliminating the racist institution of unfree labor.[71]

Despite this belief, as some abolitionists had warned Birney would happen, he did not fare well in the 1840 election. Part of the reason is that he was not active in the campaign. His attendance at the World Anti-Slavery Convention took him to London, where Henry Stanton remembered that "by his solid and varied attainments, rich fund of information, courtesy, candor, and fine debating powers [Birney] inspired confidence in his statements and reflected credit upon his country." In the months after the convention ended, Birney met antislavery leaders and gave antislavery speeches across the British Isles. He convinced the Irish leader Daniel O'Connell to write an address to Irish Americans about slavery's evils, encouraging them to support the abolitionist cause. O'Connell's address, accompanied by 60,000 signatures, reached the United States in 1842, too late to affect the 1840 election but in time to be used in the 1844 campaign. Birney did not return home until late November 1840, after the election was over.[72]

In addition to suffering from the lack of Birney's presence during the campaign, the Liberty Party (also called the Human Rights Party, the People's Party, the Abolition Party, and the Freemen's Party during the 1840 campaign) lacked national organization and coordination. The election results exposed all these weaknesses. The ticket of Birney and Earle secured only 6,946 popular votes nationwide, with just over 40 percent (2,799 votes) coming from New York. Instead of taking this defeat as an indication of the hopelessness of their cause, abolitionists used it as motivation to prepare for the next presidential campaign. Shortly after polls closed in November 1840, the National Committee of Correspondence for "the friends of Liberty and of the oppressed in the United States" issued a plan to better prepare antislavery supporters for 1844. Its members called for a national convention to meet in New York City the following spring, and they proclaimed, "The power which will overthrow slavery has been discovered; it is the terse literature of the northern ballot box." The Liberty Party did not write off antislavery southern voters, but most members understood that the abolitionists' political fight in the foreseeable future would have to take place outside of the slaveholding South.[73]

Delegates representing eleven northern states convened as requested on Wednesday, May 12, 1841. After organizing themselves, the delegates' first order of business was nominating a ticket for 1844. On the first ballot, Birney won 108 of 112 votes, overwhelmingly defeating New York judge William Jay (son of the late US Supreme Court chief justice John Jay), Thomas Morris, and prominent abolitionist businessman Gerrit Smith to become the convention's presidential candidate. Morris, a former Democrat who had represented Ohio in the US Senate, easily won the vice presidential nomination with 83 out of 104 votes; the balance was scattered among Thomas Earle, Gerrit Smith, and former Whig and active abolitionist Alvan Stewart. The delegates moved to adopt these nominations unanimously, then adjourned for the day.[74]

On Thursday morning, delegates considered several resolutions, among them one designating themselves the Liberty Party and another asking Americans to unite with them in order "to remove all oppressive laws, and to establish equal rights and the impartial administration of justice throughout" the United States. Other resolutions called on President Tyler "to liberate his slaves" and asked antislavery activists to send memorials to Congress requesting the abolition of slavery in Washington, DC, and an end to the domestic slave trade. The delegates also approved an address that focused on political and economic, instead of religious, arguments for the end of slavery. The Slave Power was propping up the slaveholding South at the expense of the free-labor North, it argued, as typified by high tariffs and the Second Bank. "The same slave power that plunders our *purses* has declared open war upon our civil, political and religious *freedom*," the address declared. Both the Democratic Party and the Whig Party were beholden to the "slave power," which left the Liberty Party no choice but to nominate its own candidate.[75]

The convention delegates also agreed on a plan of committee structure, regular communication, and national coordination of electoral efforts, from the local to the national level. To that end, they appointed one delegate to lead the effort in their home state. Because the party's development in each state rose or fell depending on who that delegate was, the result was that party members in each state, even if they agreed on certain principles, organized on their own without the national coordination envisioned at the 1841 convention. That is not to say that the Liberty Party did not experience any political success. Some antislavery Whigs unhappy with Tyler's elevation to the presidency abandoned their party to become Liberty men. Liberty candidates won local, and sometimes even statewide, elections. In the 1842 Massachusetts elections, the party forced a runoff between the Democratic and Whig gubernatorial candidates and provided the swing votes in a closely divided state legislature. Liberty newspapers sprung up, keeping members informed when mainstream newspapers ignored their party's activities and candidates. But there were cracks in the party that signaled that its lack of organization and absence of strong national leadership posed a threat to its efforts in 1844. Some Liberty politicians called for a pragmatic shifting of priorities. The party should focus on "the deliverance of the government from the control of the slave power; not the emancipation of slaves in the slave States," a group of Cincinnati Liberty leaders argued. "To reduce the principles of American liberty to practice in the administration of the government should be the aim of our party."[76]

Birney waited more than seven months before accepting the Liberty Party's nomination. During that time, he moved to the Michigan wilderness. It was a less-than-ideal situation given his political aspirations, but Birney explained to fellow abolitionist Lewis Tappan that it was necessary. Saginaw "seems almost out of the peopled world, but I can't help it. I must go where I can live cheap and where I can put my boys to doing something to support themselves." Birney was optimistic that his new state of residence would prove to be beneficial to the antislavery cause. Michiganders were "intelligent, imbued more than is common in their circumstances, with religious sentiments—law-abiding, hospitable, and generous," he told an abolitionist newspaper in his new state. "This is the mental and moral soil on which the shoot of Liberty naturally springs up and grows."[77]

Birney's much-delayed acceptance letter outlined how the United States had failed multiple groups, including enslaved African Americans, Native Americans, and Mormons. He conveyed his "faint hope" that the party would succeed, but he offset his pessimism with the assertion that "God is ever with them who contend for right, for justice, for mercy." Liberty members in Ohio, already questioning the value of Birney as a candidate, began discussing a more pragmatic nominee, someone who might not be an ideological abolitionist but who opposed slavery and had the national name recognition that could win them the election. Names bandied about included John Quincy Adams, William Jay, and New York governor William H. Seward. As abolitionist editor Gamaliel Bailey explained, he did not doubt Birney's "entire fitness for the presidential chair so far as competency and perfect integrity are concerned." The problem was that he "always appeared in the character of a Moralist, a reformer, rather than a Politician or Statesman." Birney responded by reminding Bailey that "as we are contending for the government on a single *principal* question, it is of prime importance that our candidates be wholly right on it." He let it be known, however, that he would acquiesce to whatever party members decided.[78]

In late August 1843, Liberty Party delegates reconvened in Buffalo, New

York. They set up a tent, "capable of accommodating 5,000 persons," in the park located in front of the Erie County courthouse. The convention's primary purposes were to settle once and for all the presidential and vice presidential nominations and to refine the platform that would guide the party during the 1844 campaign. On Thursday morning, the delegates voted unanimously to reaffirm the nominations of Birney and Morris. They also passed forty-four resolutions as part of their platform. Some were minor in nature, but most spoke to the concerns that the party members shared. The second resolution summarized the party's main principle: "the absolute and unqualified divorce of the General Government from Slavery." Another resolution emphasized that although the party opposed "slaveholding, as the grossest form and most revolting manifestation of Despotism," it was equally committed to defending equal rights and "every just measure conducive to individual and social freedom." Other resolutions argued that the founding generation had agreed to a future of state-initiated gradual emancipation. The United States' failure to fulfill this promise, the resolutions concluded, had produced a divided Union in which the "slave power" was "corrupting" the nation's domestic scene and "exhibiting the American people to the world in the ridiculous and contemptible character of patrons of the slave trade." Other resolutions called for party members to organize at all levels of government and disseminate the party's principles via the nation's print culture. Finally, the delegates approved resolutions that made clear their rejection of the unconstitutional laws that had proceeded from the nation's founding document.[79]

Liberty Party delegates departed Buffalo full of hope for 1844. Birney helped sustain that momentum by agreeing to undertake a speaking tour through New England, New York, and Michigan in October 1843. "Your presence will give double and triple activity to every canvasser, and tract distributor and vote distributor," one supporter wrote encouragingly. Thanks to a refocused purpose and an active presidential candidate, the Liberty Party represented itself well in the 1843 elections, not winning many offices but gaining votes. All was not right with the party, however. Birney had not been the preferred candidate of every Liberty Party member, and some still harbored reservations about him. His acceptance letter, which consisted mostly of a long diatribe against Adams's lack of antislavery principle, did not help matters. Morris's presence on the ticket also elicited concern. He had popularized the Slave Power conspiracy narrative and made it an integral part of the Liberty Party's rhetoric, but some party members remembered his Democratic past and did not trust his commitment to antislavery principles. Morris's prickly personality only exacerbated his interpersonal conflicts with other Liberty members. "A storm is brewing" between Morris and party leaders, "which may burst in fury before the winter months," William Birney reported to his father in the fall of 1843. Morris also expressed indecisiveness about being on the ticket, which hardly increased his goodwill with Liberty men such as Ohioans Gamaliel Bailey and Salmon P. Chase. Bailey was so exasperated with him that he "*privately* threatened to expose some" unnamed "long past moral evil" that Morris had been part of. By March 1844, Birney's son reported that Liberty leaders in Ohio were still uncomfortable, but "matters move along more smoothly."[80]

Despite some Liberty members' reluctant acceptance of the Birney–Morris ticket, the party put together an organized and energetic campaign in late 1843 and early 1844. Morris and Leicester King, who served as chair of the 1843 national convention, worked on strengthening the party in Ohio. Two of the party's founders, Gerrit Smith and Alvan Stewart, oversaw operations in western New York. Smith helped fund Liberty lecturers, who traveled across the North disseminating the party's message, and Stewart encouraged the party to focus on print culture as another way of spreading its influence. In New England, newspaper editors Joshua Leavitt and Elizur Wright Jr. led the party. Leavitt began writing a campaign biography of Birney, which Beriah Green eventually completed. Wright helped publicize the Liberty Party's official symbol, which was the cedar tree of Lebanon. (The symbolism came from Psalm 92:12: "The righteous . . . shall grow like a cedar in Lebanon.") "The Cedar," one abolitionist publication pronounced, "is the emblem of Constancy, of Protection, of Renown, of Immortality." Both Wright and his eleven-year-old son composed campaign songs, one of which went:

> We hail thee, Birney, just and true,
> The calm and fearless, staunch and tried,
> The bravest of the valiant few,
> Our country's hope, our country's pride!
> In Freedom's battle take the van;
> We hail thee as an honest man.[81]

Birney himself was an important part of getting the campaign off the ground. Wright invited him on a "stump" tour throughout Massachusetts. "Our leader must not be browsing on the solitary and humid plains of Saginaw, among the reeds and alders and *weeping* willows," he wrote Birney

James G. Birney, 1844. (Courtesy of the Library of Congress)

from Boston. "We want him to water the cedars which are sticking their roots down among the *granite* foundations of this continent." Helping the abolitionist cause was his primary motivation in accepting Wright's invitation, but Birney was also relieved to get away from Saginaw. Peace in the community of approximately 130 people had proven elusive. "We have a miserable population here," he reported. "They would be pirates if they had courage. Their vices are lying, drinking, gambling, backbiting etc. etc." There was no religion, no "moral restraint," among his neighbors. His debts were small, but he could not pay them off. Despite having land and cattle to sell, Birney found no one in the area who had the money to take them off his hands. He was stuck in isolation, putting him at a disadvantage in the presidential contest. "It frets and goads me to death," Birney told one correspondent. Hitting the campaign trail was just what he needed, so he headed east, making several appearances not just in the Bay State but also in Connecticut, New York, and Michigan.[82]

Birney's presidential campaign coincided with abolitionism's move away from moral suasion and toward violence as the best and quickest way to end slavery. Violence had been part of antislavery resistance since the colonial period, and in the early 1840s, it increasingly became part of the mainstream abolitionist movement. Abolitionist conventions in Maine and New Hampshire acknowledged that violence might be necessary. Henry Highland Garnet's address to the National Negro Convention in Buffalo, just two weeks before his appearance at the Liberty national convention in the same city, encouraged listeners, "Let your motto be RESISTANCE! RESISTANCE! RESISTANCE!." This push to "force freedom," in conjunction with the injection of Texas annexation into the 1844 campaign, ensured that slavery would remain at the forefront of political debate among the various candidates. Despite the shift, Birney and most of his Liberty supporters continued to use moral suasion in their effort to pull off an improbable political upset.[83]

By the end of August 1844, one presidential candidate (Joseph Smith) was dead, and one (John Tyler) had dropped out. It remained to be seen which of the three presidential candidates still in the race—Birney, Clay, or Polk—would be able to win over voters. Defining their policies was important, but so was answering questions about their personal lives. Just as critical was the effective employment of cultural politics to turn out their loyal base, attract new voters, and convince others to switch their partisan allegiance.

5

"A NATIONAL FESTIVAL" THE 1844 CAMPAIGN

The 1844 presidential campaign began in earnest once the Democratic convention ended in late May. For the next five-plus months, James G. Birney, Henry Clay, and James K. Polk faced questions about several matters that worried voters. Longtime issues, such as the tariff, political corruption, personal morality, and slavery, joined with newly urgent concerns, such as nativism and Texas annexation, to produce a campaign that signaled the United States was moving into a new era of national politics.

These political issues were crucial to turning out each party's base, but sustaining partisan interest and reaching new voters required more than just policy. Recent elections had provided the template for animating political enthusiasm, and both Democrats and Whigs knew its effectiveness. The campaign season from May to November offered the parties the opportunity to build on the cultural politics that had so energized voters in the "Log Cabin and Hard Cider" campaign of 1840. These electioneering techniques were important not only in generating support for specific issues but also for rejuvenating the partisanship among voters that could grow dormant between elections. It was cultural politics that breathed life into the issues that divided the candidates and imparted the energy the parties needed to harness votes and achieve victory.[1]

Even before the nominating convention month of May came to an end, work had already started on campaign biographies for the presidential candidates. Epes Sargent corresponded directly with Clay to expand an 1842 biography that his brother, John O. Sargent, had published about the Kentuckian. Nathan Sargent (no relation to the brothers) also published an expanded biographical sketch that he had written the previous year. Having antici- pated that Martin Van Buren would be the Democratic candidate, Clay and his supporters, taking a page from the 1840 playbook, had already created a false narrative about the Kentuckian's upbringing that emphasized the hardscrabble life he was said to have endured growing up in "the Slashes" of Hanover County. Clay supposedly spent long hours in hard labor trav- eling to, and working at, a grist mill. When Polk emerged as a candidate instead, Whigs did not abandon this narrative, finding it convenient to keep up this "Millboy of the Slashes" persona they had developed.[2]

By running a new candidate in Polk instead of someone like Van Bu- ren, Democrats found themselves lagging behind their opponents in cre- ating campaign literature. Polk's allies hoped to convince George Bancroft, whom Samuel H. Laughlin regarded as "the best Historical writer of the age in any language," to undertake an official campaign biography. They wanted Polk to provide Bancroft with a full sketch of 100 to 200 pages that he could expand or refine as needed. Bancroft, who had started a campaign biography of Van Buren when it appeared his friend would win the nomi- nation, turned down the opportunity. Another option for some Democrats was Amos Kendall, but he was too unpopular with the party to be assigned the task. The best that Democrats could muster were short biographies printed in newspaper columns and a fifty-page pamphlet by Baltimore jour- nalist George H. Hickman that included biographies of Polk and George M. Dallas and selected speeches by both.[3]

Helping these campaign biographies get the word out about the can- didates were partisan newspapers. Francis P. Blair's *Globe* was the Demo- crats' most important national newspaper, often printing extracts of letters that captured the enthusiasm that party members felt about the Polk– Dallas ticket. The two Washington, DC, Whig organs, the *National Intel- ligencer* and the *Whig Standard*, did the same for Clay and Theodore Frel- inghuysen. In addition to established newspapers in the nation's capital and elsewhere, both parties also produced campaign-specific organs. One Whig paper, *That Same Old Coon* (Dayton, OH), played on one of Clay's nicknames with its title. Democrats fought back with their own campaign organs that incorporated this nickname, including the *Coon Hunter* (Boon- ville, MO), the *Coon Skinner* (Ithaca, NY), and the *Coon Dissector* (Dayton, OH). They also published newspapers that used Polk's most-used nick- name, including the *Young Hickory* (Lynn, MA) and the *Young Hickory Ban-*

ner (New York). This print war contributed to the growth in the number of newspapers during the decade, from 1,404 in 1840 to 2,526 by 1850.[4]

Newspapers were the main source of campaign information for most voters, and there was a lot of news to keep up with. Texas remained in the headlines immediately following the nominating conventions. Just more than a week after the Democrats left the Egyptian Saloon, the Senate rejected the Texas annexation treaty by a vote of thirty-five to sixteen, nowhere close to the late Abel P. Upshur's estimation of support and far short of the two-thirds needed for passage. Twenty-seven Whigs voted against the treaty, and one voted for it. Seven Democrats (six northerners and one westerner) joined the Whigs in the opposition. These antiannexation Democrats—such as Thomas Hart Benton and Silas Wright Jr.—had close ties to Van Buren, and their willingness to buck the party majority on the annexation issue indicated that Polk's campaign had some fence-mending to do. The idea of annexation would not die, however. Tyler refused to concede defeat, moving the discussion to the House. He requested that Texas be annexed via a joint congressional resolution; this approach would only require a majority vote in both chambers. In the Senate, Benton proposed, among other things, opening treaty negotiations with both Texas and Mexico and, if annexation succeeded, dividing Texas into free and slave states. His pompous tone prompted South Carolina's George McDuffie to respond that Democrats needed to expel Benton from the party. John Quincy Adams feared that the heated rhetoric might lead the two men into an affair of honor, but cooler heads prevailed. Neither of these proposals went anywhere before Congress adjourned in mid-June, but Benton's actions reportedly led Andrew Jackson to pronounce "that ever since the explosion of the big gun [i.e., the USS *Princeton* accident] Benton has not been in his right mind."[5]

Clay had staked out his position against immediate annexation before being nominated, but because even Whig voters showed significant enthusiasm for the idea, the Kentuckian began rethinking his opinion. In July, he wrote a letter and had it published in an Alabama newspaper. In it, Clay backed away from his antiannexation stance, claiming that he possessed "no objection" to annexing Texas if it did not threaten the Union's future. A second letter, published in a different Alabama newspaper, followed later that month. In this one, Clay denied that slavery and annexation were intertwined issues and said that he might decide to annex Texas if he became president. The two "Alabama letters" seriously damaged Clay's credibility in the North, so much so that he wrote yet another letter of clarification in September. This one, appearing in a Washington newspaper, asserted that

Clay had maintained a consistent position in all his letters: opposition to immediate annexation, but openness to annexation under certain conditions. Clay's last letter was defensive and condescending in tone, and it only served to strengthen a sense of desperation and inconsistency about his "Janus-faced" candidacy at a crucial time in the campaign.[6]

Polk did not suffer from Clay's equivocation when it came to Texas. The Tennessean believed in, and was committed to, immediate annexation. But his party was divided over the question. This meant that Polk had to find ways to keep Democrats from splintering, allowing Clay to swoop in and steal the election from them. One of the ways he attempted to maintain unity was by pledging to serve only a single term. Correspondents who wrote Polk immediately after the 1844 convention advised him that making such a promise would ensure the support of disappointed contenders such as John C. Calhoun and Lewis Cass. It would allow them to "think they are yet to be President before their day is spent." The danger of a one-term pledge was that it might also encourage the more ambitious Democratic aspirants to withhold their support in 1844, calculating that running as the opposition candidate against an incumbent Clay four years later might be the more attractive strategy.[7]

Another question was whether New York would support Polk. The Empire State was critical for his election chances, and some Democrats were still unhappy about the Baltimore convention's outcome. In July, a circular letter was distributed by seven New York Democrats who found distasteful the way in which Texas annexation had been foisted on the national convention and who believed that the issue was one that was "abhorrent to the opinions and feelings of a great majority of Northern freemen." They proposed drafting a joint public letter of prominent state Democrats indicating their acceptance of the Polk–Dallas ticket but "rejecting the resolutions respecting Texas." These disaffected Democrats also wanted to focus on nominating congressional candidates who agreed with their antiannexation stance. Some Whigs reveled in this intraparty division, believing it indicated that Democrats were desperate to appeal to the antislaveryites who were abandoning their party because of the annexation issue. Others proclaimed the letter a ruse to lure abolitionists into voting for the Democrats. The Whig claim that the Democratic Party in New York was "broken up, dissolved, and . . . defunct" because of annexation was an exaggeration, but many of the state's Democrats were unhappy; placating them would be necessary if Polk was going to defeat Clay.[8]

Unlike Clay and Polk, Birney was expressly opposed to annexation. Part of his hostility to the idea was based on his constitutional interpretation of territorial acquisition and his resistance to Manifest Destiny. In his view, the Constitution did not specifically allow the United States "in any way, to accept of a cession of foreign territory." He also thought that the United States was large enough; acquiring Texas would only feed the hunger for more territory. But mostly Birney opposed annexation because it was expressly tied to the expansion of slavery. He believed that the Constitution was an antislavery document, so slavery's existence anywhere within the United States was wrong. Birney's disagreement with annexation was so pronounced that he found himself accused of being a Manchurian candidate for the British abolitionists. Whigs also suggested that the Democrats were paying him to siphon off votes from Clay.[9]

Texas drew a lot of attention throughout the campaign, but other issues, including the tariff, also generated a great deal of interest. The Tariff of 1842, which had barely passed both congressional chambers with strong Whig support but only a handful of Democratic votes, appeared to provide Whigs with plenty of political ammunition to use in 1844. They pointed to its passage as the reason for the nation's economic recovery from Van Buren's disastrous policies. Realizing the political danger it posed for their presumed presidential nominee, congressional Democrats attempted to reduce the 1842 tariff before their May 1844 nominating convention. The effort failed, allowing the tariff to remain a political test for the rest of the campaign, despite one Alabama newspaper editor's assertion that it had "lost its terrors with the people."[10]

Clay had supported tariffs throughout his political career, believing that they protected American industry and helped the nation maintain its independence from Europe. His views on the tariff aligned with the majority in his party: he was "in favor of a Tariff for Revenue, with discrimination for *Protection*, and against the repeal of the Tariff of 1842." Democrats attempted to use the Kentuckian's positions against him, claiming that he only supported tariff protection for manufacturing, not agricultural, interests. The Whig nominee quickly shot down this argument, noting that he believed protecting manufacturing would also "benefit agriculture, by opening a new and home market for its agricultural productions."[11]

The tariff issue proved more treacherous for Polk. Three months before the Baltimore convention, a political ally told him that "if nothing can be done with the Tariff we are a lost & doomed party." Once he became the nominee, Democratic friends immediately reminded Polk that his stance was important, especially when it came to convincing Pennsylvanians to

POLK VERSUS WOOL OR THE HARRY-CANE.

The 1844 campaign marked a transition period in major issues: James K. Polk looks to avoid the tariff by running toward Texas annexation. (Courtesy of the Tennessee State Library & Archives)

support him. Andrew J. Donelson recommended that he follow Jackson's approach, telling him that "your success is certain if your ground on the Tariff is wisely chosen." Cave Johnson advised his friend to stay away from discussing the tariff, except to say that as president he would sign a bill reducing it for revenue purposes. Robert Walker agreed, arguing that the tariff was the only issue that could defeat the Democrats. The best approach for Polk was to focus on Texas, the Mississippian counseled, but when he had to address the tariff, he needed to remember that "an out & out Free trade candidate cannot receive the vote of Pennsylvania. This is certain, & without her vote we are beaten." "Go as far as your principles will permit for incidental protection," Walker advised.[12]

Avoiding the issue was not an option, as Polk quickly discovered. A Louisiana congressman wrote him less than a week after the May convention asking for his views on the sugar tariff, which he wanted to share with constituents back home. John K. Kane, a prominent Pennsylvania Democrat, told Polk that on all the other issues, the Keystone State's Democrats "will be found right to the core," but the tariff was "the one question, on which in some parts of our state we are vulnerable." Realizing that remaining silent was not possible, Polk decided to send Kane an explanation of his views in mid-June. He declared himself in favor of a tariff that would produce enough revenue to support an "economically administered" national government and pronounced himself "opposed to a tariff for protection *merely*, and not for revenue." Polk also pointed voters to his previous statements and votes on tariff legislation. This letter was published and disseminated widely throughout the nation. During the remainder of the campaign, when a Democratic correspondent asked Polk what he thought about the tariff, he referred them to his Kane letter. Whig queries, meanwhile, were ignored and treated with "silent contempt."[13]

Pennsylvania and New York were two major battlegrounds for the tariff debate. Whigs were furious that Polk's support for the 1842 tariff in the Kane letter flew in the face of the position they believed he had taken throughout his political career. Consequently, they tried to force Pennsylvania Democrats to "discuss nothing but the tariff & distribution" in hopes of exposing the lie. When that proved ineffective, Whigs also spread disinformation, distributing false statements on the tariff that they attributed to Polk. Democrats in the state took heart from the Kane letter, which they saw as the antidote to any poisonous false rumors. One Pennsylvanian declared that Polk's letter had left his state's Democrats "sailing before a spanking breeze without a rock, a shoal or eddy ahead, and as sure of success as we ever were in the course of our political history." After taking a trip through "the Tariff region" of Pennsylvania, Kane himself reported that Democrats there were "never so united." New York Democrats faced similar challenges, with similar results. The Whigs "are trying to get rid of every issue but Slavery and the Tariff," one New Yorker warned. "Ingenious are they not." Silas Wright believed that by discussing the tariff "fairly and frankly and honestly," Democrats had "gained rather than lost" ground in the Empire State.[14]

Even Birney—who was focused on slavery—found himself forced to address the tariff. "I know that ours is a party with but one object," Pittsburgher Russell Errett noted in asking for his official position, "but here, we are pestered to death with this Tariff issue." "I would not on my own account have troubled you," another Pennsylvanian apologized when making a similar request. Unable to avoid these and other similar queries, Birney reluctantly responded with a statement that he hoped would not "divert our friends from our paramount object, the overthrow of the slave-power." His letter was a naïvely optimistic analysis of the nation's economic future. He asserted that a tariff sufficient to meet the regular government expenditures "will have to be the *rule*," with occasional higher duties for "extraordinary expenditure." Americans would never allow "higher duties than are necessary for revenue . . . [to] become the permanent policy of the country." Birney also considered it "altogether improbable" that the national government would "ever adopt a direct taxation of any sort as a permanent revenue system." Errett eventually decided that he had misread the public demand for Birney's views on the tariff, but the Liberty nominee published his views anyways. The reaction by one Pennsylvania newspaper suggested that it was a mistake: "The Tariff citizens of this region will understand why his letter has been hid so long."[15]

The Democrats' experience in the 1840 campaign had demonstrated what happened when a political party ignored energetic campaigning. Polk was determined to avoid Van Buren's fate in this regard. Crucial to his effort was the work of his wife, Sarah Childress Polk. She had been a powerful partner for her husband throughout his political career, with James often asking for, and following, her advice. During her husband's congressional tenure, Sarah emulated Dolley Madison by "combining politics and entertainment," providing space for Washington politicians to network under her supervision. Once James was nominated in Baltimore, Sarah had the opportunity to take on a more active role by heading up a de facto campaign headquarters at the Nashville home of US Supreme Court justice John Catron. "I desire that Mrs. Polk should be visited by Whigs and democrats, of her own sex," the judge wrote, noting that his wife, Matilda, agreed with him. Catron reminded Polk that he spoke from experience—he had been part of a committee that had defended the Jacksons' marriage in the 1824 and 1828 campaigns. That Sarah was "fit in high places, should be well known to friends and opponents," and Nashville was a better location for that intermingling than Columbia. Sarah declined their friends' offer as a matter of "*inconvenience*," preferring to assist her husband from their Columbia home.[16]

Even in taking a more geographically distant approach to campaigning, Sarah still played an important role in swaying moral voters. Clay's reputation for gambling persisted, and his refusal to rule out engaging in a duel if the circumstances required it was concerning to some. As Whig defenses of his "good private character" fell flat with voters, the door opened for Sarah to present her husband as morally upstanding. James was not particularly religious, but Sarah was, and she used her influence throughout their marriage to ensure that her husband, like the protagonist in John Bunyan's *Pilgrim's Progress*, stayed on the King's Highway and avoided the Slough of

Despond. Her devotion to the Sabbatarian cause, which called for a prohibition of work on Sunday, the traditional Christian day of worship, not only highlighted James's religiosity in comparison to the Kentuckian's rumored depravity, but it also helped counter the pious Frelinghuysen's place on the Whig ticket. Democratic newspapers reveled in repeating descriptions of Polk, found in opposition newspapers, that described him as "a man of EXEMPLARY MORALS" and "ABOVE REPROACH." One of the best attacks on Polk's character that Whigs could muster early in the campaign was that his grandfather Ezekiel had been a Tory during the American Revolution. Another indirect criticism that appeared later was that James's brother William was a "murderer" who had "shot down or butchered a gentleman in Columbia, Tenn. some years ago."[17]

Sarah Polk was the most prominent woman—Democratic or Whig—actively engaged in the campaign, but she was not the only one. One of the hallmarks of the 1844 campaign was the continued growth in women's political activity. Their inability to cast their "maiden vote" differentiated women from men in substantive ways. But even though they could not vote, women had learned during recent presidential elections that their campaign presence mattered: men "ignored them at their own risk." The Whigs had harnessed women's influence more effectively than Democrats in 1840, using their presence as moral endorsements of their ticket, but the 1844 campaign demonstrated that the playing field was evening out.[18]

"Democratic women were quieter about their politics than their Whig sisters" in 1844, but they were "no less committed." At a Winchester, Virginia, meeting, about 1,400 women were in the crowd estimated at 10,000. In New York, women made up a significant percentage of large Democratic gatherings in Albion and Granville; in Otis, Massachusetts, they made up nearly a third of an audience of 2,000. Some Democratic women went beyond simple attendance at political activities. Women in Hunterdon, New Jersey, gave the local Democratic Association a *"young hickory"* tree, which the men planted. Flag presentations also provided opportunities for women to speak publicly about the campaign. In Canton, New York, a group of women presented the town's Democratic Association a banner inscribed with the motto, "Peace we love best, War, if oppressed." The women's representatives called for a united Democratic Party that practiced "Christian charity and toleration." At Andrew J. Donelson's home Tulip Grove, located adjacent to his uncle's Hermitage plantation, his wife, Elizabeth, and his sister-in-law, Mary D. Martin, presented flags, respectively, to the Young Hickories from Lebanon and the Hermitage Texas Rangers. Martin's speech pointed out that the flag contained a star representing Texas, indicating the support "Democratic ladies" held for the people of Texas who desired annexation. Sarah Cheatham, the daughter of Tennessee Democrat Leonard P. Cheatham, echoed this sentiment in her presentation of a similar flag on another occasion. These activities by Democratic women refuted "one of the favorite dogmas of the Whigs," that "the Ladies are all Whigs."[19]

Even before Clay became the official Whig nominee, one anonymous supporter wrote to him that "although your Country-Women cannot serve you at the Ballot-box, they can, and do, remember you at the Altar" of prayer. Clay was well aware of women's significance to the cause. In a June 1842 speech given in Lexington, he had noted that Whig women "as in 1840, . . . can powerfully aid a great and good cause, without any departure from the propriety or dignity of their sex." Whig women participated in all kinds of events in 1844. At a minimum, they attended political events in large numbers; in Louisiana, they frequently averaged 20 percent of the audience. They also undertook the traditional activities expected of them. In East Tennessee, for example, an estimated 1,500 women prepared "a bountiful table" for attendees of a party meeting in Greeneville. At a Kentucky rally, Whig women presented banners inscribed with slogans such as "We will do our duty" and "Whig or no husband." On other occasions, they engaged in less traditional political endeavors. Eliza Roberts, wife of former congressman Jonathan Roberts, not only presented a banner to the Upper Merrion (PA) Clay Club, she also told the Whig men that a small group of women had persevered through sickness and the death of one of their own to produce the banner as a symbol of "their zeal in the cause which you are expected more effectively to engage." Eliza Roberts observed that some of the men thought that women should not be involved in politics and acknowledged that she herself was "no advocate" of female politicking. She wanted them to know, however, that "your wives, your mothers, your sisters, and daughters . . . look for you to aid in securing for us the peace and prosperity of our beloved country." A Zanesville, Ohio, newspaper reported an anecdote about an eighty-four-year-old woman who ordered her sons to bring twenty Whigs attending a local rally to her house for dinner. When they arrived, she told them that in her younger years, she had been "an intimate of the homes of both Washington and Jefferson" and was glad to see that the present-day Whig Party so closely resembled that of "those Revolutionary fathers." She then gave their efforts her blessing: "Eat, then, for you are welcome!"[20]

Whig men valued these types of female endorsement of their political activities. At a Pennsylvania rally, General Samuel Alexander addressed a group of women who presented the Carlisle Clay Club with a banner. "Ladies, [sic] do not often take an active or public part in political affairs," he commented, but when they did become involved "in any great cause, their advice, and feelings and judgments are on the side of integrity, truth, public good and wide spread benevolence." To Alexander, the banner represented "the free testimonial of approval of our principles and candidates by those we esteem and love; and who, as a body, never do sustain an impure or a faithless cause." Liberty men, by contrast, did not attach much importance to women's activity in the 1844 campaign, a circumstance that the party's women appeared to accept.[21]

Women's increased involvement in presidential campaigns did not occur without criticism from across the country and within both political parties. One Tennessean called Whig women "boiling political partisan politicians," and a Virginia Democrat considered them "not capable of understanding the great political questions which now agitate the country." A Whig politician in the Volunteer State invoked Frances Wright's name in noting the "notorious associations" of the Democratic Party on the East Coast. Whigs often used the famous feminist and abolitionist's nickname "Fanny Wright" as shorthand for all kinds of perceived societal ills associated with her, including atheism, racial equality, and sexual promiscuity, but they were not the only ones to reference her. An Ohio Democrat described a Whig rally at which "some dozen amazons, who have made some practical improvements in the doctrines of Fanny Wright," waved banners from a second-story window; one even gave a speech. "But to avoid any mistake, gentle reader," the correspondent wrote, "I assure you none of them had breeches on that I could see."[22]

Women found ways to assert their agency in presidential politics more frequently, but it was still primarily a man's world. That was especially true when it came to stump speaking, a form of electioneering that was beginning to mature during the 1840s. Clay and Polk abstained from speaking at public events themselves once they had been nominated, but both parties had plenty of surrogates willing to take their message to the people. Former US representative Seargent S. Prentiss was one of the most notable Whig stump speakers. The stocky, cavernous-chested Mississippian had stumped extensively for the Whig cause in 1840, and he did the same four years later, making a two-month trek from Alabama to Maine extolling the virtues of his party before taking his speaking tour to Tennessee, then Mississippi. At Natchez, the "Vicksburg Kangaroo" gave a scathing three-hour speech, in which he was described as "foaming at the mouth, convulsed in every limb, flushed almost to apoplexy, and, at times, quite black in the face, looking more like a demon than a man." When discussing Polk, Prentiss reportedly "*looked* like a savage in the act of butchering his victim." His efforts were so severe that he collapsed in Natchez and, a short time later, had a similar health episode in Rodney, Mississippi. Prentiss denied that his speeches had been as severe as reported by the Democratic press and asserted that his motivation for campaigning came "entirely from a conviction of duty," but he acknowledged that he harbored "feelings of the utmost disgust, contempt, and abhorrence" for his political opponents. For him, and for many other Whigs and Democrats, this election was not just about rational policy differences—it was personal and emotional and required using every means necessary to defeat the enemy.[23]

Democrats were not as vicious as Prentiss, but they took to the stump too. Samuel H. Laughlin and Leonard P. Cheatham were popular choices among Polk's Tennessee friends. Philadelphian John K. Kane and Bostonian George Bancroft were two of the most active and effective northern orators, and one New Yorker described Gansevoort Melville, older brother of *Moby Dick* author Herman Melville, as "one of the ablest Stump Orators we have in the Northern States. . . . His voice is so powerful that he can easily be heard by thousands." Democrats were so attuned to the power of these events that they made sure to include foreign-language speakers at political rallies to appeal to immigrants from other (mostly European) nations.[24]

Stump speakers often attended events organized by auxiliary organizations, which represented another key outlet for electioneering. The activities of these social groups usually centered on food and alcohol, with political discussion the excuse for indulging in both. From the committees of correspondence of the American Revolution to the Old Kinderhook and Old Tippecanoe Clubs of the 1840 election, auxiliary organizations had kept voters loyal and engaged between elections and energized them when it came time to support candidates at the polls. They proved especially important in attracting young men who were casting their first ballots, as this "virgin vote" often bound them to a party for life.[25]

To support their candidate during the 1844 campaign, Whigs reopened old Clay Clubs and formed new ones. Even before the Kentuckian was officially nominated, clubs named for him were "running over the State 'like wild-fire'" in South Carolina and other states. According to one newspaper description, Clay Clubs provided a venue for "the diffusion of correct information, by means of lectures and publications, the thorough organization of the party, and the concentration of effort upon the right points, and in the right way." These clubs concerned Democrats, who acknowledged that their existence prior to the Whig national convention provided their opponents with an organizational advantage throughout the campaign. Democrats did not simply cede this ground to Whigs, however. Much like the Hickory Clubs that had formed as part of Jackson's presidential campaigns, once Polk was nominated, Young Hickory Clubs popped up nationwide as places for Democrats to meet, socialize, and promote their ticket. "YOUNG HICKORY CLUBS are the institutions for ORGANIZATION, for VIGILANCE, and for PROCURING ammunition!" a Nashville newspaper proclaimed. The one established in Van Buren's native Columbia County hoped to "inspire the Democracy of the District with an increased determination to engage vigorously in the approaching contest."[26]

The actions of one auxiliary organization, the Democratic Empire Club in New York City, may have done Polk more harm than good. Its members participated in the usual pomp and circumstance, such as "erecting a tall Hickory," displaying Polk banners, and forming a brass band. They also engaged in poll watching to ensure that ineligible voters did not participate in the election. But the club also allegedly perpetrated violence and intimidation. In one minor encounter, some Empire Club members "threw lumps of *clay*" at Whigs in a large parade. In another confrontation, they reportedly used "clubs, bowie-knives, 'slang-shot'" and other dangerous weapons against a Whig procession, resulting in significant injuries. Not surprisingly, Whigs denounced the Empire Club as "a body of murderers and thieves" and accused the Democratic Party of planning to use it to intimidate voters through violence. Even staunch New York Democrat Gansevoort Melville criticized the club as "one of those fighting and bullying political clubs which disgrace our city politics," led by "men of reputed and believed suspicious and *criminal* character." Other Democrats chalked up opposition to the Empire Club as purely Whig overreaction to club members "sitting in their own club room singing Polk and Dallas songs," while occasionally "throw[ing] a stone, or pok[ing] a stick at some prancing horse."[27]

Not all auxiliary organizations engaged in or endorsed violence, but one Connecticut correspondent's general assessment of these groups probably resonated with some people during the 1844 campaign. "These workshops of despotism" were "dangerous to the liberties of a people," they argued. "A people who suffer themselves to be ruled by Political Clubs will find themselves insensibly enslaved to the will of a domination more inexorable than the rule of a single tyrant."[28]

As the summer heated up with stumping and organizational meetings, the campaign also became more impassioned. A group of South Carolina radicals was upset at what its members perceived as an antisouthern conspiracy among the presidential campaigns and began organizing with sympathetic allies immediately after the Baltimore convention. Ironically, they were not led by Calhoun, who might have had just cause to be embittered at losing the nomination to Polk. Instead, US representative Robert Barnwell Rhett headed up the malcontents. He and his coterie held the Whigs in contempt, believing abolitionists controlled both their party and their presidential candidate. Tyler and the 1842 tariff bill that he had signed also drew their wrath. But Democrats were not immune from suspicion either. Rhett argued that northern Democratic support of the tariff and opposition to Texas annexation were part of a plot to trample on southern rights. Even Calhoun was deemed complicit, suspected of having abandoned his defense of southern principles for the power and prestige of a high-ranking cabinet position. Ignoring Calhoun's advice to act pragmatically so as not to jeopardize Texas's annexation, Rhett outlined several solutions to this alleged conspiracy at a July 31 dinner in Bluffton, South Carolina. He proposed a southern convention in Nashville and the nullification of the tariff before pronouncing that the South faced so dire a situation that secession might be the only remedy. Depending on Polk to protect southern interests, especially in relation to the tariff, was "the embodyment [sic] of the vanity of hope."[29]

Dallas warned his running mate to be careful not to let the South Carolinians divert him from the ultimate objective. A united party that avoided internal strife would allow Polk to "achieve an exploit worthy of immortal fame and universal gratitude" over "the alarming strides of abolition and her kindred bigotry." "But if they distract your councils and enfeeble your measures," Dallas cautioned, "I cannot see whence you are to draw force enough to beat back the amalgamated and fierce onset that is threatened."[30]

Polk, who was intimately involved in many aspects of the campaign, understood that it was crucial to tamp down rancor over the sectional convention that Rhett and other South Carolinians were contemplating. To that end, he worked with his advisors to put together a mass meeting in Nashville. Polk told prominent Tennessee Democrats to write newspaper articles expressing support for the mass Democratic meeting and opposition to an exclusively southern convention. Originally scheduled for July, the mass meeting was postponed until August in order to allow northern Democrats to attend. Jackson and others were asked to write personal invitations to prominent northern and western Democrats, urging them to make their way to Nashville to show their support for Polk and the party.[31]

The August meeting, billed as "THE GREATEST POPULAR COUNCIL EVER HELD IN THIS COUNTRY," was one of the most significant campaign events the Democratic Party organized in 1844. The central committee produced an address that emphasized Democratic unity in support of the Polk–Dallas ticket and espoused Texas annexation as a national concern "necessary to strengthen the Union, and secure us peace, harmony and increased prosperity." The address made sure to emphasize that the proposed meeting was not "in any sense, a sectional Convention, but a NATIONAL FESTIVAL." The committee invited Democratic leaders across the nation to join them in Nashville. Several party leaders and former convention rivals were unable to make the journey and sent their public regrets and well wishes. In a private letter explaining his absence, James Buchanan warned that Democrats needed "to avoid . . . every appearance of the slightest tending towards nullification or disunion." He also cautioned that in order to put Pennsylvania in the Democratic column, "the more you say against the Bank & distribution & in favor of Texas; so much the better." Van Buren's reply declining his invitation was expectedly long-winded. He barely mentioned Polk and Dallas, focusing instead on the party's history and its principles and emphasizing Democratic unity. He specifically addressed Texas annexation as one of the issues on which Democrats needed to set aside their disagreements as "honest differences of opinion." Calhoun sent his trusted cousin and fellow South Carolinian Francis Pickens as his proxy. Unavoidably delayed, Pickens missed the meeting, but he went to Columbia, Tennessee, to meet with Polk afterward and received assurances about issues important to South Carolina, including replacing Blair at the *Globe*, annexing Texas, and supporting tariff reform. Pickens left Tennessee satisfied that Polk was a reliable southerner, a confidence that Calhoun shared when he received a report of the meeting.[32]

As Democrats gathered in Nashville in mid-August, they experienced a carefully orchestrated extravaganza. The detailed order of procession and planned festivities were published in the local Democratic newspaper and included details on which street each volunteer militia company would take and the order in which each state delegation would march. On Wednesday, August 14, Nashville was described as "a *Military Camp*," with the hotels full and tents pitched to contain those unable to find conventional lodging. As crowds lined the streets and gathered on balconies, Democrats paraded through the city, eventually reaching Camp Hickory, located "in the immediate vicinity of this city, in a large umbrageous grove, including fifty or sixty acres of beautifully enclosed land." That night, former Whig representative Thomas F. Marshall, nephew of the late Supreme Court chief justice John Marshall, gave a candlelight speech on Texas annexation, the topic over which he had parted ways with the Whigs.[33]

The meeting opened the following morning, with the official procession snaking through the city. As an estimated 50,000 attendees packed Camp Hickory and ate dinner at "two miles of table," they heard multiple Democratic speakers laud the party's ticket and deny that they were participating in "*disunion* against the democracy." One of the speakers was Lewis Cass, whose speech was lauded as "one of unsurpassed eloquence." On Friday, the list of speakers continued. Stephen A. Douglas of Illinois, a rising star in the party who would win the northern Democratic presidential nomination sixteen years later, was one of the highlights, "scattering the arguments of the opponents of immediate annexation to the winds." Kentucky congressman Linn Boyd was unable to take the platform because of a carriage accident involving his family, but Donelson made sure to remind the crowd that Boyd had "proved" the "corrupt bargain" between Clay and Adams that had stolen the presidential election from Jackson in 1825. Speeches continued until Saturday evening. The *Nashville Union* noted that despite the large crowd, "not a single incident of quarrelling, rioting, or disorder of any sort occurred"—a testament to Democratic unity as the campaign heated up.[34]

The mass meeting produced a set of resolutions endorsing the Polk–Dallas ticket, emphasizing sectional unity, welcoming back disaffected Democrats who had voted for Harrison in 1840, and criticizing Clay for "his dictatorial spirit" and willingness "to destroy the checks and balances of the Constitution." They also denounced Britain's alleged conspiracy to control both Oregon, which necessitated "the speedy occupation" of that territory by Americans, and Texas, which made the Lone Star Republic's "re-annexation" to the United States imperative. None of the resolutions were surprising, but given the rancor and division that had permeated their Baltimore convention, Democrats needed a show of partisan unity and purpose. The Nashville meeting gave them exactly that.[35]

Just days after Democrats wrapped up their mass meeting in Nashville, Whigs prepared to hold their own in the same city. Much like their opponents, Nashville Whigs went all out as they prepared to welcome loyal party members from across the nation to their city. They raised a 200-foot-high liberty pole, a political symbol dating from the American Revolution. Local

Whigs were asked to contribute "TWO or more cooked hams or shoulders" and the enslaved laborers needed to serve them. "Ladies are expected to dress in white with sky blue sashes," a local newspaper reminded Whig women, who were scheduled to ride in carriages and carry party banners. The sounds of the drum, fife, and bugle let Nashvillians know that the Whigs were on the move through the city. Auxiliary organizations who marched through Nashville's streets included companies of men in military uniform, such as the Harrison Guards and the Cedar Snags, and others less regal but just as committed, such as the pro-tariff Ore Diggers from West Tennessee. By the time all the Whigs has assembled at Camp Harrison, the outdoor meeting place named for their former president, they were a reported 50,000 to 75,000 strong. "The people are here, truly *en masse*— the hearty voters, the hard-fisted bone and sinew, the genuine hardy yeomanry of the republic," according to one sympathetic observer. The Whig meeting included speeches by several prominent party leaders, including convention president and former Jackson confidant John Bell, Tennessee governor "Lean Jimmy" Jones, the infamous duelist William J. Graves, and the long-haired "Arkansas giant" Albert Pike. Also present was the indefatigable Seargent Prentiss. On one occasion, while speaking in front of the courthouse, Prentiss suffered a "stricture of the chest"; being "exposed to a broiling sun" that produced a daytime temperature of ninety-four degrees during his earlier speech probably contributed to his distress. After a few minutes of rest, the Mississippian recovered and finished his oration.[36]

In addition to holding their Nashville meeting, Whigs organized other large rallies. An estimated 15,000 party members attended a meeting at Madison, Georgia, in late July. This rally, and every other Whig event, was overshadowed by the one held at Bunker Hill in Boston, where a reported 100,000 attended. The Whigs employed stump speakers such as Illinois lawyer Abraham Lincoln and former congressman Ebenezer J. Shields of Memphis, who gained notoriety for traveling throughout New York informing Whigs about Polk's slaveholding. Democrats deemed him "a consummate jackass" for his efforts. Sometimes these Whig events threatened to turn violent. In Murfreesboro, Tennessee, William Graves spoke at a party rally. Several times, Democrat David M. Currin attempted to interrupt his three-and-a-half-hour speech. When the Kentuckian finally ceded the floor, Currin taunted him, calling Graves a bully and telling him that he was ready to defeat him with words "or any weapons you may like better." Graves's friends rushed to find weapons for him but, as the eyewitness recounted, this time "he left no slain" as cooler heads prevailed.[37]

As it had been for the past several presidential contests, material culture—objects that symbolized one's commitment to a party or candidate—was pervasive at these public events and elsewhere, helping energize existing voters and attract future ones. Using material culture to evoke the victorious "Log Cabin and Hard Cider" campaign was common among Whigs in 1844. For their August meeting in Nashville, they constructed two log cabins on a hill outside the state capitol. The "big balls" that Jackson had criticized in the 1840 campaign also made an appearance. In an East Tennessee meeting that averaged 8,000 in attendance over three days, Whigs rolled a "GREAT BALL" beside the platform where speakers were stumping for Clay and Frelinghuysen. "The ball was guarded by hundreds of men upon foot," one newspaper reported, "ready to defend it from an attack . . . [by] their overheated adversaries." Whigs also continued to display live coons "in cages and on poles" as their official party mascot. The ubiquitous poles that had been used as political statements for decades were also a common sight. One traveling Arkansan described frequently seeing "Ash poles, with Clay flags" containing the inscription "Clay, Frelinghuysen, and the United States."[38]

Whig campaign paraphernalia did not just remind voters of the party's prior success and make general statements of support for their ticket. It also conveyed subtle, yet powerful, political messages. One Whig campaign banner showed the hand of Providence holding a scale tilted in favor of a bowl containing "Clay & Our Country." In the other bowl was "Polk & Texas." Across the top was written "Mene, mene, tekel, parsin." Those familiar with the Bible would have recognized the reference to the Old Testament story of King Belshazzar and the mysterious handwriting that appeared to him on the palace wall. The Hebrew prophet Daniel's interpretation to Belshazzar was that "God hath numbered thy kingdom, and finished it. . . . Thou art weighed in the balances, and art found wanting." The implication was that the views of Polk and the Democrats had been compared to those of Clay and the Whigs and had proven unsatisfactory.[39]

Not to be outdone by their opponents, Democrats also utilized material culture to support their ticket. In Nashville, Polk-supporting members of a militia company displayed transparencies, or "boxed display signs illuminated from within." Samuel H. Laughlin reported seeing "long poles, true young hickory trees . . . planted, with green tops, and surmounted by green poke stalks of large size" in Elkton, Maryland, and Brownsville, Pennsylvania. A month before their meeting in the state's capital, Nashville Democrats raised "a Hickory Pole 184 feet." Flags with "Polk, Dallas, and Texas" inscribed on them were also a common sight. At Fort Lee in New Jersey, Democrats saw symbolism in "a proud and stately Eagle perched" on top of a recently erected hickory pole. The majestic bird's frequent returns were hailed as its attempt "to have a smell of pure democratic air."[40]

Both parties enjoyed mocking their opponents' material culture. Drawing special Democratic ire was the Whigs' prodigious use of the coon. The sight of "the childish, silly, ridiculous display of coon tails sticking in the hats of the mass" at a Whig "Coon Festival" in Columbia, where Polk lived, was "disgusting," one Democrat fumed. "They have completely adopted the *coon* as their *idol* and their *God*." On his way back from a meeting at Rochester, New York, Cassius M. Clay passed through Wheeling, Virginia. As he made his way down the mountain into town, he saw "a newly-erected hickory-pole, with leaves still green on the top. From a limb was suspended a skinned coon; and then we knew the Whigs, nicknamed 'Coons,' were lost!" Whigs, meanwhile, pointed out the hypocrisy of Democratic ridicule of their material culture. At a Centreville, Indiana, meeting, Democrats displayed a banner with Polk and Dallas riding "two red Roosters," another with "a charicature [sic]" of Clay "shooting some one," and "several others equally ridiculous." "Yet they denounce the banners of their political opponents as 'vile mummery,'" one Whig newspaper reflected sarcastically. Another Whig paper pointed out that at the Democratic mass meeting in Nashville, Cass dispensed "some very grave advice against the use of songs, banners, the coon, and other Whig appliances," which prompted applause from a Democrat audience ironically "assembled under banners, and some few polk stalks."[41]

Although retired and in poor health, Andrew Jackson loomed large as a campaign symbol. "We thank the coons for their unintended kindness" in giving Polk the name "Young Hickory," one Democratic newspaper remarked, because it reminded voters of all of Jackson's positive contributions to the nation. (This origin story conveniently omitted that Democrats had assigned Polk the nickname in the 1840 campaign.) Polk supporters used "Young Hickory" extensively in 1844 to ensure that voters could not forget his connection to the party's elder statesman. A resolution by a mass meeting of New York Democrats, for example, stated that the "old hickory tree . . . cannot live forever," so a "tall and noble sapling," a "young Hickory," was needed and would "be transplanted by the People to the People's House at Washington." Whigs, meanwhile, found Jackson a convenient symbol by which to attack Polk. A Whig transparency that depicted Clay standing on Polk with one foot and "stamping Jackson in the dust" with his

Democratic "hunter" James K. Polk trees the Whig "coons" Henry Clay and Theodore Frelinghuysen. (Courtesy of the Library of Congress)

other foot left one Democrat "indignant" at the disrespect shown the former president and the current nominee. Whigs also utilized the "humbug cognomen" of "Young Hickory" to ridicule their opponents. "Old Hickory is full of courage, and the sapling Hickory is full of cowardice," the *Louisville Daily Journal* said. "To call Polk 'Young Hickory' is the most absurd of all designations. He is no more like Jackson than a lank, long-legged, filthy fly-up-the-creek is like a South American condor."[42]

The advancements in lithography had allowed visual culture to play an increasingly larger role in presidential elections since 1836, a change that was apparent in 1844. Before the national nominating conventions in May, political cartoons and illustrations focused on the expected contest between Clay and Van Buren. Once Polk was nominated, attention turned to contrasting him visually with the Kentuckian. Common motifs included depicting the candidates and their supporters as animals. The Clay-as-a-coon motif was popular with both Whigs and Democrats. The Whig newspaper *That Same Old Coon* frequently displayed an illustrated raccoon on its borders as an inspirational symbol for Whigs, and the Democratic newspaper *Coon Dissector* lined its borders with raccoons in nooses. Another newspa-

Texas annexation provided a clear contrast between James K. Polk and Henry Clay. Here Polk welcomes Texas (depicted as a young woman) as a sister, while Clay says, "Stand back, Madam Texas!" (Courtesy of the Library of Congress)

per illustration showed a rooster crowing at a raccoon slinking away, "You're a gone coon." In "Treeing Coons," Clay and Frelinghuysen appeared as raccoons who had climbed a hickory tree to escape the buckskin-clad Polk, while various anti-Clay politicians, including Calhoun and John Tyler's son Robert, exclaimed, "Down with the Coons."[43]

The number of political cartoons that placed Polk and the Democrats in a positive light were few and far between. Those that appeared in print primarily emphasized Texas annexation as the issue that would catapult Polk to victory. "Virtuous Harry, or Set a Thief to Catch a Thief!" contrasted Polk's and Dallas's gallant courting of "Madam Texas" with Clay's self-righteous pronouncement, "Do you think we will have anything to do with gamblers, horse-racers, and licentious profligates?" A Quaker stood to Clay's side, telling him, "Softly, Softly, friend Harry. Thou hast mentioned the very reason that we cannot Vote for thee!" Another lithograph, "The Masked Battery or Loco-Foco Strategy," credited Jackson with crafting a winning campaign strategy for his party's ticket. It showed Polk and Walker firing a cannon from behind the cover of the armor-clad Calhoun, Tyler, Richard M. Johnson, and Van Buren, striking Clay and other Whigs with a "Texas" cannon-

Texas drew significant attention during the campaign season, and it overpowered discussion of the Bank, which had been a prominent issue since 1832. (Courtesy of the Library of Congress)

ball. Jackson's "General Orders" appeared at the top of the print, encouraging "the veteran candidates" to help hide "the big Gun charged with Texas" until the right moment to fire on their political enemies. Another print emphasized one of the Democrats' main lines of attack. It depicted Satan encouraging Clay to use Frelinghuysen as a shield against accusations of gambling, swearing, and dueling. One of the most optimistic Democratic prints showed a funeral procession for a coon in the foreground, while in the background Democrats surrounded an elevated platform to help Polk celebrate his victory. Balloons with the different states' names dotted the sky, and Jackson appeared headed for a cemetery, saying, "My country is saved! I am now ready for my last resting place."[44]

As in 1840, however, most published campaign images were pro-Whig. Polk was frequently depicted as being under the influence of Jackson. "Balloon Ascension to the Presidential Chair," for example, showed the former president using his cane to help Polk's hot air balloon get off the ground in a race with Clay's. Jackson's commentary played on his protégé's name: "I'll use my best endeavours to 'poke' it up. But it's harder work than gaining the battle of New Orleans!" A companion piece, "Bursting the Balloon," employed the familiar theme of "Salt River," which was a contemporary

THE HUNTER OF KENTUCKY.

Whigs tapped into the western mythology of the time by portraying Henry Clay as a frontiersman hunting his campaign competitors. (Courtesy of the Library of Congress)

symbol for political failure. It showed Clay popping Polk's balloon, causing him and Dallas to fall into the river, where Jackson and Van Buren were already floundering. Whig political cartoons addressed not just long-standing political issues but also specific criticisms. Clay himself was portrayed positively in many lights, none more dramatically than in an 1843 print in which he appeared as the rising sun chasing away the evil spirits of the Democratic Party. Another cartoon depicted him as a Kentucky hunter who had captured a rattlesnake (Tyler), a fox (Van Buren), and a goose (Polk).[45]

Political music remained an important part of presidential campaigning in 1844. It served several purposes, depending on who was using it. Political music could reinforce the ruling power of the elite but also unify the nation during a divisive time. In 1844, the parties used it to encapsulate campaign themes and energize voters to turn out for a specific candidate. Whigs held the prior advantage over their opponents and now produced dozens of songs, often compiled in songbooks called "songsters" or "minstrels," in support of Clay and Frelinghuysen. Even before Clay received the nomination, his party was issuing songs backing him as their standard-bearer against a confused, hapless Democracy. Once the party's nominations were made, another Whig song warned Democrats to "Get out of the way, the country's rising / For Harry Clay and Frelinghuysen." Whig music did not simply ask for unquestioned loyalty. One ballad, entitled "A Song for the Man," extolled Clay for ten verses, covering the highlights of his political career and refuting in stanza form some of the scandals associated with him. "Now Let Us Try Harry!" urged Whigs to vote for Clay, "who was always true," unlike Tyler, who was "a Traitor to you." Many Whig songs referenced Van Buren, Jackson, and other Democrats, but the two names atop the Democratic ticket were the most important musical targets. "Oh! Polk and Dallas are men of doubt / They cant poke in and must stay out / And in November they will find / Their party poking far behind," went one song that was set to the well-known tune of "Old Dan Tucker." "Jimmy Polk of Tennessee" referenced Dallas's previous work for the Second Bank of the United States when it pointed out that he "went the Bank and Biddle" before becoming "second fiddle" to Polk. "Now 'choke' and Polk will always rhyme," the lyrics continued, "And Dallas and gallows is very sublime."[46]

Democrats frequently commented on the constant singing of "Clay and coon songs," "ridiculous songs," and "vulgar songs" and made clear that their campaign would emphasize "rational enthusiasm" and not the "frothy excitement produced by song singing & clamorous addresses to the cupidity and the worst passions of men." Democrats did not produce as many campaign songs as their opponents, but they nevertheless found it prudent to embrace music as means to gin up support for their ticket. They often did so with enthusiasm when it came to mass meetings. "Have 300 volunteers, a fine Band of Music, and in Mass Prominade [sic] the Streets," Robert Armstrong reported from Nashville in late June. A week later, he announced that he was "arranging to send 200 Texan volunteers Equipt & the Company of Hickory Dragoons with the Bands of musicians, and all the Transparencies" to Columbia for another campaign rally. Democrats crowed about their efforts to "out Herod Herod" and "fight the Devil with fire" when it came to music: "Nothing plagues the coons more than to turn their songs against them."[47]

And turn they did. In "New Yankee Doodle," Democrats sang, "Their coons are dead, their cabins down, / Hard Cider grown quite stale, sirs." The theme of Whig death was not uncommon. "The Dying Coon" described Clay's response to his pending political doom: "I feel the sharp knife o'er my furry hide going, / I feel its sharp point in my very heart's core." Another anti-Whig song mocked Clay's lust for the presidency. The lyrics had the Kentuckian admitting, "I do not want to stay at home; you know I've long been bent / On sitting in the Chair of State, as your great

President," to which "THE PEOPLE" responded, "You shall never enter in the White House as your home." One of the harshest songs invoked biblical allusions against Clay, whom the lyrics described as "Lucifer" before he was thrown out of heaven to become "Old Harry." Like their opponents, Democrats also made sure to support the men heading their ticket. "The True-Hearted Statesman" recounted Polk's time as Speaker of the House. When Whigs "sought to repulse him with insults and lies," the lyrics bragged, "he showed their corruption, their measures he foiled." In "The Farmer of Ashland," Whigs lamented, "We've been licked by old Dallas, and poisoned by Polk," while "Democratic Ticket" observed that "when we did choose George M. Dallas / The Coons they all cried out *alas!*" Democratic music also spoke to the campaign issues. "A Song of the Hickories" declared about Texas, "Young Hickory shall shelter her / In spite of Harry Clay." Another pro-annexation song proclaimed that Democrats would give up the Union "before we'd give up our Texas and Polk." "Texas we'll have by the gods, right or wrong" was its concluding lyric.[48]

The onslaught of objects and images and the cacophony of music frequently focused on personalities and high-visibility issues, such as Texas annexation, but other issues took on importance as the campaign progressed through the summer and into the fall. The place of immigrants in US society was one such concern. Between 1841 and 1844, more than 300,000 foreigners came to the United States, with more than 104,000 entering in 1842 alone. The annual average of nearly 79,000 immigrants was comparable to the rate witnessed during Van Buren's administration. While the number of immigrants arriving in the United States remained relatively stable, the nativist movement had grown since Van Buren's administration, particularly in New York and Pennsylvania. In New York, Whig governor William H. Seward had inadvertently stoked nativist fires by supporting the idea of parochial schools as an educational option in New York City. Catholic bishop John Hughes endorsed the proposal, as did many Democrats, whose political majority in the city came from foreign-born Catholics; most Whigs opposed the idea. The pairing of Catholicism with education led to the creation of the American Republican Party (known colloquially as "Native Americans" or the "Native American Party") in 1843. This party opposed parochial education, wanted longer residency requirements before naturalization, and supported a policy of American-only officeholders. The American Republicans drew 23 percent of the vote in the fall 1843 elections, and their candidate became New York City mayor, with Whig assistance, in April 1844, just before the national nominating conventions.[49]

RIOT IN PHILADELPHIA
JUNE 7. 1844.

Immigration had been growing as a political issue, and the violent clashes in Philadelphia in the summer of 1844 ensured that the presidential nominees would have to address it as part of their campaign strategies. (Courtesy of the Library of Congress)

An outbreak of nativist violence in Philadelphia in the summer of 1844 ensured that immigration remained at the forefront of voters' minds in the Northeast. Just like in New York City, an attempt to provide a more Catholic-friendly educational environment—in this case, allowing the use of a Catholic Bible in public schools—led to controversy in the city. The American Republican Party paired the economic resentments of unskilled working-class men with fears about sociocultural threats posed by immigrants to win the spring 1844 elections in the City of Brotherly Love. Attempts to expand the party's reach into immigrant communities led to violence in May, with six deaths and property damage, including the burning of two Catholic churches, estimated at $250,000. One observer relayed the common belief among Philadelphians that "a large number of desperate men have vowed that every Catholic church in the country shall be burnt & every Catholic expelled from it." Another violent clash in July, this time because of rumors that Irish Catholics were stockpiling weapons, led Whig city leaders sympathetic to the nativist cause to use militia troops to confront the perceived threat. By the time this second conflict ended, at least a dozen people were dead, and several dozen more were wounded.[50]

Immigration was not just a concern on the East Coast. In Ohio, it was the primary issue, according to some of Polk's correspondents. An estimated 20,000 German American voters wanted to know what the presidential candidates thought about naturalization laws before casting their votes. A group of Dayton, Ohio, citizens cited the nativist violence in the East as the reason for an interrogatory they sent the Liberty Party candidates. Correspondents suggested to Polk that his views on immigration would prove important in Indiana, Illinois, Louisiana, and Missouri. His allies also believed that it was critical for them to reach out to German and Dutch communities in his home state.[51]

These questions about the place of immigrants in society begged for a response from the presidential candidates. Birney's campaign was forced to confront nativism more directly than his opponents when Clay newspapers questioned why Birney's son Dion was enrolled at St. Xavier's College in Cincinnati. Was a Catholic institution "the most appropriate and desirable literary institutiun [sic] in these United States for the education of his son?" As one newspaper observed, the Clay campaign was insinuating that James G. Birney "was courting the Romanists." Birney's oldest son, James Jr., explained that Dion had moved to Cincinnati to live with their brother William, who enrolled him in St. Xavier's in part to protect him from "the temptations and allurements of a large city." William "did so on his own responsibility, without consulting his father or any other member of the family." William and Dion also wrote a short public letter denying their father's involvement in the decision. "The wording of this denial is quite ingenious," one newspaper noted. "While it fully exonerates the father, it leaves the impression that the young men themselves could, without much labor, become proficients [sic] to Jesuitry [sic]." Unmentioned in the Birney sons' public letters was an important detail: Dion had left home under acrimonious circumstances and was estranged from his father. Birney could have used this omission to further refute the accusation that he was pro-Catholic, but he chose instead to protect his family's privacy.[52]

Even before the kerfuffle over Dion's schooling became a campaign topic, Birney had made an explicit public statement about his views on immigrants. Earlier that spring, a group of Dayton, Ohio, citizens had sent him an interrogatory asking two questions: Did he support naturalized citizens' "enjoying the rights and privileges secured to them by the present naturalization laws," and did he uphold the right of freedom of religion for everyone, including Catholics? In answer to the first question, Birney gave an emphatic "yes." "Shall we confer rights on others to-day, and tomorrow say, they shall not use them?" he asked rhetorically. "This would be deceitful—base." As for the second question, he pointed out that the guarantee of religious freedom already existed. Birney believed that the government "*ought* to be conducted in strict accordance with the principles of Christianity," but Americans were free to worship as they saw fit "so long as their religious forms encroach not on the rights of others, . . . or on those rules of public morality, decency and good order universally received as binding by all civilized communities." He made sure to link the issue of nativism to slavery by noting that he could not dismiss immigrants' fears about their rights as long as the "slave power" and its northern "minions" controlled the government.[53]

Unlike Birney, both Clay and Polk largely tried to avoid disclosing their opinions about immigration. Clay recognized the Whigs' difficulty in attracting immigrants, especially those who were Irish and Catholic. Publicly he cited the United States as a beacon of liberty for immigrants, but he also emphasized the need for law and order when it came to voting. Privately, Clay expressed stronger nativist views. He had no issue treating immigrants who were already US citizens and those residing in the United States awaiting citizenship under existing laws fairly and equitably; however, he thought that stringent naturalization laws should be imposed on those who had not yet made it to the United States. Throughout the campaign, Clay sought counsel from friends all over the nation about whether to speak out on the issue. Former Treasury secretary Thomas Ewing, whose foster son and future general William Tecumseh Sherman came out as a Whig supporter during this election, told Clay that discussing a change to the naturalization laws would be used to tie him "to the savage & intolerant spirit" that spawned the Philadelphia violence, an assessment with which other advisors agreed. Some Whigs, however, believed remaining silent posed a risk for their chances. One Pittsburgher claimed that his service on a local committee of naturalization revealed that newly arrived immigrants were becoming citizens within three months, which would make it difficult for the Whig Party to do well at the polls. Clay followed the counsel that most advisors gave him by remaining silent and letting his career speak for him. "Every pulsation of my heart is American and nothing but American. I am utterly opposed to all foreign influence in every form and shape," he told one correspondent. At the same time, Clay wanted the United States "to remain a sacred asylum for all unfortunate and oppressed men whether from religious or political causes."[54]

As the summer progressed, some of Polk's correspondents warned him to take a wait-and-see approach to the immigration issue, but others deemed it "a good subject" capable of gaining him votes. A New Yorker told him that John Tyler was using immigration as a last-ditch effort to form a winning coalition before deciding whether he should drop out of the race. Whichever way Polk approached the issue posed a risk. Dallas, who advised silence, nevertheless told his running mate that one Catholic leader had informed him that there were 5,000 church members in his Philadelphia district waiting to be convinced to vote for one of the presidential candidates. Other correspondents recommended taking a pragmatic course to ensure that Democrats were able to "get all the votes we can, without any abandonment of our principles."[55]

Polk decided to refer those who asked questions about naturalization laws to his party's platform, which included a resolution opposing attempts to alter existing pathways to citizenship. His correspondents, especially Dallas, kept him updated on the progress of the issue in the mid-Atlantic states. Polk remained concerned about how the nativist parties were faring in local and state elections. Sometimes he was convinced that their alliance to ensure the Democrats' defeat was a local one and not something that would work effectively in the presidential election. At other times, Polk thought that his allies were underestimating the danger that the nativists posed to his success. Still, he did not wade into the debate with an official statement. Democrats made sure, however, to point out that Frelinghuysen's involvement with Protestant proselytizing organizations smelled suspiciously like a nativist conspiracy against the newly enfranchised immigrants who supported Polk.[56]

Concern about society's corruption, particularly politicians who placed self-interest above the good of community, constituted another issue. Tyler's conduct as president—ignoring his own party and picking fights with Congress—understandably enhanced this anxiety. Given this context, one anti-Polk argument that Whigs chose was the Democrat's alleged connection to "the system of public stealing" undertaken by Jackson and Van Buren. A Polk administration, they argued, would simply be a continuation of that "dark and iniquitious [sic] history of Locofocoism." Clay was the only candidate who could save the nation from the "internal corruption and decay" that infected all great civilizations; Polk would only accelerate the United States' collapse.[57]

Added to these denunciations about political corruption was a charge that combined the political and the personal. The growing antislavery movement provided Whigs the opportunity to make Polk's enslavement

CLEANSING THE AUGEAN STABLE.

In looking to Henry Clay to clean out the Democrats' corruption, Whigs
employed a familiar trope used during Andrew Jackson's presidency. (Courtesy
of the Library of Congress)

of African Americans a campaign issue. He owned nearly forty enslaved
African Americans in 1844, with most of them laboring on his plantation
in Yalobusha County, Mississippi. Like many absentee enslavers, Polk relied on overseers and male relatives to run day-to-day operations, and, as
in many such arrangements, the enslaved people sometimes found themselves whipped or sold for not acquiescing to the enslaver's power. Many
southern voters would have understood, accepted, and even approved of
Polk's status as an enslaver, but to win the presidency, he had to appeal to
voters outside of the region, many of whom might be uncomfortable with
his ownership and treatment of enslaved people.[58]

Democrats tried to downplay the slavery issue for their candidate. New
Yorker Samuel Darling told Polk that local Democrats denied that he even
was an enslaver, while their opponents insisted that he was "one of the
most ardent Slave holders in [the] South." Darling advised Polk that many
Democrats and Whigs in the area "have gone over to the Abolition party."
Correspondents in other northern states, such as Maine, inquired directly
about whether Polk had previously, or currently, owned enslaved people.
Several Ohioans were concerned enough about this issue that they asked

Polk to respond to queries. An Akronite, for example, told Polk that Whigs there claimed that he held 300 and 400 African Americans in bondage and rented them out. He asked the Democratic candidate to confirm how many enslaved people he owned, assuring Polk that his Akron supporters were "not exactly opposed to Slavery." Unlike other northern correspondents, one Michigander challenged Polk to wear his enslaver status proudly. J. G. High told him that Whigs were spreading the rumor that Polk had freed the people he enslaved in order to court northern abolitionists. "We prefer you to continue to own them and use them as you had done," he wrote, "thereby showing the people, you did not seek any low groveling device to obtain votes."[59]

To answer these questions, Polk's supporters crafted a narrative of their candidate that acknowledged his enslaver status but provided disinformation about his support of the institution and mistreatment of the people he enslaved. A Democratic Nashville newspaper published the most comprehensive version of this false narrative. According to this editorial, the people Polk enslaved came from his and Sarah's parents. These enslaved people did not want to be emancipated or owned by anyone else; they wanted to remain under Polk's "constant guardianship and protection." This information, the writer asserted, came not from Polk but from "some of his older servants" and from neighbors. Further, the Democratic nominee "never has bought, or sold, or exchanged one slave for another, except at the entreaty of the slave," and only then to maintain family units. Polk's status as an enslaver was legal and constitutional, the editorial continued, and "he stands justified in the eyes of God and man." "IT IS AN HONOR TO HIM," the writer concluded.[60]

This defense of Polk appeared on the verge of collapsing as the summer drew to a close. In late August, a New York newspaper published an article that told of an encounter a German baron named Roorback reportedly had near Polk's home in Middle Tennessee. The account, submitted by a contributor going by the pseudonym "An Abolitionist," described a coffle of approximately 300 enslaved people headed to work on Louisiana sugar plantations, with "forty-three of these unfortunate beings" having Polk's initials branded on their shoulders as a mark of his former ownership of them. The story received little media attention until Thurlow Weed's *Albany Evening Journal* published it in mid-September. At that point, other Whig newspapers picked up the story, and it spread quickly to every region of the country. Polk's opponents gleefully used the story to attack him as unfit for the presidency. Were voters expected to "elevate to the Presidency

James K. Polk's tariff views were seen as an obstacle to winning over Pennsylvania voters, but so was his treatment of enslaved people, as described in the Roorback hoax. (Courtesy of the Division of Rare and Manuscript Collections, Cornell University Library)

a man who sells human beings—men, women and children—to be driven off with chains, WITH HIS NAME BRANDED INTO THEIR FLESH?" Weed asked. "Polk ought to be damned for this cruel deed to perpetual infamy," the *Richmond Whig* pronounced. Jackson and Van Buren were preferable to "this inhuman coward." The story even made it into a campaign cartoon: "James K. Polk Going through Pennsylvania for the Tariff" focused attention on the Democratic candidate's purported contradictory views on protective duties, but those examining the image closely could not have missed the presence of an enslaved African American man who had "JKP" branded on his arm.[61]

The problem for Whigs was that the Roorback story was not true. It was a cannibalized version of an account from George W. Featherstonhaugh's recently published memoir of traveling through the South. When it became clear that the story was false, Weed and other Whig editors were forced to retract the story, allowing Democrats to pillory their opponents. Democrats had proven the story a lie, Dallas told Polk, "and I think what was intended to injure you will yet be made the means of extensive benefit." "The *'Roorback' forgery & falsehood*, is the grossest & basest I have ever known,"

Polk pronounced. "It is in all its facts an infamous falsehood. I am glad the Democratic press, at the East, have been able so promptly to meet and expose it." It was an embarrassing moment for the Whigs, on an issue that they hoped would convince antislavery voters, and maybe even Liberty men, that supporting Clay was best way to avoid putting a violent enslaver in the White House.[62]

Some Americans were less interested in Polk's personal involvement with slavery and more concerned about learning his views on the intersection of slavery and national politics. A group of Massachusetts Democrats asked if he supported adding more slave states, if he believed Congress could legislate slavery in the District of Columbia, and if he thought citizens of a state could replace its proslavery government with one "more equal just & liberal." This discussion became more controversial in September when Robert J. Walker published, through the Democratic Association in Washington, a pamphlet entitled *The South in Danger*. It used scaremongering to argue that Whigs were infusing the political discourse with a "demoniac feeling" intended "to *taboo the South*," deride its character, and take away its enslaved property. After listing the prominent Whigs who were unjustly attacking the South, the pamphlet ended with a plea to southern Whigs to "pause and consider well all the dreadful consequences, before you sink us all together into one common abyss of ruin and degradation." Some Democrats accused their opponents of forging the document; Whigs responded that Walker's strategy had been to circulate the pamphlet in the South to sway voters and to claim it was a forgery if it made it into the hands of northern voters. Walker asserted in a public letter that he had focused on distributing the pamphlet in the southern states, but he would happily help Whigs put it in the hands of voters everywhere.[63]

This pamphlet did Polk no favors in the North. It proved especially detrimental in the Ohio gubernatorial race, where copies reportedly made their way to abolitionists and cost Democrats the state's electoral votes. This result lent credence to one New York Democrat's prediction that putting "annexation solely on the grounds of *extending* and *perpetuating Slavery*" would lead to a Whig landslide by "tens of thousands" in the presidential contest. William E. Cramer expressed frustration that Polk's chances depended on swaying voters in New York, Ohio, and Pennsylvania, not the South, yet Walker's actions threatened Democratic appeals in these northern states. "It is important fully to appreciate the difficulties under which we are thrown," he told Polk.[64]

Making things easier for Polk and the Democrats was the fact that Clay had to answer for his own alleged involvement in corruption and his dependence on enslaved labor. As he had for nearly two decades, the Kentuckian found it impossible to duck the "corrupt bargain" allegation. Once the Whigs nominated Clay, Democrats issued THE BARGAIN AND INTRIGUE between Clay and Adams, a sixteen-page pamphlet available for two dollars per one hundred copies. Nineteen years of facing this "stale and discredited" charge had made Clay prickly. His frustration was evident shortly after he received the Whig nomination, when he told a correspondent that he was thinking about "carrying the war into Africa," that is, turning the tables on the Democrats by accusing Jackson of attempting his own "corrupt bargain." This Whig conspiracy theory had Jacksonian supporters Buchanan and Sam Houston intriguing on behalf of Old Hickory. According to former Ohio congressman John Sloane, Houston had approached him about convincing his state's delegation to vote for Jackson in the 1825 House election that decided the presidency. If Sloane was successful, Houston allegedly implied, Clay could become secretary of state. Clay said that James Buchanan made a similar proposition to both him and Robert P. Letcher about Kentucky's vote. Ultimately, Letcher refused to cooperate with this campaign strategy, saying he could "perceive no earthly good" coming from it. Buchanan, meanwhile, declared himself "as innocent as a sucking dove of any improper intention."[65]

Clay's enslaver status allowed some to dismiss Polk's own complicity in the institution. By his own count, Clay owned approximately fifty enslaved people in 1842. One Democratic newspaper correspondent explained that "as a slaveholder, he [Polk] has been distinguished for his love of justice and his humanity." "As a master and a slaveholder," Clay, meanwhile, was recognized as "cruel and unjust." There was even a rumor that one of his former overseers would testify under oath that Clay, like Richard M. Johnson, had engaged in a relationship with an enslaved woman at Ashland. According to the story, when Clay's wife, Lucretia, reportedly discovered him "attending to the yellow Girl more [l]ovingly than suited her feelings," she forced her husband to sell the enslaved woman and all her children. "Much as has been said about Col. Johnsons Negro wife," observed the Democrat who was sharing this rumor, "he did not sell his Children as Mr Clay has done."[66]

Clay's identity as an enslaver provided him with credibility among southern voters, but like Polk, he needed to appeal to the increasingly antislavery North as well. This line proved difficult to walk. Facing an onslaught of criticism on the issue of slavery, Clay asked his cousin Cassius M. Clay—an abolitionist—to embark on a campaign in the North to solidify his support among those opposed to slavery. Cassius agreed to help. In July, he wrote a letter that found its way into the *New-York Daily Tribune*. It called on Whigs to reject tyranny and embrace "*Union, and Liberty.*" The letter also asked northern states to rally to Henry Clay and help him overcome the loss of electoral votes in the South. So far, so good. Then Cassius Clay made an egregious political error. In framing the election as a contest between "Slavery and Liberty," he wrote, "I do not mean to say that Mr. [Henry] Clay is an emancipationist—but I believe his feelings are with the cause." Cassius went on to add that "those most immediately within his [Henry Clay's] influence approximate to myself in sentiment upon the subject of Slavery." It was a damning statement about a candidate trying to appeal to those on opposite sides of the slavery issue. Understanding that the letter was problematic, Henry Clay repudiated his abolitionist cousin in early September. Democrats seized the opportunity to publish a "purloined" private letter between the two cousins in which the Whig nominee said he was at neither extreme on the issue. These letters did him no favors with southern Whigs.[67]

Staunch Liberty men understandably did not trust Clay on the slavery issue, and late in the campaign, Birney took advantage of the Kentuckian's awkward position to write an exposé of his slaveholding. Entitled "Headlands in the Life of Henry Clay," this projected series covered Clay's defense of slavery up to 1827. It demonstrated that the Whig Party was playing a "gross deception" on voters by portraying itself and its presidential candidate as antislavery, according to the editors of the newspaper in which the exposé appeared. One of these editors, Joshua Leavitt, encouraged Birney to finish the series, telling him, "I cannot, and have no other man to put to it." Only the first installment appeared in print, however, initially in an abolitionist newspaper, then as a separately published eight-page pamphlet. Even while attacking Clay, Birney himself was not immune to questions about his former status as an enslaver. An editor in his native state of Kentucky accused him of being a hypocrite for profiting from the sale of the people he had enslaved immediately prior to going public as an abolitionist. Birney defended himself at length, noting that when he was an enslaver, he had never sold someone to a slave trader and was regarded by his neighbors as so "indulgent" that they called him "a 'negro spoiler.'" Critics also charged Birney with using the sale of his enslaved people to cheat his law partner and his creditors. These accusations were so baseless that his estranged pro-slavery brother-in-law, John J. Marshall, went public to defend him.[68]

Late in the campaign, Birney also faced a charge of political corruption. Both Whigs and Democrats in his Michigan community reportedly respected his leadership ability and appreciated his attempts to weed out corruption in local politics. As a result, before Birney left on his New England electioneering tour in the late summer of 1844, he was informed that his neighbors wanted him to run for a seat in the state legislature. Birney agreed to the proposal, but he made it clear that if he received a party nomination, he would only serve as a representative of the people, not a party. Once he was gone, and Michigan Democrats had nominated him for the legislature, Whigs began accusing Birney of colluding with their opponents to ensure Clay's defeat. They went as far as to forge documents and affidavits. The most damning piece of fake evidence was a letter Birney purportedly wrote fellow Saginawan Jerome B. Garland, in which he supposedly stated, "I AM NOW AND EVER HAVE BEEN, a Democrat of the 'Jeffersonian School,'" and in which he claimed that he was secretly posing as an abolitionist to help advance the Democratic cause. Whigs made sure that word of Birney's alleged treachery reached communities on his tour but only after he had left town. Birney and the Liberty Party were caught flat-footed by this intrigue. He reiterated to the public that his nomination for the Michigan legislature was nonpartisan. Once his nomination by the state's Democrats was announced, Birney told Liberty Party members that "no pledge of party service was proposed—none was given." Because the "Garland forgery" came so late in the contest—at the end of October—Birney and his supporters had little chance to refute it before polls closed in many places. Most Liberty members probably stayed true to their plans to vote for the Birney–Morris ticket, but the Whigs' "October surprise" may have changed some minds.[69]

Birney's opponents found it difficult to identify credible lines of attack when it came to his personal life. Some Libertyites asked him to explain his former connection to Freemasonry. Given the concerns that some Americans still had about the immorality of the secret society, which were similar to those they shared about Catholics and Mormons, it was not an inconsequential question for a presidential candidate running on a moral platform. Birney went further than asked, outlining why he had joined the Masons, why he had left, and the deficiencies he found in the fraternal order. He concluded that however much Freemasons wanted to see their order as contributing to society, it did more harm than good in terms of moral, religious, and political practices. Birney's answer seemed to reassure those concerned. One contributor to a Vermont Liberty newspaper encouraged

Anti-Masons to ignore the Masonic politicians "who play pig to-day and puppy tomorrow" and to employ the energy they used against Freemasonry to help Birney fight slavery.[70]

The songs, speeches, meetings, cartoons, and other electioneering machinations that permeated the United States in 1844 created an atmosphere of excitement comparable to that of the 1840 campaign. None of these practices were new in 1844, but both Whigs and Democrats had witnessed their efficacy in generating partisan enthusiasm about the candidates and the issues the nation faced. Voters could not escape cultural politics, but it remained to be seen which party had been able to turn campaign zeal into electoral success.

ELECTION RESULTS

The days and weeks leading up to the end of the 1844 presidential campaign produced a flurry of political activity. Betting on the election outcome was common, with rumors of partisan women using enslaved people as stakes. Accusations of voter fraud were also prevalent. This form of electoral corruption was not uncommon in the mid-nineteenth-century United States. Dallas told Polk, "We have nothing to fear but fraud, and against that every precaution which ingenuity and zeal could devise, has been taken." In Louisiana, US representative John Slidell used a steamboat to ferry men unable to vote in New Orleans to Plaquemines Parish, where Democratic poll workers allowed them to cast their ballots. The parish counted only 290 votes in 1840; in 1844, Polk won 1,007 of its 1,044 votes, providing enough of a margin to carry the state for the Democrats. Whigs protested and investigated, but to no avail. Rumors of planned and actual violence also permeated the final days of the campaign. Democrat John McKeon was relieved that rain had postponed a nativist parade in New York City because Whigs reportedly were going to attack the participants and blame Democrats for the fighting and bloodshed that would likely ensue. One Middle Tennessee Whig suffered a broken jaw and lost several teeth when someone in the crowd threw a rock at him after he called Polk and his supporters "tories." Another Tennessean lost his life when one member of a group of "swearing & abusing" Whigs threw a rock at a group of Democrats. The projectile hit an eighteen-year-old Whig instead, fracturing his skull "from one ear to the other across the head."[71]

The 1844 presidential election was the last one to take place on different days in different states. Over the course of twelve days, beginning on November 1 and ending on November 12, voters made their way to polling places, a journey that buzzed with activity. First-time voters cleaned themselves up and put on their best clothing to make one of the most momentous decisions of their lives; more experienced voters proceeded through the familiar ritual of presenting their ticket, or verbally announcing their choices, to polling officials in front of the rambunctious crowds that often gathered to witness the spectacle. In the case of one Polk supporter, former US representative David Petrikin, neighbors carried him "on a bed" to cast his vote. Petrikin has been "confined to his room for 18 months," but "one of the last desirse [sic] he had to gratify" was helping to "defeat Clay."[72]

As votes were being cast across the nation, enthusiasm ran high on the Democratic side. A November 1 parade in New York City drew an estimated 60,000 participants and reportedly attracted between 100,000 and 200,000 spectators. By November 9, Philadelphia Democrats were so certain of victory that they marched to Dallas's residence, where the presumptive vice president-elect regaled them with a half-hour speech. But some Democrats recognized that there was a realistic chance that Polk would lose. Andrew J. Donelson, in New Orleans on leave from his recent diplomatic appointment to Texas, tried not to think about what would happen if Clay came out on top, but he could not help speculating. "What a dark cloud [sic] will at once hang over the prospect of all our southern states," he told Polk. "Great Britain will forthwith resume her projects for the abolition of slavery, and with the aid of Webster and Adams will consider that her game is insured." Polk realized the danger to his own chances. If efforts "to unite the *Natives & Abolitionists* with the *Whig party proper*" succeeded in New York, the Empire State might decide the election in Clay's favor. "We look to New York," Robert Armstrong wrote Polk. "Every thing depends on her."[73]

Whigs were similarly animated with optimism, but like their opponents, they also sensed that the election was going to be close. One North Carolinian observed that even though the party was "holding mass meetings all over the State, to try to rouse our people, . . . it is difficult to induce them to believe that J. K. Polk is serious opposition." In late October, Clay told a supporter that the Whig ticket had "a fair prospect" of exceeding that of "Tippecanoe and Tyler Too" four years earlier. He wrote Adams that the fall elections had been close, but he believed that "the Whigs will succeed by a large Electoral majority." Clay was not immune to pessimistic thoughts, however, telling his biographer Epes Sargent that he was "looking with anxiety to New York."[74]

As darkness descended on the evening of Friday, November 15, Nashville postmaster Robert Armstrong penned a letter to Polk. A Louisville Demo-

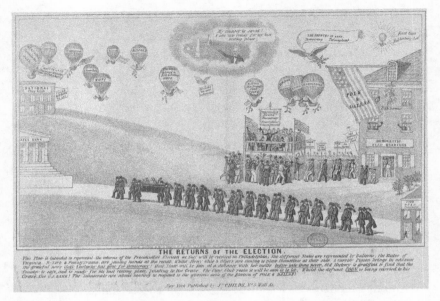

THE RETURNS OF THE ELECTION.

This Plate is intended to represent the returns of the Presidential Election as they will be received in Philadelphia. The different States are represented by balloons; the States of Virginia, N. York, & Pennsylvania are giving words as the result. Whilst Jersey, Ohio & others are rising to place themselves at their side. A carrier Pigeon brings to advance the grateful news that Kentucky had gone for Democracy; that State will be seen all a distance with her noble feather take than ever. Old Hickory is gratified to find that the Country is safe, and is ready for its last resting place. Pointing to the Grave. The Clay Club room it will be seen is to let. Whilst the defunct COON is being carried to his Grave, the CLANK! The Democrats are about marching to respond to the glorious news of the Election of POLK & DALLAS.

New York Published by J.ⁿ CHILDS, N.ⁿ5 Wall St.

Democratic optimism was best represented in this print, which shows party members celebrating James K. Polk's victory, as Whigs carry a dead raccoon (Henry Clay) to its grave. (Courtesy of the Boston Public Library)

crat had sent him "the *Glorious* News that New York is Yours," Armstrong informed his friend in Columbia. "This settles the matter and put Whiggery & Mr Clay to *rest*." The postmaster dispatched a local merchant with this letter to Columbia. By the time the messenger had made the forty-five-mile trek southward, arriving at the Polk home early Saturday morning, Nashvillians were already celebrating. Excitement had been mounting daily in the state capital as election results trickled in. Newspaper headlines had reassured Polk's supporters that their candidate was doing "O.K." in Pennsylvania and that Indiana was "*Right side up.*" With confirmation that New York was "ALL RIGHT!" arriving later on the evening of the 15th, Democrats could finally breathe a sigh of relief and begin to celebrate.[75]

Polk had, indeed, won the election. He secured 170 electoral votes to Clay's 105. This margin of victory masked the closeness of the race, however. Polk surpassed his Whig opponent's popular vote total by a little more than 40,000, or just 1.48 percent. He won fifteen states to Clay's eleven, flipping eight states, totaling 110 electoral votes, that had gone to the Whigs in 1840. He also increased the Democratic hold on Illinois, where many Mormons stayed home; those who voted probably heeded calls from some church leaders to vote for Polk.[76]

Table 5.1. 1844 Presidential Election Results

State	Total votes	JKP Pop.	JKP Pop. %	JKP Electoral	HC Pop.	HC Pop. %	HC Electoral	JGB Pop.	JGB Pop. %	JGB Electoral
Alabama	63,403	37,401	58.99	9	26,002	41.01	0	0	0	0
Arkansas	15,150	9,546	63.01	3	5,604	36.99	0	0	0	0
Connecticut	64,617	29,841	46.18	0	32,832	50.81	6	1,944	3.01	0
Delaware	12,241	5,970	48.77	0	6,271	51.23	3	0	0	0
Georgia	85,372	43,397	50.83	10	41,975	49.17	0	0	0	0
Illinois	108,346	58,982	54.44	9	45,931	42.39	0	3,433	3.17	0
Indiana	140,156	70,183	50.07	12	67,866	48.42	0	2,107	1.5	0
Kentucky	113,220	52,053	45.98	0	61,167	54.02	12	0	0	0
Louisiana	26,862	13,782	51.31	6	13,080	48.69	0	0	0	0
Maine	84,913	45,719	53.84	9	34,378	40.49	0	4,816	5.67	0
Maryland	68,660	32,676	47.59	0	35,984	52.41	8	0	0	0
Massachusetts	131,295	53,403	40.67	0	67,062	51.08	12	10,830	8.25	0
Michigan	55,559	27,737	49.92	5	24,185	43.53	0	3,637	6.55	0
Mississippi	45,800	25,926	56.61	6	19,874	43.39	0	0	0	0
Missouri	72,574	41,324	56.94	7	31,250	43.06	0	0	0	0
New Hampshire	49,161	27,232	55.39	6	17,769	36.14	0	4,160	8.46	0
New Jersey	75,644	37,495	49.57	0	38,018	50.26	7	131	0.17	0
New York	485,884	237,588	48.90	36	232,482	47.85	0	15,814	3.25	0
North Carolina	82,519	39,287	47.61	0	43,232	52.39	11	0	0	0
Ohio	312,173	149,011	47.73	0	155,112	49.69	23	8,050	2.58	0

(continued on the next page)

Table 5.1. *Continued*

State	Total votes	JKP Pop.	JKP Pop. %	JKP Electoral	HC Pop.	HC Pop. %	HC Electoral	JGB Pop.	JGB Pop. %	JGB Electoral
Pennsylvania	331,871	167,535	50.48	26	161,203	48.57	0	3,133	0.94	0
Rhode Island	12,198	4,876	39.97	0	7,322	60.03	4	0	0	0
South Carolina*	-	-	-	9	-	-	-	-	-	'
Tennessee	119,947	59,917	49.95	0	60,030	50.05	13	0	0	0
Vermont	48,796	18,049	36.99	0	26,777	54.88	6	3,970	8.14	0
Virginia	96,174	51,383	53.43	17	44,791	46.57	0	0	0	0
Total	2,702,535	1,340,313	49.59	170	1,300,197	48.11	105	62,025	2.30	0

*South Carolina's state legislature cast its nine electoral votes.

Note: States in italics switched from Whig to Democrat in 1844.

Source: Dubin, *U.S. Presidential Elections*, 83.

"What a Triumph," Armstrong wrote Polk. "Our friends are *happy* and rejoicing, *after* a *Gloomy* night & *day*." Thousands gathered in downtown Nashville to listen to Democratic speakers try to be heard over the cannon fire. Messengers had already been to the Hermitage to tell Jackson the news. "The Republic is safe," Old Hickory pronounced. "Like Simeon of old having seen my country safe, I am prepared to depart in peace." Polk's immediate response to the news went undocumented. Decades later, two of Sarah Childress Polk's friends, in a memoir they wrote with her input, recorded that James and Sarah kept the news secret until the official mail delivery made it public on Sunday, November 17. Once Polk's victory was announced, Columbia went into a frenzy. Democrats feted the president-elect in public and assembled at his home "with a band of music, and with noisy hurrahs and other manifestations of pleasure usual on such occasions." When one man told Sarah that her husband's friends would keep the well-wishers outside "because the street is muddy and your carpets and furniture will be spoiled," she replied, "The house is thrown open to everybody. . . . Let them all come in; they will not hurt the carpets." James "heartily seconded the enthusiastic invitation."[77]

Those who went to the Polk home that day (and who, according to Sarah's memory, were careful to keep it clean) encountered a man who had just turned forty-nine years old. One individual who visited Columbia just a month earlier described Polk's "features" as "strongly marked by evidences of intellect, blandness, firmness and benevolence." The president-elect's mostly white hair was swept back and sat at the top of a "high, broad and full" forehead, with strong widow's peaks on both sides. Nineteenth-century phrenologists, who used the human skull's physical appearance to draw conclusions about "character, intellect, or sentiment," would have considered Polk's "a splendid model," according to this visitor, because "the intellectual and moral faculties are largely predominant . . . [and] [t]he organs of benevolence, veneration and firmness, are prominently developed." Most Americans had never met, and would never meet, the incoming president in person, but this visitor was impressed. "If elected," they had predicted, Polk would "make, an able, judicious, sound and safe President of the United States; one that will aim to maintain the rights and honor of the country, in our foreign relations, and secure as far as practicable, the peace and prosperity of our people at home."[78]

6

"THE REPUBLIC IS SAFE"
UNDERSTANDING POLK'S VICTORY

Attempts to understand the Democratic victory in 1844, then and since, have focused on three major explanations. The first concerns the role of Texas annexation. This one loomed large in the immediate postelection analysis. Many Democrats thought annexation had harmed more than helped their cause. Samuel Medary blamed Ohio's loss on the rumor that James K. Polk would send the state's men "as soldiers into Texas or Mexico to be butchered by Spaniards and Indians!" A New Orleans Democrat believed that his party lost several Louisiana counties when Whigs convinced voters that acquiring Texas "would completely destroy the stock and grazing business" of the state. According to outgoing New York governor William C. Bouck, "the tariff and Texas question" hurt Polk among Democrats in his state; Tennessean Adam Huntsman thought annexation cost the ticket "many ten thousands." Some Whigs agreed with their opponents. William H. Seward, for example, was discouraged about Henry Clay's prospects "until the annexation of Texas was made a political question." He believed that it brought Liberty and Democratic voters to their side. Massachusetts abolitionist and former Quaker I. C. Ray told Clay that the "wicked scheme" of annexation and "extend[ing] the withering curse of slavery" had galvanized New England opposition to Polk's election. Tennessee, "the very cradle and nurse of the Texas conspiracy," the *New-York Tribune* noted, "has voted for the Anti-Texas candidate." Other Whigs believed Texas harmed Clay, however, helping elect "a mere *Tom Tit* over the old Eagle."[1]

In hindsight, annexation probably produced Democratic gains in the South in 1844, especially in Georgia and Louisiana, and it also likely won the Democrats Indiana's and Maine's twenty-one combined electoral votes. But annexation also helped Whigs substantially in the northern states. Most significantly, Ohio's twenty-three votes likely went to the Whigs because of the annexation issue. Texas annexation garnered a lot of press attention and was unquestionably a political flashpoint in 1844, but it was only one contributing factor in Polk's victory.[2]

A second explanation centers on the abolitionist Liberty Party as the determining factor in New York's vote. According to this argument, absent the Liberty Party ticket, abolitionists would have had no choice but to vote Clay as the lesser of two evils, giving Whigs New York and the White House. At the same time, and relatedly, Birney's entry in the race provided antiannexation Whigs a place to go if they wanted to protest their party's support of Manifest Destiny. As one New Yorker observed after the election, "The Whigs are now pretending that the Abolitionists have killed them. This is all nonsense." Staunch Liberty men did not want to support any enslaver, no matter who they were, and the argument that they would have backed Clay by default in a close election if their party had not run a ticket simply does not hold up to scrutiny. The Liberty Party had considered, then abandoned, a pragmatic approach and had committed to running on principle in 1844. It seems likely that they would simply have stayed home if Birney had not been in the campaign. Another important consideration is the demographic change that had taken place in New York. Birney did remarkably well in the national election; after winning just under 7,000 votes in 1840, he collected 62,025 in 1844, a significant increase. The Liberty Party's overall vote total in the Empire State, however, barely grew between 1843 and 1844, and its vote actually declined 0.9 percentage points. During that same time, Whigs added more than 75,000 voters and increased their share of the total vote by 4.1 percent. If Whigs abandoned Clay for the Liberty Party, which the evidence does not bear out, those losses were offset by the huge gain in voters the Whig Party made in New York.[3]

A third explanation centers on nativism. Theodore Frelinghuysen's place on the Whig ticket seemed innocuous enough at the time he was nominated, but the nativist violence that broke out in Philadelphia in the weeks and months following the Whig national convention highlighted the party's opposition to Catholic immigrants and drew attention to Frelinghuysen's ties to nativist groups, such as the American Missionary Society. One Whig noted in his postelection commentary, "Mr. F.s nomination made

Table 6.1. Comparison of Whig, Democratic, and Liberty Votes in New York, 1843–1844

Party	1843 State Senate Election*		1844 Presidential Election	
	% of vote	# of votes	% of vote	# of votes
Whig	43.7	156,878	47.8	232,482
Democratic	49.7	178,317	48.9	237,588
Liberty	4.2	15,159	3.3	15,814
	Total	350,354	Total	485,884

*One American Republican candidate received 8,712 votes, or 2.4% of the total, in District 1's Kings and New York counties. Those votes are omitted here.

Source: *The Whig Almanac and United States Register for 1844* (New York: Greeley & McElrath, 1844), 56; Dubin, *United States Presidential Elections*, 90–91.

the Catholic opposition intense." Nativism proved a particularly important campaign issue in Pennsylvania and New York. Pennsylvania had moved safely into the Democratic column since barely supporting Harrison in 1840; however, the Philadelphia nativist riots during the summer of 1844 threatened the Democratic stranglehold on the state's politics. Adding to the party's concerns was the death of Henry A. P. Muhlenberg, its gubernatorial candidate, in mid-August. Nativists accused his replacement Francis R. Shunk not just of being a Catholic but of conspiring to force Catholicism on children via the state's school system. The fall elections witnessed the Whigs gaining significant ground on their opponents. They allegedly struck a bargain with the nativist American Republican Party, which was not running a statewide ticket: if the American Republicans helped persuade its supporters to defeat Polk and Shunk, then Whigs would help them win offices in the counties surrounding Philadelphia, where the nativists were strongest. The deal paid off for the American Republicans, who secured victories at the county level, in the state legislature, and in Congress. Whigs gained less from the partnership. Contrary to their expectations, American Republicans did not help them overtake the Democrats in either the gubernatorial or the presidential election. Whigs lost both by just more than 4,000 and 6,000 votes, respectively.[4]

In New York, the nativist movement had also demonstrated growing strength. In November 1843, American Republican senatorial candidate Mangle M. Quackenboss received only 8,550 votes. By the following April, the party's mayoral candidate James Harper garnered more than 24,000 votes in the New York City election, defeating his Democratic opponent by more than 4,000 votes and the Whig candidate by more than 19,000 votes. Nativism was on the rise and appeared ready to play an important role in deciding the state's presidential vote. Efforts to organize nativism statewide largely failed in the months leading up to the November election; the exception was in New York City, where Whigs and American Republicans formed a partnership like the one in Philadelphia. Unfortunately for Clay, the outcome in New York City was similar to that in Philadelphia. Nativists ended up benefiting more from the political alliance than the Whig Party did. New Yorkers cast their presidential ballots on November 5, four days after Pennsylvanians had gone to the polls. This gap allowed Democrats to ascertain the closeness of the vote in Philadelphia and to react accordingly, something Whigs failed to do. When it came time to cast their votes, a large number of Democratic nativists, between 2,000 and 3,500, chose to support Polk over Clay. They were joined at the polls by an influx of newly naturalized citizens, many of them Irish Catholics predisposed to support a Democratic Party that generally embraced them with open arms.[5]

These issues—Texas annexation, the Liberty vote, and nativism—were only three pieces of the political puzzle that brought Polk victory in New York and in the national election, however. Two other factors were also important. One was Silas Wright's gubernatorial candidacy. Democrats had lost faith in incumbent New York governor William C. Bouck, so they chose Wright to replace "The Old White Horse" on the party ticket. This decision mollified Democrats who were still miffed at Van Buren's rejection in Baltimore and helped unite the party statewide. It also terrified Whigs. "We are in danger," New Yorker Nicholas Carroll wrote. Wright "is the hardest man for us to beat," and if allying with the American Republicans required "even a temporary yielding of principle, the emergency & the occasions, would more than justify the momentary forgetfulness." Otherwise, the Whig businessman warned, "we are whipped." The strategy Carroll recommended failed. Wright defeated the reluctant Whig candidate Millard Fillmore by more than 10,000 votes, and received nearly 4,000 more votes than Polk. This success indicated that Wright's "great personal popularity," in Benjamin F. Butler's words, and delicate handling of the annexation controversy helped turn out the Democratic base. Butler also credited the economic focus of Wright's campaign with convincing "many Whigs, Native Americans, & Abolitionists, who feared the consequences of a Whig triumph, on the financial interest & character of the state, to give him their votes."[6]

The other factor—the role of cultural politics in turning out old and new

Table 6.2. States in the 1844 Presidential Election Where Polk and Clay Were Separated by 3 percent or Less of the Popular Vote

State	Polk	% difference	Popular vote difference	Electoral votes	Clay	% difference	Popular vote difference	Electoral votes
Delaware					X	2.46	301	3
Georgia	X	1.66	1,422	10				
Indiana	X	1.65	2,317	12				
Louisiana	X	2.62	702	6				
New Jersey					X	.69	523	7
New York	X	1.05	5,106	36				
Ohio					X	1.96	6,101	23
Pennsylvania	X	1.91	6,332	26				
Tennessee					X	.1	113	13
Total			15,879	90			7,038	46

Source: Dubin, *United States Presidential Elections*, 83–96.

voters in 1844—has gone largely unrecognized. Often derided by contemporaries as noise and nonsense and by later historians as inconsequential entertainment, the electioneering techniques employed in the 1844 campaign did not just attract women to political events and make the Whig coon a ubiquitous symbol—it convinced newly enfranchised men to make a lifelong commitment by casting their "virgin vote" and helped send eligible voters of all ages to the ballot box. Almost 79 percent of eligible voters cast a vote for president in 1844. This represented a slightly lower percentage than in 1840, but the total number of votes increased by nearly 300,000. Voter consistency between the 1840 and 1844 presidential elections was remarkably high. In the important state of New York, for example, 92.1 percent of eligible voters cast a vote, slightly higher than the 91.9 percent that voted in 1840. This stability indicated that parties had landed on a successful strategy to maintain voter enthusiasm that not only rallied the party faithful but also enticed newly eligible voters in 1844. Twenty-three-year-old William Saunders Brown was one such new voter. The Virginia clerk did not just vote the Whig ticket—he also raised a seventy-foot "Clay pole" that flew a thirty-five-foot-long banner. Clay's loss to Polk "haunted" Brown and made him ashamed of his fellow Americans.[7]

All five of these factors contributed to the election's outcome. Partisan stability made it possible for issues like annexation or nativism, individually or collectively, to effect small enough changes in voter identity to move states into either the Whig or Democratic column. So did state-level reactions to politicians such as Wright or Andrew Jackson. An influx of new voters, whether native-born or foreign-born, could produce similar nudges. The cultural politics in which the parties engaged not only attracted these new voters but also renewed the commitment of previous supporters. In a closely contested election such as 1844, even one of these factors could prove decisive. In New York, the shift of thirty-six electoral votes from Polk to Clay would have given the Whig a 141 to 134 victory. But if Whigs or Democrats had won the other close states they lost, New York would not have made a difference. For example, Polk lost four states, worth forty-six electoral votes, by a combined 7,038 popular votes: Delaware, New Jersey, Ohio, and Tennessee. Clay also suffered narrow defeats. He lost five states, worth ninety electoral votes, by a combined 15,879 popular votes: Georgia, Indiana, Louisiana, New York, and Pennsylvania. In an election this close, every vote mattered.[8]

Table 6.3. Results of Gubernatorial Elections Held in 1844

State	Democratic % of vote	Whig % of vote	Liberty % of vote	Other % of vote	Date of Election	Party switch from previous election? (Y/N)
New Hampshire	53.59	30.42	11.89	4.1	March 12	N
Connecticut	47.36	49.41	3.24	—	April 3	Y
Rhode Island	—	—	—	96.39*	April 3	N
Arkansas	47.58	38.91	—	13.5	August 5	N
Kentucky	47.98	52.02	—	—	August 5	N
Missouri	54.11	45.89	—	—	August 5	N
North Carolina	47.9	52.1	—	—	August 8	N
Vermont	38.18	51.57	10.25	—	September 3	N
Maine	52.24	41.09	6.67	—	September 9	N
Maryland	49.61	50.39	—	—	October 2	Y
New Jersey	49.06	50.94	—	—	October 8	Y
Ohio	48.31	48.73	2.96	—	October 8	Y
Pennsylvania	50.27	48.93	0.8	—	October 8	N
Delaware	49.82	50.18	—	—	November 5	N
New York	49.48	47.42	3.11	—	November 5	N
Massachusetts	40.86	51.95	7.19	—	November 11	N

* Law and Order Party; 3.61 (scattered)

Source: Dubin, *Gubernatorial Elections*, xxxv, 10, 23, 27, 76, 91, 97, 114–115, 139–140, 155, 158, 172–173, 184, 203–204, 224–225, 235, 277–278.

Table 6.4. Changes in Party Control in State Legislatures, 1844

State	Legislative Chamber	Party Seats after Previous Election*	Party Seats after 1844 Election
Connecticut	House	113–75 Dem.	104–83 Whig
	Senate	16–5 Dem.	15–6 Whig
Indiana	House	55–45 Dem.	54–45–1 Whig
	Senate	26–24 Whig	25–25 Tie
Louisiana	Senate	9–8 Whig	9–8 Dem.
New Jersey	House	35–23 Dem.	40–18 Whig
	Senate	12–6 Dem.	13–6 Whig
North Carolina	House	67–53 Dem.	70–50 Whig
	Senate	30–20 Whig	25–25 Tie
Ohio	Senate	20–16 Dem.	22–14 Whig
Virginia	House	75–59 Dem.	73–61 Whig

*Note: In Louisiana and North Carolina, the previous election was held in 1842; in all other states, it was 1843.

Source: Michael J. Dubin, *Party Affiliations in the State Legislatures: A Year by Year Summary, 1796–2006* (Jefferson, NC: McFarland, 2007), 9, 34, 60, 76, 127, 140, 147, 176, 192.

The presidential election was not the only contest in 1844. In Congress, Whigs increased their minority in the House by seven members, and the nativist American Party gained six seats of its own. The most consequential change was in the Senate. There, Democrats made gains that eventually turned a 23–29 deficit in the 28th Congress (1843–1845) into a 34–22 majority in the 29th Congress (1845–1847). Helping Democrats assume control of the Senate was Lewis Cass, who was elected in Michigan. (In February 1846, the addition of two seats from the new state of Texas, held by Sam Houston and Thomas J. Rusk, further increased the Democratic majority.) The effects on national politics were almost immediate. In March 1845, Vice President Dallas appointed expansionist William Allen chair of the Senate Foreign Relations committee; from this powerful seat, the Ohioan served as a major voice in pushing for US control of Oregon at the 54° 40 line.[9]

At the state level, Whigs demonstrated strength in the gubernatorial elections held in 1844. They won ten of the sixteen races held between March 12 and November 11, capturing four seats from the Democrats. Examining the results, however, shows that the gubernatorial elections were a series of close races, mirroring the competitiveness of the presidential election. Elections affecting the composition of the state legislatures also demonstrated the small gap between voters' support of the parties. In 1843, Democrats controlled fifteen state legislatures, Whigs seven. By the end of 1844, the two parties were evenly matched, with command of ten legislatures each. In some cases, the shift in partisan power in a state capitol was by the narrowest of margins. In Louisiana, for example, a flip of one seat moved the state senate from the Whigs to the Democrats. In other instances, the change represented a repudiation of the ruling party. In each of these cases, the swing from being a decided minority to becoming a comfortable majority favored the Whigs. Democrats may have won the presidency and control of Congress, but the nation was still divided by thin partisan margins.[10]

EPILOGUE

"Your troubles now begin," a correspondent warned James K. Polk as the election results started coming into focus in November 1844. Indeed, the Tennessean found that organizing his administration revealed cracks in the Democratic Party that his campaign had temporarily spackled over. His cabinet choices put him at odds with the Van Buren wing and even brought criticism from Andrew Jackson. John Tyler's last-minute signing of a joint congressional resolution inviting Texas into the Union also ensured that Polk would from the start be forced to focus on western expansion, a not unwelcome scenario for the president-elect.[1]

Polk delivered his inaugural address on a dreary, rainy Tuesday in early March. Drafted with the help of experienced Democratic rhetorician Amos Kendall, it ran less than 5,000 words, almost half as long as the one William Henry Harrison had delivered four years earlier. In it, Polk assured Americans that he would be the president of the people, not of a party. He emphasized some of his specific concerns, such as the need to protect individual freedom, shore up minority rights, practice government frugality, and preserve, in the words of Old Hickory, "our Federal Union." Polk also touched on many of the previous year's campaign issues. He promised to hold public officials accountable for corruption. He saw no need for banks and wanted a revenue tariff that spread out the tax burden "justly and equally among all classes of our population." Alluding to the divisiveness Polk saw in abolitionism, he lectured listeners on the dangers posed by those "misguided persons" who sought to destroy constitutionally established "domestic institutions." Given Tyler's last-minute signing of House legislation offering Texas immediate annexation, the incoming president spent several paragraphs on the issue that had made him the Democratic candidate. In Polk's telling, Texas had been part of the United States, so its "re-annexation" was appropriate, as was the addition of the Oregon territory. "The bonds of our Union, so far from being weakened, will become stronger" by this territorial expansion, he confidently asserted.[2]

Polk's one term in the White House proved his prediction wrong. Americans witnessed some of their nation's most divisive moments over Manifest Destiny between 1845 and 1849, as Young Hickory oversaw the completion of the Texas annexation process and provoked a controversial war with Mexico, based on questionable justification, shortly thereafter. The Mexican-American War (1846–1848) broke open the congressional debate over slavery's expansion westward and elevated its importance in the national political discourse. The Treaty of Guadalupe Hidalgo (1848) that resolved the conflict did not keep the United States from continuing to pursue the ideology of Manifest Destiny that privileged Christian nationalism, white supremacy, and capitalism at the expense of enslaved African Americans, displaced Native Americans, and other racial and ethnic minorities.[3]

Other issues important to the 1844 election had lasting value. Both the tariff and nativism played an important role in swinging Pennsylvania into the Whig column in the 1848 presidential election, allowing Zachary Taylor to defeat Lewis Cass. The tariff persisted as a contentious issue into the 1850s. The Republicans, who eventually replaced the Whigs as the second major political party later in the decade, used it as part of their "free-labor" appeal, explicitly noting how the Slave Power supported low tariffs in order to protect its system of enslaved labor. As European immigrants continued to pour into the United States in the 1840s and 1850s, nativism became more entrenched. By 1856, the movement had become a national political party—the American Party, or Know-Nothing Party—powerful enough to run a ticket in that year's election: former vice president and president Millard Fillmore, a former Whig, for president, and former Democrat Andrew J. Donelson as vice president.[4]

Political corruption remained a cause for concern. Accusations of voter fraud, financial malfeasance by government officials, selling political offices—all of these problems and more haunted both Democrats and Whigs in the 1850s. Republicans were the beneficiary, as corruption "helped destroy the Whig party and . . . helped wreck the [James] Buchanan Administration." Personal character remained a valuable commodity. Democrats denounced religious interference in politics and state enforcement of moral codes; at the same time, they pronounced themselves arbiters of maintaining sexual and racial purity. Whigs, and then Republicans, had no trouble focusing on personal character, especially when it meant critiquing the ways in which the Slave Power corrupted Americans' moral code, individually and collectively. The violence that pervaded Congress during these years gave the lie to the effectiveness of this moral posturing.[5]

Finally, the 1844 campaign confirmed that cultural politics had become a permanent, and critical, part of presidential elections. The different manifestations of electioneering normalized in 1840 and 1844 continued to turn out voters. After slight dips in eligible voter turnout in 1848 (72.7%) and 1852 (69.6%), the 1856 election matched 1844 turnout (78.9%), and the 1860 election (81.2%) exceeded even the Log Cabin and Hard Cider campaign of 1840. These voters grew up in a culture that cultivated political engagement via song, literature, objects, public events, and other activities, even as the United States denied the majority of people living within its borders the right to cast a vote. Cultural politics proved critical in helping parties ensure their voters made it to the polls, a lesson the 1848 presidential election reinforced. A shift of about 6,000 votes in Georgia and Maryland would have left Taylor and Cass tied with 145 electoral votes each, producing a House vote as had occurred after the 1824 election. In local, state, and national elections that remained close, every vote counted.[6]

"Who is James K. Polk?" some Americans wanted to know in 1844. Looking back, we can see that he was the man whose victorious presidential campaign served as a tipping point for the nation, ensuring that slavery remained at the forefront of the national conversation and pushing the United States to aggressively pursue Manifest Destiny on the continent. Polk was also the man whose election swiftened the current of sectionalism and made it increasingly difficult for the United States to avoid the treacherous waters of disunion and civil war.

APPENDIX

JAMES K. POLK'S INAUGURAL
ADDRESS, MARCH 4, 1845

FELLOW-CITIZENS:

Without solicitation on my part, I have been chosen by the free and voluntary suffrages of my countrymen to the most honorable and most responsible office on earth. I am deeply impressed with gratitude for the confidence reposed in me. Honored with this distinguished consideration at an earlier period of life than any of my predecessors, I can not disguise the diffidence with which I am about to enter on the discharge of my official duties.[1]

If the more aged and experienced men who have filled the office of President of the United States even in the infancy of the Republic distrusted their ability to discharge the duties of that exalted station, what ought not to be the apprehensions of one so much younger and less endowed now that our domain extends from ocean to ocean, that our people have so greatly increased in numbers, and at a time when so great diversity of opinion prevails in regard to the principles and policy which should characterize the administration of our Government? Well may the boldest fear and the wisest tremble when incurring responsibilities on which may depend our country's peace and prosperity, and in some degree the hopes and happiness of the whole human family.

In assuming responsibilities so vast I fervently invoke the aid of that Almighty Ruler of the Universe in whose hands are the destinies of nations and of men to guard this Heaven-favored land against the mischiefs which without His guidance might arise from an unwise public policy.

With a firm reliance upon the wisdom of Omnipotence to sustain and direct me in the path of duty which I am appointed to pursue, I stand in the presence of this assembled multitude of my countrymen to take upon myself the solemn obligation "to the best of my ability to preserve, protect, and defend the Constitution of the United States."

A concise enumeration of the principles which will guide me in the administrative policy of the Government is not only in accordance with the examples set me by all my predecessors, but is eminently befitting the occasion.

The Constitution itself, plainly written as it is, the safeguard of our federative compact, the offspring of concession and compromise, binding together in the bonds of peace and union this great and increasing family of free and independent States, will be the chart by which I shall be directed.

It will be my first care to administer the Government in the true spirit of that instrument, and to assume no powers not expressly granted or clearly implied in its terms. The Government of the United States is one of delegated and limited powers, and it is by a strict adherence to the clearly granted powers and by abstaining from the exercise of doubtful or unauthorized implied powers that we have the only sure guaranty against the recurrence of those unfortunate collisions between the Federal and State authorities which have occasionally so much disturbed the harmony of our system and even threatened the perpetuity of our glorious Union.

"To the States, respectively, or to the people" have been reserved "the powers not delegated to the United States by the Constitution nor prohibited by it to the States." Each State is a complete sovereignty within the sphere of its reserved powers. The Government of the Union, acting within the sphere of its delegated authority, is also a complete sovereignty. While the General Government should abstain from the exercise of authority not clearly delegated to it, the States should be equally careful that in the maintenance of their rights they do not overstep the limits of powers reserved to them. One of the most distinguished of my predecessors attached deserved importance to "the support of the State governments in all their rights, as the most competent administration for our domestic concerns and the surest bulwark against antirepublican tendencies," and to the "preservation of the General Government in its whole constitutional vigor, as the sheet anchor of our peace at home and safety abroad."

To the Government of the United States has been intrusted the exclusive management of our foreign affairs. Beyond that it wields a few general enumerated powers. It does not force reform on the States. It leaves individuals, over whom it casts its protecting influence, entirely free to improve their own condition by the legitimate exercise of all their mental and physical powers. It is a common protector of each and all the States; of every man who lives upon our soil, whether of native or foreign birth; of every religious sect, in their worship of the Almighty according to the dictates of their own conscience; of every shade of opinion, and the most free inquiry; of every art, trade, and occupation consistent with the laws of the States. And we rejoice in the general happiness, prosperity, and advancement of our country, which have been the offspring of freedom, and not of power.

This most admirable and wisest system of well-regulated self-government among men ever devised by human minds has been tested by its successful operation for more than half a century, and if preserved from the usurpations of the Federal Government on the one hand and the exercise by the States of powers not reserved to them on the other, will, I fervently hope and believe, endure for ages to come and dispense the blessings of civil and religious liberty to distant generations. To effect objects so dear to every patriot I shall devote myself with anxious solicitude. It will be my desire to guard against that most fruitful source of danger to the harmonious action of our system which consists in substituting the mere discretion and caprice of the Executive or of majorities in the legislative department of the Government for powers which have been withheld from the Federal Government by the Constitution. By the theory of our Government majorities rule, but this right is not an arbitrary or unlimited one. It is a right to be exercised in subordination to the Constitution and in conformity to it. One great object of the Constitution was to restrain majorities from oppressing minorities or encroaching upon their just rights. Minorities have a right to appeal to the Constitution as a shield against such oppression.

That the blessings of liberty which our Constitution secures may be enjoyed alike by minorities and majorities, the Executive has been wisely invested with a qualified veto upon the acts of the Legislature. It is a negative power, and is conservative in its character. It arrests for the time hasty, inconsiderate, or unconstitutional legislation, invites reconsideration, and transfers questions at issue between the legislative and executive departments to the tribunal of the people. Like all other powers, it is subject to be abused. When judiciously and properly exercised, the Constitution itself may be saved from infraction and the rights of all preserved and protected.

The inestimable value of our Federal Union is felt and acknowledged by all. By this system of united and confederated States our people are permitted collectively and individually to seek their own happiness in their own way, and the consequences have been most auspicious. Since the Union was formed the number of the States has increased from thirteen to twenty-eight; two of these have taken their position as members of the Confederacy within the last week. Our population has increased from three to twenty millions. New communities and States are seeking protection under its ægis, and multitudes from the Old World are flocking to our shores to participate in its blessings. Beneath its benign sway peace and prosperity prevail. Freed from the burdens and miseries of war, our trade and intercourse have extended throughout the world. Mind, no longer tasked in devising means to accomplish or resist schemes of ambition, usurpation, or conquest, is devoting itself to man's true interests in developing his faculties and powers and the capacity of nature to minister to his enjoyments. Genius is free to announce its inventions and discoveries, and the hand is free to accomplish whatever the head conceives not incompatible with the rights of a fellow-being. All distinctions of birth or of rank have been abolished. All citizens, whether native or adopted, are placed upon terms of precise equality. All are entitled to equal rights and equal protection. No union exists between church and state, and perfect freedom of opinion is guaranteed to all sects and creeds.

These are some of the blessings secured to our happy land by our Federal Union. To perpetuate them it is our sacred duty to preserve it. Who shall assign limits to the achievements of free minds and free hands under the protection of this glorious Union? No treason to mankind since the organization of society would be equal in atrocity to that of him who would lift his hand to destroy it. He would overthrow the noblest structure of human wisdom, which protects himself and his fellow-man. He would stop the progress of free government and involve his country either in anarchy or despotism. He would extinguish the fire of liberty, which warms and animates the hearts of happy millions and invites all the nations of the earth to imitate our example. If he say that error and wrong are committed in the administration of the Government, let him remember that nothing human can be perfect, and that under no other system of government revealed by Heaven or devised by man has reason been allowed so free and broad a scope to combat error. Has the sword of despots proved to be a safer or surer instrument of reform in government than enlightened reason? Does he expect to find among the ruins of this Union a happier abode for our swarming millions than they now have under it? Every lover of his country must shudder at the thought of the possibility of its dissolution, and will be ready to adopt the patriotic sentiment, "Our Federal Union—it must be preserved."

To preserve it the compromises which alone enabled our fathers to form a common constitution for the government and protection of so many States and distinct communities, of such diversified habits, interests, and domestic institutions, must be sacredly and religiously observed. Any attempt to disturb or destroy these compromises, being terms of the compact of union, can lead to none other than the most ruinous and disastrous consequences.

It is a source of deep regret that in some sections of our country misguided persons have occasionally indulged in schemes and agitations whose object is the destruction of domestic institutions existing in other sections—institutions which existed at the adoption of the Constitution and were recognized and protected by it. All must see that if it were possible for them to be successful in attaining their object the dissolution of the Union and the consequent destruction of our happy form of government must speedily follow.

I am happy to believe that at every period of our existence as a nation there has existed, and continues to exist, among the great mass of our people a devotion to the Union of the States which will shield and protect it against the moral treason of any who would seriously contemplate its destruction. To secure a continuance of that devotion the compromises of the Constitution must not only be preserved, but sectional jealousies and heartburnings must be discountenanced, and all should remember that they are members of the same political family, having a common destiny. To increase the attachment of our people to the Union, our laws should be just. Any policy which shall tend to favor monopolies or the peculiar interests of sections or classes must operate to the prejudice of the interest of their fellow-citizens, and should be avoided. If the compromises of the Constitution be preserved, if sectional jealousies and heartburnings be discountenanced, if our laws be just and the Government be practically administered strictly within the limits of power prescribed to it, we may discard all apprehensions for the safety of the Union.

With these views of the nature, character, and objects of the Government and the value of the Union, I shall steadily oppose the creation of those institutions and systems which in their nature tend to pervert it from its legitimate purposes and make it the instrument of sections, classes, and individuals. We need no national banks or other extraneous institutions planted around the Government to control or strengthen it in opposition to the will of its authors. Experience has taught us how unnecessary they are as auxiliaries of the public authorities—how impotent for good and how powerful for mischief.

Ours was intended to be a plain and frugal government, and I shall regard it to be my duty to recommend to Congress and, as far as the Executive is concerned, to enforce by all the means within my power the strictest economy in the expenditure of the public money which may be compatible with the public interests.

A national debt has become almost an institution of European monarchies. It is viewed in some of them as an essential prop to existing governments. Melancholy is the condition of that people whose government can be sustained only by a system which periodically transfers large amounts from the labor of the many to the coffers of the few. Such a system is incompatible with the ends for which our republican Government was instituted. Under a wise policy the debts contracted in our Revolution and during the War of 1812 have been happily extinguished. By a judicious application of the revenues not required for other necessary purposes, it is not doubted that the debt which has grown out of the circumstances of the last few years may be speedily paid off.

I congratulate my fellow-citizens on the entire restoration of the credit of the General Government of the Union and that of many of the States. Happy would it be for the indebted States if they were freed from their liabilities, many of which were incautiously contracted. Although the Government of the Union is neither in a legal nor a moral sense bound for the debts of the States, and it would be a violation of our compact of union to assume them, yet we can not but feel a deep interest in seeing all the States meet their public liabilities and pay off their just debts at the earliest practicable period. That they will do so as soon as it can be done without imposing too heavy burdens on their citizens there is no reason to doubt. The sound moral and honorable feeling of the people of the indebted States can not be questioned, and we are happy to perceive a settled disposition on their part, as their ability returns after a season of unexampled pecuniary embarrassment, to pay off all just demands and to acquiesce in any reasonable measures to accomplish that object.

One of the difficulties which we have had to encounter in the practical administration of the Government consists in the adjustment of our revenue laws and the levy of the taxes necessary for the support of Government. In the general proposition that no more money shall be collected than the necessities of an economical administration shall require all parties seem to acquiesce. Nor does there seem to be any material difference of opinion as to the absence of right in the Government to tax one section of country, or one class of citizens, or one occupation, for the mere profit of another.

"Justice and sound policy forbid the Federal Government to foster one branch of industry to the detriment of another, or to cherish the interests of one portion to the injury of another portion of our common country." I have heretofore declared to my fellow-citizens that "in my judgment it is the duty of the Government to extend, as far as it may be practicable to do so, by its revenue laws and all other means within its power, fair and just protection to all of the great interests of the whole Union, embracing agriculture, manufactures, the mechanic arts, commerce, and navigation." I have also declared my opinion to be "in favor of a tariff for revenue," and that "in adjusting the details of such a tariff I have sanctioned such moderate discriminating duties as would produce the amount of revenue needed and at the same time afford reasonable incidental protection to our home industry," and that I was "opposed to a tariff for protection merely, and not for revenue."

The power "to lay and collect taxes, duties, imposts, and excises" was an indispensable one to be conferred on the Federal Government, which without it would possess no means of providing for its own support. In executing this power by levying a tariff of duties for the support of Government, the raising of *revenue* should be the *object* and *protection* the *incident*. To reverse this principle and make *protection* the *object* and *revenue* the *incident* would be to inflict manifest injustice upon all other than the protected interests. In levying duties for revenue it is doubtless proper to make such discriminations within the *revenue principle* as will afford incidental protection to our home interests. Within the revenue limit there is a discretion to discriminate; beyond that limit the rightful exercise of the power is not conceded. The incidental protection afforded to our home interests by discriminations within the revenue range it is believed will be ample. In making discriminations all our home interests should as far as practicable be equally protected. The largest portion of our people are agriculturists. Others are employed in manufactures, commerce, navigation, and the mechanic arts. They are all engaged in their respective pursuits, and their joint labors constitute the national or home industry. To tax one branch of this home industry for the benefit of another would be unjust. No one of these interests can rightfully claim an advantage over the others, or to be enriched by impoverishing the others. All are equally entitled to the fostering care and protection of the Government. In exercising a sound discretion in levying discriminating duties within the limit prescribed, care should be taken that it be done in a manner not to benefit the wealthy few at the expense of the toiling millions by taxing *lowest* the luxuries of life, or articles of superior quality and high price, which can only be consumed by the wealthy, and *highest* the necessaries of life, or articles of coarse quality and low price, which the poor and great mass of our people must consume. The burdens of government should as far as practicable be distributed justly and equally among all classes of our population. These general views, long entertained on this subject, I have deemed it proper to reiterate. It is a subject upon which conflicting interests of sections and occupations are supposed to exist, and a spirit of mutual concession and compromise in adjusting its details should be cherished by every part of our widespread country as the only means of preserving harmony and a cheerful acquiescence of all in the operation of our revenue laws. Our patriotic citizens in every part of the Union will readily submit to the payment of such taxes as shall be needed for the support of their Government, whether in peace or in war, if they are so levied as to distribute the burdens as equally as possible among them.

The Republic of Texas has made known her desire to come into our Union, to form a part of our Confederacy and enjoy with us the blessings of liberty secured and guaranteed by our Constitution. Texas was once a part of our country—was unwisely ceded away to a foreign power—is now independent, and possesses an undoubted right to dispose of a part or the whole of her territory and to merge her sovereignty as a separate and independent state in ours. I congratulate my country that by an act of the late Congress of the United States the assent of this Government has been given to the reunion, and it only remains for the two countries to agree upon the terms to consummate an object so important to both.

I regard the question of annexation as belonging exclusively to the United States and Texas. They are independent powers competent to contract, and foreign nations have no right to interfere with them or to take exceptions to their reunion. Foreign powers do not seem to appreciate the true character of our Government. Our Union is a confederation of independent States, whose policy is peace with each other and all the world. To enlarge its limits is to extend the dominions of peace over additional territories and increasing millions. The world has nothing to fear from military ambition in our Government. While the Chief Magistrate and the popular branch of Congress are elected for short terms by the suffrages of those millions who must in their own persons bear all the burdens and miseries of war, our Government can not be otherwise than pacific. Foreign powers should therefore look on the annexation of Texas to the United States not as the conquest of a nation seeking to extend her dominions by arms and violence, but as the peaceful acquisition of a territory once her own, by adding another member to our confederation, with the consent of that member, thereby diminishing the chances of war and opening to them new and ever-increasing markets for their products.

To Texas the reunion is important, because the strong protecting arm of our Government would be extended over her, and the vast resources of her fertile soil and genial climate would be speedily developed, while the safety of New Orleans and of our whole southwestern frontier against hostile aggression, as well as the interests of the whole Union, would be promoted by it.

In the earlier stages of our national existence the opinion prevailed with some that our system of confederated States could not operate successfully over an extended territory, and serious objections have at different times been made to the enlargement of our boundaries. These objections were earnestly urged when we acquired Louisiana. Experience has shown that they were not well founded. The title of numerous Indian tribes to vast tracts of country has been extinguished; new States have been admitted into the Union; new Territories have been created and our jurisdiction and laws extended over them. As our population has expanded, the Union has been cemented and strengthened. As our boundaries have been enlarged and our agricultural population has been spread over a large surface, our federative system has acquired additional strength and security. It may well be doubted whether it would not be in greater danger of overthrow if our present population were confined to the comparatively narrow limits of the original thirteen States than it is now that they are sparsely settled over a more expanded territory. It is confidently believed that our system may be safely extended to the utmost bounds of our territorial limits, and that as it shall be extended the bonds of our Union, so far from being weakened, will become stronger.

None can fail to see the danger to our safety and future peace if Texas remains an independent state or becomes an ally or dependency of some foreign nation more powerful than herself. Is there one among our citizens who would not prefer perpetual peace with Texas to occasional wars, which so often occur between bordering independent nations? Is there one who would not prefer free intercourse with her to high duties on all our products and manufactures which enter her ports or cross her frontiers? Is there one who would not prefer an unrestricted communication with her citizens to the frontier obstructions which must occur if she remains out of the Union? Whatever is good or evil in the local institutions of Texas will remain her own whether annexed to the United States or not. None of the present States will be responsible for them any more than they are for the local institutions of each other. They have confederated together for certain specified objects. Upon the same principle that they would refuse to form a perpetual union with Texas because of her local institutions our forefathers would have been prevented from forming our present Union. Perceiving no valid objection to the measure and many reasons for its adoption vitally affecting the peace, the safety, and the prosperity of both countries, I shall on the broad principle which formed the basis and produced the adoption of our Constitution, and not in any narrow spirit of sectional policy, endeavor by all constitutional, honorable, and appropriate means to consummate the expressed will of the people and Government of the United States by the reannexation of Texas to our Union at the earliest practicable period.

Nor will it become in a less degree my duty to assert and maintain by all constitutional means the right of the United States to that portion of our territory which lies beyond the Rocky Mountains. Our title to the country of the Oregon is "clear and unquestionable," and already are our people preparing to perfect that title by occupying it with their wives and children. But eighty years ago our population was confined on the west by the ridge of the Alleghanies. Within that period—within the lifetime, I might say, of some of my hearers—our people, increasing to many millions, have filled the eastern valley of the Mississippi, adventurously ascended the Missouri to its headsprings, and are already engaged in establishing the blessings of self-government in valleys of which the rivers flow to the Pacific. The world beholds the peaceful triumphs of the industry of our emigrants. To us belongs the duty of protecting them adequately wherever they may be upon our soil. The jurisdiction of our laws and the benefits of our republican institutions should be extended over them in the distant regions which they have selected for their homes. The increasing facilities of intercourse will easily bring the States, of which the formation in that part of our territory can not be long delayed, within the sphere of our federative Union. In the meantime every obligation imposed by treaty or conventional stipulations should be sacredly respected.

In the management of our foreign relations it will be my aim to observe a careful respect for the rights of other nations, while our own will be the subject of constant watchfulness. Equal and exact justice should characterize all our intercourse with foreign countries. All alliances having a tendency to jeopard the welfare and honor of our country or sacrifice any one of the national interests will be studiously avoided, and yet no opportunity will be lost to cultivate a favorable understanding with foreign governments by which our navigation and commerce may be extended and the ample products of our fertile soil, as well as the manufactures of our skillful artisans, find a ready market and remunerating prices in foreign countries.

In taking "care that the laws be faithfully executed," a strict performance of duty will be exacted from all public officers. From those officers, especially, who are charged with the collection and disbursement of the public revenue will prompt and rigid accountability be required. Any culpable failure or delay on their part to account for the moneys intrusted to them at the times and in the manner required by law will in every instance terminate the official connection of such defaulting officer with the Government.

Although in our country the Chief Magistrate must almost of necessity be chosen by a party and stand pledged to its principles and measures, yet in his official action he should not be the President of a part only, but of the whole people of the United States. While he executes the laws with an impartial hand, shrinks from no proper responsibility, and faithfully carries out in the executive department of the Government the principles and policy of those who have chosen him, he should not be unmindful that our fellow-citizens who have differed with him in opinion are entitled to the full and free exercise of their opinions and judgments, and that the rights of all are entitled to respect and regard.

Confidently relying upon the aid and assistance of the coordinate departments of the Government in conducting our public affairs, I enter upon the discharge of the high duties which have been assigned me by the people, again humbly supplicating that Divine Being who has watched over and protected our beloved country from its infancy to the present hour to continue His gracious benedictions upon us, that we may continue to be a prosperous and happy people.

March 4, 1845

NOTES

PREFACE

1   For the profane version of the question and its variations as used in 1844, see *Vermont Journal* (Windsor), 27 June 1844, and *New York Herald*, 11 November 1844. Examples of the less-profane version used in 1844 can be found in *Old Warrior and "That Same Old Coon"* (Harrisburg, PA), 1 June 1844; *Pittsfield (MA) Sun*, 6 June 1844; George L. Brown to Edward S. Aldrich, 4 July 1844, in *The Letters of George Long Brown: A Yankee Merchant on Florida's Antebellum Frontier*, ed. James M. Denham and Keith L. Huneycutt (Gainesville: University Press of Florida, 2019), 64; Joseph B. Anthony to James K. Polk, September 25, 1844, and Joseph Favor to James K. Polk, 10 November 1844, Polk Papers, DLC. For examples of the profane version in the post–Civil War era, see *Cincinnati Enquirer*, 20 February 1868; *Reading (PA) Adler*, 27 June 1876; *Public Ledger* (Memphis, TN), 16 July 1880; *Louisiana Democrat* (Alexandria), 28 July 1897.

2   "James K. Polk," in *BDUSC*; Sam Haynes, *James K. Polk and the Expansionist Impulse* (New York: Longman, 1997), 43–50. For examples of the question in the post–Civil War era, see *Cincinnati Enquirer*, 20 February 1868; *Reading (PA) Adler*, 27 June 1876; *Public Ledger* (Memphis, TN), 16 July 1880; *Louisiana Democrat* (Alexandria), 28 July 1897.

3   A search of online newspaper databases in 1844–1845 did not turn up the use of "dark horse" in reference to Polk. The term, which could refer either to a little-known competitor or to someone who emerges as an unexpected success story, was still relatively new in 1844. See "dark horse, *fig.*," *OED Online*.

CHAPTER 1. "A POLITICAL SATURNALIA"

1   Mark R. Cheathem, *Andrew Jackson and the Rise of the Democratic Party* (Knoxville: University of Tennessee Press, 2018), 63–64, 71–79; Donald J. Ratcliffe, *The One-Party Presidential Contest: Adams, Jackson, and 1824's Five-Horse Race* (Lawrence: University Press of Kansas, 2015), 253–257.

2   *Vermont Patriot and State Gazette* (Montpelier, VT), September 24, 1827; Cheathem, *Andrew Jackson and the Rise of the Democratic Party*, 55–56, 61–62; "John Quincy Adams," Prints and Photographs Division, DLC, https://www .loc.gov/resource/ppmsc.02936/; William J. Cooper, *The Lost Founding Father: John Quincy Adams and the Transformation of American Politics* (New York: Liveright, 2017), 202; "John Quincy Adams," in *BDUSC*; Daniel Walker Howe,

What Hath God Wrought: The Transformation of America, 1815–1848 (New York: Oxford University Press, 2007), 211.

3   "Henry Clay," in *BDUSC*; John R. Van Atta, *Wolf by the Ears: The Missouri Crisis, 1819–1821* (Baltimore: Johns Hopkins University Press, 2015), 24, 92–99; Robert V. Remini, *Henry Clay: Statesman for the Union* (New York: W. W. Norton, 1991), 229; "Portrait of Henry Clay," Historic Art Collection, Transylvania University, https://hub.catalogit.app/6735/folder/entry/e0016640-05cf-11ec -9007-9790faeo0011; Willie P. Mangum to Duncan Cameron, December 10, 1823, in *Papers of Willie Person Mangum*, ed. Henry T. Shanks (Raleigh, NC: State Department of Archives and History, 1950–1956), 1:83; Diary entries, 8 and 21 September 1814, and 9 March 1821, in John Quincy Adams, *Memoirs of John Quincy Adams, Comprising Portions of His Diary from 1795 to 1848*, ed. Charles Francis Adams (Freeport, NY: Books for Libraries Press, 1969), 3:32, 39; 5:325; David S. Heidler and Jeanne T. Heidler, *Henry Clay: The Essential American* (New York: Random House, 2010), 45, 111, 169–170. The nickname "Prince Hal" was a reference to Shakespeare's depiction of Henry V's youthful indiscretions before ascending the throne; see Heidler and Heidler, *Henry Clay*, 45; and Alan Gerald Gross, "The Justification of Prince Hal," *Texas Studies in Literature and Language* 10 (Spring 1968): 27–35.

4   Cheathem, *Andrew Jackson and the Rise of the Democratic Party*, 35, 40, 46; Mark R. Cheathem, *Andrew Jackson, Southerner* (Baton Rouge: Louisiana State University Press, 2013), 99–117; Ludwig M. Deppisch, "Andrew Jackson and American Medical Practice: Old Hickory and His Physicians," *Tennessee Historical Quarterly* 62 (Summer 2003): 131–132.

5   Donald B. Cole, *Martin Van Buren and the American Political System* (Princeton, NJ: Princeton University Press, 1984), 1–181; Chase C. Mooney, *William H. Crawford: 1772–1834* (Lexington: University Press of Kentucky, 1974), 302–341; Martin Van Buren to Thomas Ritchie, 13 January 1827, PMVB (mvb00528).

6   Cheathem, *Andrew Jackson and the Rise of the Democratic Party*, 23; "John C. Calhoun," ca. 1823, National Portrait Gallery, https://npg.si.edu/object/npg _NPG.65.58; Diary entry, 15 October 1821, in Adams, *Memoirs of John Quincy Adams*, 5:361; Robert Elder, *Calhoun: American Heretic* (New York: Basic Books, 2021), 209, 221–222.

7   Cheathem, *Andrew Jackson and the Rise of the Democratic Party*, xvi–xvii, 83–110.

8   James Parton, *Life of Andrew Jackson* (New York: Mason Brothers, 1861), 3:287; Andrew Jackson to John Overton, 31 December 1829, in *PAJ*, 7:656; Cheathem, *Andrew Jackson and the Rise of the Democratic Party*, 121. The Eaton affair is ably covered in John F. Marszalek, *The Petticoat Affair: Manners, Mutiny, and Sex in Andrew Jackson's White House* (New York: Free Press, 1997).

9   Cheathem, *Andrew Jackson and the Rise of the Democratic Party*, 1–10, 83–91, 135; "Democrats" and "Locofocos," in *HDJEMD*, 118–120, 224–225. The "Locofoco" label originated at an 1835 Democratic meeting in New York where those supporting urban workers were forced to continue the meeting using candles, lit by "locofoco" matches, after their opponents threw Tammany Hall in the dark by extinguishing the gaslights.

10 Cheathem, *Andrew Jackson and the Rise of the Democratic Party*, 183; Mark R. Cheathem, *The Coming of Democracy: Presidential Campaigning in the Age of Jackson* (Baltimore: Johns Hopkins University Press, 2018), 71; Norman K. Risjord, *The Old Republicans: Southern Conservatism in the Age of Jefferson* (New York: Columbia University Press, 1965), 1–127; Cheathem, *Andrew Jackson, Southerner*, 125, 133–135.

11 "Presidential Election, 1832," "Whigs," in *HDJEMD*, 137, 405–407; Cheathem, *Andrew Jackson and the Rise of the Democratic Party*, 1–10, 201–202; Stephen White to Daniel Webster, 27 December 1833, in *PDW:Corr.*, 3:296–97; "King Andrew the First," Prints and Photographs Division, DLC, http://www.loc.gov /pictures/item/2008661753/; James G. Barber, *Andrew Jackson: A Portrait Study* (Seattle: University of Washington Press, 1991), 157 fig. 118; Michael F. Holt, *The Rise and Fall of the American Whig Party: Jacksonian Politics and the Onset of the Civil War* (New York: Oxford University Press, 1999), 17–32.

12 Steven C. Bullock, *Revolutionary Brotherhood: Freemasonry and the Transformation of the American Social Order, 1730–1840* (Chapel Hill: University of North Carolina Press, 1996), 281–282; Cooper, *Lost Founding Father*, 283–285; Holt, *Rise and Fall*, 13–14, 29–30, 37–39; "Anti-Masonic Party," in *HDJEMD*, 39–40; Anthony Gene Carey, *Parties, Slavery, and the Union in Antebellum Georgia* (Athens: University of Georgia Press, 1997), 31–38, 47–49.

13 Cheathem, *Coming of Democracy*, 119; Michael J. Dubin, *United States Presidential Elections, 1788–1860: The Official Results by County and State* (Jefferson, NC: McFarland, 2002), 61.

14 James Buchanan to Benjamin Carpenter et al., 17 December 1836, in *The Works of James Buchanan, Comprising His Speeches, State Papers, and Private Correspondence*, ed. John Bassett Moore (Philadelphia: J. B. Lippincott, 1908–11), 3:130.

15 Cheathem, *Andrew Jackson, Southerner*, 114–115; Cheathem, *Andrew Jackson and the Rise of the Democratic Party*, 161–166.

16 Cheathem, *Andrew Jackson, Southerner*, 125, 133–135; Donald B. Cole, *The Presidency of Andrew Jackson* (Lawrence: University Press of Kansas, 1993), 143–144; Andrew Jackson, Nullification Proclamation, 10 December 1832, in *A Compilation of the Messages and Papers of the Presidents, 1789–1902*, comp. James D. Richardson (Washington, DC: Bureau of National Literature and Art, 1907), 2:652, 654; Diary entry, 19 December 1832, in Charles H. Ambler, *The Life and Diary of John Floyd: Governor of Virginia, an Apostle of Secession, and the Father of the Oregon Country* (Richmond, VA: Richmond Press, 1918), 204; William K. Bolt, *Tariff Wars and the Politics of Jacksonian America* (Nashville: Vanderbilt University Press, 2017), 134–144.

17 Cheathem, *Andrew Jackson and the Rise of the Democratic Party*, 178–191; Andrew Jackson, Veto message, 10 July 1832, in Richardson, comp., *Messages and Papers*, 2:576–591.

18 Andrew Jackson to James K. Polk, 16 December 1832, in *CJKP*, 1:575; Andrew Jackson, Paper read to the cabinet, 18 September 1833, Andrew Jackson, "Protest" message, 15 April 1834, in Richardson, comp., *Messages and Papers*, 3:19, 90; Cheathem, *Andrew Jackson and the Rise of the Democratic Party*, 196–198,

203; Nicholas Biddle to Joseph Hopkinson, 21 February 1834, in *The Correspondence of Nicholas Biddle Dealing with National Affairs, 1807–1844*, ed. Reginald C. McGrane (Boston: Houghton Mifflin, 1919), 222; Henry Clay, Speech, 26 December 1833, in US Senate, *Register of Debates*, 23rd Cong., 1st Sess., 60, 94.

19 Cheathem, *Coming of Democracy*, 122–125; Jessica M. Lepler, *The Many Panics of 1837: People, Politics, and the Creation of a Transatlantic Financial Crisis* (Cambridge: Cambridge University Press, 2013), 122; Sharon Ann Murphy, *Other People's Money: How Banking Worked in the Early American Republic* (Baltimore: Johns Hopkins University, 2017), 45–47, 99–102, 106–109; Major L. Wilson, *The Presidency of Martin Van Buren* (Lawrence: University Press of Kansas, 1984), 124.

20 Cheathem, *Andrew Jackson and the Rise of the Democratic Party*, 1–3; Gordon S. Wood, "Conspiracy and the Paranoid Style: Causality and Deceit in the Eighteenth Century," *William & Mary Quarterly* 39 (July 1982): 401–441.

21 Memorandum on appointments, 23 February 1829, and Memorandum book entry, 21 May 1829, in *PAJ*, 7:60–61, 193.

22 Fowler's Garden Speech, 16 May 1829, in *PHC*, 8:43, 45; "King Andrew the First" [1833], Prints and Photographs Division, DLC, https://www.loc.gov/pictures/item/2008661753/; Barber, *Andrew Jackson*, 157 fig. 118. In defending Jackson's philosophy on the Senate floor in 1832, New Yorker William L. Marcy argued that successful politicians "see nothing wrong in the rule, that to the victor belong the spoils of the enemy"; see *Register of Debates*, Senate, 22nd Cong., 1st Sess. (24–25 January 1832): 1325.

23 Cheathem, *Andrew Jackson and the Rise of the Democratic Party*, 131–137; Richard R. John, *Spreading the News: The American Postal System from Franklin to Morse* (Cambridge, MA: Harvard University Press, 1995), 212–13; Leo Hershkowitz, "'The Land of Promise': Samuel Swartwout and Land Speculation in Texas, 1830–1838," *New York Historical Society Quarterly* 48 (October 1964): 307–325; Wilson, *Presidency of Martin Van Buren*, 125–126; Leonard D. White, *The Jacksonians: A Study in Administrative History, 1829–1861* (New York: Macmillan, 1954), 422; Stephen W. Campbell, *The Bank War and the Partisan Press: Newspapers, Financial Institutions, and the Post Office in Jacksonian America* (Lawrence: University Press of Kansas, 2019), 127–132; Robert V. Remini, *Andrew Jackson* (New York: Harper & Row, 1977–1984), 3:241; US Senate, *Register of Debates*, 23rd Cong., 1st Sess. (9 June 1834): 229; Howe, *What Hath God Wrought*, 353; Cole, *Presidency of Andrew Jackson*, 111–112; Ronald N. Satz, *American Indian Policy in the Jacksonian Era* (Lincoln: University of Nebraska Press, 1975), 30, 87, 193–195.

24 James S. Chase, *Emergence of the Presidential Nominating Convention, 1789–1832* (Urbana: University of Illinois Press, 1973), 267; *United States' Telegraph*, 3 February 1835; Barber, *Andrew Jackson*, 157 fig. 118; Cole, *Martin Van Buren*, 226. For examples of the use of "Little Magician" during Van Buren's presidency, see *Boston Traveler*, 27 June 1837; *Alexandria (VA) Gazette*, 22 September 1838; *National Gazette and Literary Register* (Philadelphia), 15 October 1838; *Cabinet* (Schenectady, NY), 12 November 1839. For the use of "sly fox," see *Madisonian for the Country* (Washington, DC), 18 June 1840.

25 Cole, *Martin Van Buren*, 9–13; Richard J. Ellis, *Old Tip vs. the Sly Fox: The 1840 Election and the Making of a Partisan Nation* (Lawrence: University Press of Kansas, 2020), 213; Robert Gray Gunderson, "Ogle's Omnibus of Lies," *Pennsylvania Magazine of History and Biography* 80 (October 1956): 444; Holt, *Rise and Fall*, 40–41, 54, 91–93, 101–104; "Francis Granger" and "Landaff Watson Andrews," in *BDUSC*; US House, *Congressional Globe*, 26th Cong., 1st Sess. (April 14, 1840): 327; *New Haven (CT) Evening Palladium*, quoted in *Hartford Courant*, 24 March 1840; Charles Ogle, *Speech of Mr. Ogle, of Pennsylvania, on the Regal Splendor of the President's Palace. Delivered in the House of Representatives, April 14, 1840* ([Washington?]: [1840]), 1–8; A Workingman, *More Than One Hundred Reasons Why William Henry Harrison Should and Will Have the Support of the Democracy [. . .]* (Boston: Tuttle, Dennett and Chisholm, 1840), 8.

26 M. J. Heale, *The Presidential Quest: Candidates and Images in American Political Culture, 1787–1852* (New York: Longman, 1982), 8, 12–13, 17, 20; Andrew S. Trees, *The Founding Fathers and the Politics of Character* (Princeton, NJ: Princeton University Press, 2004), xi–xii.

27 Cheathem, *Andrew Jackson, Southerner*, 105–117; Craig Bruce Smith, *American Honor: The Creation of the Nation's Ideals during the Revolutionary Era* (Chapel Hill: University of North Carolina Press, 2018), 213–240; *Eastern Argus* (Portland, ME), 8 July 1828; *New Hampshire Patriot and State Gazette* (Concord), 27 August 1832; Robert V. Remini, *Daniel Webster: The Man and His Time* (New York: W. W. Norton, 1997), 307–309.

28 Ogle, *Speech of Mr. Ogle*, 1–2, 5–6, 8; Bryan C. Rindfleisch, "'What It Means to Be a Man': Contested Masculinity in the Early Republic and Antebellum America," *History Compass* 10 (November 2012): 852–865; David Crockett [Augustin S. Clayton], *The Life of Martin Van Buren . . .* (Philadelphia: Robert Wright, 1835), 80–81; see "dandy, n.1, adj., and adv.," *OED Online*; Cheathem, *Coming of Democracy*, 111, 118–119; *Washington (DC) Daily Globe*, 19 January 1836.

29 Cave Johnson to James K. Polk, 29 January 1843, in *CJKP*, 6:197; Jonathan Milnor Jones, "The Making of a Vice President: The National Political Career of Richard M. Johnson of Kentucky" (PhD diss., University of Memphis, 1998), 5–7; Stuart S. Sprague, "The Death of Tecumseh and the Rise of Rumpsey Dumpsey: The Making of a Vice President," *Filson Club Quarterly* 59 (October 1985): 455–461; Christina Snyder, *Great Crossings: Indians, Settlers, and Slaves in the Age of Jackson* (New York: Oxford University Press, 2017), 53–64, 194–218; *Indiana American* (Brookville), 17 July 1835.

30 *Providence (RI) Journal*, 2 June 1835; *United States' Telegraph Extra*, 5 June 1835; *Richmond (VA) Whig*, 2 June 1835, and 20 July 1835. White American society found the use of "Negro" acceptable during the Jacksonian era, but even then, it contained negative connotations. See Jabari Asim, *The N Word: Who Can Say It, Who Shouldn't, and Why* (Boston: Houghton Mifflin, 2007), 11–12.

31 Jones, "Making of a Vice President," 310–314; Cheathem, *Coming of Democracy*, 119.

32 Mark R. Cheathem, "African-American Revolutionaries," in *Jacksonian and Antebellum Age: People and Perspectives*, ed. Mark R. Cheathem (Santa Barbara,

CA: ABC-CLIO, 2008), 1–5; Kellie Carter Jackson, *Force and Freedom: Black Abolitionists and the Politics of Violence* (Philadelphia: University of Pennsylvania Press, 2019), 17–24.

33 Paul Finkelman, *Defending Slavery: Proslavery Thought in the Old South* (Boston: Bedford/St. Martin's, 2003), 25–40; John Patrick Daly, *When Slavery Was Called Freedom: Evangelicalism, Proslavery, and the Causes of the Civil War* (Lexington: University Press of Kentucky, 2002), 30–56; Lewis Cecil Gray, *History of Agriculture in the Southern United States to 1860* (Gloucester, MA: Peter Smith, 1958), 2:1026; Adam Rothman, *Slave Country: American Expansion and the Origins of the Deep South* (Cambridge, MA: Harvard University Press, 2005), 187–189; Steven Deyle, *Carry Me Back: The Domestic Slave Trade in American Life* (New York: Oxford University Press, 2005), 140; Michael Tadman, *Speculators and Slaves: Masters, Traders, and Slaves in the Old South* (Madison: University of Wisconsin Press, 1989), 12; Cheathem, *Andrew Jackson, Southerner*, 58–78, 90–98; Edward E. Baptist, *The Half Has Never Been Told: Slavery and the Making of American Capitalism* (New York: Basic Books, 2014), 117–118; Joshua D. Rothman, *The Ledger and the Chain: How Domestic Slave Traders Shaped America* (New York: Basic Books, 2021), 104.

34 Michael Feldberg, *The Philadelphia Riots of 1844: A Study of Ethnic Conflict* (Westport, CT: Greenwood Press, 1975), 43–50; David Grimsted, *American Mobbing, 1828–1861: Toward Civil War* (New York: Oxford University Press, 1998), 1–82; Leonard L. Richards, *"Gentlemen of Property and Standing": Anti-Abolition Mobs in Jacksonian America* (New York: Oxford University Press, 1970), 1–46; Cheathem, *Andrew Jackson, Southerner*, 172–173; Andrew Jackson to Amos Kendall, 9 August 1835, Andrew Jackson Papers, DLC.

35 Thomas Cooper to the editor of the *Columbia (SC) Telescope*, 18 March 1837, PMVB (mvb11775); Cole, *Martin Van Buren*, 329, 361, 363–364.

36 Richard Bruce Winders, *Crisis in the Southwest: The United States, Mexico, and the Struggle over Texas* (Wilmington, DE: Scholarly Resources, 2002), 10–11, 79–82; Cole, *Martin Van Buren*, 317–319.

37 Cole, *Martin Van Buren*, 319–321; John H. Schroeder, "Annexation or Independence: The Texas Issue in American Politics, 1836–1845," *Southwestern Historical Quarterly* 89 (October 1985): 145–147; Leonard L. Richards, *The Slave Power: The Free North and Southern Domination, 1780–1860* (Baton Rouge: Louisiana State University Press, 2000), 136; Daniel Carpenter, *Democracy by Petition: Popular Politics in Transformation, 1790–1870* (Cambridge, MA: Harvard University Press, 2021), 356; *Fifth Annual Report of the Executive Committee of the American Anti-Slavery Society . . .* (New York: William S. Dorr, 1838), 48.

38 On Manifest Destiny in this era, see Thomas R. Hietala, *Manifest Design: Anxious Aggrandizement in Late Jacksonian America* (Ithaca, NY: Cornell University Press, 1985); Anders Stephanson, *Manifest Destiny: American Expansionism and the Empire of Right* (New York: Hill & Wang, 1995).

39 Andrew Jackson, First Annual Message, 8 December 1829, in Richardson, comp., *Messages and Papers*, 2:455–59; "The Removal Act of May 28, 1830," in Satz, *American Indian Policy*, 296–98; Tim Alan Garrison, "United States In-

dian Policy in Sectional Crisis: Georgia's Exploitation of the Compact of 1802," in *Congress and the Emergence of Sectionalism: From the Missouri Compromise to the Age of Jackson*, ed. Paul Finkelman and Donald R. Kennon (Athens: Ohio University Press, 2008), 122–123; Cheatham, *Andrew Jackson and the Rise of the Democratic Party*, 153–156; C. S. Monaco, *The Second Seminole War and the Limits of American Aggression* (Baltimore: Johns Hopkins University Press, 2018), 200.

40 *Pennsylvania Freeman* (Philadelphia), 10 May 1838; Wilson, *Presidency of Martin Van Buren*, 185–186; Howe, *What Hath God Wrought*, 416; Cheatham, *Andrew Jackson and the Rise of the Democratic Party*, 153–156.

41 Martin Van Buren, First Annual Message, 5 December 1837, in Richardson, comp., *Messages and Papers*, 3:391; Monaco, *Second Seminole War*, 55, 76–81, 93–97; *Boston Courier*, 4 October 1838; *Auburn (NY) Journal and Advertiser*, 28 March 1838; *Hampshire Gazette* (Northampton, MA), 26 September 1838.

42 Maxime Dagenais and Julien Mauduit, eds., *Revolutions across Borders: Jacksonian American and the Canadian Rebellion* (Montreal and Kingston: McGill-Queen's University Press, 2019), 3–6; Sam Y. Haynes, *Unfinished Revolution: The Early American Republic in a British World* (Charlottesville: University of Virginia Press, 2010), 209–210; Wilson, *Presidency of Martin Van Buren*, 166.

43 Gordon S. Wood, *Empire of Liberty: A History of the Early Republic, 1789–1815* (New York: Oxford University Press, 2009), 247–250; Padraig Riley, *Slavery and the Democratic Conscience: Political Life in Jeffersonian America* (Philadelphia: University of Pennsylvania Press, 2016), 71–77; Terri Diane Halperin, *The Alien and Sedition Acts of 1798: Testing the Constitution* (Baltimore: Johns Hopkins University Press, 2016), 15–16, 34–38, 44–45, 47–48, 56–57, 76.

44 Angela F. Murphy, *American Slavery, Irish Freedom: Abolition, Immigrant Citizenship, and the Transatlantic Movement for Irish Repeal* (Baton Rouge: Louisiana State University Press, 2010), 10; Holt, *Rise and Fall*, 117–118; US Census Bureau, *Historical Statistics of the United States: Colonial Times to 1970* (Washington, DC: GPO, 1975), 1:106; Tyler Anbinder, *Nativism and Slavery: The Northern Know Nothings and the Politics of the 1850s* (New York: Oxford University Press, 1992), 1–10.

45 Anbinder, *Nativism and Slavery*, 5–10; David Brion Davis, "Some Themes of Counter-Subversion: An Analysis of Anti-Masonic, Anti-Catholic, and Anti-Mormon Literature," *Mississippi Valley Historical Review* 47 (September 1960): 205–24; "Samuel F. B. Morse," in *HDJEMD*, 251–252; Murphy, *American Slavery, Irish Freedom*, 11; Cassandra Yacovazzi, *Escaped Nuns: True Womanhood and the Campaign against Convents in Antebellum America* (New York: Oxford University Press, 2018), 26–47.

46 Ellen M. Hanson to Andrew Jackson, 12 March 1835, and Andrew Jackson to Ellen M. Hanson, 25 March 1835, Jackson Papers, DLC; Jason K. Duncan, "'Plain Catholics of the North': Martin Van Buren and the Politics of Religion, 1807–1836," *U.S. Catholic Historian* 38 (Winter 2020): 25–48; Martin Van Buren to Felix Cicognani, 20 July 1829, PMVB (mvb00954); Cole, *Martin Van Buren*,

269; *Vermont Phoenix* (Brattleboro), 2 August 1839; *Tennessee Whig* (Elizabethton), 5 March 1840; *South-Western Virginian* (Abingdon), 1 August 1840; *Pilot and Transcript* (Baltimore), 26 October 1840. My thanks to Tom Coens at the Papers of Andrew Jackson for providing transcriptions of the Hanson–Jackson correspondence (Email, 21 January 2021).

47   Ray A. Billington, *The Protestant Crusade, 1800–1860: A Study of the Origins of American Nativism* (New York: Macmillan, 1938), 97–98; Thomas M. Brown, "The Image of the Beast: Anti-Papal Rhetoric in Colonial America," in *Conspiracy: The Fear of Subversion in American History*, ed. Richard O. Curry and Thomas M. Brown (New York: Holt, Rinehart and Winston, 1972), 1–20; Jenny Franchot, *Roads to Rome: The Antebellum Protestant Encounter with Catholicism* (Berkeley: University of California Press, 1994), 135–161; Marie Anne Pagliarini, "The Pure American Woman and the Wicked Catholic Priest: An Analysis of Anti-Catholic Literature in Antebellum America," *Religion and American Culture: A Journal of Interpretation* 9 (Winter 1999): 97–128; James L. Gray, "Culture, Gender, and the Slave Narrative," *Proteus: A Journal of Ideas* 7 (Spring 1990): 37–42; Frances Smith Foster, *Witnessing Slavery: The Development of Ante-bellum Slave Narratives*, 2nd ed. (Madison: University of Wisconsin Press, 1994), 44–61; Cindy Weinstein, "The Slave Narrative and Sentimental Literature," in *The Cambridge Companion to the African American Slave Narrative*, ed. Audrey A. Fisch (New York: Cambridge University Press, 2007), 115–134.

48   US Census Bureau, *Historical Statistics*, 1:106; Anbinder, *Nativism and Slavery*, 1–10; Billington, *Protestant Crusade*, 118–120, 123, 132–135.

49   Howe, *What Hath God Wrought*, 455, 557; Cheathem, *Coming of Democracy*, 9.

50   Jon Grinspan, *The Virgin Vote: How Young Americans Made Democracy Social, Politics Personal, and Voting Popular in the Nineteenth Century* (Chapel Hill: University of North Carolina Press, 2016), 10–11, 66–69, 163.

51   Cheathem, *Coming of Democracy*, 129–131; Richard J. Ellis, *Presidential Travel: The Journey from George Washington to George W. Bush* (Lawrence: University Press of Kansas, 2008), 15–59.

52   Edward J. Crapol, *John Tyler: The Accidental President* (Chapel Hill: University of North Carolina Press, 2006), 30–32, 41, 50; Cheathem, *Coming of Democracy*, 106–107.

53   William Henry Harrison, Speech, 28 July 1840, in *Portland (ME) Advertiser*, 1 September 1840; Heale, *Presidential Image*, 119; "King Matty and Blair," in *Wabash Courier* (Terre Haute, IN), September 19, 1840; *New York Morning Express*, May 9, 1840; *Richmond (IN) Weekly Palladium*, 28 December 1839; *Cincinnati Chronicle*, quoted in *Daily Republican Banner* (Nashville, TN), 19 March 1840; *Richmond (VA) Whig*, 10 July 1840.

54   Snyder, *Great Crossings*, 215–216; Andrew Jackson to Francis P. Blair, 22 May 1840, in *CAJ*, 6:61; Unknown to Amos Kendall, 12 August 1839, PMVB (mvb02830); Amos Kendall to Martin Van Buren, 22 August 1839, PMVB (mvb02836); Nicholas P. Cox, "The White, Black and Indian Families of Richard Mentor Johnson" (PhD diss., University of Houston, 2012), 83–84. My

thanks to Amrita Chakrabarti Myers for help with the question of Dinah Chinn (Email, 11 July 2022).

55 *Boston Nettle*, 10 July 1840; *New Bedford (MA) Register*, 30 July 1840; *Mecklenburg (NC) Jeffersonian*, 16 April 1844; *New York Daily Herald*, 5 June 1844; *The Age* (Woodstock, VT), 25 July 1844; Charles G. Sellers Jr., *James K. Polk* (Princeton, NJ: Princeton University Press, 1966), 1:399–403, 406, 410–416; Diary entry, April 14, 1840, in St. George L. Sioussat, ed., "Diaries of S. H. Laughlin, of Tennessee, 1840, 1843," *Tennessee Historical Magazine* 2 (March 1916): 46; Andrew Jackson to Martin Van Buren, 29 April 1840, PMVB (mvb02959); Martin Van Buren to Andrew Jackson, 17 April 1840, PMVB (mvb09900); Alexander O. Anderson to James K. Polk, 2 March 1840, Felix Grundy to James K. Polk, 15 April 1840, and James K. Polk to Felix Grundy, 27 May 1840, in *CJKP*, 5:398–399, 428, 470–471; *Niles' Weekly Register*, 9 May 1840, 151; Roderick Heller III, *Democracy's Lawyer: Felix Grundy of the Old Southwest* (Baton Rouge: Louisiana State University Press, 2010), 254–257; Richard M. Johnson to Linn Boyd and William O. Butler, 25 April 1840, in *Washington (DC) Daily Globe*, 7 May 1840; Richard M. Johnson to Humphrey Marshall, 26 May 1840, Humphrey Marshall Papers, folder 1, Filson Historical Society.

56 Cheathem, *Coming of Democracy*, 136–169; Andrew Jackson to Francis P. Blair, 26 September 1840, in *CAJ*, 6:78; *Baltimore Chronicle*, n.d., quoted in *Phoenix Civilian* (Cumberland, MD), December 21, 1839; Heidler and Heidler, *Henry Clay*, 371–372; David R. Roediger, *The Wages of Whiteness: Race and the Making of the American Working Class*, rev. ed. (Brooklyn, NY: Verso, 1999), 98. For examples of Whig parades containing these elements, see *Augusta (GA) Chronicle*, 22 July 1840, and *Albany (NY) Argus*, 18 August 1840.

57 Martin Van Buren, "Thoughts on New York," [March 1840], 1, 6, 74, Martin Van Buren Papers, DLC. This manuscript draft has many additions, deletions, and emendations. For that reason, I have edited the text for clarity and added page numbers for each manuscript page in the above citation.

58 Cheathem, *Coming of Democracy*, 145–147; Andrew Jackson to Charles F. M. Dancy and Thomas B. M. Murphy, 3 July 1840, and Andrew Jackson to Francis P. Blair, 26 September 1840, in *CAJ*, 6:67–68, 78; Sellers, *James K. Polk*, 1:420–423; James K. Polk to Samuel H. Laughlin, August 2, 1840, James K. Polk to Alexander O. Anderson, August 16, 1840, and James K. Polk to Robert M. Burton, 20 August 1840, in *CJKP*, 5:524–525, 541–543, 544–545; Andrew Jackson to Francis P. Blair, 26 September 1840, in *CAJ*, 6:78.

59 Dubin, *United States Presidential Elections*, 71–82; US Senate, "Party Division," http://www.senate.gov/pagelayout/history/one_item_and_teasers/partydiv .htm; and US House, "Party Divisions of the House of Representatives," History, Art and Archives: United States House of Representatives, http://history .house.gov/Institution/Party-Divisions/Party-Divisions/; Mark R. Cheathem, "'It has caused me considerable embarrassment and not a little pain': The Ruptured Relationship of Martin Van Buren and James K. Polk," in *Polk and His Time: Essays on the Conclusion of the Correspondence of James K. Polk*, ed. Michael

D. Cohen (Knoxville: University of Tennessee Press, 2022), 111–133; Ellis, *Old Tip vs. the Sly Fox*, 260–266.

60 Cheathem, *Coming of Democracy*, 169; Martin Van Buren, "The Autobiography of Martin Van Buren," ed. John C. Fitzpatrick, in *Annual Report of the American Historical Association for 1918* (Washington, DC: Government Printing Office, 1920), 2:394; Andrew Jackson to Martin Van Buren, 24 November 1840, in *CAJ*, 6:83–84.

CHAPTER 2. "OLL FOR KLAY"

1 Diary entry, 4 December 1840, in Adams, *Memoirs*, 10:366.

2 Philip Hone, *The Diary of Philip Hone, 1828–1851* (New York: Dodd, Mead, 1889), 2:67; *Daily National Intelligencer* (Washington, DC), 5 March 1841; *Alexandria (VA) Gazette*, 11 March 1841; Freeman Cleaves, *Old Tippecanoe: William Henry Harrison and His Time* (New York: Scribner's, 1939; Norwalk, CT: Easton Press, 1986), 335; Christopher J. Leahy, *President without a Party: The Life of John Tyler* (Baton Rouge: Louisiana State University Press, 2020), 134; Jane McHugh and Philip A. Mackowiak, "Death in the White House: President William Henry Harrison's Atypical Pneumonia," *Clinical Infectious Diseases* 59 (October 2014): 990–995; Thomas Miller, "Case of the Late William H. Harrison, President of the United States," *Boston Medical and Surgical Journal* 24 (June 2, 1841): 266; Cabinet circular letter, 4 April 1841, in *Salem (MA) Register*, 5 April 1841; *Hartford Daily Courant*, 6 April 1841.

3 John Tyler to Littleton W. Tazewell, 11 October 1841, in *The Letters and Times of the Tylers*, ed. Lyon G. Tyler (Richmond, VA: Whittet & Shepperson, 1884–96), 2:127; Fred Shelley, ed., "The Vice President Receives Bad News in Williamsburg," and James Lyons to John Tyler, 3 April 1841, *Virginia Magazine of History and Biography* 76 (July 1968): 337–338, 339; Leahy, *President without a Party*, 127–131; Diary entry, 16 April 1841, in Adams, *Memoirs*, 10:463–464; Stephen W. Stathis, "John Tyler's Succession: A Reappraisal," *Prologue* 8 (Winter 1976): 234–235; Aaron Scott Crawford, "'I am President': John Tyler, Presidential Succession, the Crisis of Legitimacy, and the Defense of Presidential Power," in *When Life Strikes the President: Scandal, Death, and Illness in the White House*, ed. Jeffrey A. Engel and Thomas J. Knock (New York: Oxford University Press, 2017), 45; *Daily National Intelligencer* (Washington, DC), April 7, 1841; Peterson, *Presidencies of Harrison and Tyler*, 45–50; "25th Amendment," National Constitution Center, https://constitutioncenter.org/interactive-constitution/amendment/amendment-xxv. For early examples of the use of "His Accidency" in newspapers, see *Milledgeville (GA) Journal*, 11 May 1841; *Flag of the Union* (Tuscaloosa, AL), 19 May 1841; and *Mobile (AL) Daily Commercial Register and Patriot*, July 2, 1844.

4 Leahy, *President without a Party*, 14, 16–21, 36–37, 62, 68, 92–93, 109, 113, 116, 118, 121–122; Ellis, *Old Tip vs. the Sly Fox*, 89.

5 *Daily National Intelligencer* (Washington, DC), 7 April 1841; Henry Clay to John L. Lawrence, 13 April 1841, Henry Clay to Nathaniel Beverly Tucker, 15 April 1841, and Henry Clay to Henry B. Bascom, 17 April 1841, in *PHC*, 9: 519, 520,

520; Diary entry, 4 April 1841, in Adams, *Memoirs*, 10:457; James Kirke Paulding to Martin Van Buren, 11 April 1841, PMVB (mvb03239); Francis P. Blair to Andrew Jackson, 4 and 11 April 1841, and Andrew Jackson to Francis P. Blair, 19 April 1841, in *CAJ*, 6:98, 103–104.

6   John Tyler to Samuel Rush et al., 19 February 1842, in *Daily Madisonian* (Washington, DC), 26 February 1842; *Madisonian* (Washington, DC), 6 March 1841; John Tyler to William C. Rives, 9 April 1841, in Tyler, *Letters and Times*, 2:20.

7   Richard E. Ellis, "The Persistence of Antifederalism after 1789," in *Beyond Confederation: Origins of the Constitution and American National Identity*, ed. Richard Beeman et al. (Chapel Hill: University of North Carolina Press, 1987), 297; John Tyler, Speech, April 30, 1834, in US Senate, *Register of Debates*, 23rd Cong., 1st Sess., 1573–81; Craig M. Simpson, *A Good Southerner: The Life of Henry A. Wise of Virginia* (Chapel Hill: University of North Carolina Press, 1985), 45; William Henry Harrison, Inaugural Address, 9 April 1841, in Richardson, comp., *Messages and Papers*, 4:36–39.

8   William Henry Harrison to Henry Clay, November 2 and 15, 1840; Henry Clay to Robert P. Letcher, 4 November 1840; Henry Clay to Peter B. Porter, 8 December 1840; Henry Clay to James T. Austin, December 10, 1840; and Henry Clay to John M. Clayton, 17 and 29 December 1840, and 12 February 1841, in *PHC*, 9:450, 452, 451, 459, 460, 466, 469, 499–500; Remini, *Henry Clay*, 372–373, 492, 568–572; Norma Lois Peterson, *The Presidencies of William Henry Harrison and John Tyler* (Lawrence: University Press of Kansas, 1989), 31–34; William Henry Harrison to Daniel Webster, 1 December 1840, and Daniel Webster to William Henry Harrison, 11 December 1840, in *PDW:Dipl.*, 1:3–4, 4–5. Nicholas Biddle to Daniel Webster, 13 December 1840, in McGrane, ed., *Correspondence of Nicholas Biddle*, 337; Remini, *Daniel Webster*, 469–470; *Louisville (KY) Daily Journal*, December 2, 1840; *Cincinnati Republican*, n.d., quoted in *Louisville (KY) Daily Journal*, 10 December 1840; *Washington Globe*, 14 December 1840.

9   John Tyler to Nathaniel Beverley Tucker, 28 July 1841, in Tyler, *Letters and Times*, 2:53–54; Ebenezer Pettigrew to James Cathcart Johnston, 17 May 1841, in *The Pettigrew Papers*, ed. Sarah McCulloh Lemmon (Raleigh, NC: State Department of Archives and History, 1971, 1988), 2:467.

10   *Charleston (SC) Daily Courier*, 15 September 1841; Peterson, *Presidencies of Harrison and Tyler*, 80; Simpson, *A Good Southerner*, 53–55; "Thomas Walker Gilmer" and "Francis Mallory," in *BDUSC*.

11   Peterson, *Presidencies of Harrison and Tyler*, 37–39; William Henry Harrison, Proclamation, 17 March 1841, in Richardson, *Messages and Papers*, 4:21.

12   John Tyler to Henry Clay, 30 April 1841, in *PHC*, 9:527–528.

13   Henry Clay to Charles L. Peyton, 11 May 1841, Thomas Ewing to Henry Clay, 8 May 1841, and Henry Clay to Francis T. Brooke, 14 May 1841, in *PHC*, 9:533, 530, 534.

14   Dan Monroe, *The Republican Vision of John Tyler* (College Station: Texas A&M University Press, 2003), 90; John Tyler, Special session message, 1 June 1841, in Richardson, *Messages and Papers*, 4:40–42, 50; Leahy, *President without a*

Party, 210; Crapol, *John Tyler*, 58–61, 74–80; Howard Jones and Donald A. Rakestraw, *Prologue to Manifest Destiny: Anglo-American Relations in the 1840s* (Wilmington, DE: Scholarly Resources, 1997), 78.

15   Monroe, *Republican Vision*, 90–101, 208n49; Henry Clay to Robert P. Letcher, 11 June 1841, in *PHC*, 9:544; Peterson, *Presidencies of Harrison and Tyler*, 62–71; John Tyler, Statement, ca. August 1842, and Thomas W. Gilmer to Franklin Minor, 7 August 1841, in Tyler, *Letters of Tylers*, 2:70, 706; Daniel Webster to Caroline Le Roy Webster, 8 August 1841, in *The Private Correspondence of Daniel Webster*, ed. Fletcher Webster (Boston: Little, Brown and Co., 1857), 2:107–108.

16   Daniel Webster, Memorandum on the banking bills and the vetoes, [1841], in *PDW, Corr.*, 5:177; Tyler, "Veto Message," 16 August 1841, in Richardson, *Messages and Papers*, 4:63–68; Monroe, *Republican Vision*, 100–101; Peterson, *Presidencies of Harrison and Tyler*, 71–72; Thomas W. Gilmer to Franklin Minor, 7 August 1841, in Tyler, *Letters of Tylers*, 2:707; William E. Ames, *A History of the "National Intelligencer"* (Chapel Hill: University of North Carolina Press, 1972), 249–250, 259–260; *Daily National Intelligencer* (Washington, DC), 19 and 20 August 1841; *Daily Madisonian* (Washington, DC), 19 and 21 August 1841; *State Capitol Gazette* (Harrisburg, PA), 27 August 1841; *Gettysburg (PA) Compiler*, 30 August 1841; *The Democrat* (Huntsville, AL), 11 September 1841; Wilhelmus Bogart Bryan, *A History of the National Capital, from Its Foundation through the Period of the Adoption of the Organic Act* (New York: Macmillan, 1914, 1916), 2:271–273.

17   *Illinois State Register* (Springfield), 3 September 1841; *Louisville (KY) Daily Journal*, 25 and 28 August 1841; *Mississippi Free Trader* (Natchez), 10 September 1841; *Alton (IL) Weekly Telegraph*, 28 August 1841; *Cincinnati Enquirer*, 27 August 1841; *Ohio Statesman* (Columbus), 1 September 1841; *Boston Post*, 7 September 1841; *Weekly Arkansas Gazette* (Little Rock), 15 September 1841; *The Democrat* (Huntsville, AL), 11 September 1841; James D. Birchfield, "Porter Clay, 'A Very Excellent Cabinetmaker'—Part One: Biographical Account," *Journal of Early Southern Decorative Arts* 35 (2014): 105–146, https://www.mesda journal.org/2014/porter-clay-a-excellent-cabinetmaker-part-one-biographical -account/.

18   Robert E. Shalhope, *The Baltimore Bank Riot: Political Upheaval in Antebellum Maryland* (Urbana: University of Illinois Press, 2009), 1–5.

19   Leahy, *President without a Party*, 166, 171–176; John M. Botts to "Coffee House, Richmond," 16 August 1841, in *Madisonian* (Washington, DC), 21 August 1841; Daniel Webster, Memorandum on the banking bills and the vetoes, 1841, in *PDW:Corr.*, 5:178; Henry Clay, Speech, 19 August 1841, in *Congressional Globe*, Senate, 27th Cong., 1st Sess., Appendix: 368; Nigel Graeme Barber, "The Corporal's Guard in Congress, 1841–1843" (Master's thesis, College of William & Mary, 1970).

20   Joanne B. Freeman, *Field of Blood: Violence in Congress and the Road to Civil War* (New York: Farrar, Straus and Giroux, 2018), 43, 128–129, 348–349n133; Ebenezer Pettigrew to James Cathcart Johnston, 15 September 1841, in Lemmon, ed., *Pettigrew Papers*, 2:483; Diary entry, 13 September 1841, in Benjamin

Brown French, *Witness to the Young Republic: A Yankee's Journal, 1828–1870*, ed. Donald B. Cole and John J. McDonough (Hanover, NH: University Press of New England, 1989), 125; Leahy, *President without a Party*, 177–185; Monroe, *Republican Vision*, 102; Henry A. Wise to Beverley Tucker, 29 August 1841, in Tyler, *Letters and Times*, 2:90–91.

21 Peterson, *Presidencies of Harrison and Tyler*, 86–87; Thomas Ewing to John Tyler, 11 September 1841, in *Madisonian* (Washington, DC), 14 September 1841; Remini, *Daniel Webster*, 528–530; Daniel Webster to Hiram Ketchum, 11 September 1841, in *PDW:Corr.*, 5:149–150; John Tyler to Littleton W. Tazewell, 11 October 1841, John Tyler Papers, DLC; Claude H. Hall, *Abel Parker Upshur: Conservative Virginian, 1790–1844* (Madison: State Historical Society of Wisconsin, 1964), 5, 75–76, 113–114; Crapol, *John Tyler*, 43, 47; Leahy, *President without a Party*, 62, 188; Michael O'Brien, *A Character of Hugh Legaré* (Knoxville: University of Tennessee Press, 1985), 163–166.

22 John Tyler to Daniel Webster, 11 October 1841, in *PDW:Corr.*, 5:166–167; Ebenezer Pettigrew to James Cathcart Johnston, 15 September 1841, in Lemmon, ed., *Pettigrew Papers*, 2:483; Leahy, *President without a Party*, 189–190; Whig address, 13 September 1841, in *Daily Madisonian* (Washington, DC), 16 September 1841; Andrew R. Black, *John Pendleton Kennedy: Early American Novelist, Whig Statesman, and Ardent Nationalist* (Baton Rouge: Louisiana State University Press, 2016), 185–186; Henry Clay to Robert P. Letcher, 11 June 1841, in *PHC*, 9:543.

23 Whig address, 13 September 1841, in *Daily Madisonian* (Washington, DC), 16 September 1841; Holt, *Rise and Fall*, 75 (table 6), 139–140; Diary entry, 15 August 1841, in French, *Witness to the Young Republic*, 121.

24 Peterson, *Presidencies of Harrison and Tyler*, 96–108; Leahy, *President without a Party*, 166, 176–177, 210–222; Monroe, *Republican Vision*, 142, 148–149; Henry Clay to John J. Crittenden, 3 June 1842, 16 and 26 July 1842, and Henry Clay to Willie P. Mangum, 11 July 1842, in *PHC*, 9:706, 735–736, 739–740, 731.

25 John J. Crittenden to Henry Clay, 12 August 1842, in *PHC*, 9:755; Peterson, *Presidencies of Harrison and Tyler*, 104–108, 169–173; US House, "Congress Profiles," https://history.house.gov/Congressional-Overview/Profiles/27th/, and https://history.house.gov/Congressional-Overview/Profiles/28th/; US Senate, "Party Divisions," https://www.senate.gov/pagelayout/history/one_item_and_teasers/partydiv.htm. Daniel Webster to Edward Everett, 31 October 1842, in *PDW:Corr.*, 5:250; Daniel Webster to Fletcher Webster, 8 November 1842, in *Private Correspondence of Daniel Webster*, 2:152.

26 Thomas Richards Jr., *Breakaway Americas: The Unmanifest Future of the Jacksonian United States* (Baltimore: Johns Hopkins University Press, 2020), 28, 39–40; Drew R. McCoy, *The Elusive Republic: Political Economy in Jeffersonian America* (Chapel Hill: University of North Carolina Press, 1996), 120–135; Crapol, *John Tyler*, 21, 37, 43, 47–50, 53, 59–61; Robert H. Gudmestad, *A Troublesome Commerce: The Transformation of the Interstate Slave Trade* (Baton Rouge: Louisiana State University Press, 2003), 166–167; Leahy, *President without a Party*, 119–120; Lawrence A. Peskin, "Conspiratorial Anglophobia and the War of

1812," *Journal of American History* 98 (December 2011): 647–669; Haynes, *Unfinished Revolution*, 118–122, 271–272, 280; US House, *Annals of Congress*, 16th Cong., 1st Sess., 1383, 1393.

27   Crapol, *John Tyler*, 25.

28   Leahy, *President without a Party*, 262–281; Donald A. Rakestraw, *Daniel Webster: Defender of Peace* (Lanham, MD: Rowman & Littlefield, 2018), 69–93; Peterson, *Presidencies of Harrison and Tyler*, 135; Frederick Merk, *Albert Gallatin and the Oregon Problem: A Study in Anglo-American Diplomacy* (Cambridge, MA: Harvard University Press, 1950), viii; "Oregon Treaty," in *HDJEMD*, 274.

29   Richards, *Breakaway Americas*, 183–184, 187–190, 197–198, 204; John Suval, "'The Nomadic Race to Which I Belong': Squatter Democracy and the Claiming of Oregon," *Oregon Historical Quarterly* 118 (Fall 2017): 307–308, 311–320; Michael B. Husband, "Senator Lewis F. Linn and the Oregon Question," *Missouri Historical Review* 66 (October 1971): 4–8, 10–14, 17–19; Peterson, *Presidencies of Harrison and Tyler*, 140; Matthew S. Warshauer, *Andrew Jackson and the Politics of Martial Law: Nationalism, Civil Liberties, and Partisanship* (Knoxville: University of Tennessee Press, 2006), 77–83; John M. Belohlavek, *Broken Glass: Caleb Cushing and the Shattering of the Union* (Kent, OH: Kent State University Press, 2005), 92–94, 152–153; Diary entry, 30 January 1843, in Adams, *Memoirs*, 11:304.

30   David M. Pletcher, *The Diplomacy of Annexation: Texas, Oregon, and the Mexican War* (Columbia: University of Missouri Press, 1973), 76–84; Herbert Gambrell, "Lamar, Mirabeau Buonaparte," *Handbook of Texas Online*, https://www.tshaonline.org/handbook/entries/lamar-mirabeau-buonaparte.

31   Simpson, *A Good Southerner*, 50; Hall, *Abel Parker Upshur*, 196; Leahy, *President without a Party*, 147; John Tyler to Daniel Webster, 11 October 1841, in *PDW:Corr.*, 5:167; Monroe, *Republican Vision*, 116; Crapol, *John Tyler*, 35–37, 58–61.

32   Rakestraw, *Daniel Webster*, 93–94; Leahy, *President without a Party*, 212, 288–290; Schroeder, "Annexation or Independence," 149–151.

33   Henry A. Wise, *Seven Decades of the Union* (Philadelphia: J. B. Lippincott, 1876), 181–182; Simpson, *A Good Southerner*, 50, 55–57; *Daily National Intelligencer* (Washington, DC), 15 April 1842; William G. Shade, *Democratizing the Old Dominion: Virginia and the Second Party System, 1824–1861* (Charlottesville: University Press of Virginia, 1996), 251; Thomas W. Gilmer to unknown, 10 January 1843, in *Daily Madisonian* (Washington, DC), 23 January 1843; Schroeder, "Annexation or Independence," 150.

34   John Quincy Adams, Speech, 17 September 1842, in *Boston Daily Atlas*, 17 and 28 October 1842; Richards, *Slave Power*, 24–25; Schroeder, "Annexation or Independence," 150–151; *Daily National Intelligencer* (Washington, DC), 4 May 1843; Diary entry, 25 March 1843, in Adams, *Memoirs*, 11:344–347. For examples of Adams's research, see diary entries for 1, 3, 5, 7 April 1843, in Adams, *Memoirs*, 11:350–351, 352–353, 354, 355–356.

35   Daniel Webster to Nicholas Biddle, 2 March 1843, in *PDW:Corr.*, 5:277; Daniel Webster to Hiram Ketchum, 1 March 1843, Daniel Webster to Nicholas Biddle,

11 March 1843, and Daniel Webster to John Tyler, 8 May 1843, in *PDW:Dipl.*, 1:929, 26–27, 931; Rakestraw, *Daniel Webster*, 93–94; John B. Wilder, rev. Randolph B. Campbell and Brett J. Derbes, "Van Zandt, Isaac," *Handbook of Texas Online*, https://www.tshaonline.org/handbook/entries/van-zandt-isaac; Herbert Gambrell, "Jones, Anson," *Handbook of Texas Online*, https://www.tsha online.org/handbook/entries/jones-anson; Isaac Van Zandt to Anson Jones, 19 April 1843, in "Diplomatic Correspondence of the Republic of Texas," in *Annual Report of the American Historical Association for the Year 1908*, ed. George P. Garrison (Washington, DC: Government Printing Office, 1911), 2:164–165; Isaac Van Zandt to Anson Jones, 15 March 1843, in Anson Jones, *Memoranda and Official Correspondence Relating to the Republic of Texas, Its History and Annexation* (New York: D. Appleton, 1859), 213.

36 Hall, *Abel Parker Upshur*, 195, 197–198; Sam W. Haynes, "Anglophobia and the Annexation of Texas: The Quest for National Security," in *Manifest Destiny and Empire: American Antebellum Expansionism*, ed. Sam W. Haynes and Christopher Morris (College Station: Texas A&M Press, 1997), 115–128; Haynes, *Unfinished Revolution*, 230–242; Abel P. Upshur to John C. Calhoun, 14 August 1843, in *PJCC*, 17:354–357.

37 Duff Green to William Henry Harrison, 28 February 1841, and 23 March 1841, William Henry Harrison Papers, DLC; W. Stephen Belko, *The Invincible Duff Green: Whig of the West* (Columbia: University of Missouri Press, 2006), 332–358; Duff Green, *Facts and Suggestions, Biographical, Historical, Financial and Political: Addressed to the People of the United States* (New York: C. S. Westcott, 1866), 141; *Niles' National Register* 65 (4 November 1843): 149; St. George L. Sioussat, "Duff Green's 'England and the United States': With an Introductory Study of American Opposition to the Quintuple Treaty of 1841," *Proceedings of the American Antiquarian Society* 40 (October 1930): 177–180, 206; Elizabeth Silverthorne, "Smith, Ashbel," in *Handbook of Texas Online*, https://www .tshaonline.org/handbook/entries/smith-ashbel; Justin H. Smith, *The Annexation of Texas* (New York: Baker & Taylor, 1911), 83; Hietala, *Manifest Design*, 17; Pletcher, *Diplomacy of Annexation*, 123; Duff Green to Abel P. Upshur, 3 August 1843, in *Diplomatic Correspondence of the United States: Inter-American Affairs, 1831–1860*, ed. William R. Manning (Washington, DC: Carnegie Endowment for International Peace, 1932–39), 12:296–297; Matthew Mason, *Apostle of Union: A Political Biography of Edward Everett* (Chapel Hill: University of North Carolina Press, 2016), 144–147; Hall, *Abel Parker Upshur*, 198.

38 Hall, *Abel Parker Upshur*, 199–200; *Daily Madisonian* (Washington, DC), 19 October 1843.

39 Thomas W. Cutrer, "Thompson, Waddy," *Handbook of Texas Online*, https://www.tshaonline.org/handbook/entries/thompson-waddy; John Tyler to Waddy Thompson, 28 August 1843, in "Correspondence of President Tyler," *William & Mary Quarterly* 12 (January 1904): 140–141; Hall, *Abel Parker Upshur*, 200–202; Abel P. Upshur to William S. Murphy, 21 November 1843, in Manning, ed., *Diplomatic Correspondence*, 12:56–57; Mason, *Apostle of Union*, 147; Abel P. Upshur to Edward Everett, 28 September 1843, and Edward Everett to Abel P.

Upshur, 3 and 16 November 1843, in Manning, ed., *Diplomatic Correspondence*, 7:6, 246–248, 248–250.

40 Leahy, *President without a Party*, 319; Peterson, *Presidencies of Harrison and Tyler*, 192–195; Virgil Maxcy to John C. Calhoun, 10 December 1843, in *PJCC*, 17:601–602; James L. Haley, *Sam Houston* (Norman: University of Oklahoma Press, 2002), 277–278; Pletcher, *Diplomacy of Annexation*, 127–128.

41 John Tyler, "Third Annual Message," 5 December 1843, in Richardson, *Messages and Papers*, 4:260–262; Pletcher, *Diplomacy of Annexation*, 129–130, 136–137; Andrew Jackson to William B. Lewis, 15 December 1843, New York Public Library Digital Collections, http://digitalcollections.nypl.org/items/17aece10 -2924-0135-1111-237219ca8cac; Abel P. Upshur to William S. Murphy, 16 and 23 January 1844, in Manning, ed., *Diplomatic Correspondence*, 12:61, 64, 69; Timothy S. Huebner, *The Southern Judicial Tradition: State Judges and Sectional Divisiveness, 1790–1890* (Athens: University of Georgia Press, 1999), 63–65; Editorial note, in *CJKP*, 3:14n2; J. K. Greer, "The Committee on the Texan Declaration of Independence, III," *Southwestern Historical Quarterly* 31 (October 1927): 130–149; Isaac Van Zandt to Anson Jones, 20 January 1844, in Garrison, ed., "Diplomatic Correspondence," 2:240–242; Henry Clay to John J. Crittenden, 15 February 1844, in *PHC*, 10:6–7.

42 Frederick Merk and Lois Bannister Merk, *Fruits of Propaganda in the Tyler Administration* (Cambridge, MA: Harvard University Press, 1971), 97; James P. Shenton, *Robert John Walker: A Politician from Jackson to Lincoln* (New York: Columbia University Press, 1961), 31, 34–35; J. F. H. Claiborne, *Mississippi, as a Province, Territory, and State, With Biographical Notices of Eminent Citizens* (Jackson, MS: Power & Barksdale, 1880), 419–420; Paul E. Sturdevant, "Robert John Walker and Texas Annexation: A Lost Champion," *Southwestern Historical Quarterly* 109 (October 2005): 189, 197; Peterson, *Presidencies of Harrison and Tyler*, 209; "William Wilkins," in *BDUSC*; Laura Ellyn Smith, "Southerners Divided: The Opposition of Mississippi Whigs to Texas Annexation during the Presidential Election of 1844 as Portrayed by *The Republican* of Woodville, Mississippi," *Journal of Mississippi History* 80 (Fall/Winter 2018): 133–153; Cheathem, *Andrew Jackson, Southerner*, 198.

43 Hall, *Abel Parker Upshur*, 206–207; Robert J. Walker, *Letter of Mr. Walker, of Mississippi, Relative to the Annexation of Texas: In Reply to the Call of the People of Carroll County, Kentucky, to Communicate His View on That Subject* (Washington, DC: Globe, 1844), 14, 26; Merk and Merk, *Fruits of Propaganda*, 99–104.

44 Robert J. Walker to Andrew Jackson, 10 January 1844, in *CAJ*, 6:255; Andrew Jackson to William B. Lewis, 15 December 1843, New York Public Library Digital Collections, http://digitalcollections.nypl.org/items/17aece10-2924-0135 -1111-237219ca8cac; William B. Lewis to Andrew Jackson, 9 January 1844, Andrew Jackson Papers, DLC; Andrew Jackson to William B. Lewis, 18 January 1844, New York Public Library Digital Collections, http://digitalcollections.ny pl.org/items/2950eba0-2924-0135-b471-153faaa4a9a0; Andrew Jackson to Sam Houston, 18 January 1844, Andrew Jackson Papers, Scholarly Resources, Inc., Wilmington, DE.

45 Llerena B. Friend, *Sam Houston: The Great Designer* (Austin: University of Texas Press, 1954), 127–134; Claude Elliott, "Henderson, James Pinckney," *Handbook of Texas Online*, https://www.tshaonline.org/handbook/entries/henderson-james-pinckney; Anonymous, "Miller, Washington D.," *Handbook of Texas Online*, https://www.tshaonline.org/handbook/entries/miller-washington-d; Sam Houston to Andrew Jackson, 16 February 1844, and Andrew Jackson to Sam Houston, 15 March 1844, in *The Writings of Sam Houston, 1813–1863*, ed. Amelia W. Williams and Eugene C. Barker (Austin: University of Texas Press, 1938–1943), 4:260–265, 265–267.

46 Thomas P. Govan, *Nicholas Biddle: Nationalist and Public Banker, 1786–1844* (Chicago: University of Chicago Press, 1959), 49, 396–398, 411; Diary entry, 28 February 1844, 3 March 1844, in *A Philadelphia Perspective: The Diary of Sidney George Fisher Covering the Years, 1834–1871*, ed. Nicholas B. Wainwright (Philadelphia: Historical Society of Pennsylvania, 1967), 154, 159–160; Hall, *Abel Parker Upshur*, 210–13; *New York World*, 28 October 1888; Patrick Calhoun to John C. Calhoun, 28 February 1844, in *PJCC*, 17:806–807; John Tyler, "The Dead of the Cabinet," 24 April 1856, in Tyler, *Letters and Times*, 2:391.

47 *Baltimore Sun*, 4 March 1844; George Sykes to Ann Sykes, 5 March 1844, in St. George L. Sioussat, ed., "The Accident on Board the U.S. Steamer 'Princeton,' February 28, 1844: A Contemporary News-Letter," *Pennsylvania History* 4 (July 1937): 168–180; Hall, *Abel Parker Upshur*, 210–13; Patrick Calhoun to John C. Calhoun, 28 February 1844, in *PJCC*, 17:806–807; John Tyler, "The Dead of the Cabinet," 24 April 1856, in Tyler, *Letters and Times*, 2:390–391; John Tyler to the US Congress, 29 February 1844, in Richardson, *Messages and Papers*, 4:279–280; Matthew Costello, "The Enslaved Households of President John Tyler," White House Historical Association, https://www.whitehousehistory.org/the-enslaved-households-of-president-john-tyler; "Bursting of the Paixhan Gun," in *A Collection from the Miscellaneous Writings of Nathaniel Peabody Rogers*, 2nd ed. (Boston: Benjamin B. Mussey, 1849), 375–377; *New York World*, 28 October 1888.

48 A. H. Miles, "The 'Princeton' Explosion," *United States Naval Institute Proceedings* 52 (November 1926): 2238; John Tyler, "The Dead of the Cabinet," 24 April 1856, and John Tyler to Mary Tyler Jones, 4 March 1844, in Tyler, *Letters and Times*, 2:391, 289; Thomas Hart Benton, *Thirty Years' View, or, A History of the Workings of the American Government for Thirty Years, From 1820 to 1850* (New York: D. Appleton, 1857), 2:568; *Washington (DC) Globe*, 4 March 1844.

49 Leahy, *President without a Party*, 123, 326–327; "John Young Mason," in *BDUSC*; Patrick Calhoun to John C. Calhoun, 28 February 1844; George McDuffie to John C. Calhoun, 1 and 5 March 1844; Ker Boyce to John C. Calhoun, 4 March 1844; James G. Holmes to John C. Calhoun, 5 March 1844; Robert Barnwell Rhett to John C. Calhoun, 5 March 1844; William Anderson to John C. Calhoun, 6 March 1844; Aaron V. Brown to John C. Calhoun, 6 March 1844; Hugh A. Haralson to John C. Calhoun, 6 March 1844; Isaac E. Holmes to John C. Calhoun, 6 March 1844; Dixon H. Lewis to John C. Calhoun, 6 March 1844; Samuel S. Phelps to John C. Calhoun, 6 March 1844; Henry A. Wise

to Robert M. T. Hunter, 7 March 1844; and John Tyler to John C. Calhoun, 6 March 1844 (two letters), in *PJCC*, 17:806–807, 809–810, 815–816, 811–812, 814–815, 816–817, 819, 819–820, 820–821, 821–825, 826–827, 844–845, 828, 828–829; Simpson, *A Good Southerner*, 57–58; Peterson, *Presidencies of Harrison and Tyler*, 206; Isaac Van Zandt to Anson Jones, 5 March 1844, in Garrison, *Diplomatic Correspondence*, 2:262.

50 John C. Calhoun to George McDuffie, 9 March 1844; John C. Calhoun to Anna Maria Calhoun Clemson, 15 March 1844; John C. Calhoun to Thomas G. Clemson, 16 March 1844; John C. Calhoun to John Tyler, 16 March 1844; John C. Calhoun to Andrew Pickens Calhoun, 17 March 1844; Oath of Office as Secretary of State, 30 March 1844; and John C. Calhoun to Isaac Van Zandt and J. Pinckney Henderson, 11 April 1844, in *PJCC*, 17:848–851, 867–868, 869, 870, 870–871, 906, 18:208–209; Pletcher, *Diplomacy of Annexation*, 136; Hall, *Abel Parker Upshur*, 205–209.

51 Elder, *Calhoun*, 417–418; Richard Pakenham to Abel P. Upshur, 26 February 1844, and Lord Aberdeen to Richard Pakenham, 26 December 1843, in Manning, ed., *Diplomatic Correspondence*, 7:252, 252–253.

52 Peterson, *Presidencies of Harrison and Tyler*, 214–215; John C. Calhoun to Richard Pakenham, 18 April 1844; Richard Pakenham to John C. Calhoun, 19 and 30 April 1844; and John C. Calhoun to Richard Pakenham, 27 April 1844, in *PJCC*, 18:273–278, 286–289, 370–371, 348–352.

53 Peterson, *Presidencies of Harrison and Tyler*, 215–219; *New York Evening Post*, 27 April 1844; Francis P. Blair to Andrew Jackson, 2 May 1844, and William B. Lewis to Andrew Jackson, 26 April 1844, Andrew Jackson Papers, DLC; Benton, *Thirty Years' View*, 2:589–590; Daniel Webster to Robert C. Winthrop, 28 April 1844, in *PDW:Corr.*, 6:46; Diary entry, 1 May 1844, in Wainwright, ed., *A Philadelphia Perspective*, 164.

54 Peterson, *Presidencies of Harrison and Tyler*, 215–218; Elder, *Calhoun*, 418; John C. Calhoun to James Henry Hammond, 5 March 1844, 17 May 1844, and John C. Calhoun to Francis Wharton, 28 May 1844, in *PJCC*, 17:649–650, 18:534, 649–650; Diary entry, 6 August 1834, in Wainwright, ed., *A Philadelphia Perspective*, 3; John Tyler to Robert Tyler, 17 April 1850, in Tyler, *Letters and Times*, 2:483; John Tyler to Daniel Webster, 17 April 1850, John Tyler Papers, DLC; Leahy, *President without a Party*, 330–331; John Tyler to Andrew Jackson, 18 April 1844, Andrew Jackson Papers, DLC.

55 Frederick Merk, *Slavery and the Annexation of Texas* (New York: Alfred A. Knopf), 1972), 69–79; Ken S. Mueller, *Senator Benton and the People: Master Race Democracy on the Early American Frontier* (Dekalb: Northern Illinois University Press, 2014), 200–201.

56 Charles G. Sellers Jr., "Election of 1844," in *History of American Presidential Elections, 1789–1968*, ed. Arthur M. Schlesinger Jr. and Fred L. Israel (New York: Chelsea House, 1971), 1:758–759; *North-Carolina Standard* (Raleigh), 18 October 1843; *New York Spectator*, 7 December 1842; *New-Bedford (MA) Register*, 24 May 1843; Francis P. Weisenburger, *The Life of John McLean: A Politician on the United States Supreme Court* (Columbus: Ohio State University Press,

1937), 2, 7–9, 15–16, 20–22, 33–35; Cheathem, *Andrew Jackson and the Rise of the Democratic Party*, 112.

57 Weisenburger, *Life of John McLean*, 31–33, 69–80, 82–99, 103–105; Cheathem, *Coming of Democracy*, 99; Allen Sharp, "Justices Seeking the Presidency," *Journal of Supreme Court History* 29 (November 2004): 290; *Democratic Free Press* (Detroit, MI), 26 October 1842; *New York Spectator*, 3 December 1842.

58 Henry Clay to John M. Clayton, 27 May 1843, in *PHC*, 9:821; John McLean to unknown, 10 August 1843, in *Richmond (VA) Whig*, 26 September 1843; *North-Carolina Standard* (Raleigh), 22 November 1843.

59 Timothy D. Johnson, *Winfield Scott: The Quest for Military Glory* (Lawrence: University Press of Kansas, 1998), 12, 136–138; Scott Kaufman and John A. Soares, "'Sagacious beyond Praise'? Winfield Scott and Anglo-American-Canadian Border Diplomacy, 1837–1860," *Diplomatic History* 30 (January 2006): 57–82; Maxime Dagenais, "The Canadian Rebellion and Jacksonian America: A Connection Decades in the Making," in Dagenais and Mauduit, eds., *Revolutions across Borders*, 6; Cheathem, *Coming of Democracy*, 128–130; Winfield Scott to Henry Clay, 5 February 1839, in *PHC*, 9:277; *Baltimore Sun*, 9 December 1839.

60 Winfield Scott to Henry Clay, 5 February 1839, in *PHC*, 9:277; Sarah H. Hill, "'To Overawe the Indians and Give Confidence to the Whites': Preparations for the Removal of the Cherokee Nation from Georgia," *Georgia Historical Quarterly* 95 (Winter 2011): 465–497; Fred S. Rolater, "The American Indian and the Origin of the Second American Party System," *Wisconsin Magazine of History* 76 (Spring 1993): 180–203; Johnson, *Winfield Scott*, 2, 139–146; Winfield Scott to T. P. Atkinson, 9 February 1843, in *Newark (NJ) Daily Advertiser*, 25 March 1843.

61 Cheathem, *Coming of Democracy*, 99, 119; Rakestraw, *Daniel Webster*, 99–101; Remini, *Daniel Webster*, 587–602; [John Haven et al.] to Daniel Webster, [ca. 13 September 1843], in *New Hampshire Sentinel* (Keene), 13 September 1843; Daniel Webster to John Haven et al., 3 January 1844, in *Boston Courier*, 5 February 1844; James Alfred Pearce to Ebenezer Pettigrew, 7 August 1843, in Lemmon, ed., *Pettigrew Papers*, 2:582; *Richmond (VA) Whig and Public Advertiser*, 7 February 1843, and 12 May 1843; *Alexandria (VA) Gazette*, 19 May 1843.

62 Heidler and Heidler, *Henry Clay*, 363–369; *Raleigh (NC) Register*, 8 April 1842; *Georgia Reporter* (Milledgeville), 21 June 1842; *New York Evening Post*, 23 June 1842; *Niles' National Register* 62 (9 July 1842): 295; Robert P. Letcher to John J. Crittenden, 21 June 1842, and John J. Crittenden to Robert P. Letcher, 23 June 1842, in [Ann Mary Butler Crittenden] Coleman, *The Life of John J. Crittenden, with Selections from His Correspondence and Speeches* (Philadelphia: J. B. Lippincott, 1873), 1:183, 184.

63 Robert P. Letcher to John J. Crittenden, 21 June 1842, in Coleman, *Life of Crittenden*, 1:183; Heidler and Heidler, *Henry Clay*, 372–374; *Daily Cleveland Herald*, 7 October 1842; *True Republican* (Rushville, IN), 14 October 1842; *Richmond (IN) Palladium*, 8 October 1842; Leonard S. Kenworthy, "Henry Clay at Richmond in 1842," *Indiana Magazine of History* 30 (December 1934): 353–359; Hiram Mendenhall et al. to Henry Clay, 1 October 1842, in *PHC*, 9:777.

64 Petition, ca. September 1842, in *Richmond (IN) Palladium*, 17 September 1842; Henry Clay, Speech, 1 October 1842, in *PHC*, 9:777–782. Eric Brooks, email message to author, 10 November 2020. The relative value was calculated using the latest value of the consumer price index at MeasuringWorth.com, https://www.measuringworth.com/dollarvaluetoday/?amount=15000&from=1844.

65 Eric Burin, *Slavery and the Peculiar Solution: A History of the American Colonization Society* (Gainesville: University Press of Florida, 2005), 14, 23; Weisenburger, *Life of John McLean*, 188–210; Johnson, *Winfield Scott*, 145–146; Remini, *Daniel Webster*, 433–434, 591.

66 Henry Clay, Speech, 5 and [7] October 1842, in *PHC*, 9:782–784, 785; *Indiana State Sentinel* (Indianapolis), 11 October 1842, and 1 November 1842; Henry Clay to Jacob Strattan, 13 September 1842, in *Georgetown (DC) Advocate*, 24 September 1842; *Republican and Daily Argus* (Baltimore), n.d., quoted in *Daily Mercantile Courier and Democratic Economist* (Buffalo, NY), 8 November 1842.

67 *Louisville (KY) Weekly Journal*, 30 November 1842; Henry Clay to J. F. Farrington et al., 18 September 1842, in *New Orleans Bee*, 17 October 1842; Henry Clay to Francis T. Brooke, 30 December 1842; Henry Clay to Lucretia Hart Clay, 9 December 1842, and 3 January 1843; Deed of trust for Ashland, 15 November 1842; Partial statement of debts, 23 November 1842; Henry Clay to Thomas Hart Clay, 25 December 1842, and 22 January 1843; and Speech, 25 February 1843, in *PHC*, 9:795, 790, 795, 789–790, 790, 793, 795, 799, 801–803; *Louisville (KY) Daily Journal*, 6 March 1843. To make the comparison for Clay's wealth then and now, I used the latest value of the consumer price index at MeasuringWorth.com, https://www.measuringworth.com/dollarvaluetoday/?amount=19391&from=1842.

68 Henry Clay, Speech, 10 April 1843, and Henry Clay to Chambersburg (PA) Clay Club, 25 July 1843, in *PHC*, 9:808–810, 839–840.

69 Henry Clay to Peter B. Porter, 3 October 1843, and 17 September 1843; Henry Clay to Benjamin W. Leigh, 20 June 1843; Henry Clay to John M. Clayton, 21 June 1843; Henry Clay to Robert P. Letcher, 26 June 1843; Henry Clay to William L. Hodge, 10 August 1843; and Henry Clay to Epes Sargent, 26 September 1843, in *PHC*, 9:864–865, 857, 826–827, 827, 830, 844, 862.

70 Henry Clay to Henry A. S. Dearborn, 13 July 1842; Henry Clay to John M. Berrien, 17 July 1843, and 23 April 1843; Henry Clay to Buckner S. Morris, 27 August 1842; and Henry Clay to John M. Clayton, 27 May 1843, and 28 June 1843, in *PHC*, 9:732–733, 834–835, 812, 759, 821, 831. Heidler and Heidler, *Henry Clay*, 375–376.

71 Henry Clay to John M. Clayton, 27 May 1843, and 28 June 1843; Henry Clay to John Davis, 21 August 1843; Henry Clay to John M. Berrien, 4 and 22 September 1843; Henry Clay to Peter B. Porter, 17 September 1843; and Henry Clay to James K. Polk, 20 May 1843, in *PHC*, 9:820, 831–832, 849, 854, 859, 857, 818–820.

72 Henry Clay to John M. Clayton, 27 May 1843; Henry Clay to B. F. Moore et al., 10 July 1843; Editorial note; Henry Clay to Richard H. Bayard, 10 November 1843; William Browne to Henry Clay, 5 January 1844; Henry Clay to William

Browne, 6 February 1844; Francis Y. Porcher to Henry Clay, 6 January 1844; Henry Clay to Francis Y. Porcher, 5 February 1844; Henry Clay to William C. Preston, 19 January 1844; and Henry Clay to William A. Graham, 6 February 1844, in *PHC*, 9:820, 833, 833–834, 886, 10:1, 1–2, 2, 2, 2, 6.

73   Henry Clay, Speech, 29 February 1844, in *Richmond (VA) Whig*, 8 March 1844; Henry Clay, Speech, 19 and 22 March 1844, and Henry Clay to William C. Preston, 20 March 1844, in *PHC*, 10:10–11, 12, 12–13; Donnie Summerlin, "George W. Crawford (1798–1872)," *New Georgia Encyclopedia* https://www.georgiaen cyclopedia.org/articles/government-politics/george-w-crawford-1798-1872. In addition to the previously cited speeches, see Clay's speeches of 27 January 1844, in *Opelousas (LA) Gazette*; 10 February 1844 (New Orleans), and 11 March 1844 (Columbus, GA), in *Daily National Intelligencer* (Washington, DC), 22 March 1844; 18 March 1844 (Macon, GA), in *Fayetteville North-Carolinian*, 30 March 1844; 26 March 1844 (Augusta, GA), in *Clay Banner* (Mobile, AL), 6 April 1844, and *Easton (MD) Star*, 30 April 1844; and ca. April 2 (Columbia, SC), April 6 (Charleston, SC), and April 9 (Wilmington, NC), in *PHC*, 10:16, 17–18, 18.

74   Dorman Picklesimer Jr., "To Campaign or Not to Campaign: Henry Clay's Speaking Tour through the South," *Filson Club Historical Quarterly* 42 (July 1968): 240; Henry Clay, Speech, 13 April 1844, in *PHC* 10:18–38; Cheatham, *Coming of Democracy*, 57–59, 81–82.

75   Henry Clay to John J. Crittenden, 5 December 1843, in *PHC*, 9:897–900; Heidler and Heidler, *Henry Clay*, 382.

76   Picklesimer, "Henry Clay's Speaking Tour," 241; Remini, *Henry Clay*, 634–635; Henry Clay to John J. Crittenden, 15 February 1844, and 24 March 1844; and Henry Clay to Willie P. Mangum, 14 April 1844, in *PHC*, 10:6–7, 14, 39.

77   Henry Clay to John J. Crittenden, 24 March 1844, and 17 April 1844; Henry Clay to Willie P. Mangum, 14 April 1844; and Henry Clay, Speech, 13 April 1844, in *PHC*, 10:14, 40, 39, 32. Remini, *Henry Clay*, 638–639; Heidler and Heidler, *Henry Clay*, 385–386; "George Edmund Badger" and "Benjamin Watkins Leigh," in *BDUSC*; C. T. Neu, "Hunt, Memucan," *Handbook of Texas Online*, https://www.tshaonline.org/handbook/entries/hunt-memucan; Memucan Hunt to Willie P. Mangum, 27 February 1844, and 27 March 1844, and Benjamin Watkins Leigh to Willie P. Mangum, 28 March 1844, and 22 April 1844, in *Papers of Willie Person Mangum*, 4:57, 76–78, 79–83, 114–115.

78   Henry Clay to John J. Crittenden, 17, 19, and 21 April 1844, in *PHC*, 10:40, 46, 48.

79   Henry Clay to Joseph Gales Jr. and William W. Seaton, 17 April 1844, in *Daily National Intelligencer* (Washington, DC), 27 April 1844.

80   *Newburyport (MA) Herald*, 30 April 1844; *Philadelphia Public Ledger*, 30 April 1844; *Richmond (VA) Whig*, 30 April 1844; *Daily Madisonian* (Washington, DC), 30 April 1844; Andrew Jackson to Francis P. Blair, 7 May 1844, in *CAJ*, 6:283.

81   *American and Commercial Daily Advertiser* (Baltimore), 30 April 1844; *Wabash Courier* (Terre Haute, IN), 7 October 1843; *Boston Evening Transcript*, 27 April

1844; "John Johnston," Ohio History Central, https://ohiohistorycentral.org/index.php?title=John_Johnston&rec=216; *Boston Weekly Messenger*, 1 May 1844; *Daily National Intelligencer*, 29 April 1844, and 2 May 1844; *Newark (NJ) Daily Advertiser*, 30 April 1844; *Alexandria (VA) Gazette*, 1 May 1844.

82   *Daily National Intelligencer*, 2 May 1844; *Philadelphia Inquirer*, 30 April 1844; *Portland (ME) Weekly Advertiser*, 30 April 1844.

83   *Baltimore Sun*, 30 April 1844, 2 May 1844; *American and Commercial Daily Advertiser* (Baltimore), 27 April 1844; *Richmond (VA) Whig*, 30 April 1844; *Public Ledger* (Philadelphia), 30 April 1844; *Daily National Intelligencer*, 2 May 1844.

84   *Daily National Intelligencer*, 2 May 1844; *Universalist Union*, 6 (5 June 1841): 464; "Ambrose Spencer," in *BDUSC*.

85   Henry Clay to Reverdy Johnson, 29 April 1844, in *PHC*, 10:51–52; *Daily National Intelligencer*, 2 May 1844.

86   David Francis Bacon to Henry Clay, 7 October 1843, in *PHC*, 9:867; John M. Clayton to the editors of the *Delaware Journal*, 17 June 1843, in *Daily National Intelligencer*, 23 June 1843; *Daily National Intelligencer*, 2 May 1844; Weisenburger, *Life of John McLean*, 103–105. Unless noted otherwise, biographical details of these potential nominees come from *BDUSC*.

87   *Portland (ME) Advertiser*, 30 January 1844; Willie P. Mangum to John M. Clayton, 16 March 1844; Reverdy Johnson to Willie P. Mangum, 23 March 1844; Benjamin W. Leigh to Willie P. Mangum, 28 March 1844; and Richard H. Atwell to Willie P. Mangum, 17 April 1844, in *Papers of Willie Person Mangum*, 4:66, 74, 81–83, 105–106; *Daily National Intelligencer*, 2 May 1844; Holt, *Rise and Fall*, 104, 189; Kinley J. Brauer, "The Webster–Lawrence Feud: A Study in Politics and Ambitions," *Historian* 29 (November 1966): 35–47; Ivor D. Spencer, *The Victor and the Spoils: A Life of William L. Marcy* (Providence, RI: Brown University Press, 1959), 91–96; Robert G. Gunderson, *The Log Cabin Campaign* (Lexington: University Press of Kentucky, 1957), 46, 63, 88; Henry Clay to Nathaniel P. Tallmadge, 10 October 1839, in *PHC*, 9:351; Oliver Perry Chitwood, *John Tyler: Champion of the Old South* (New York: D. Appleton-Century, 1939), 267; *Troy (NY) Daily Whig*, 20 March 1844; *Boston Mercantile Journal*, n.d., in *New York Commercial Advertiser*, 16 April 1844; *Richmond (VA) Whig*, 12 April 1844.

88   Richard F. Miller, ed., *States at War*, Vol. 4, *A Reference Guide for Delaware, Maryland, and New Jersey in the Civil War* (Lebanon, NH: University Press of New England, 2015), 798, n665; *Daily National Intelligencer*, 2 May 1844; Robert J. Eells, *Forgotten Saint: The Life of Theodore Frelinghuysen: A Case Study of Christian Leadership* (New York: University Press of America, 1987), 41; Arthur B. Darling, *Political Changes in Massachusetts, 1824–1848: A Study of Liberal Movements in Politics* (New Haven, CT: Yale University Press, 1925), 115–118, 184–185, 260–270, 289–293; Russel B. Nye, *George Bancroft: Brahmin Rebel* (New York: Knopf, 1944), 107, 120, 123–125, 127; Brauer, "Webster-Lawrence Feud," 37–38, 44, 49; Remini, *Daniel Webster*, 426, 430, 435–436, 570–573; Daniel Wirls, "'The Only Mode of Avoiding Everlasting Debate': The Overlooked Senate Gag Rule for Antislavery Petitions," *Journal of the Early Repub-*

lic 27 (Spring 2007): 127–129; Elizabeth B. Monroe, "*Charles River Bridge v. Warren Bridge*," in *The Oxford Companion to the Supreme Court of the United States*, ed. Kermit L. Hall (New York: Oxford University Press, 1992), 135–136; John Davis to Daniel Webster, 10 April 1836; Daniel Webster to Phineas Davis, 16 and 30 May 1836; Phineas Davis to Daniel Webster, 5 June 1836; Joseph Ricketson Williams to Daniel Webster, 17 June 1836; Daniel Fletcher Webster to Daniel Webster, 2 March 1837; and John T. Haight to Daniel Webster, 31 March 1837, in *PDW:Corr.*, 4:102, 110, 118, 125, 127, 202, 208–209; Speech, 30 September 1842, in *Papers of Daniel Webster: Speeches & Formal Writings*, ed. Charles M. Wiltse and Alan R. Berolzheimer (Hanover, NH: University Press of New England, 1988), 2:331–360.

89 "Millard Fillmore," in *BDUSC*; Robert J. Rayback, *Millard Fillmore: Biography of a President* (Buffalo, NY: Buffalo Historical Society, 1959), 22–25, 65–82, 106, 147–159; Paul Finkelman, *Millard Fillmore* (New York: Times Books, 2011), 13–14; Henry Clay to John M. Berrien, 23 April 1843, in *PHC*, 9:812; Millard Fillmore to Francis Bacon, 12–23 March 1844, United States Presidents Collection, box 1, folder 29, Beinecke Rare Book Library, Yale University; Millard Fillmore to Gideon Hard, 11 February 1844; Millard Fillmore to Francis Granger, 7 April 1844; and Millard Fillmore to Ann L. Dixson, 30 May 1844, draft transcriptions by the Correspondence of Zachary Taylor and Millard Fillmore Project, ed. Michael David Cohen, American University, Washington, DC. My thanks to Michael David Cohen for providing copies of the Fillmore letters.

90 "John Sergeant," in *BDUSC*; Chase, *Emergence of the Presidential Nominating Convention*, 220; Andrew R. L. Cayton, "The Debate over the Panama Congress and the Origins of the Second American Party System," *Historian* 47 (February 1985): 220, 236; Charles M. Snyder, *The Jacksonian Heritage: Pennsylvania Politics, 1833–1848* (Harrisburg: Pennsylvania Historical and Museum Commission, 1958), 220; Holt, *Rise and Fall*, 189.

91 "Theodore Frelinghuysen," in *BDUSC*; Eells, *Forgotten Saint*, xiv, 5, 15, 19, 22–26, 38–40, 47–48, 55, 61–65, 73–77; [Theodore Frelinghuysen], *An Inquiry into the Moral and Religious Character of the American Government* (New York: Wiley and Putnam, 1838), 18; Richard Carwardine, "Evangelicals, Whigs, and the Election of William Henry Harrison," *Journal of American Studies* 17 (April 1983): 47–75; Holt, *Rise and Fall*, 188.

92 *Daily National Intelligencer* (Washington, DC), 2 May 1844.

93 *American and Commercial Daily Advertiser* (Baltimore), 2 May 1844; Eells, *Forgotten Saint*, 41–42; Holt, *Rise and Fall*, 188–190.

94 Henry Clay to Thurlow Weed, 6 May 1844, in *PHC*, 10:53; John H. Haughton to Willie P. Mangum, 23 May 1844, in *Papers of Willie Person Mangum*, 4:126; *New York Evening Express*, 3 May 1844; *New York Journal of Commerce*, 3 May 1844.

95 *Daily National Intelligencer* (Washington, DC), 2 May 1844; Henry Clay, Speech, 22 March 1844, in *Niles' National Register* 66 (13 April 1844): 107.

96 Heidler and Heidler, *Henry Clay*, 387–388; Remini, *Henry Clay*, 645–646; Holt, *Rise and Fall of the American Whig Party*, 164–172, 190–191; Ira M. Leon-

ard, "The Rise and Fall of the American Republican Party in New York City, 1843–1845," *New-York Historical Society Quarterly* 50 (April 1966): 154–155. On the intersections of the political and social worlds in Washington, see Rachel A. Shelden, *Washington Brotherhood: Politics, Social Life, and the Coming of the Civil War* (Chapel Hill: University of North Carolina Press, 2013), 1–40.

97   *Ohio Democrat* (New Philadelphia), 9 May 1844; Samuel H. Laughlin to John P. Heiss, 31 May 1844, in *Tri-Weekly Nashville (TN) Union*, 11 June 1844; Cave Johnson to James K. Polk, 3 May 1844, in *CJKP*, 7:117; *Democrats' Companion* (Troy, NY), 1 May 1844.

CHAPTER 3. "AN ENTIRELY NEW MAN"

1   Andrew Jackson to Martin Van Buren, 31 July 1840, PMVB (mvb03029); Martin Van Buren to Isaac Stoutenburgh Hone et al., 4 May 1837, PMVB (mvb11932); Lepler, *Many Panics of 1837*, 188, 215. For the consequences of the 1839 depression, see Alasdair Roberts, *American's First Great Depression: Economic Crisis and Political Disorder after the Panic of 1837* (Ithaca, NY: Cornell University Press, 2012).

2   Diary entry, 23 March 1841, in George Templeton Strong, *Diary*, ed. Allan Nevins and Milton Halsey Thomas (New York: Macmillan, 1952), 1:158.

3   Reeve Huston, "The 'Little Magician' after the Show: Martin Van Buren, Country Gentleman and Progressive Farmer, 1841–1862," *New York History* 85 (Spring 2004): 93–99, 112–114; Martin Van Buren to William L. Marcy, 27 August 1841, PMVB (mvb08375); Martin Van Buren to Garrit Gilbert and Edward Patterson, 4 September 1841, PMVB (mvb03281); Martin Van Buren to Andrew Jackson, 12 October 1841, PMVB (mvb03293); Martin Van Buren to John Milton Niles, 30 October 1841, PMVB (mvb08387); Martin Van Buren to Henry Horn, 26 November 1841, PMVB (mvb08562); Francis W. Pickens to Martin Van Buren, 29 August 1841, PMVB (mvb03279); Robert McClellan to Martin Van Buren, 7 August 1841, PMVB (mvb03270); Samuel Hart to Martin Van Buren, 28 June 1841, PMVB (mvb03256); Nathaniel West to Martin Van Buren, 30 January 1842, PMVB (mvb03340). For Van Buren's domestic concerns, see, for example, Martin Van Buren to Harriet Allen Butler, ca. 15 May 1841, PMVB (mvb08334); Martin Van Buren to Levi Woodbury, 24 July 1841, PMVB (mvb08365). References to his cabbage-growing appeared frequently in newspapers; see, for example, *Greensborough (NC) Patriot*, 17 August 1841; *State Capitol Gazette* (Harrisburg, PA), 3 December 1841; *American Protector* (Bennington, VT), 19 March 1844.

4   Cheathem, *Coming of Democracy*, 143–144; James K. Polk to Andrew Jackson, 7 February 1839, in *CJKP*, 5:53; Martin Van Buren to Andrew Jackson, 12 October 1841, PMVB (mvb03293); Martin Van Buren to Albert Haller Tracy, 13 December 1841, PMVB (mvb08492); Martin Van Buren to Joel Roberts Poinsett, 12 January 1842, PMVB (mvb08689); James Kirke Paulding to Martin Van Buren, 24 January 1842, PMVB (mvb09841); Martin Van Buren to James Kirke Paulding, 3 February 1842, PMVB (mvb09842); Martin Van Buren to George Bancroft, 4 February 1842, PMVB (mvb08683); Martin Van Buren to Andrew Jackson, 7 February 1842, PMVB (mvb03347).

5   *Philadelphia Inquirer and National Gazette*, 14 February 1842; *Albany (NY) Argus*, 25 February 1842; *Daily Pennsylvanian* (Philadelphia), 24 February 1842, 6 June 1842; *Baltimore Sun*, 25 February 1842; *Louisville (KY) Daily Journal*, 4 March 1842; *Charleston (SC) Mercury*, 28 February 1842; *Wetumpka (AL) Argus*, 6 April 1842; Cole, *Martin Van Buren*, 384; Martin Van Buren to Andrew Jackson, 7 February 1842, PMVB (mvb03347); Andrew Jackson to Martin Van Buren, 22 February 1842, PMVB (mvb03352); Martin Van Buren to Andrew Jackson, 26 March 1842, PMVB (mvb03355); *Mississippi Free Trader* (Natchez), 14 April 1842; *Mississippi Creole* (Canton), 23 April 1842; *Jackson (MS) Southron*, 28 April 1842; *Weekly Mississippian* (Jackson), 18 March 1842; *Nashville Union*, 3 and 10 May 1842; Henry Clay to Martin Van Buren, 17 March 1842, in *PHC*, 9:680; Martin Van Buren to Henry Clay, 26 March 1842, PMVB (mvb08697); *Cincinnati Enquirer*, 31 May 1842; *Indiana State Sentinel* (Indianapolis), 14 June 1842; *Illinois Free Trader* (Ottawa), 1 July 1842; *Boon's Lick Times* (Fayette, MO), 2 July 1842; *Washington (DC) Weekly Globe*, 30 July 1842; *Milwaukee Sentinel*, 9 July 1842; *Democratic Free Press* (Detroit, MI), 9 July 1842; *Cleveland Herald and Gazette*, 13 July 1842; *New York Evening Express*, 18 July 1842; Martin Van Buren to Charles Wilkes, 22 July 1842, PMVB (mvb08704).

6   Martin Van Buren to Joel Roberts Poinsett, 6 February 1842, PMVB (mvb08684); Martin Van Buren to James K. Paulding, ca. 3 February 1832, PMVB (mvb09842); *Charleston (SC) Mercury*, 4 March 1842; Franklin H. Elmore et al. to Martin Van Buren, ca. 3 March 1842, PMVB (mvb08694); Franklin H. Elmore et al. to Martin Van Buren, 3 March 1842, PMVB (mvb08693); *Winyah (SC) Observer*, 12 March 1842; Robert F. W. Allston to Martin Van Buren, ca. 20 March 1842, PMVB (mvb08699); Martin Van Buren to Robert F. W. Allston, 20 March 1842, PMVB (mvb08700); C. Robinson et al. to Martin Van Buren, 8 April 1842, and Martin Van Buren to C. Robinson et al., 8 April 1842, in *Albany (NY) Argus*, 26 April 1842; *Wetumpka (AL) Argus*, 13 April 1842; John Slidell to Martin Van Buren, 10 March 1842, PMVB (mvb03354); *Daily Picayune* (New Orleans), 12, 13, 15, 16, April 1842; George W. Campbell et al. to Martin Van Buren, 27 April 1842, and Martin Van Buren to George W. Campbell, 29 April 1842, in *Nashville Union*, 3 May 1842; James K. Polk to Franklin H. Elmore, 13 June 1842, in *CJKP*, 6:72; Henry Clay to Nathan Sargent, 31 May 1842, and Henry Clay to John J. Crittenden, 3 June 1842, in *PHC*, 9:704, 706.

7   Martin Van Buren, Speech, 8 July 1842, in *Democratic Free Press* (Detroit, MI), 9 July 1842; Martin Van Buren to Andrew Jackson, 30 July 1842, PMVB (mvb03378); Martin Van Buren to Andrew Jackson, 19 October 1842, PMVB (mvb03409); US House, "Party Divisions of the House of Representatives, 1789 to Present," https://history.house.gov/Institution/Party-Divisions/Party -Divisions/; Michael J. Dubin, *Party Affiliations in the State Legislatures: A Year by Year Summary, 1796–2006* (Jefferson, NC: McFarland, 2007), 135, 192, 92; Andrew Jackson to Francis P. Blair, 25 November 1842, in *CAJ*, 6:178; Amos Kendall to Martin Van Buren, 3 January 1843, PMVB (mvb03453). Van Buren visited at least eighteen states: New York, Pennsylvania, Maryland, Virginia, North Carolina, South Carolina, Georgia, Alabama, Louisiana, Mississippi,

Tennessee, Kentucky, Ohio, Indiana, Illinois, Missouri, Wisconsin, and Michigan. He may also have visited Delaware and Arkansas along the way, but I was unable to uncover documentation of those visits. Adding those two states brings the total to twenty, as Van Buren indicated in his speech.

8   John Niven, *Martin Van Buren: The Romantic Age of American Politics* (New York: Oxford University Press, 1983), 505–507; *Daily Pennsylvanian* (Philadelphia), 7, 9 January 1843; *Indiana State Sentinel* (Indianapolis), 17 January 1843; Ethan Allen Brown et al. to Martin Van Buren, 10 January 1843, PMVB (mvb03462); Resolutions of the Democratic State Convention of Indiana, 9 January 1843, PMVB (mvb12137); Martin Van Buren to Ethan Allen Brown et al., 15 February 1843, PMVB (mvb12176).

9   Niven, *Martin Van Buren*, 507–509; John Arthur Garraty, *Silas Wright* (New York: Columbia University Press, 1949), 239–242; Henry Dilworth Gilpin to Martin Van Buren, 5 May 1843, PMVB (mvb03545); John Bragg to Martin Van Buren, 7 May 1843, PMVB (mvb03546); George Bancroft to Martin Van Buren, 10 and 23 May 1843, PMVB (mvb03551 and mvb03561).

10 Cole, *Martin Van Buren*, 387–390; *Daily Globe* (Washington, DC), 13 April 1843; Andrew Jackson to Martin Van Buren, 29 November 1843, PMVB (mvb03686); David C. Skerrett et al. to Martin Van Buren, 9 December 1843, PMVB (mvb03697); Martin Van Buren to George Bancroft, 25 February 1844, PMVB (mvb05053).

11 Claude G. Berube and John A. Rodgaard, *A Call to the Sea: Captain Charles Stewart of the USS Constitution* (Washington, DC: Potomac Books, 2005), 11–12, 14–21, 26–28, 73–93, 110–132, 137–155, 208–215, 234–239; "Congressional Gold Medal Recipients," History, Art & Archives: U.S. House of Representatives, https://history.house.gov/Institution/Gold-Medal/Gold-Medal-Recipients/.

12 Berube and Rodgaard, *A Call to the Sea*, 179–195, 203–204; Jane M. Côté, *Fanny and Anna Parnell: Ireland's Patriot Sisters* (New York: St. Martin's Press, 1991), 20–25, 36–37, 270–271n53; John D. Fair, "Letters of Mourning from Katharine O'Shea Parnell to Delia Tudor Stewart Parnell," *Irish Historical Studies* 31 (November 1998): 242.

13 Berube and Rodgaard, *Call to the Sea*, 95, 218–219; *Pittsburgh Gazette*, 29 January 1838; *Iowa News* (Dubuque), 17 March 1838; *Carlisle (PA) Weekly Herald and Expositor*, 7 August 1838; *Vicksburg (MS) Daily Whig*, 18 February 1840; "Old Ironsides," *Hours at Home* 10 (March 1870): 472–473; Matthew J. Karp, "Slavery and American Sea Power: The Navalist Impulse in the Antebellum South," *Journal of Southern History* 77 (May 2011): 301; Stephen B. Kingston et al. to Charles Stewart, 24 April 1841, in *Charleston (SC) Daily Courier*, 4 June 1841; Charles Stewart to Stephen B. Kingston et al., 22 May 1841, in *New York Evening Post*, 27 May 1841; "The Great American Steeple Chase for 1844," 1843, Prints and Photographs Division, DLC, https://www.loc.gov/pictures/item/2008661408/; *Illinois Free Trader and LaSalle County Commercial Advertiser* (Ottawa), 18 August 1843; *Hartford Daily Courant*, 13 December 1843; "Commodore Chs. Stewart," ca. 1841, Prints and Photographs Division, DLC, https://www.loc.gov/pictures/item/2004666064/; *New York Daily Herald*, 25

December 1843; *Pittsburgh Weekly Gazette*, 26 January 1844; *New-York Tribune*, 5 February 1844; *Public Ledger* (Philadelphia), 17 February 1844; *Charleston (SC) Daily Courier*, 21 February 1844; *Jeffersonian* (Stroudsburg, PA), 22 February 1844; Herbert D. A. Donovan, *The Barnburners: A Study of the Internal Movements in the Political History of New York State and of the Resulting Changes in Political Affiliation, 1830–1852* (Philadelphia: Porcupine Press, 1974), 32–33, 52–54; Louis H. Fox, "New York City Newspapers, 1820–1850: A Bibliography," *Papers of the Bibliographical Society of America* 21, no. 1/2 (1927): 110; *New York True Sun*, 27 January 1844, 5 February 1844.

14 "Jacob Thompson," in *BDUSC*; Jacob Thompson to Charles Stewart, 29 April 1844, and Charles Stewart to Jacob Thompson, 2 May 1844, in *Washington (DC) Globe*, 6 May 1844; *New York True Sun*, 18, 20 April 1844, 6, 7 May 1844; *Buffalo Commercial Advertiser*, 30 May 1844; *Daily Madisonian* (Washington, DC), 10 May 1844; *Philadelphia Gazette*, 7 May 1844.

15 Matthew S. Warshauer, *Andrew Jackson and the Politics of Martial Law: Nationalism, Civil Liberties, and Partisanship* (Knoxville: University of Tennessee Press, 2006), 77–83; Frederick Moore Binder, *James Buchanan and the American Empire* (Selinsgrove, PA: Susquehanna University Press, 1994), 13, 40–41, 45–46, 48–49; Haynes, *Unfinished Revolution*, 127; Thomas J. Balcerski, *Bosom Friends: The Intimate World of James Buchanan and William Rufus King* (New York: Oxford University Press, 2019), 51, 67; *Lancaster (PA) Intelligencer and Journal*, 17 January 1843.

16 Balcerski, *Bosom Friends*, 24–25, 30–31, 43, 52, 66–97, 102, 105–106; Binder, *James Buchanan*, 13–14; Thomas J. Balcerski, "The Bachelor's Mess: James Buchanan and the Domestic Politics of Doughfacery in Jacksonian America," in *The Worlds of James Buchanan and Thaddeus Stevens: Place, Personality, and Politics in the Civil War Era*, ed. Michael J. Birkner, Randall M. Miller, and John W. Quist (Baton Rouge: Louisiana State University Press, 2019), 31–61; *Congressional Globe*, 27th Cong., 2nd Sess., 287–288; Diary entry, 10 May 1844, in Adams, *Memoirs*, 12:25; Lewis O. Saum, "'Who Steals My Purse': The Denigration of William R. King, the Man for Whom King County Was Named," *Pacific Northwest Quarterly* 92 (Fall 2001): 187–189; Aaron V. Brown to Sarah Childress Polk, 14 January 1844, James K. Polk Papers, DLC; Amy S. Greenberg, *Lady First: The World of First Lady Sarah Polk* (New York: Alfred A. Knopf, 2019), 91–92, 112–113; John Gilbert McCurdy, *Citizen Bachelors: Manhood and the Creation of the United States* (Ithaca, NY: Cornell University Press, 2009), 198–200.

17 Philip S. Klein, *President James Buchanan: A Biography* (University Park: Pennsylvania State University Press, 1962), 155–157; James Buchanan to the Democrats of Pennsylvania, 14 December 1843, in *Lancaster (PA) Intelligencer and Journal*, 26 December 1843; Binder, *James Buchanan*, 55.

18 John Niven, *John C. Calhoun and the Price of Union: A Biography* (Baton Rouge: Louisiana State University Press, 1988), 239–244; Elder, *Calhoun*, 382, 385.

19 Niven, *John C. Calhoun*, 159–163, 248, 252–255, 260; Francis W. Pickens to

John C. Calhoun, 2 October 1841, John C. Calhoun to Armistead Burt, 28 November 1841, and John C. Calhoun to Duff Green, 31 August 1842, in *PJCC*, 15:782, 828–829, 16:437–438; Charles M. Wiltse, *John C. Calhoun* (Indianapolis: Bobbs-Merrill, 1944–51), 3:87; *Congressional Globe*, Senate, 27th Cong., 2nd Sess., 958; Frederick W. Moore, ed., "Calhoun as Seen by His Political Friends: Letters of Duff Green, Dixon H. Lewis, Richard K. Crallé during the Period from 1831 to 1848," *Publications of the Southern History Association* 7 (May 1903): 159–163; Cole, *Martin Van Buren*, 387; Shade, *Democratizing the Old Dominion*, 247–252; Sellers, *James K. Polk*, 2:25.

20 Niven, *John C. Calhoun*, 239, 256; Elder, *Calhoun*, 406–408; Erik J. Chaput, *The People's Martyr: Thomas Wilson Dorr and His 1842 Rhode Island Rebellion* (Lawrence: University Press of Kansas, 2013), 127–131; William McKendree Gwin to Andrew Jackson, 14 March 1842, Andrew Jackson Papers, DLC; Nomination resolution by the South Carolina legislature, 19 December 1842, in *PJCC*, 16:574–576; *New-York Tribune*, 2 January 1843.

21 Niven, *Martin Van Buren*, 508; *Charleston (SC) Mercury*, 21 December 1842; Niven, *John C. Calhoun*, 249, 252–253, 257–260; Wiltse, *John C. Calhoun*, 2:111–113, 136–138; Sellers, *James K. Polk*, 2:25–26, 52; Joseph A. Scoville to Robert M. T. Hunter, 11 September 1842, 21 November 1842, in *Correspondence of Robert M. T. Hunter, 1826–1876*, in *Annual Report of the American Historical Association for the Year 1916*, ed. Charles H. Ambler (Washington, DC: GPO, 1918), 2:41–48, 52; James L. Anderson and W. Edwin Hemphill, "The 1843 Biography of John C. Calhoun: Was R. M. T. Hunter Its Author?," *Journal of Southern History* 38 (August 1972): 469–474.

22 Niven, *John C. Calhoun*, 258–263; John C. Calhoun to Robert M. T. Hunter, 2 April 1843, in *PJCC*, 17:133; Sellers, *James K. Polk*, 2:52; *Congressional Globe*, House of Representatives, 28th Cong., 1st Sess., 3; Donald B. Cole, *A Jackson Man: Amos Kendall and the Rise of American Democracy* (Baton Rouge: Louisiana State University Press, 2004), 241–242.

23 "The Address of Mr. Calhoun to His Political Friends and Supporters," 21 December 1843, John C. Calhoun to Jacob Bond I'On, 21 December 1843; John C. Calhoun to Franklin H. Elmore 16 January 1844; "The Address of Mr. Calhoun to His Political Friends and Supporters," 29 January 1844; and John C. Calhoun to James Edward Colhoun, 7 February 1844, in *PJCC*, 17:617–633, 633, 710–711, 729–742, 772; Niven, *John C. Calhoun*, 263.

24 "Lewis Cass," in *BDUSC*; William Carl Klunder, *Lewis Cass and the Politics of Moderation* (Kent, OH: Kent State University Press, 1996), 120–124, 176; Henry D. Gilpin to Martin Van Buren, 14 December 1842, PMVB (mvb03434).

25 Klunder, *Lewis Cass*, 113–114, 120–129, 176; Moses Dawson to Martin Van Buren, 4 February 1843, PMVB (mvb12153).

26 Klunder, *Lewis Cass*, 124–127, 132–133; Mahlon Dickerson to Lewis Cass, 10 December 1842, and Lewis Cass to Mahlon Dickerson, 10 December 1842, in *Newark (NJ) Daily Advertiser*, 12 December 1842; Lewis Cass to Ethan A. Brown et al., 8 February 1843, in *Indiana State Sentinel* (Indianapolis), 11 April 1843; Lewis Cass to Thomas Worthington et al., 19 June 1843, in *New-York*

Tribune, 18 July 1843; Speech, 4 July 1843, in *Detroit Democratic Free Press*, 15 July 1843.

27 Louis R. Harlan, "Public Career of William Berkeley Lewis [Part 2]," *Tennessee Historical Quarterly* 7 (June 1948): 126–145; Remini, *Andrew Jackson*, 2:182; William B. Lewis to Andrew Jackson, 30 August 1839, Andrew Jackson to William B. Lewis, 30 August 1839, 19 October 1839, and William B. Lewis to Andrew Jackson, 6 October 1839, in *CAJ*, 6:20–21, 18, 33–35, 30; William Berkeley Lewis to Andrew Jackson, 26 January 1843, 10 July 1843, and Lewis Cass to Andrew Jackson, 26 May 1843, Andrew Jackson Papers, DLC; *Sketch of the Life and Services of Gen. Lewis Cass, of Ohio* (Harrisburg, PA, 1843); Klunder, *Lewis Cass*, 131–132; William B. Lewis to Lewis Cass, 2 July 1843, Lewis Cass Papers, Clements Library, University of Michigan; Andrew Jackson to Lewis Cass, 8 July 1843, Andrew Jackson Papers, Scholarly Resources, Inc., Wilmington, DE.

28 Klunder, *Lewis Cass*, 113–114, 120–134, 176.

29 Jones, "Making of a Vice President," 60–62, 73–88, 182–188, 237–255; Richard M. Johnson, Speech, 20 January 1819, in US House, *Annals of Congress*, 15th Cong., 2nd Sess., 658; Marszalek, *Petticoat Affair*, 116–118, 255n19.

30 Jones, "Making of a Vice President," 65–72, 93–142, 194–216, 233–235, 239–240, 292–295, 307, 310–331, 349–351; C. Edward Skeen, *1816: America Rising* (Lexington: University Press of Kentucky, 2003), 79–80; *Daily National Intelligencer* (Washington, DC), 25 May 1835; Cheathem, *Coming of Democracy*, 143–146; Deborah Bingham Van Broekhoven, "'Let Your Names Be Enrolled': Method and Ideology in Women's Antislavery Petitioning," in *The Abolitionist Sisterhood: Women's Political Culture in Antebellum America*, ed. Jean Fagan Yellin and John C. Van Horne (Ithaca, NY: Cornell University Press, 1994), 179–199.

31 Jones, "Making of a Vice President," 3, 24–25, 39–40, 48–49, 49n2.

32 Cox, "White, Black and Indian Families of Richard Mentor Johnson," 122; Miles J. Smith, "The Kentucky Colonel: Richard M. Johnson and the Rise of Western Democracy, 1780–1850" (PhD diss., Texas Christian University, 2013), 293–297; Richard M. Johnson to Samuel Medary et al., 30 May 1842, in *Ohio Statesman* (Columbus), 15 June 1842; Jones, "Making of a Vice President," 358; *Lancaster (PA) Examiner*, 20 July 1842; *Daily Cleveland Herald*, 16 January 1843; *Ohio Democrat* (New Philadelphia), 8 December 1842; *New-Hampshire Sentinel* (Keene), 1 March 1843; *Niles' National Register*, 63 (18 February 1843): 386.

33 Leland Winfield Meyer, *The Life and Times of Colonel Richard M. Johnson of Kentucky* (New York: Columbia University Press, 1932), 401; Smith, "Kentucky Colonel," 15; *Washington (DC) Globe*, 1 June 1843; *Weekly Mississippian* (Jackson), 13 April 1843; *Mississippi Free Trader*, 29 March 1843; *Daily Pennsylvanian* (Philadelphia), 1 May 1843; *Boston Traveler*, 2 May 1843; *Sentinel and Expositor for the Country* (Vicksburg, MS), 2 May 1843; *New York Herald*, 30 April 1843, 15 August 1843; *Republican Banner* (Nashville, TN), 12 May 1843; *New-York Tribune*, 16 May 1843; "The Visit to Springfield of Richard M. Johnson, May 18–20, 1843," *Journal of the Illinois State Historical Society* 13 (July 1920):

192–209; *New York Evening Post*, 23 May 1843; *Republican Herald* (Providence, RI), 7 June 1843, 15 July 1843; Jones, "Making of a Vice President," 359–360, 364–365; *Daily Madisonian* (Washington, DC), 11 August 1843; *Natchez (MS) Weekly Courier*, 12 April 1843; Richard M. Johnson to the Oregon General Committee of Ohio, 31 May 1843, in *American and Commercial Daily Advertiser* (Baltimore), 22 June 1843; *Salem (MA) Register*, 26 June 1843; *New Hampshire Sentinel* (Keene), 11 October 1843; *Boston Daily Atlas*, 13 October 1843.

34 Cox, "White, Black and Indian Families of Richard Mentor Johnson," 123; Smith, "Kentucky Colonel," 295–299; *Louisville (KY) Daily Journal*, 6 July 1842; Richard M. Johnson to Francis P. Blair, 29 January 1844, in *Washington (DC) Daily Globe*, 5 February 1844; Meyer, *Life and Times of Colonel Richard M. Johnson*, 461.

35 Amos Kendall, *Mr. Kendall's Address to the People of the United States* (1840), 2; Sellers, *James K. Polk*, 1:465; "Levi Woodbury," "Silas Wright Jr.," and "Joel R. Poinsett," in *BDUSC*; Joel R. Poinsett to Gouverneur Kemble, 13 September 1843, in *Calendar of Joel R. Poinsett Papers in the Henry D. Gilpin Collection*, ed. Grace E. Heilman and Bernard S. Levin (Philadelphia: Historical Society of Pennsylvania, 1941), 173–174; Catherine M. Wright, "John Letcher," *Encyclopedia Virginia*, https://www.encyclopediavirginia.org/Letcher_John_1813-1884; John Letcher to Thomas Hart Benton, 15 December 1842, PMVB (mvb03436).

36 A. O. P. Nicholson to James K. Polk, 13 January 1841, in *CJKP*, 5:616; Sellers, *James K. Polk*, 1:430, 432–433, 438–444; *Pittsburgh Weekly Gazette*, 21 June 1844; Greenberg, *Lady First*, 77, 80–81; Andrew Jackson to Martin Van Buren, 16 August 1841, PMVB (mvb03274).

37 Joseph M. Pukl Jr., "James K. Polk's Congressional Campaigns of 1835 and 1837," *Tennessee Historical Quarterly* 41 (Summer 1982): 106; William Dusinberre, *Slavemaster President: The Double Career of James Polk* (New York: Oxford University Press, 2003), 15–16; Greenberg, *Lady First*, 72, 75, 83–84; James K. Polk to Robert B. Reynolds, 19 August 1841, and James K. Polk to Samuel H. Laughlin, 24 August 1841, in *CJKP*, 5:728–729, 733; Sellers, *James K. Polk*, 1:447–448, 450–452, 460; *Speech of Governor James K. Polk, . . . October 23, 1841* ([1841]), James K. Polk Papers, DLC.

38 Sellers, *James K. Polk*, 1:462–469.

39 Sellers, *James K. Polk*, 1:470–490; James K. Polk to Martin Van Buren, 8 December 1842, PMVB (mvb06151); *Nashville Tri-Weekly Union*, 25 April 1843; Jonathan Atkins, *Parties, Politics, and the Sectional Conflict in Tennessee, 1832–1861* (Knoxville: University of Tennessee Press, 1997), 120–125; Henry Clay to James K. Polk, 20 May 1843, in *CJKP*, 7:311–312.

40 Sellers, *James K. Polk*, 1:489–491, 2:9–13; Robert P. Letcher to John J. Crittenden, 6 January 1844, John J. Crittenden Papers, DLC.

41 Sellers, *James K. Polk*, 2:50–51, 56; Thomas W. Gilmer to unknown, 10 January 1843, in *Daily Madisonian* (Washington, DC), 23 January 1843; Aaron V. Brown to Andrew Jackson, 23 January 1843, Andrew Jackson Papers, Scholarly Resources; Aaron V. Brown to Francis P. Blair and John C. Rives, 20 March 1844, in *Washington (DC) Daily Globe*, 20 March 1844; Andrew Jackson to Aaron V.

Brown, 12 February 1843, Andrew Jackson to Amos Kendall, 9 August 1844, in *CAJ*, 6:201–202, 5:361; Cheathem, *Andrew Jackson, Southerner*, 172–174.

42 Sellers, *James K. Polk*, 2:50–51; Francis P. Blair to Martin Van Buren, 18 March 1844, PMVB (mvbo3814).

43 Martin Van Buren to Andrew Jackson, 23 and 29 March 1844, PMVB (mvbo3820 and mvbo3833).

44 "The Election of House Chaplain William Henry Hammett," US House of Representatives, https://history.house.gov/HistoricalHighlight/Detail/36718; William Henry Hammett to Martin Van Buren, 27 March 1844, PMVB (mvbo3827); Silas Wright Jr. to Martin Van Buren, 6 April 1844, PMVB (mvbo3845); Silas Wright Jr. to Martin Van Buren, 11 April 1844, PMVB (mvbo3850).

45 Benjamin Franklin Butler to Martin Van Buren, 6 April 1844, PMVB (mvbo3843); Jabez Delano Hammond to Martin Van Buren, 7 April 1844, PMVB (mvbo3846).

46 Martin Van Buren to William Henry Hammett, 20 April 1844, PMVB (mvbo3868); Niven, *Martin Van Buren*, 526–527; Pletcher, *Diplomacy of Annexation*, 66–73; Winders, *Crisis in the Southwest*, 19–26; Haynes, *Unfinished Revolution*, 217–221, 231, 241–242.

47 James Kirke Paulding to Martin Van Buren, 16 April 1844, PMVB (mvbo3863); Silas Wright Jr. to Martin Van Buren, 29 April 1844, PMVB (mvbo3878); Garraty, *Silas Wright*, 104–106; John Fairfield to Anna Fairfield, 3 December 1843, in *The Letters of John Fairfield*, ed. Arthur G. Staples (Lewiston, ME: Lewiston Journal Company, 1922), 311; "Lemuel Stetson," "Preston King," and "William Allen," in *BDUSC*.

48 Silas Wright Jr. to Martin Van Buren, 29 April 1844, PMVB (mvbo3878); "Charles Jared Igersoll," "William Wilkins," "George Coke Dromgoole," and "Lewis Steenrod," in *BDUSC*.

49 Niven, *Martin Van Buren*, 527–530; Silas Wright Jr. to Martin Van Buren, 29 April 1844, PMVB (mvbo3878); Cole, *Martin Van Buren*, 393–394. On speculation that Van Buren and Clay reached an agreement on a joint approach to Texas annexation in 1842, see, especially, James C. N. Paul, *Rift in the Democracy* (Philadelphia: University of Pennsylvania Press, 1951), 37–38. Robert Remini accepted this claim in his Jackson biography (Remini, *Andrew Jackson*, 3:497), but he later dismissed it as "totally without foundation" in his Clay biography (Remini, *Henry Clay*, 613n7).

50 John Worth Edmonds to Martin Van Buren, 30 April 1844, PMVB (mvbo3884); Samuel Jones Tilden to Martin Van Buren, ca. 30 April 1844, PMVB (mvbo3885); Smith Thompson Van Buren to Martin Van Buren, 23 April 1844, PMVB (mvbo3872); "William John Brown" and "James McDowell," in *BDUSC*; William John Brown to Martin Van Buren, 29 April 1844, PMVB (mvbo3879); Alfred Balch to Martin Van Buren, 22 May 1844, PMVB (mvbo3956); Amos Kendall to Martin Van Buren, 29–30 April 1844, PMVB (mvbo3880); James McDowell to the members of the Central Democratic Committee at Richmond, 6 May 1844, in Charles H. Ambler, ed., "Virginia and Texas, 1844," *John P. Branch Historical Papers of Randolph-Macon College* 4 (June 1913): 126;

Republican Banner (Nashville, TN), 6 May 1844; Benjamin Franklin Butler to Martin Van Buren, 29 March 1844, PMVB (mvb03831); Arthur A. Ekirch Jr., "Benjamin F. Butler of New York: A Personal Portrait," *New York History* 68 (January 1977): 64; Andrew Jackson to Francis P. Blair, 7 May 1844, in *CAJ*, 6:283–285.

51 Andrew Jackson to Francis P. Blair, 7 May 1844, in *CAJ*, 6:284; Salmon P. Chase et al. to James K. Polk, 30 March 1844, and James K. Polk to Salmon P. Chase et al., 23 April 1844, in *Nashville Union*, 30 April 1844. Leonard P. Cheatham to James K. Polk, 7 May 1844; Editorial note; Samuel H. Laughlin to James K. Polk, 24 April 1844; James K. Polk to Cave Johnson, 4 May 1844; and James K. Polk to Samuel H. Laughlin, 9 May 1844, in *CJKP*, 7:124, 106, 107, 119–120, 130. For Andrew Jackson's claims about "re-annexation," see Andrew Jackson to John C. Calhoun, 21 December 1820, and Andrew Jackson to John Overton, 8 June 1829, in *PAJ*, 4:409–410, 7:270; Andrew Jackson to Francis P. Blair, 26 July 1844, 24 October 1844, Jackson Papers, DLC.

52 Cave Johnson to James K. Polk, 30 April 1844, 8 May 1844, in *CJKP*, 7:113–114, 125–126.

53 Robert Armstrong to James K. Polk, 10 May 1844, Andrew J. Donelson to James K. Polk, 10 May 1844, and James K. Polk to Cave Johnson, 13 and 14 May 1844, in *CJKP*, 7:131, 131–132, 134–136, 137; Mark R. Cheathem, *Old Hickory's Nephew: The Political and Private Struggles of Andrew Jackson Donelson* (Baton Rouge: Louisiana State University Press, 2007), 158–159; Sellers, *James K. Polk*, 2:70–71; Andrew Jackson to Francis P. Blair, 11 May 1844, in *CAJ*, 6:287.

54 James K. Polk to Cave Johnson, 13 and 14 May 1844, in *CJKP*, 7:134–136, 136–138.

55 James K. Polk to Cave Johnson, 14 May 1844, in *CJKP*, 7:136; Andrew Jackson to John P. Heiss, 13 May 1844, in *Nashville Union*, 16 May 1844; Remini, *Andrew Jackson*, 3:502; *Nashville Tri-Weekly Union*, 23 May 1844.

56 Martin Van Buren to George Bancroft, 8 May 1844, PMVB (mvb05070).

57 Benjamin F. Butler to Martin Van Buren, 29 April 1844, 4 May 1844, PMVB (mvb03881); Benjamin F. Butler to Andrew Jackson, 10 May 1844, Andrew Jackson Papers, DLC; Sellers, *James K. Polk*, 2:65–66; George C. Dromgoole to Thomas Ritchie, 3 May 1844, and William Allen et al. to Ohio Democrats, 1 May 1844, in *Washington (DC) Semi-Weekly Globe*, 6 May 1844; Silas Wright Jr. to Martin Van Buren, 29 April 1844, PMVB (mvb03878); Amos Kendall to Martin Van Buren, 13 May 1844, PMVB (mvb03920); Mueller, *Senator Benton*, 199–200; Andrew Jackson to Francis P. Blair, 7, 11, and 18 May 1844, Andrew Jackson to William B. Lewis, 11 May 1844, and Andrew Jackson to Thomas Hart Benton, 14 May 1844, in *CAJ*, 6:284–285, 285–286, 294, 288, 291–293; Reginald C. McGrane, *William Allen: A Study in Western Democracy* (Columbus: Ohio State Archeological and Historical Society, 1925), 94; Elbert B. Smith, *Magnificent Missourian: The Life of Thomas Hart Benton* (Philadelphia: J. B. Lippincott, 1958), 203; Cave Johnson to James K. Polk, 5 May 1844, in *CJKP*, 7:121.

58 Amos Kendall to Martin Van Buren, 13 May 1844, PMVB (mvb03920).

59   James E. Winston, "The Lost Commission: A Study in Mississippi History," *Mississippi Valley Historical Review* 5 (September 1918): 158–166; Sellers, *James K. Polk*, 2:61–62; Cave Johnson to James K. Polk, 30 April 1844, in *CJKP*, 7:113; *Washington (DC) Semi-Weekly Globe*, 6 May 1844; George Bancroft to Martin Van Buren, 23 May 1844, PMVB (mvb03972); Henry Clay to Thurlow Weed, 6 May 1844, in *PHC*, 10:54.

60   *Richmond (VA) Enquirer*, 3 February 1844, 3 May 1844, 25 July 1854; Thomas Ritchie to Howell Cobb, 8 February 1844, 6 and 23 May 1844, in *Correspondence of Robert Toombs, Alexander H. Stephens, and Howell Cobb*, in *Annual Report of the American Historical Association for the Year 1911*, ed. Ulrich B. Phillips (Washington, DC: GPO, 1913), 2:55, 56–57, 59; Austin Brockenbrough to Thomas Ritchie, 21 April 1844; William Byars to Thomas Ritchie, 27 April 1844; James Hoge to the Central Democratic Committee, 3 May 1844; R. J. Poulson to Thomas Ritchie, 3 May 1844; Thomas J. Randolph to Thomas Ritchie, 4 May 1844; James McDowell to the Central Democratic Committee, 6 May 1844; W. M. Watkins to Thomas Ritchie, 7 May 1844; John R. Edmunds to Thomas Ritchie, 12 May 1844; R. Hubbard to Thomas Ritchie, 18 May 1844; and S. Bassett French to Thomas Ritchie, 23 May 1844, in Ambler, ed., "Virginia and Texas, 1844," 117–118, 118–119, 119–121, 121–122, 122–125, 125–127, 127–130, 130–134, 134–137, 137; Thomas Ritchie to Silas Wright Jr., 20 March 1844, PMVB (mvb03817); Silas Wright Jr. to Martin Van Buren, 29 April 1844, PMVB (mvb03878); Charles H. Ambler, *Thomas Ritchie: A Study in Virginia Politics* (Richmond, VA: Bell Book & Stationery, 1913), 237–242; Anonymous to Martin Van Buren, 1 May 1844, PMVB (mvb12449); Thomas Ritchie to Martin Van Buren, 5 May 1844, PMVB (mvb12450); Lewis Cass to Edward A. Hannegan, 10 May 1844, in *New York Evening Post*, 18 May 1844.

61   *Richmond (VA) Enquirer*, 25 July 1854; Martin Van Buren to Thomas Ritchie, 16 May 1844, PMVB (mvb03937); Martin Van Buren to Anderson Hutchinson et al., 3 May 1844, PMVB (mvb03892); Martin Van Buren to George Bancroft, 8 May 1844, PMVB (mvb05070); Martin Van Buren to Silas Wright Jr., 10 May 1844, PMVB (mvb06158).

62   Sellers, *James K. Polk*, 2:77–78; Silas Wright Jr. to Martin Van Buren, 26 May 1844, PMVB (mvb03976).

63   Samuel Rhea Gammon Jr., *The Presidential Campaign of 1832* (Baltimore: Johns Hopkins University Press, 1922), 100–101; William E. Beard, "Democracy's Two-Thirds Rule Rounds Out a Century," *Tennessee Historical Magazine* 2 (January 1932): 87–94; Chase, *Emergence of the Presidential Nominating Convention*, 264–266; Laura Ellyn Smith, "Anti-Jacksonian Democratization: The First National Political Party Conventions," *American Nineteenth Century History* 21 (August 2020): 161–162; George Bancroft to Martin Van Buren, 23 May 1844, PMVB (mvb03972); George Bancroft to Martin Van Buren, 24 May 1844, PMVB (mvb03970); Sherman Croswell to Edwin Croswell, 24 May 1844, PMVB (mvb03977); Silas Wright Jr. to Martin Van Buren, 26 May 1844, PMVB (mvb03976); Levi Woodbury to J. H. Reid et al., 9 May 1844, in *Richmond (VA) Enquirer*, 24 May 1844.

64 Andrew Johnson to A. O. P. Nicholson, 12 February 1844, and Andrew Johnson to David T. Patterson, 13 May 1844, in *The Papers of Andrew Johnson*, ed. Paul H. Bergeron et al. (Knoxville: University of Tennessee Press, 1967–2000), 1:149–150, 162–163; Sellers, *James K. Polk*, 2:76–83; William G. Childress to James K. Polk, 25 May 1844, in *CJKP*, 7:153.

65 Sellers, *James K. Polk*, 2:84–85; Gideon J. Pillow to James K. Polk, 25 May 1844, in *CJKP*, 7:155–156.

66 *Emporium and True American* (Trenton, NJ), 24 May 1844.

67 *Lancaster (PA) Intelligencer*, 28 May 1844; William Tyack to Martin Van Buren, 27 May 1844, PMVB (mvb03979); Daniel S. Dickinson to Lydia Dickinson, 27 May 1844, in Daniel S. Dickinson, *Speeches, Correspondence, Etc., of the Late Daniel S. Dickinson of New York*, ed. John R. Dickinson (New York: Putnam, 1867), 2:369; *Baltimore Sun*, 27 May 1844.

68 Gideon J. Pillow to James K. Polk, 22 May 1844, Samuel H. Laughlin to James K. Polk, 23 May 1844, and William G. Childress to James K. Polk, 25 May 1844, in *CJKP*, 7:145, 147, 153; Henry Dilworth Gilpin to Martin Van Buren, 26 May 1844, PMVB (mvb03975); Diary entry, 28 May 1844, in Hone, *Diary*, 2:223–224.

69 *Brooklyn Evening Star*, 29 May 1844; Daniel S. Dickinson to Lydia Dickinson, 27 May 1844, in Dickinson, ed., *Speeches, Correspondence, Etc., of the Late Daniel S. Dickinson*, 2:369; Cave Johnson to James K. Polk, 27 May 1844, in *CJKP*, 7:157; *New-York Tribune*, 29 May 1844; John Louis O'Sullivan to Martin Van Buren, 27 May 1844, PMVB (mvb03981).

70 Sellers, *James K. Polk*, 2:80, 87; "Political Portraits with Pen and Pencil. No. XXV. Henry Hubbard, of New Hampshire," *United States Magazine and Democratic Review* 9 (August 1841): 188; "Henry Hubbard," in *BDUSC*; Cole, *Martin Van Buren*, 210; H. G. Jones, "Saunders, Romulus Mitchell," *NCpedia*, https://www.ncpedia.org/biography/saunders-romulus-mitchell; John Louis O'Sullivan to Martin Van Buren, 27 May 1844, PMVB (mvb03981); Cave Johnson to James K. Polk, 27 May 1844, in *CJKP*, 7:157; *New York Evening Post*, 28 May 1844; *Washington (DC) Daily Globe*, 4 June 1844.

71 *Washington (DC) Daily Globe*, 4 June 1844; Sellers, *James K. Polk*, 2:87; Anonymous to John Van Buren, 21 May 1846, PMVB (mvb04233).

72 *Washington (DC) Daily Globe*, 4 June 1844; *Daily Madisonian* (Washington, DC), 1 June 1844; Francis W. Pickens to John C. Calhoun, 3 March 1844, in *PJCC*, 17:810–811; *Charleston (SC) Mercury*, 19 March 1844; Francis W. Pickens to James E. Colhoun, 17 May 1844, F. W. Pickens Papers, South Caroliniana Library, University of South Carolina; Daniel S. Dickinson to Lydia Dickinson, 27 May 1844, in Dickinson, ed., *Speeches, Correspondence, Etc., of the Late Daniel S. Dickinson*, 2:369.

73 *Washington (DC) Daily Globe*, 4 June 1844; John Louis O'Sullivan to Martin Van Buren, 27 May 1844, PMVB (mvb03981); Cave Johnson to James K. Polk, 27 May 1844, in *CJKP*, 7:157; Francis W. Pickens to John C. Calhoun, 28 May 1844, in *PJCC*, 18:646.

74 John Louis O'Sullivan to Martin Van Buren, 27 May 1844, PMVB (mvb03981);

William Tyack to Martin Van Buren, 27 May 1844, PMVB (mvb03979); Cave Johnson to James K. Polk, 27 May 1844, in *CJKP*, 7:157.

75 *Washington (DC) Daily Globe*, 5 June 1844; Sellers, *James K. Polk*, 2:88.

76 *Louisville (KY) Daily Journal*, 4 June 1844; *Washington (DC) Daily Globe*, 5 June 1844.

77 *Washington (DC) Daily Globe*, 5 June 1844; "John Krepps Miller" and "John Hickman," in *BDUSC*; Julius W. Blackwell to James K. Polk, 28 May 1844, James K. Polk Papers, DLC; Gideon J. Pillow to James K. Polk, 28 May 1844, in *CJKP*, 7:158.

78 *Washington (DC) Daily Globe*, 4 June 1844.

79 *Washington (DC) Daily Globe*, 4 June 1844; Francis W. Pickens to John C. Calhoun, 28 May 1844, in *PJCC*, 18: 646–647.

80 Cave Johnson to James K. Polk, 25 May 1844, in *CJKP*, 7:154; Silas Wright Jr. to John Fine, 23 May 1844, in Jabez Delano Hammond, *The History of Political Parties in the State of New-York, from the Ratification of the Federal Constitution to 1840* (Cooperstown, NY: H. & E. Phinney, 1846), 3:456–459; Garraty, *Silas Wright*, 265–266; Martin Van Buren to Benjamin F. Butler, 20 May 1844, PMVB (mvb06155).

81 Nye, *George Bancroft*, 115–117, 130–131, 300; Paul H. Bergeron, "James K. Polk and the Jacksonian Press in Tennessee," *Tennessee Historical Quarterly* 41 (Fall 1982): 275–277; James K. Polk to Andrew J. Donelson, 3 January 1839, George Bancroft to James K. Polk, 6 July 1844, and Gideon J. Pillow to James K. Polk, 28 May 1844, in *CJKP*, 5:9, 7:317, 158–159.

82 Benjamin F. Butler to Martin Van Buren, 31 May 1844, PMVB (mvb03993).

83 Thomas Hart Benton to Andrew Jackson, 28 May 1844, Andrew Jackson Papers, DLC; Mueller, *Senator Benton*, 197–198.

84 Benjamin F. Butler to Martin Van Buren, 31 May 1844, PMVB (mvb03993); Sellers, *James K. Polk*, 2:95.

85 Alexander Harris, *A Biographical History of Lancaster County . . .* (Lancaster: Elias Barr, 1872), 217; *Washington (DC) Daily Globe*, 6 June 1844; Mark I. Greenberg, "Becoming Southern: The Jews of Savannah, Georgia, 1830–1870," *American Jewish History* 86 (March 1998): 55–75; Solomon Cohen and Miriam Gratz Moses Cohen, Cohen/Gratz/Moses Family Papers, 1818–1972 (bulk 1858–1868) [finding aid], https://galileo-georgiaarchives.primo.exlibrisgroup.com/perma link/01GALI_GADEPT/l2nkgs/alma99188873902963; Nathaniel B. Sylvester, *History of Saratoga County, New York* (Philadelphia: Everts & Ensign, 1878), 140–142; Garraty, *Silas Wright*, 275; *Niles' Register* 66 (1 June 1844): 217; *Washington (DC) Daily Globe*, 4 June 1844; "Edward Junius Black," in *BDUSC*; Carey, *Parties, Slavery, and the Union*, 36–37, 43–44, 48–49, 66–67; Freeman, *Field of Blood*, 11; Bertram Wyatt-Brown, *Southern Honor: Ethics and Behavior in the Old South* (New York: Oxford University Press, 1982), 43; Kenneth S. Greenberg, *Honor and Slavery: Lies, Duels, Noses, Masks, Dressing as a Woman, Gifts, Strangers, Humanitarianism, Death, Slave Rebellions, the Proslavery Argument, Baseball, Hunting, and Gambling in the Old South* (Princeton, NJ: Princeton University Press, 1996), 62. See "mongrel," *Oxford English Dictionary*.

86 *Washington (DC) Daily Globe*, 6 June 1844; *Baltimore Sun*, 14 September 1863; "Francis Wilkinson Pickens" and "Franklin Harper Elmore," in *BDUSC*.

87 Howe, *What Hath God Wrought*, 7, 691–692; *Washington (DC) Daily Globe*, 6 June 1844; Andrew J. Donelson to Andrew Jackson, 29 May 1844, and Andrew Jackson to Francis Preston Blair, 7 June 1844, Andrew Jackson Papers, DLC.

88 Gideon J. Pillow to James K. Polk, 29 May 1844, 2 June 1844, and Andrew J. Donelson to James K. Polk, 31 May 1844, in *CJKP*, 7:162, 182, 169–170; George Bancroft to Jeremiah George Harris, 30 August 1887, in Jesse S. Reeves, ed., "Letters of Gideon J. Pillow to James K. Polk, 1844," *American Historical Review* 11 (July 1906): 841n1.

89 William G. Childress to James K. Polk, 28 May 1844, James K. Polk Papers, DLC; Williamson Smith to James K. Polk, 29 May 1844, and George Bancroft to James K. Polk, 6 July 1844, in *CJKP*, 7:165, 317; "Cave Johnson," in *HD-JEMD*, 206–207; Howard C. Perkins, "A Neglected Phase of the Movement for Southern Unity, 1847–1852," *Journal of Southern History* 12 (May 1946): 162–164; Ellwood Fisher to John C. Calhoun, ca. 7 April 1845, in *PJCC*, 21:476; Jeremiah George Harris to George Bancroft, 13 September 1887, in Lyon Tyler, ed., "Some Letters of Tyler, Calhoun, Polk, Murphy, Houston and Donelson," *Tyler's Quarterly Historical and Genealogical Magazine* 7 (July 1925): 12–13.

90 *Washington (DC) Daily Globe*, 6 June 1844; Diary entry, 30 May 1844, in Hone, *Diary*, 2:224.

91 *Washington (DC) Daily Globe*, 6 June 1844.

92 *New York Herald*, 31 May 1844, 4 June 1844; *Albany (NY) Argus*, 4 June 1844; *Daily National Intelligencer* (Washington, DC), 30 May 1844; Sellers, *James K. Polk*, 2:98; Garraty, *Silas Wright*, 282.

93 *Niles' National Register* 66 (1 June 1844): 218; *Washington (DC) Daily Globe*, 30 May 1844.

94 *Washington (DC) Daily Globe*, 30 May 1844.

95 Silas Wright Jr. to Benjamin F. Butler, 29 May 1844, in *Niles' National Register* 66 (1 June 1844): 218; Silas Wright Jr. to Benjamin F. Butler, 3 June 1844, Silas Wright Letters to Benjamin F. Butler, A. C. Flagg, and John Tyler, Manuscripts and Archives Division, The New York Public Library, Astor, Lenox, and Tilden Foundations; Diary entry, 31 May 1844, in Hone, *Diary*, 2:225; *Niles' National Register* 66 (1 June 1844): 218; John Fairfield to Anna Fairfield, 2 June 1844, in Staples, ed., *Letters of John Fairfield*, 340; *Washington (DC) Daily Globe*, 6 June 1844; Sellers, *James K. Polk*, 2:96–97; Niven, *Martin Van Buren*, 540; John Belohlavek, *George Mifflin Dallas: Jacksonian Patrician* (University Park: Pennsylvania State University Press, 1977), 83–86.

96 *Niles' National Register* 66 (1 June 1844): 218; *Washington (DC) Daily Globe*, 6 June 1844.

97 Diary entry, 31 May 1844, in Hone, *Diary*, 2:225; Staples, ed., *Letters of John Fairfield*, 53; John Fairfield to Anna Fairfield, 30 May 1844, in Staples, 340; Merk and Merk, *Fruits of Propaganda*, 57, 64–67; Robert J. Walker to James K. Polk, 30 May 1844, in *CJKP*, 7:168; Belohlavek, *George Mifflin Dallas*, 86–87.

98 *Washington (DC) Daily Globe*, 30 May 1844; *New York Daily Herald*, 1 June 1844; *Niles' National Register* 66 (1 June 1844): 218. Magenis's name did not appear on the list of official Missouri delegates; see *New York Daily Herald*, 1 June 1844; *Washington (DC) Daily Globe*, 6 June 1844.

99 *Nashville Tri-Weekly Union*, 11 June 1844; *Washington (DC) Daily Globe*, 1 June 1844, 3 June 1844; *Richmond (VA) Enquirer*, 4 June 1844; "Andrew Kennedy," in *BDUSC*; see "brickbat, n.," *OED Online*.

100 Cave Johnson to James K. Polk, 2 June 1844, and Gideon J. Pillow to James K. Polk, 2 June 1844, in *CJKP*, 7:180–181, 182; *Washington (DC) Daily Globe*, 3 June 1844.

101 Robert Armstrong to James K. Polk, 4 and 5 June 1844, and William M. Gwin to James K. Polk, 8 June 1844, in *CJKP*, 7:197, 198, 216–217; *Nashville Tri-Weekly Union*, 6 June 1844, 8 June 1844.

102 James K. Polk to Charles J. Ingersoll, 8 June 1844; James K. Polk to Cave Johnson, 8 June 1844; James K. Polk to John K. Kane, 8 June 1844; James K. Polk to Robert J. Walker; 8 June 1844; and James K. Polk to Silas Wright Jr., 12 June 1844, in *CJKP*, 7:218, 218–219, 220, 221, 244–245; Sellers, *James K. Polk*, 2:114–116; Garraty, *Silas Wright*, 286.

103 Cole, *A Jackson Man*, 242–243; Amos Kendall to Martin Van Buren, 16 May 1844 (2 letters), PMVB (mvb03932 and mvb09676); Martin Van Buren to Amos Kendall, 12 June 1844, PMVB (mvb04018); Churchill Caldom Cambreleng to Martin Van Buren, 8 June 1844, PMVB (mvb04010); Andrew Jackson Donelson to Martin Van Buren, 2 June 1844, PMVB (mvb12000); Anthony Ten Eyck to Martin Van Buren, 4 June 1844, PMVB (mvb04005); Martin Van Buren to Gansevoort Melville et al., 3 June 1844, PMVB (mvb04003); Martin Van Buren to A. Noble et al., 14 June 1844, PMVB (mvb04021); Martin Van Buren to Thomas J. Morgan et al., 15 June 1844, PMVB (mvb09677); Martin Van Buren to Samuel Hart et al., 17 June 1844, PMVB (mvb04029); Martin Van Buren to John Francis Hamtramck Claiborne, 21 June 1844, PMVB (mvb04032); Martin Van Buren to Peter Vivian Daniel, 21 June 1844, PMVB (mvb04033); Martin Van Buren to John L. O'Sullivan, 30 October 1844, PMVB (mvb04079); Niven, *Martin Van Buren*, 542–548; Belohlavek, *George Mifflin Dallas*, 88; US Senate, "John W. Forney, Secretary of the Senate, 1861–1868," https://www.senate.gov/artandhistory/history/common/generic/SOS_John_Forney.htm; Peter Vivian Daniel to Martin Van Buren, 11 June 1844, PMVB (mvb04016); Anthony Ten Eyck to Martin Van Buren, 4 June 1844, PMVB (mvb04005). Van Buren's letter to Kendall has been edited here for readability.

104 Robert P. Letcher to James Buchanan, 7 July 1844, in George Ticknor Curtis, *Life of James Buchanan: Fifteenth President of the United States* (New York: Harper & Bros., 1883), 1:510; Willie P. Mangum to Priestley H. Mangum, 29 May 1844, George S. Yerby to Willie P. Mangum, 29 June 1844, in *Papers of Willie Person Mangum*, 4:128, 141; *New-York Tribune*, 1 June 1844; Diary entry, 3 June 1844, in Strong, *Diary*, 237; Nicholas B. Wainwright, "Sidney George Fisher—The Personality of a Diarist," *Proceedings of the American Antiquarian*

Society (April 1962): 27–28; "The Diary of Sidney George Fisher, 1844," *Pennsylvania Magazine of History and Biography* 79 (October 1955): 498–499.

105 *New-York Daily Tribune*, 31 May 1844.

CHAPTER 4. "IN THE HANDS OF THE SLAVE POWER"

1 Spencer W. McBride and Jennifer Hull Dorsey, eds., *New York's Burned-over District: A Documentary History* (Ithaca, NY: Cornell University Press, 2023); Richard Lyman Bushman and Dean C. Jesse, "Joseph Smith and His Papers," in *JSP:J*, 1:xv–xli.

2 Bushman and Jesse, "Joseph Smith and His Papers," in *JSP:J*, 1:xv–xli; Richard L. Bushman, *Joseph Smith: Rough Stone Rolling* (New York: Alfred A. Knopf, 2005), 162–168, 215–230, 338–346; William G. Hartley, "Missouri's 1838 Extermination Order and the Mormons' Forced Removal to Illinois," *Mormon Historical Studies* 2 (Spring 2001): 5–27; Lilburn W. Boggs to John B. Clark, 27 October 1838, Missouri State Archives: The Missouri Mormon War, https://www.sos.mo.gov/cmsimages/archives/resources/findingaids/miscMormRecs/eo/18381027_ExtermOrder.pdf; Benjamin E. Park, *Kingdom of Nauvoo: The Rise and Fall of a Religious Empire on the American Frontier* (New York: Liveright, 2020), 16–21, 23, 28–31, 16–21.

3 Park, *Kingdom of Nauvoo*, 36–38, 42–44; Carpenter, *Democracy by Petition*, 67; Spencer W. McBride, "When Joseph Smith Met Martin Van Buren: Mormonism and the Politics of Religious Liberty in Nineteenth-Century America," *Church History* 85 (March 2016): 153–158; "John Reynolds," in *BDUSC*; Joseph Smith to Hyrum Smith and the Nauvoo High Council, 5 December 1839, Joseph Smith to Seymour Brunson and the Nauvoo High Council, 7 December 1839, and Senate report, 4 March 1840, in *JSP:D*, 7:69–70, 77–81, 541–543.

4 Park, *Kingdom of Nauvoo*, 45; Discourse, 1 March 1840, in *JSP:D*, 7:202; McBride, "When Joseph Smith Met Martin Van Buren," 154, 158; *Alexandria (VA) Gazette*, 11 July 1840.

5 Park, *Kingdom of Nauvoo*, 75–77, 80, 158–160; Joseph Smith to "my friends in Illinois," 20 December 1841, in *Times and Seasons* 3 (1 January 1842): 651, https://contentdm.lib.byu.edu/digital/collection/NCMP1820-1846/id/9736; Robert W. Johannsen, *Stephen A. Douglas* (New York: Oxford University Press, 1973), 106–110.

6 Park, *Kingdom of Nauvoo*, 53–56, 97–98, 125–131, 155–157; Editorial notes, in *JSP:D*, 7:xxiii, 369n302.

7 Park, *Kingdom of Nauvoo*, 58, 61–67, 88–92, 104–114; Brian C. Hales, *Joseph Smith's Polygamy* (Salt Lake City: Greg Kofford Books, 2013), 2:263–314.

8 Park, *Kingdom of Nauvoo*, 60.

9 Journal entries, 2 and 4 November 1843, in *JSP:J*, 3:124; Joseph Smith to Martin Van Buren, Lewis Cass, Richard M. Johnson, John C. Calhoun, and Henry Clay, 4 November 1844, in JSP, https://www.josephsmithpapers.org/paper-summary/letter-to-presidential-candidates-4-november-1843-draft/2.

10 Cheatham, *Coming of Democracy*, 11; Brent M. Rogers, "To the 'Honest and Patriotic Sons of Liberty': Mormon Appeals for Redress and Social Justice,

1843–44," *Journal of Mormon History* 39 (Winter 2013): 40–67; William W. Phelps et al. to Daniel Dunklin, 10 April 1834, W. W. Phelps Collection of Missouri Documents, 1833–1837, CHL, https://catalog.churchofjesuschrist.org/as sets?id=1455b1ae-8788-404f-ad0b-a464679f23b8&crate=0&index=0; Petition, 10 April 1834, W. W. Phelps Collection of Missouri Documents, 1833–1837, CHL, https://catalog.churchofjesuschrist.org/assets?id=5233cc7a-8909-4545 -b9ce-2911ad6a67be&crate=0&index=0; Lewis Cass to Algernon S. Gilbert et al., 2 May 1834, W. W. Phelps Collection of Missouri Documents, 1833–1837, CHL, https://catalog.churchofjesuschrist.org/assets?id=1a377cdb-f056-48e6 -a1cc-ba71ebbbcdfb&crate=0&index=0; Lewis Cass to Joseph Smith, 9 December 1844, in JSP, https://www.josephsmithpapers.org/paper-summary/letter -from-lewis-cass-9-december-1843/4; John C. Calhoun to Joseph Smith, 2 December 1843, in *PJCC*, 17:583; Henry Clay to Joseph Smith, 15 November 1843, in *PHC*, 9:890–891; Joseph Smith to John C. Calhoun, 2 January 1844, in *PJCC*, 17:662–667.

11   Journal entries, 27 December 1843, 5, 19 January 1844, 29 January 1844, in *JSP:J*, 3:152, 157, 166, 169–171. The Quorum of the Twelve Apostles, modeled on Jesus's most important disciples in the New Testament, was charged with assisting the First Presidency in leading the Mormon Church. The First Presidency was (and is) the church's highest governing body. During these early years, as has been true for most of Mormonism's history, it consisted of the Prophet and two counselors; see "Twelve Apostles," JSP, https://www .josephsmithpapers.org/topic/twelve-apostles; "First Presidency," JSP, https:// www.josephsmithpapers.org/topic/first-presidency.

12   Journal entry, 29 January 1844, in *JSP:J*, 3:169–171; Discourse, 7 April 1840, in *JSP:D*, 7:260; McBride, "When Joseph Smith Met Martin Van Buren," 153–154.

13   *Times and Seasons* (Nauvoo, IL), 15 February 1844.

14   Richards, *Breakaway Americas*, 89–91; *General Smith's Views of the Powers and Policy of the Government of the United States* (Nauvoo, IL: John Taylor, 1844), in JSP, https://www.josephsmithpapers.org/paper-summary/general-smiths -views-of-the-powers-and-policy-of-the-government-of-the-united-states-7-feb ruary-1844/3.

15   Journal entries, 24, 25, and 27 February 1844, in *JSP:J*, 3:183–184; "History, 1838–1856, volume E-1 [1 July 1843–30 April 1844]," 1907, JSP, https://www .josephsmithpapers.org/paper-summary/history-1838-1856-volume-e-1-1-ju ly-1843-30-april-1844/279; Park, *Kingdom of Nauvoo*, 8; "History, 1838–1856, volume E-1 [1 July 1843–30 April 1844]," 1913–1914, JSP, https://www.jo sephsmithpapers.org/paper-summary/history-1838-1856-volume-e-1-1-july -1843-30-april-1844/285.

16   Spencer W. McBride, *Joseph Smith for President: The Prophet, the Assassins, and the Fight for American Religious Freedom* (New York: Oxford University Press, 2021), 3, 89–105.

17   "History, 1838–1856, volume E-1 [1 July 1843–30 April 1844]," 1911, 1913, JSP, https://www.josephsmithpapers.org/paper-summary/history-1838-1856-vol ume-e-1-1-july-1843-30-april-1844/285; Park, *Kingdom of Nauvoo*, 8; Journal

entry, 8 February 1844, in *JSP:J*, 3:175; Discourse, 8 February 1844, in JSP, https://www.josephsmithpapers.org/paper-summary/discourse-8-february -1844-as-reported-by-wilford-woodruff/1; "History, 1838–1856, volume E-1 [1 July 1843–30 April 1844]," p. 1886, in JSP, https://www.josephsmithpapers.org/pa per-summary/history-1838-1856-volume-e-1-1-july-1843-30-april-1844/258.

18 Introduction, *JSP:C50*, xxx–xxi, xxxiv–xl; Patrick Q. Mason, "God and the People: Theodemocracy in Nineteenth-Century Mormonism," *Journal of Church and State* 53 (Summer 2011): 350–358; Benjamin E. Park, "Joseph Smith's Kingdom of God: The Council of Fifty and the Mormon Challenge to American Democratic Politics," *Church History* 87 (December 2018): 1031–1041.

19 Introduction, *JSP:C50*, xxiii–xxxvii; Derek R. Sainsbury, *Storming the Nation: The Unknown Contributions of Joseph Smith's Political Missionaries* (Salt Lake City: RSC BYU/Deseret Book, 2020), 17, 45; Meeting minutes, 11 April 1844, in *JSP:C50*, 88, 90, 92–93, 95–96, 101; "Sidney Rigdon," JSP, https://www .josephsmithpapers.org/person/sidney-rigdon.

20 Meeting minutes, 19 March 1844, and 18 April 1844, in *JSP:C50*, 54, 110–114; Park, "Joseph Smith's Kingdom of God," 1041–1044.

21 Meeting minutes, 25 April 1844, in *JSP:C50*, 133–136; Park, "Joseph Smith's Kingdom of God," 1042.

22 *Nauvoo (IL) Neighbor*, 20 March 1844; Mark Ashurst-McGee, "The King Follett Discourse and Joseph Smith's Preaching Style," JSP, https://www.jo sephsmithpapers.org/articles/the-king-follett-discourse-and-joseph-smiths -preaching-style; Donald Q. Cannon, "The King Follett Discourse: Joseph Smith's Greatest Sermon in Historical Perspective," *BYU Studies Quarterly* 18 (April 1978): 180–182; Bushman, *Rough Stone Rolling*, 533–537; "King Follett Sermon," 7 April 1844, in "History, 1838–1856, volume E-1 [1 July 1843–30 April 1844]," 1972, JSP, https://www.josephsmithpapers.org/paper-summary /history-1838-1856-volume-e-1-1-july-1843-30-april-1844/344.

23 Sainsbury, *Storming the Nation*, 50–51; "History, 1838–1856, volume E-1 [1 July 1843–30 April 1844]," 1982, JSP, https://www.josephsmithpapers.org/pa per-summary/history-1838-1856-volume-e-1-1-july-1843-30-april-1844/354; Richard S. Van Wagoner, *Sidney Rigdon: A Portrait of Religious Excess* (Salt Lake City: Signature Books, 2006), 333; "Minutes and Discourses, 6–7 April 1844, as Published by Times and Seasons," 524, JSP, https://www.josephsmith papers.org/paper-summary/minutes-and-discourses-6-7-april-1844-as-pub lished-by-times-and-seasons/3; "Minutes and Discourses, 6–7 April 1844, as Published by Times and Seasons," 578, JSP, https://www.josephsmithpapers .org/paper-summary/minutes-and-discourses-6-7-april-1844-as-published -by-times-and-seasons/5; Journal entries, 29 January 1844, 25 February 1844, in *JSP:J*, 3:169–171, 183; "Minutes and Discourses, 6–9 April 1844, as Reported by Thomas Bullock," 32, JSP, https://www.josephsmithpapers.org/pa per-summary/minutes-and-discourses-6-9-april-1844-as-reported-by-thomas -bullock/35; "Minutes and Discourses, 6–9 April 1844, as Reported by Thomas Bullock," 36, JSP, https://www.josephsmithpapers.org/paper-summary/min utes-and-discourses-6-9-april-1844-as-reported-by-thomas-bullock/39; "History,

1838–1856, volume E-1 [1 July 1843–30 April 1844]," 1993, JSP, https://www
.josephsmithpapers.org/paper-summary/history-1838-1856-volume-e-1-1-ju-
ly-1843-30-april-1844/365; "Journal, December 1842–June 1844; Book 4, 1
March–22 June 1844," [77], JSP, https://www.josephsmithpapers.org/paper
-summary/journal-december-1842-june-1844-book-4-1-march-22-june
-1844/79; "History, 1838–1856, volume E-1 [1 July 1843–30 April 1844]," 1998–
1999, JSP, https://www.josephsmithpapers.org/paper-summary/history-1838–
1856-volume-e-1-1-july-1843-30-april-1844/370; "John Taylor," JSP, https:// www
.josephsmithpapers.org/person/john-taylor; "Hyrum Smith," JSP, https://
www.josephsmithpapers.org/person/hyrum-smith; "Brigham Young," JSP,
https://www.josephsmithpapers.org/person/brigham-young.

24 Sainsbury, *Storming the Nation*, 59, 60–62, 65–68, 78; McBride, *Joseph Smith*,
57; "Amasa Mason Lyman," JSP, https://www.josephsmithpapers.org/person
/amasa-mason-lyman; Meeting minutes, 11 April 1844, in *JSP:C50*, 103.

25 Lyndon W. Cook, "James Arlington Bennet and the Mormons," *BYU Studies Quarterly* 19 (April 1979): 247–248; McBride, *Joseph Smith*, 139–142;
"James Arlington Bennet," JSP, https://www.josephsmithpapers.org/person
/james-arlington-bennet; James Arlington Bennet to Joseph Smith, 24 October 1843, in JSP, https://www.josephsmithpapers.org/paper-summary/letter
-from-james-arlington-bennet-24-october-1843/1.

26 Journal entry, 4 March 1844, in *JSP:J*, 3:189; "Willard Richards," JSP, https://
www.josephsmithpapers.org/person/willard-richards; Willard Richards to
James Arlington Bennet, 4 March 1844, in "History, 1838–1856, volume E-1
[1 July 1843–30 April 1844]," 1902–4, JSP, https://www.josephsmithpapers
.org/paper-summary/history-1838-1856-volume-e-1-1-july-1843-30-april
-1844/274; McBride, *Joseph Smith*, 140, 150; Willard Richards to James Arlington Bennet, 24 March 1844, in Willard Richards Journals and Papers,
1821–1854, Outgoing correspondence, Letters, 1844 February–June 20, CHL,
https://catalog.churchofjesuschrist.org/assets?id=411ac303-7faf-4919-852c
-b1456e983141&crate=0&index=0; *Nauvoo (IL) Neighbor*, 13 March 1844,
http://boap.org/LDS/Nauvoo-Neighbor/1844/3-13-1844.pdf; James Arlington
Bennet to Willard Richards, 14 April 1844, in Willard Richards Journals and
Papers, 1821–1854, Outgoing Correspondence, Letters, 1844 February–June
20, CHL, https://catalog.churchofjesuschrist.org/assets?id=01661856-cc07
-4229-a1a9-28702580600e&crate=0&index=0.

27 McBride, *Joseph Smith*, 150; Journal entries, 8, 20 March 1844, in *JSP:J*, 3:198–
199, 206; "Solomon Copeland," JSP, https://www.josephsmithpapers.org/per
son/solomon-copeland?highlight=Solomon%20Copeland; Robert M. McBride
and Dan M. Robison, *Biographical Directory of the Tennessee General Assembly*
(Nashville: Tennessee State Library and Archives and the Tennessee Historical Commission, 1975), 1:166–167; Wilford Woodruff to Solomon Copeland,
19 March 1844, in Joseph Smith's Office Papers, 1835–1844, Correspondence,
Letters, 1844, CHL, https://catalog.churchofjesuschrist.org/assets?id=b0df75
bf-3247-4bbd-9a0d-8f8f23db3f99&crate=0&index=0.

28 Richard T. Hughes, *Reviving the Ancient Faith: The Story of Churches of Christ in*

America (Grand Rapids, MI: Eerdmans, 1996),1–2, 21–46; Van Wagoner, *Sidney Rigdon*, 17–61, 294–302; "Sidney Rigdon," JSP, https://www.josephsmith papers.org/person/sidney-rigdon; Editorial note, *JSP:D*, 7:58n50; Park, *Kingdom of Nauvoo*, 36–38, 42, 106–109, 242; *JSP:D*, 7:31n142; Bushman, *Rough Stone Rolling*, 298–299, 510–511; McBride, *Joseph Smith*, 151–152.

29 Meeting minutes, 6 May 1844, in *JSP:C50*, 157–159, 157–158n491, 158–159n494; Van Wagoner, *Sidney Rigdon*, 4, 331.

30 Meeting minutes, 3 May 1844, in *JSP:C50*, 139; Sainsbury, *Storming the Nation*, 97–101; Josiah Quincy, *Figures of the Past, from the Leaves of Old Journals* (Boston: Roberts Brothers, 1883), 380, 397, 399; Jed L. Woodworth, "Josiah Quincy's 1844 Visit with Joseph Smith," *BYU Studies Quarterly* 39 (October 2000): 71–87; "Autobiography of Dr. Ephraim Ingals," *Journal of the Illinois State Historical Society* 28 (January 1936): 295.

31 "Heber Chase Kimball," JSP, https://www.josephsmithpapers.org/person /heber-chase-kimball; "History, 1838–1856, volume E-1 [1 July 1843–30 April 1844]," 1998, JSP, https://www.josephsmithpapers.org/paper-summary/histo ry-1838-1856-volume-e-1-1-july-1843-30-april-1844/370; *Nauvoo (IL) Neighbor*, 29 May 1844; Sainsbury, *Storming the Nation*, 93, 95–96, 105–109, 115–119, 120–133; Brigham Young and Willard Richards to Reuben Hedlock, 3 May 1844, in "History, 1838–1856, volume F-1 [1 May 1844–8 August 1844]," 2, JSP, https://www.josephsmithpapers.org/paper-summary/history-1838-1856-vol ume-f-1-1-may-1844-8-august-1844/8; Van Wagoner, *Sidney Rigdon*, 331.

32 Journal entry, 23 April 1844, in *JSP:J*, 3:233; David S. Hollister to Joseph Smith, 9 May 1844, in JSP, https://www.josephsmithpapers.org/paper-summary/let ter-from-david-s-hollister-9-may-1844/; Sainsbury, *Storming the Nation*, 96, 129, 138; *Nauvoo (IL) Neighbor*, 24 April 1844; David S. Hollister to Joseph Smith, 26 June 1844, in JSP, https://www.josephsmithpapers.org/paper-sum mary/letter-from-david-s-hollister-26-june-1844/; McBride, *Joseph Smith*, 173–174.

33 Sainsbury, *Storming the Nation*, 98, 101–104; *Nauvoo (IL) Neighbor*, 22 May 1844; Journal entry, 17 May 1844, in *JSP:J*, 3:253; *Nauvoo (IL) Neighbor*, 22 May 1844.

34 Sainsbury, *Storming the Nation*, 87–89, 113–114, 132–138; LeGrand L. Baker, *Murder of the Mormon Prophet: Political Prelude to the Death of Joseph Smith* (Salt Lake City: Eborn Books, 2006), 236–239, 245–247; *Christian Journal* (Exeter, NH), 6 June 1844; *Warsaw (IL) Signal*, 8 May 1844; *New York Herald*, 23 May 1844; Unknown to the editors of the *Missouri Republican* (St. Louis), 25 April 1844, in *Watchman* (Montpelier, VT), 7 June 1844; Park, *Kingdom of Nauvoo*, 208–212; *New York Daily Herald*, 27 May 1844; Unknown to the editors of the *Louisville (KY) Journal*, 25 May 1844, in *Louisville (KY) Daily Journal*, 31 May 1844; *Richmond (IN) Weekly Palladium*, 24 May 1844; *New-York Tribune*, 23 May 1844; "Alfred Morrison, 1821–1897," The Correspondence of James McNeill Whistler, https://www.whistler.arts.gla.ac.uk/correspondence/biog /display/?bid=Morr_A; Diary entry, 30 June 1844, in Wainwright, ed., *A Philadelphia Perspective*, 172; *Hawk-Eye* (Burlington, IA), 6 May 1844.

35 *Nauvoo (IL) Neighbor*, 22 May 1844; Charles A. Foster to James G. Bennett, 12 June 1844, in *New York Daily Herald*, 26 June 1844; Park, *Kingdom of Nauvoo*, 223–238; Richards, *Breakaway Americas*, 86; McBride, *Joseph Smith*, 191–195.

36 *Indiana American* (Brookville, IN), 12 July 1844; Sainsbury, *Storming the Nation*, 142–145, 153–165; Baker, *Murder of the Mormon Prophet*, 616–618, 644–645, 698; David Hollister to Ellis Sanders, 9 July 1844, Ellis M. Sanders Papers, CHL; McBride, *Joseph Smith*, 200; *Daily National Intelligencer* (Washington, DC), 15 July 1844; Van Wagoner, *Sidney Rigdon*, 335–343; Park, *Kingdom of Nauvoo*, 242–245; Lee Davidson, "LDS Presidential Candidates: One GOP Nomination, One Assassination, Many Attacks for Church Views—but Never a Win," *Salt Lake Tribune*, 29 September 2020.

37 Monroe, *Republican Vision*, 87–89, 100, 104–106, 109, 111; Leahy, *President without a Party*, 4–6, 10–11, 15–16; Wyatt-Brown, *Southern Honor*, 14.

38 Leahy, *President without a Party*, 227–230; Christopher J. Leahy, "Playing Her Greatest Role: Priscilla Cooper Tyler and the Politics of the White House Social Scene, 1841–44," *Virginia Magazine of History and Biography* 120 (September 2012): 242–249, 254–264; Frank Thomas, "Personal Traits of President Tyler and His Family," *The Knickerbocker, or New-York Monthly Magazine* 22 (July 1843): 49–50, 53.

39 Diary entry, 9 March 1842, in Wainwright, ed., *A Philadelphia Perspective*, 132–133.

40 Daniel Webster to John Tyler, 29 August 1843, in *PDW:Corr.*, 5:311–313.

41 John Tyler to George Roberts, 28 September 1843, in "Letter of President Tyler," *William & Mary Quarterly* 19 (January 1911): 216; *New York Evening Post*, 19 December 1843; Cole, *Martin Van Buren*, 392; Silas Wright Jr. to Martin Van Buren, 2 January 1844, PMVB (mvb03719); Robert Bruce Blake, "Mason, John Thomson," *Handbook of Texas Online*, https://www.tshaonline.org/handbook/entries/mason-john-thomson; Silas Wright Jr. to Martin Van Buren, 8 January 1844, PMVB (mvb03724); "John Canfield Spencer," in *BDUSC*.

42 Robert M. Ireland, "Spencer, John C.," in Hall, ed., *Oxford Companion to the Supreme Court*, 816; Cole, *Martin Van Buren*, 392; Silas Wright Jr. to Martin Van Buren, 6 March 1844, PMVB (mvb03800).

43 Theophilus Fisk to Polk, March 9, 1844; Aaron V. Brown to Polk, March 10, 1844; Robert Armstrong to James K. Polk, March 21, 1844; James K. Polk to Theophilus Fisk, 20 March 1844; James K. Polk to Cave Johnson, 21 March 1844; and Cave Johnson to James K. Polk, 15 April 1844, in *CJKP*, 7:82–83, 83–86, 93, 92, 93–95, 103–105.

44 Niven, *Martin Van Buren*, 517; Niven, *John C. Calhoun*, 277; Nye, *George Bancroft*, 128.

45 Niven, *John C. Calhoun*, 277; John Tyler to Henry A. Wise, 20 April 1852, and John Tyler to Alexander Gardiner, 11 July 1846, in Tyler, *Letters and Times*, 3:170, 2:341; *Daily Madisonian* (Washington, DC), 27 May 1844.

46 *Baltimore Sun*, 27 May 1844; *Richmond (VA) Enquirer*, 28 May 1844; "Cathedral Hill," National Register of Historic Places Inventory—Nomination Form (1987), 13, https://mht.maryland.gov/secure/medusa/PDF/NR_PDFs

/NR-977.pdf; Sherman Croswell to Edwin Croswell, 24 May 1844, PMVB (mvb03977); *Daily National Intelligencer* (Washington, DC), 31 May 1844; *Philadelphia Gazette*, 27 May 1844; John B. Jones to the *Madisonian*, 25 May 1844, in *Daily Madisonian* (Washington, DC), 27 May 1844; *Daily Madisonian* (Washington, DC), 1 June 1844.

47 *Daily Madisonian* (Washington, DC), 28 May 1844; *Baltimore Sun*, 28 May 1844; *Daily Picayune* (New Orleans), 5 June 1844; "Andrew T. McReynolds," Michigan Legislative Biography, https://mdoe.state.mi.us/legislators/Legislator/LegislatorDetail/4791; *New Hampshire Sentinel* (Keene), 5 June 1844; *Charleston (SC) Courier*, 31 May 1844.

48 *Daily Madisonian* (Washington, DC), 28 May 1844, 4 June 1844; D. Hamilton Hurd, comp., *History of New London County, Connecticut* . . . (Philadelphia: J. W. Lewis, 1882), 306–307; Leahy, *President without a Party*, 82–83, 114–118; C. M. L. Wiseman, *Centennial History of Lancaster, Ohio, and Lancaster People* (Lancaster, OH: C. M. L. Wiseman, 1898), 195–196; *Whig Standard* (Washington, DC), 24 January 1844; *Buffalo Daily Gazette*, 27 January 1844, 29 April 1844; *New York Evening Post*, 4 April 1844; *Baltimore Sun*, 28 May 1844; *New Hampshire Sentinel* (Keene), 5 June 1844; *Charleston (SC) Courier*, 31 May 1844; "Lathrop Storrs Eddy," https://www.findagrave.com/memorial/50368164/lathrop-storrs-eddy; *Daily Alta California* (San Francisco), 11 December 1851.

49 "Amendment XXV. Presidential Vacancy and Disability," Legal Information Institute, Cornell Law School, https://www.law.cornell.edu/constitution-conan/amendment-25; *Daily Madisonian* (Washington, DC), 29 May 1844, 4 June 1844.

50 Thomas T. Cropper et al. to John Tyler, 28 May 1844, and John Tyler to Thomas T. Cropper et al., 30 May 1844, in *Daily Madisonian* (Washington, DC), 30 May 1844.

51 Lathrop Eddy to John C. Calhoun, 28 May 1844, in *PJCC*, 18:641; Willie P. Mangum to Priestley H. Mangum, 29 May 1844, in *Papers of Willie Person Mangum*, 4:128; Diary entry, 28 May 1844, in Adams, *Memoirs*, 12:37; Robert Armstrong to James K. Polk, 5 June 1844, in *CJKP*, 7:198; Andrew Jackson to Francis P. Blair, 7 June 1844, Andrew Jackson Papers, DLC.

52 *Baltimore Sun*, 27 May 1844; *Sunbury (PA) American*, 15 June 1844.

53 Karen Halttunen, *Confidence Men and Painted Women: A Study of Middle-Class Culture in America, 1830–1870* (New Haven, CT: Yale University Press, 1982), 137; Elisabeth Celnart, *The Gentleman and Lady's Book of Politeness and Propriety of Deportment: Dedicated to the Youth of Both Sexes*, 5th ed. (Philadelphia: Grigg, Elliot, 1848), 210–212; Leahy, *President without a Party*, 307–309, 334–337; Diary entry, 26 June 1844, in Strong, *Diary*, 238; Margaret Gardiner to Julia Gardiner Tyler, 8 July 1844, in "Letters from Tyler Trunks," *Tyler's Quarterly Historical and Genealogical Magazine* 18 (January 1937): 141; Juliana Gardiner to Julia Gardiner Tyler, July 1844, in "Letters from Tyler Trunks," *Tyler's Quarterly Historical and Genealogical Magazine* 18 (October 1936): 94–95.

54 Sellers, *James K. Polk*, 2:135; Robert Seager II, *And Tyler Too: A Biography of John and Julia Gardiner Tyler* (New York: McGraw-Hill Books, 1963), 232.

55 Alexander Gardiner to Julia Gardiner Tyler, [June] 1844, in "Letters from Tyler Trunks," (October 1936): 90; Sellers, *James K. Polk*, 2:135–136; Monroe, *Republican Vision*, 177; John Tyler to Robert Tyler, 6 July 1844, in Tyler, *Letters and Times*, 2:710; Robert J. Walker to James K. Polk, 10 July 1844, in *CJKP*, 7:337.

56 Robert J. Walker to James K. Polk, 10 July 1844, in *CJKP*, 7:337.

57 Robert J. Walker to James K. Polk, 10 and 11 July 1844, James K. Polk to Andrew J. Donelson, 23 July 1844, and James K. Polk to Andrew Jackson, 23 July 1844, in *CJKP*, 7:337–338, 344, 384–385, 388–389; Nathaniel Cheairs Hughes and Roy P. Stonesifer, *The Life and Wars of Gideon J. Pillow* (Chapel Hill: University of North Carolina Press, 1993), 38.

58 Andrew Jackson to James K. Polk, 26 July 1844, in *CJKP*, 7:401; Andrew Jackson to Francis P. Blair, 26 July 1844, Andrew Jackson to John Y. Mason, 1 August 1844, Andrew Jackson Papers, DLC; Andrew Jackson to William B. Lewis, 1 August 1844, Jackson–Lewis Correspondence, New York Public Library; Leahy, *President without a Party*, 4–6; Cheathem, *Andrew Jackson, Southerner*, 4.

59 John Tyler to Andrew Jackson, 18 August 1844, Andrew Jackson Papers, DLC; John Tyler to the American people, 20 August 1844, in *Daily Madisonian* (Washington, DC), 20 August 1844; Jimmy Carter–Ronald Reagan presidential debate, 28 October 1980, C-SPAN, https://www.c-span.org/video/?33229 -1/1980-presidential-candidates-debate; John Tyler to Henry A. Wise, 20 April 1852, and John Tyler to Alexander Gardiner, 11 July 1846, in Tyler, *Letters and Times*, 3:170–171, 2:341; Leahy, *President without a Party*, 288–291.

60 Julia Tyler to unknown, 22 August 1844, in Tyler, *Letters and Times*, 2:342n1; *Whig Standard* (Washington, DC), 21 August 1844; *New York Daily Herald*, 22 August 1844; *Washington (DC) Daily Globe*, 22 August 1844; Joel B. Sutherland to Andrew Jackson, 20 August 1844, in Tyler, *Letters and Times*, 3:147–148; Andrew Jackson to James K. Polk, 2 September 1844, Alexander O. Anderson to James K. Polk, 22 August 1844, 12 September 1844, in *CJKP*, 8:3, 7:458–459, 8:48–49.

61 Robert P. Lamb, "James G. Birney and the Road to Abolitionism," *Alabama Review* 47 (April 1994): 87–88; Eli Pullman, "Alexander Dallas," *The Digital Encyclopedia of George Washington*, https://www.mountvernon.org/library/dig italhistory/digital-encyclopedia/article/alexander-dallas/.

62 Lamb, "James G. Birney," 88–91, 102–104; Plantation record book, 1824, James G. Birney to Gerrit Smith, 13 September 1835, in *LJGB*, 1:52, 242; Cheathem, *Andrew Jackson, Southerner*, 4, 63–66, 69–74.

63 Lamb, "James G. Birney," 104–107, 109–111; Benjamin Labaree diary entry, n.d., in *LJGB*, 1:242n4.

64 Betty Fladeland, *James Gillespie Birney: Slaveholder to Abolitionist* (Ithaca, NY: Cornell University Press, 1955), 52–53; Robert H. Abzug, *Passionate Liberator: Theodore Dwight Weld and the Dilemma of Reform* (New York: Oxford University Press, 1980), 86; William Birney, *James G. Birney and His Times: The Genesis of the Republican Party with Some Account of Abolition Movements in the South Before 1828* (New York: D. Appleton, 1890), 105–106; Lamb, "James G. Birney," 113–126; Benjamin Labaree diary entry, n.d.; and James G. Birney to Ralph R. Gurley, 24 January 1833, in *LJGB*, 1:242n4, 52.

65 James G. Birney to Ralph R. Gurley, 11 December 1833, Address of the Kentucky Society for the Gradual Relief of the State from Slavery, [December 1833], in *LJGB*, 1:98–99, 100; Lamb, "James G. Birney," 121–122, 125–129.

66 Cathy Rogers Franklin, "James Gillespie Birney, the Revival Spirit, and 'The Philanthropist,'" *American Journalism* 17 (April 2000): 32, 37–41, 43, 45–47; Lewis Bond to James G. Birney, 31 August 1835, in *LJGB*, 1:240; Executive Committee of the Ohio Anti-Slavery Society, *Narrative of the Late Riotous Proceedings Against the Liberty of the Press, in Cincinnati. With Remarks and Historical Notices Relating to Emancipation* (Cincinnati, OH, 1836), 16–17; Howe, *What Hath God Wrought*, 433; Fladeland, *James Gillespie Birney*, 141–148, 154–159.

67 D. Laurence Rogers, *Apostles of Equality: The Birneys, the Republicans and the Civil War* (Lansing: Michigan State University Press, 2011), 114–115, 46; Fladeland, *James Gillespie Birney*, 93–95, 155–160; Diary entry, 17 September 1834, in *LJGB*, 1:135; James G. Birney to Henry Clay, 22 December 1837; and Henry Clay to James G. Birney, 16 September 1834, 3 November 1838, in *PHC*, 9:111–113, 8:748, 9:244–245; Joseph A. Boromé, "Henry Clay and James G. Birney: An Exchange of Views," *Filson Club History Quarterly* 35 (April 1961): 122–124.

68 Reinhard O. Johnson, *The Liberty Party, 1840–1848: Antislavery Third-Party Politics in the United States* (Baton Rouge: Louisiana State University Press, 2009), 11–14, 357.

69 Johnson, *Liberty Party*, 14–16, 339; Edwin B. Bronner, *Thomas Earle as a Reformer* (Philadelphia: Press of International Printing Company, 1948), 53–55; *The Emancipator*, 9 April 1840; Myron Holley, Joshua Leavitt, and Elizur Wright Jr. to James G. Birney, 2 April 1840, in *LJGB*, 1:550.

70 Fladeland, *James Gillespie Birney*, 194–198; Editorial note, and James G. Birney to Myron Holley, Joshua Leavitt, and Elizur Wright Jr., 11 May 1840, in *LJGB*, 1:xvi, 565, 567, 569–570, 574.

71 Corey M. Brooks, *Liberty Power: Antislavery Third Parties and the Transformation of American Politics* (Chicago: University of Chicago Press, 2016), 9, 27–28; David Brion Davis, *The Slave Power Conspiracy and the Paranoid Style* (Baton Rouge: Louisiana State University Press, 1969); Richards, *Slave Power*.

72 Elizabeth Cady Stanton, *Eighty Years and More, 1815–1897: Reminiscences of Elizabeth Cady Stanton* (New York: European Publishing Co., 1898), 79; Henry B. Stanton, *Random Recollections*, 2nd ed. (New York: Macgowan & Slipper, 1886), 48; Rogers, *Apostles of Equality*, 125, 128–132; Murphy, *American Slavery, Irish Freedom*, 52.

73 Francis J. LeMoyne to James G. Birney, 24 March 1840, John Greenleaf Whittier to James G. Birney, 16 April 1840, and Gamaliel Bailey to James G. Birney, 18 April 1840, in *LJGB*, 1:543–545, 555, 556–558; Johnson, *Liberty Party*, 16–21; Dubin, *United States Presidential Elections*, 71–72; Alvan Stewart, "An Address by the 'National Committee of Correspondence,' . . ." November 1840, in *The Emancipator*, 17 December 1840; Stanley C. Harrold Jr., "The Southern Strategy of the Liberty Party," *Ohio History* 87 (Winter 1978): 21–28.

74 *The Friend of Man* (Utica, NY), 25 May 1841; Fladeland, *James Gillespie Birney*, 215–219; Johnson, *Liberty Party*, 362, 370–371, 373.

75 *The Friend of Man* (Utica, NY), 25 May 1841; *The Emancipator*, 27 May 1841.

76 *The Friend of Man* (Utica, NY), 25 May 1841; Johnson, *Liberty Party*, 22–35; Thomas Morris et al. to Joshua Leavitt, 9 February 1842, in *Emancipator and Free American* (Boston), 16 June 1842.

77 Fladeland, *James Gillespie Birney*, 211–213; James G. Birney to Lewis Tappan, 4 and 25 October 1841, and James G. Birney to Joshua Leavitt et al., 10 January 1842, in *LJGB*, 2:637, 640, 645–656; James G. Birney to Theodore Foster and Guy Beckley, 29 September 1841, in *Signal of Liberty* (Ann Arbor, MI), 6 October 1841; Carol E. Mull, "The *Signal of Liberty* Newspaper," Ann Arbor District Library, https://aadl.org/signalofliberty; John W. Quist, "'The Great Majority of Our Subscribers Are Farmers': The Michigan Abolitionist Constituency of the 1840s," *Journal of the Early Republic* 14 (Autumn 1994): 325–358.

78 Fladeland, *James Gillespie Birney*, 215–219, 224; James G. Birney to Joshua Leavitt et al., 10 January 1842, Gamaliel Bailey to James G. Birney, 31 March 1843, and James G. Birney to Gamaliel Bailey, 16 April 1843, in *LJGB*, 2:645–656, 726, 732; Johnson, *Liberty Party*, 324.

79 *New-York Daily Tribune*, 4 September 1843; *Buffalo Commercial Advertiser*, 30 and 31 August 1843; *Spirit of Liberty* (Pittsburgh), 16 September 1843; Johnson, *Liberty Party*, 37–38.

80 Elizur Wright Jr. to James G. Birney, 16 September 1843; James G. Birney to Leicester King, 1 January 1844; and William Birney to James G. Birney, 24 September 1843, 12 and 26 January 1844, 26 February 1844, 28 March 1844, in *LJGB*, 2:760, 766–773, 762, 774, 776, 794, 802; Johnson, *Liberty Party*, 34, 40–42; Eric Foner, *Free Soil, Free Labor, Free Men: The Ideology of the Republican Party before the Civil War* (New York: Oxford University Press, 1970), 90–91; Brooks, *Liberty Power*, 25–26.

81 Fladeland, *James Gillespie Birney*, 227–229; Johnson, *Liberty Party*, 235–237, 353–354, 356, 370–371, 373; Erika Pribanic-Smith, "Partisan News and the Third-Party Candidate: Press Coverage of James G. Birney's 1844 Presidential Campaign," *Journalism History* 39 (Fall 2013): 170–176; *American Anti-Slavery Almanac*, 2, no. 1 (1842), 18–19, https://transcription.si.edu/view/26316 /NMAAHC-2010_01_12_010-000001; Psalm 92:12, King James Version; Elizur Wright Jr. to James G. Birney, 16 September 1843, in *LJGB*, 2:759–761; "Ode to James G. Birney," in George W. Clark, *The Liberty Minstrel* (New York: Saxton and Miles, 1844), https://www.gutenberg.org/files/22089/22089 -h/22089-h.htm#ODE_TO_JAMES_G_BIRNEY.

82 Fladeland, *James Gillespie Birney*, 227–229; Elizur Wright Jr. to James G. Birney, 16 September 1843, and James G. Birney to Elizur Wright Jr., 4 March 1844, in *LJGB*, 2:759–761, 798.

83 Jackson, *Force and Freedom*, 36–39, 45, 47; "Address to the Slaves of the U.S.," 16 August 1843, Project Gutenberg, https://www.gutenberg.org/files /16516/16516-h/16516-h.htm#ADDRESS_TO_THE_SLAVES_OF_THE_US; Howard H. Bell, "National Negro Conventions of the Middle 1840's: Moral Suasion vs. Political Action," *Journal of Negro History* 42 (October 1957): 247–260; Johnson, *Liberty Party*, 42.

CHAPTER 5. "A NATIONAL FESTIVAL"

1   Joseph E. Uscinski, *Conspiracy Theories: A Primer* (New York: Rowman & Little-field, 2020), 90–91; Cheathem, *Coming of Democracy*, 9.

2   Heidler and Heidler, *Henry Clay*, 5–6, 11–12, 371–372; Harold D. Moser, comp., *John Tyler: A Bibliography* (Westport, CT: Greenwood Press, 2001), 176–178; Henry Clay to John O. Sargent, 2 June 1841, Nathan Sargent to Henry Clay, 6 August 1842, and Henry Clay to Epes Sargent, 13 September 1842, 7 August 1844, in *PHC*, 9:536, 751, 765, 10:93; *The New World*, 24 September 1842, 162, 206; *The New World Extra* [3 September 1842], 1–16; James C. Klotter, *Henry Clay: The Man Who Would Be President* (New York: Oxford University Press, 2018), 303–304.

3   Aaron V. Brown to James K. Polk, 30 May 1844, Samuel H. Laughlin to James K. Polk, 31 May 1844, Gideon J. Pillow to James K. Polk, 2 June 1844, and Editorial note, in *CJKP*, 7:166–168, 173–176, 182, 229n8; Nye, *George Bancroft*, 132; Cole, *A Jackson Man*, 242–243; George H. Hickman, *The Life and Public Services of the Hon. James K. Polk, with a Compendium of His Speeches on Various Public Measures. Also, A Sketch of the Life of the Hon. George Mifflin Dallas* (Baltimore: N. Hickman, 1844); Moser, comp., *John Tyler*, 175.

4   Lorman A. Ratner and Dwight L. Teeter Jr., *Fanatics and Fire-eaters: Newspapers and the Coming of the Civil War* (Urbana: University of Illinois Press, 2004), 9; William A. Dill, "Growth of Newspapers in the United States" (Master's thesis, University of Kansas, 1928), 11; US Census, 1850, lxiv–lxv; *That Same Old Coon* (Dayton, OH), 12 April 1844; *Coon Hunter* (Boonville, MO), 26 April 1844; *Coon Skinner* (Ithaca, NY), 23 August 1844; *Coon Dissector* (Dayton, OH), 6 September 1844; *Young Hickory* (Lynn, MA), 14 September 1844; *Young Hickory Banner* (New York), 10 August 1844; *Washington (DC) Semi-Weekly Globe*, 1 July 1844.

5   Merk, *Slavery and the Annexation of Texas*, 81–84; William Nisbet Chambers, *Old Bullion Benton, Senator from the New West: Thomas Hart Benton, 1782–1858* (Boston: Little, Brown, 1956), 276–277; *Senate Executive Journal*, 28th Cong., 1st Sess. (8 June 1844): 312; Peterson, *Presidencies of Harrison and Tyler*, 229–233; Mueller, *Senator Benton*, 203–206; Jeremiah George Harris to James K. Polk, 25 June 1844, in *CJKP*, 7:282. Democrat Edward Hannegan of Indiana, an ardent expansionist, did not vote; see John J. Wickre, "Indiana's Southern Senator: Jesse Bright and the Hoosier Democracy" (PhD diss., University of Kentucky, 2013), 39–41.

6   Rachel A. Shelden, "Not So Strange Bedfellows: Northern and Southern Whigs and the Texas Annexation Controversy, 1844–1845," in *A Political Nation: New Directions in Mid-Nineteenth-Century American Political History*, ed. Gary W. Gallagher and Rachel A. Shelden (Charlottesville: University of Virginia Press, 2012), 11–23; Heidler and Heidler, *Henry Clay*, 390; Henry Clay to Stephen Miller, 1 July 1844, in *PHC*, 10:78–79; Henry Clay to Thomas M. Peters and John M. Jackson, 27 July 1844, and Henry Clay to Joseph Gales Jr. and William W. Seaton, 23 September 1844, in *PHC*, 10:89–91, 122–124; Sellers, *James K. Polk*, 2:146–148; David Zarefsky, "Henry Clay and the Election of 1844: The

Limits of a Rhetoric of Compromise," *Rhetoric & Public Affairs* 6 (Spring 2003): 79–96; Klotter, *Henry Clay*, 312.

7   James K. Polk to Henry Hubbard et al., 12 June 1844, Alvin Cullom to James K. Polk, 30 May 1844, and Jacob Thompson to James K. Polk, 7 June 1844, in *CJKP*, 7:241, 492, 212–213; Sellers, *James K. Polk*, 2:113–114.

8   *New York Commercial Advertiser*, 25 July 1844; *Daily Madisonian* (Washington, DC), 25 July 1844; *Whig Standard* (Washington, DC), 26 July 1844.

9   Fladeland, *James Gillespie Birney*, 233–237, 239–240; James G. Birney to William E. Austin et al., 23 February 1844, in *LJGB*, 2:787–789.

10   Bolt, *Tariff Wars*, 158–165; Stephen F. Miller to Henry Clay, 20 June 1844, in Stephen F. Miller, *The Bench and Bar of Georgia: Memoirs and Sketches* (Philadelphia: J. B. Lippincott, 1858), 2:386.

11   Heidler and Heidler, *Henry Clay*, 124, 167; Henry Clay to Job W. Ray, 26 September 1844, in *PHC*, 10:127; Robert L. Caruthers to Henry Clay, 12 August 1844, and Henry Clay to Robert L. Caruthers, 20 August 1844, in *Knoxville (TN) Register*, 11 September 1844.

12   J. G. M. Ramsey to James K. Polk, 4 January 1844; Aaron V. Brown to James K. Polk, 25 February 1844; Robert J. Walker to James K. Polk, 30 May 1844; Andrew J. Donelson to James K. Polk, 31 May 1844; Cave Johnson to James K. Polk, 2 June 1844; and Samuel H. Laughlin to James K. Polk, 10 June 1844, in *CJKP*, 7:8, 68, 168, 169–170, 180–182, 499; Sellers, *James K. Polk*, 2:116.

13   John Slidell to James K. Polk, 1 June 1844; James K. Polk to John Kintzing Kane, 19 June 1844 (2 letters); John W. Goode et al. to James K. Polk, 21 September 1844; David M. Currin to James K. Polk, 23 September 1844; James K. Polk to John W. Goode et al., 25 September 1844 (2 drafts); and John Catron to James K. Polk, 26 September 1844, in *CJKP*, 7:179, 265–267, 267–268, 8:106, 111, 122, 123, 125–126, 130–131, 152–153; Matthew J. Grow, *"Liberty to the Downtrodden": Thomas L. Kane, Romantic Reformer* (New Haven, CT: Yale University Press, 2009), 1–7; John Kintzing Kane to James K. Polk, 30 May 1844, James K. Polk Papers, DLC.

14   Francis R. Shunk to James K. Polk, 14 October 1844; John K. Kane to James K. Polk, 13, 14–15 October 1844, 9 August 1844; John Law to James K. Polk, 26 September 1844; James K. Polk to John K. Kane, 4 October 1844; William E. Cramer to James K. Polk, 4 October 1844; and Silas Wright Jr. to James K. Polk, 31 October 1844, in *CJKP*, 8:188, 181, 186, 7:445–446, 8:130–131, 152–153, 150, 250; Bolt, *Tariff Wars*, 169–171.

15   Russell Errett to James G. Birney, 13 July 1844, 27 August 1844; William M. Stephenson to James G. Birney, 23 July 1844; Richard H. Brackin to James G. Birney, 31 July 1844; and James G. Birney to Russell Errett, 5 August 1844, in *LJGB*, 2:820–821, 836–839, 822–823, 827–829, 829–832; *Signal of Liberty*, 16 September 1844; *Pittsburgh Gazette*, 28 September 1844.

16   Cheathem, *Coming of Democracy*, 141–150, 152–153; John Catron to James K. Polk, 17, 23 July 1844; James K. Polk to John B. Bratton et al., 3 July 1844; James K. Polk to James H. Stark et al., 9 July 1844; James K. Polk to William Kennon Jr. et al., 10 July 1844; James K. Polk to Robert Armstrong, 16 September 1844;

James K. Polk to Boling Gordon, 7 October 1844; John P. Heiss to James K. Polk, 29 July 1844; John K. Kane to James K. Polk, 2 July 1844; William E. Cramer to James K. Polk, 21 July 1844; Cave Johnson to James K. Polk, 4 September 1844; Barnabas Bates to James K. Polk, 21 September 1844; and Franklin Pierce to James K. Polk, 23 September 1844, in *CJKP*, 7:355–356, 383, 508, 511, 514, 8:69–70, 162, 7:410–411, 306, 376–377, 8:16–17, 102–103, 117; Greenberg, *Lady First*, xvi, 45, 51, 99–101, 107.

17 Greenberg, *Lady First*, 29, 32, 101–103; *Spirit of the Age* (Woodstock, VT), 13, 27 June 1844; B. F. Bussey to James K. Polk, 13 June 1844; William H. Haywood to James K. Polk, 28 June 1844; J. G. M. Ramsey to James K. Polk, 16 and 29 July 1844, 5 August 1844; Cave Johnson to James K. Polk, 22 July 1844; and Julius W. Blackwell to James K. Polk, 10 August 1844, in *CJKP*, 7:501, 507, 353, 440–441, 518, 516, 522; Lisa N. Oakley, "James Gettys McGready Ramsey," *Tennessee Encyclopedia*, http://tennesseeencyclopedia.net/entries/james-gettys -mcgready-ramsey/; Heale, *Presidential Quest*, 197; *Whig Standard* (Washington, DC), 11 June 1844; John M. McCalla to Daniel Bradford, 24 May 1844, in *Tri-Weekly Nashville (TN) Union*, 13 June 1844; Editorial note, in *CJKP*, 6:66n3; *Liberty Hall and Cincinnati Gazette*, 5 September 1844; *Nashville (TN) Tri-Weekly Union*, 27 August 1844; Moses Montgomery Henkle, *The Life of Henry Bidleman Bascom . . .* (Morton & Griswold, 1854), 105–107, 136; Alexander Plumer et al. to Henry Clay, 15 July 1844, in *Kendall's Expositor* (Washington, DC) 4 (3 September 1844): 331–333; *New Hampshire Patriot and State Gazette* (Concord), 15 August 1844; Henry Clay to Alexander Plumer et al., 1 August 1844, in *PHC*, 10:92–93; Samuel Darling to James K. Polk, 29 August 1844, James K. Polk Papers, DLC. William H. Polk's 1838 altercation had started when local lawyer Richard H. Hays had insulted him. A "street fight" ended with Hayes shot in the head and Polk paying a $750 fine and serving a six-month jail sentence for assault; see Sellers, *James K. Polk*, 1:331; Hughes and Stonesifer, *Life & Wars of Gideon J. Pillow*, 16; *Tri-Weekly Nashville (TN) Union*, 10 December 1838; *National Gazette* (Philadelphia), 12 December 1838; and *Nashville (TN) Daily Republican Banner*, 22 January 1839.

18 Cheathem, *Coming of Democracy*, 164–169; Grinspan, *Virgin Vote*, 43, 76–78; Greenberg, *Lady First*, 107–108.

19 Auguste D'Avezac to James K. Polk, 31 August 1844, in *CJKP*, 7:481; *Weekly Argus* (Albany, NY), 6 and 27 July 1844; *Boston Statesman*, 13 July 1844; *New England (Boston) Democrat*, 18 July 1844; *Nashville (TN) Tri-Weekly Union*, 8, 22 August 1844; Elizabeth R. Varon, *We Mean to Be Counted: White Women and Politics in Antebellum Virginia* (Chapel Hill: University of North Carolina Press, 1998), 86–87; *Wilmington (NC) Journal*, 4 October 1844; Editorial note, in *CJKP*, 7:434n12.

20 Anonymous ("A True Northern Friend") to Henry Clay, 13 July 1842, in *PHC*, 9:733–734; Henry Clay, Speech, 9 June 1842, in *Niles' Register* 62 (9 July 1842): 291; Jayne Crumpler DeFiore, "'COME, and Bring the Ladies': Tennessee Women and the Politics of Opportunity during the Presidential Campaigns of 1840 and 1844," *Tennessee Historical Quarterly* 51 (Winter 1992): 201, 203; John

M. Sacher, "'The Ladies Are Moving Everywhere': Louisiana Women and An-
tebellum Politics," *Louisiana History* 42 (Autumn 2001): 444–451; *Tri-Weekly
Nashville (TN) Republican Banner*, 31 July 1844, 12 August 1844; "Jonathan
Roberts," in *BDUSC*; Philip S. Klein, ed., "Notes and Documents: Memoirs
of a Senator from Pennsylvania: Jonathan Roberts, 1771–1854 [pt. 1]," *Pennsylvania Magazine of History and Biography* 61 (October 1937): 449; Philip S.
Klein, ed., "Notes and Documents: Memoirs of a Senator from Pennsylvania:
Jonathan Roberts, 1771–1854 [pt. 2]," *Pennsylvania Magazine of History and Biography* 62 (October 1938): 514, 525; *Evansville (IN) Weekly Journal*, 3 October
1844.

21   John Hays II Family Papers [finding aid], 2–3, http://archives.dickinson.edu
      /sites/all/files/files_collection/mc2001.01_1.pdf; *Carlisle (PA) Weekly Herald*,
      21 August 1844; Michael D. Pierson, *Free Hearts and Free Homes: Gender and
      American Antislavery Politics* (Chapel Hill: University of North Carolina Press,
      2003), 35.

22   DeFiore, "'COME, and Bring the Ladies,'" 207–208; *Nashville (TN) Whig*,
      28 September 1844; *Tri-Weekly Republican Banner* (Nashville, TN), 2 October
      1844; Varon, *We Mean to Be Counted*, 87; *Alexandria (VA) Gazette*, 5 September
      1844; Cheathem, *Coming of Democracy*, 117–118, 142–143; *Cadiz (OH) Sentinel*,
      31 July 1844.

23   Dallas C. Dickey, *Seargent S. Prentiss: Whig Orator of the Old South* (Baton
      Rouge: Louisiana State University Press, 1946), 66–67, 171, 174–192, 229–
      236, 241–244, 250, 256–259, 369–370; *Mississippi Free Trader* (Natchez), 12
      September 1844; Joseph Dunbar Shields, *The Life and Times of Seargent Smith
      Prentiss* (New York: J. B. Lippincott, 1883), 345; Seargent S. Prentiss to Richard
      T. Archer, 17 October 1844, in George Lewis Prentiss, *A Memoir of S. S. Prentiss*
      (New York: Scribner, 1855, 1856), 2:337–338.

24   James K. Polk to John B. Bratton et al., 3 July 1844; James K. Polk to James
      H. Stark et al., 9 July 1844; James K. Polk to William Kennon Jr. et al., 10 July
      1844; James K. Polk to Robert Armstrong, 16 September 1844; James K. Polk
      to Boling Gordon, 7 October 1844; John P. Heiss to James K. Polk, 29 July
      1844; John K. Kane to James K. Polk, 2 July 1844; William E. Cramer to James
      K. Polk, 21 July 1844; Cave Johnson to James K. Polk, 4 September 1844; Barn-
      abas Bates to James K. Polk, 21 September 1844; and Franklin Pierce to James
      K. Polk, 23 September 1844, in *CJKP*, 7:508, 511, 514, 8:69–70, 162, 7:410–411,
      306, 376–377, 8:16–17, 102–103, 117; Sean Scalmer, *On the Stump: Campaign
      Oratory and Democracy in the United States, Britain, and Australia* (Philadelphia:
      Temple University Press, 2017), 70–72.

25   Cheathem, *Coming of Democracy*, 13–14, 150–153; Grinspan, *Virgin Vote*, 11.

26   *Clay Bugle* (Harrisburg, PA), 1 January 1844; *Washington (DC) Daily Globe*, 2
      January 1844, 9 October 1844; *Salem (MA) Register*, 1 February 1844; Charles
      S. Wallach to James K. Polk, 14 June 1844, and Christian M. Straub et al. to
      James K. Polk, 23 August 1844, in *CJKP*, 7:502, 526; *Nashville (TN) Tri-Weekly
      Union*, 13 June 1844; *Weekly Argus* (Albany, NY), 13 July 1844; *Sober Second
      Thought, for the Presidential Campaign of 1844* (New York), 10 August 1844.

27 Andrew T. Judson to James K. Polk, 14 September 1844, George M. Dallas to James K. Polk, 8 October 1844, and Gansevoort Melville to James K. Polk, 26 October 1844, in *CJKP*, 8:60, 165–166, 227; *Washington (DC) Daily Globe*, 5 October 1844; *New York Herald*, 24 October 1844; *Richmond (VA) Whig*, 10 October 1844; *Nashville (TN) Tri-Weekly Union*, 28 August 1844; *Portland (ME) Weekly Advertiser*, 8 October 1844; Janet Galligani Casey, "New Letters of Gansevoort Melville: 1845–1846," *Studies in the American Renaissance* (1991): 141–142; *New York Evening Post*, 2 November 1844.

28 *Republican Farmer* (Bridgeport, CT), 30 January 1844.

29 Silas Wright Jr. to Benjamin F. Butler, 3 June 1844, Silas Wright Letters to Benjamin F. Butler, A. C. Flagg, and John Tyler, Manuscripts and Archives Division, New York Public Library, Astor, Lenox, and Tilden Foundations; Sellers, *James K. Polk*, 2:114–116; Wiltse, *John C. Calhoun*, 3:187–190; Elizabeth R. Varon, *Disunion! The Coming of the American Civil War, 1789–1859* (Chapel Hill: University of North Carolina Press, 2008), 170–171; William C. Davis, *Rhett: The Turbulent Life and Times of a Fire-Eater* (Columbia: University of South Carolina Press, 2001), 193, 196–201; *Southern Patriot* (Charleston, SC), 12 August 1844; *Charleston (SC) Mercury*, 8 August 1844; Erika Pribanic-Smith, "Southern Values and the 1844 Election in South Carolina Newspapers," *Journalism History* 41 (Winter 2016): 200–210.

30 George M. Dallas to James K. Polk, 16 October 1844, in *CJKP*, 8:196.

31 Sellers, *James K. Polk*, 2:116, 138–139.

32 *Nashville (TN) Union*, 1 August 1844; *Nashville (TN) Tri-Weekly Union*, 2 July 1844; Felix Robertson et al. to Martin Van Buren, 17 June 1844, PMVB (mvb04027). James Buchanan to Felix Robertson et al., 6 July 1844; John Fairfield to Felix Robertson et al., 8 July 1844; George McDuffie to Felix Robertson et al., 12 July 1844; Marcus Morton to Felix Robertson et al., 13 July 1844; Richard M. Johnson to Felix Robertson et al., 21 July 1844; Robert J. Walker to Felix Robertson et al., 30 July 1844; and Romulus M. Saunders to Felix Robertson et al., 3 August 1844, in *Nashville (TN) Tri-Weekly Union*, 17 August 1844; Martin Van Buren to Felix Robertson et al., 29 July 1844, PMVB (mvb04042). A. P. Bagby to Felix Robertson et al., 11 July 1844; Henry Horn to Felix Robertson et al., 13 July 1844; Jesse Speight to Felix Robertson et al., 3 August 1844; Richard French to Felix Robertson et al., 8 August 1844; and Benjamin F. Butler to Felix Robertson et al., 15 August 1844, in *Nashville (TN) Tri-Weekly Union*, 20 August 1844; William B. Lewis to Andrew J. Donelson, 3 July 1844; George Bancroft to Andrew J. Donelson, 6 July 1844; Thomas Hart Benton to Andrew J. Donelson, 10 August 1844; and James Buchanan to Andrew J. Donelson, 17 July 1844, Andrew Jackson Donelson Papers, DLC; Martin Van Buren to Felix Robertson et al., 29 July 1844, PMVB (mvb04042); Sellers, *James K. Polk*, 2:128; Elder, *Calhoun*, 303, 435; John B. Edmunds Jr., *Francis W. Pickens and the Politics of Destruction* (Chapel Hill: University of North Carolina Press, 1986), 20.

33 *Nashville (TN) Tri-Weekly Union*, 13 and 17 August 1844; "Thomas F. Marshall," in *BDUSC*; "Reminiscences of Tom Marshall," *The Galaxy* 17 (March 1874): 300.

34 Lewis Cass to Andrew J. Donelson, 29 July 1844, Andrew Jackson Donelson Papers, DLC; *Nashville (TN) Tri-Weekly Union*, 17, 19 August 1844; Johannsen, *Stephen A. Douglas*, 139; "Linn Boyd," in *BDUSC*.

35 *Nashville (TN) Tri-Weekly Union*, 20 August 1844.

36 *Weekly Arkansas Gazette* (Little Rock), 4 September 1844; Walter Lee Brown, *A Life of Albert Pike* (Fayetteville: University of Arkansas Press, 1997), 225; *Tri-Weekly Republican Banner* (Nashville, TN), 21, 23 August 1844; *Jamestown (NY) Journal*, 20 September 1844; Cheathem, *Coming of Democracy*, 13–14; *Cincinnati Daily Gazette*, 15 August 1844; "O. K." to unknown, 22 August 1844, in *Whig Standard* (Washington, DC), 30 August 1844; Dickey, *Seargent S. Prentiss*, 248; James C. Jones to George Prentiss, 12 February 1851, in *Memoirs of S. S. Prentiss*, 2:321–324; *Mill Boy* (St. Louis, MO), 31 August 1844; *Sandusky (OH) Clarion*, 7 September 1844. In 1838, Graves, a Kentucky congressman, and fellow representative Jonathan Cilley of Maine fought a duel that resulted in the latter's death. Henry A. Wise served as Graves's second in the affair of honor, and Henry Clay participated in the preduel preparations; see Jeffrey L. Pasley, "Minnows, Spies, and Aristocrats: The Social Crisis of Congress in the Age of Martin Van Buren," *Journal of the Early Republic* 27 (Winter 2007): 629–649.

37 *Republican Banner* (Nashville, TN), 16 August 1844; *Vermont Phoenix* (Brattleboro), 27 September 1844; William E. Bartelt, "Aiding Mr. Clay: Abraham Lincoln's 1844 Visit to Indiana," *Traces of Indiana and Midwestern History* 32 (Winter 2020): 28–39; Scalmer, *On the Stump*, 19–24; "Ebenezer J. Shields," in *BDUSC*; William Carroll Jr. to William Cullen Bryant, 14 August 1844, in *New York Evening Post*, 14 August 1844; Gilbert H. Muller, *William Cullen Bryant: Author of America* (Albany: SUNY Press, 2008), 180; *Nashville (TN) Tri-Weekly Union*, 27, 29, 30 August 1844; *New-York Tribune*, 24 September 1844; Editorial note, in *CJKP*, 7:471n13.

38 *Nashville (TN) Republican Banner*, 5 and 12 August 1844; Andrew Jackson to Francis P. Blair, 26 September 1840, in *CAJ*, 6:78; *Nashville (TN) Tri-Weekly Union*, 22 and 29 August 1844; *Weekly Arkansas Gazette* (Little Rock), 4 September 1844.

39 "Henry Clay Campaign Banner, 1844," Collections of The Henry Ford, https://www.thehenryford.org/collections-and-research/digital-collections/artifact/93395; Daniel 5:26b–28 (KJV).

40 Robert Armstrong to James K. Polk, 5, 19 July 1844; Editorial note; and Samuel H. Laughlin to James K. Polk, 28 June 1844, in *CJKP*, 7:310–311, 364, 294; *Weekly Arkansas Gazette* (Little Rock,), 4 September 1844; *Nashville (TN) Tri-Weekly Union*, 29 August 1844.

41 Heidler and Heidler, *Henry Clay*, 371–372; *Nashville (TN) Tri-Weekly Union*, 30 August 1844; Cassius M. Clay, *The Life of Cassius Marcellus Clay: Memoirs, Writings, and Speeches, Showing His Conduct in the Overthrow of American Slavery, the Salvation of the Union, and the Restoration of the Autonomy of the States* (Cincinnati: J. F. Brennan, 1886), 102–103; *Richmond (IN) Palladium*, 30 August 1844; *Mill Boy* (St. Louis, MO), 24 August 1844. "Polk stalks" referred to pokeweed,

"a large-leaved, coarse, succulent North American plant . . . of which the young leaves are eaten as a vegetable or salad" (see "pokeweed, n.," *OED Online*).

42 *Nashville (TN) Tri-Weekly Union*, 18 June 1844; *Springfield (MO) Advertiser*, 16 July 1844; *Vicksburg (MS) Whig*, 24 June 1844; *Boone's Lick Time* (Fayette, MO), 24 August 1844; Unknown to John P. Heiss, 20 September 1844, in *Tri-Weekly Nashville (TN) Union*, 30 September 1844; *Nashville (TN) Republican Banner*, 5 August 1844; *Louisville (KY) Daily Journal*, 13 August 1844.

43 Cheathem, *Coming of Democracy*, 9, 12–13, 17–21, 23, 26–28, 30–32, 37, 44–48, 53, 57–61, 81–88, 101, 109–115, 136–140, 154–158, 160–164; Grinspan, *Virgin Vote*, 31–32; *That Same Old Coon* (Dayton, OH), 12 April 1844; *Coon Hunter* (Boonville, MO), 26 April 1844; *Coon Skinner* (Ithaca, NY), 23 August 1844; *Coon Dissector* (Dayton, OH), 6 September 1844; *Young Hickory* (Lynn, MA), 14 September 1844; *Young Hickory Banner* (New York), 10 August 1844; *Washington (DC) Semi-Weekly Globe*, 1 July 1844; *Nashville (TN) Tri-Weekly Union*, 22 August 1844; "Treeing Coons" (1844), Prints and Photographs Division, DLC, https://www.loc.gov/pictures/item/2008661421/.

44 "Virtuous Harry, or Set a Thief to Catch a Thief!" (1844), Prints and Photographs Division, DLC, https://www.loc.gov/pictures/item/2008661428/; "The Masked Battery or Loco-Foco Strategy" (1844), Prints and Photographs Division, DLC, https://www.loc.gov/pictures/item/2008661430/; "Doings of the *Decency* or 'Charity Covering a Multitude of Sins,'" Heritage Auctions, https://historical.ha.com/itm/political/henry-clay-doings-of-decency-or-charity-covering-a-multitude-of-sins-lithograph-print/a/6032-47123.s; "The Returns of the Election," Digital Commonwealth, Boston Public Library, https://ark.digitalcommonwealth.org/ark:/50959/9880w9931.

45 "Balloon Ascension to the Presidential Chair," Prints and Photographs Division, DLC, https://www.loc.gov/pictures/item/2008661433/; "Bursting the Balloon" (1844), Prints and Photographs Division, DLC, https://www.loc.gov/pictures/item/2008661434/; Liz Hutter, "'HO FOR SALT RIVER!'" *Commonplace: The Journal of Early American Life*, http://commonplace.online/article/ho-for-salt-river/; "Impure Spirits Disappearing before the Rising Sun" (1843), Susan H. Douglas Political Americana Collection, #2214, Division of Rare and Manuscript Collections, Cornell University Library, https://digital.library.cornell.edu/catalog/ss:10637512; "The Hunter of Kentucky" (1844), Prints and Photographs Division, DLC, https://www.loc.gov/pictures/item/2008661440/. This claim is based on an analysis of fifty-five political cartoons found in various archives and online auction sites.

46 Billy Coleman, *Harnessing Harmony: Music, Power, and Politics in the United States, 1788–1865* (Chapel Hill: University of North Carolina Press, 2020), 1–13; Kirsten E. Wood, "'Join with Heart and Soul and Voice': Music, Harmony, and Politics in the Early American Republic," *American Historical Review* 119 (October 2014): 1083–1089; Gavin James Campbell, "'He Put His Thumb up to His Nose, And Twirl'd His Fingers at His Foes': Presidential Campaign Songs in 1844," *Southern Cultures* 4 (Spring 1998): 139–140; Cheathem, *Coming of Democracy*, 2–3, 15–17; "Clear the Track for Old Kentucky!," Susan H. Douglas

Political Americana Collection, #2214, Division of Rare and Manuscript Collections, Cornell University Library, https://digital.library.cornell.edu/catalog/ss:10638508; *Harry of the West* (Lexington, MO), 9 August 1844; "A Song for the Man, A Henry Clay Ballad for 1844," Susan H. Douglas Political Americana Collection, #2214, Division of Rare and Manuscript Collections, Cornell University Library, https://digital.library.cornell.edu/catalog/ss:10638507; "Now Let Us Try Harry!," in *The Clay Minstrel, or National Songster*, 2nd ed. enlarged (New York: Greeley & M'Elrath, 1844), 309–310; "The Second Polk Song," "Clay and Frelinghuysen," and "Jimmy Polk of Tennessee," in *National Clay Minstrel, and Frelinghuysen Melodist, for the Presidential Canvass of 1844* (Philadelphia: George Hood, 1844), 16–17, 7, 8–9. William Miles, *Songs, Odes, Glees and Ballads: A Bibliography of Presidential Campaign Songsters* (Westport, CT: Greenwood, 1990), 9–22, includes thirty Whig songsters and only eight Democratic for 1844. In Danny O. Crew, *Presidential Sheet Music: An Illustrated Catalogue* (Jefferson, NC: McFarland, 2001), 297–308, 381–382, 96 of the 119 examples of published sheet music focused on Clay were produced between 1842 and 1844; by comparison, the examples of Polk music totaled a mere nineteen, with thirteen items from 1844.

47   *Nashville (TN) Tri-Weekly Union*, 21 August 1844; Austin E. Wing to James K. Polk, 11 June 1844; John M. Davis to James K. Polk, 9 September 1844; Robert Armstrong to James K. Polk, 28 June 1844, 5 July 1844; and Julius W. Blackwell to James K. Polk, 28 September 1844, in *CJKP*, 7:237, 8:34, 7:290, 310–311 8:134–135.

48   "New Yankee Doodle," "Harry Clay," in George Stuyvesant Jackson, *Early Songs of Uncle Sam* (Boston: Bruce Humphries, 1933), 114–115, 116–117; Campbell, "Presidential Campaign Songs in 1844," 144; *Wilmington (NC) Journal*, 27 September 1844; "The Brave Patriot Boys," in *Spirit of the Age* (Woodstock, VT), 1 August 1844; "The True-Hearted Statesman," in Jackson, *Early Songs of Uncle Sam*, 115; "The Coon Exterminator," in *Polk and Dallas Songster* (New York: Turner & Fisher, 1844), 64, Albert Gore Research Center, Middle Tennessee State University, https://www.mtsu.edu/gorecenter/political-songs-tennessee-presidents.php; "The Farmer of Ashland," in *The Plaindealer* (Lancaster, PA), 3 October 1844; "Democratic Ticket," in *New York Daily Herald*, 1 June 1844; "A Song of the Hickories," in *Pittsburgh Daily Post*, 2 September 1844; "Texas and Polk—A Locofoco Song," in *Alton (IL) Weekly Telegraph*, 14 September 1844.

49   US Census Bureau, *Historical Statistics of the United States: Colonial Times to 1970* (Washington, DC: GPO, 1975), 1:106; Anbinder, *Nativism and Slavery*, 10–11; Leonard, "Rise and Fall of the American Republican Party," 153, 170.

50   Anbinder, *Nativism and Slavery*, 11–12; Feldberg, *Philadelphia Riots*, 5, 51, 58–59, 78, 96, 115–116, 139, 143–146; Zachary M. Schrag, *The Fires of Philadelphia: Citizen-Soldiers, Nativists, and the 1844 Riots over the Soul of a Nation* (New York: Pegasus, 2021), 61–63; Diary entry, 12 May 1844, in Wainwright, ed., *A Philadelphia Perspective*, 167.

51   Jeremiah Y. Dashiell to James K. Polk, 27 July 1844; Samuel H. Laughlin to

James K. Polk, 3 August 1844; C. T. H. Willgohs and Ernest Moffett to James K. Polk, 20 August 1844; J. G. M. Ramsey to James K. Polk, 9 October 1844; J. G. M. Ramsey to James K. Polk, 14 October 1844; and Samuel P. Walker to James K. Polk, 9 October 1844, in *CJKP*, 7:406, 433, 457, 8:172, 187, 188; Patrick Kelly et al. to James G. Birney, Thomas Morris, and Leicester King, 17 May 1844, in *Emancipator and Republican* (Boston), 29 May 1844.

52 *New-York Observer*, 10 August 1844; James Birney Jr. to unknown, 21 August 1844, in *New-York Observer*, 24 August 1844; *Christian Mirror* (Portland, ME), 17 October 1844; *Emancipator and Republican* (Boston), 4 September 1844; William Birney and Dion Birney to the Editors of the *New York Observer*, 20 August 1844, in *Emancipator and Republican* (Boston), 4 September 1844; Gabriel Mützenberg, "Merle d'Aubigné, Jean-Henri," in *Historical Dictionary of Switzerland (DHS)*, version dated 7 January 2010, https://hls-dhs-dss.ch/fr/articles/011272/2010-01-07/; Fladeland, *James Gillespie Birney*, 238; William Birney to James G. Birney, 10 October 1843; James M. Birney to James G. Birney, 23 August 1844, 14 September 1844; and Orson Parker to James G. Birney, 9 September 1844, James G. Birney Papers, Clements Library.

53 Fladeland, *James Gillespie Birney*, 233; Patrick Kelly et al. to James G. Birney, Thomas Morris, and Leicester King, 17 May 1844, in *Emancipator and Republican* (Boston), 29 May 1844; James G. Birney to Patrick Kelly et al., 10 June 1844, in *Emancipator and Republican* (Boston), 14 August 1844.

54 John F. Marszalek, *Sherman: A Soldier's Passion for Order* (New York: Vintage, 1994), 9, 45; Thomas Ewing to Henry Clay, 23 June 1844; Henry Clay to George M. Davis, 31 August 1844; Henry Clay to Theodore Frelinghuysen, 22 May 1844; Joseph Knore to Henry Clay, 11 October 1844; Henry Clay to Peter Sken Smith, 17 June 1844; Henry Clay to Thomas Ewing, 19 June 1844; Henry Clay to William P. Thomasson, 8 July 1844; and Henry Clay to James Watson Webb, 25 October 1844, in *PHC*, 10:73–74, 107, 63, 132, 70, 71, 83, 136; Heidler and Heidler, *Henry Clay*, 379–380. Joseph Knore's claim about immediate voting rights for new immigrants does not appear to comport with the Naturalization Act of 1802, which required a five-year residency for citizenship. That legislation, however, largely ceded citizenship and its accompanying privileges to the states, so his reporting may have been accurate; see Douglas Bradburn, *The Citizenship Revolution: Politics and the Creation of the American Union, 1774–1804* (Charlottesville: University of Virginia Press, 2009), 285–286.

55 John Catron to James K. Polk, 8 June 1844; George M. Dallas to James K. Polk, 26 June 1844, 6 July 1844; Samuel H. Laughlin to James K. Polk, 5 July 1844; Elijah F. Purdy to James K. Polk, 16 July 1844; Auguste D'Avezac to James K. Polk, 4 August 1844; and John McKeon to James K. Polk, 7 August 1844, in *CJKP*, 7:215, 285, 322–323, 314, 352, 437, 444.

56 James K. Polk to George M. Dallas, 29 August 1844, 21 October 1844; James K. Polk to John K. Kane, 17 October 1844; James K. Polk to William Allen, 18 October 1844; James K. Polk to Aaron Vanderpoel, 22 October 1844; and James K. Polk to Fernando Wood, 26 October 1844, in *CJKP*, 7:477–478, 8:210, 199,

203, 215, 233. Democratic Party platform, 30 May 1844, in *Washington (DC) Daily Globe*, 30 May 1844; Heidler and Heidler, *Henry Clay*, 389.

57 Holt, *Rise and Fall*, 150; Watson, *Liberty and Power: The Politics of Jacksonian America*, rev. ed. (New York: Hill & Wang, 2006), 42–72; *Louisville (KY) Daily Journal*, 7 and 18 September 1844, 5 October 1844; *Nashville (TN) Tri-Weekly Republican Banner*, 20 September 1844, 28 October 1844; *Lancaster (PA) Examiner and Democratic Herald*, 17 July 1844.

58 Dusinberre, *Slavemaster President*, 11–22, 23–39, 46–48, 73–74, 87–89, 164, 242n34, appendix A.

59 Samuel Darling to James K. Polk, 29 August 1844; John F. Russ, Abraham S. Harmon, and Joshua Saule to James K. Polk, 24 August 1844; Enos Page to James K. Polk, 26 August 1844; William J. May et al. to James K. Polk, 29 August 1844; and F. Adams to James K. Polk, 8 August 1844, James K. Polk Papers, DLC; J. G. High to James K. Polk, 7 August 1844, in *CJKP*, 7:443–444.

60 *Tri-Weekly Nashville (TN) Union*, 7 September 1844; Dusinberre, *Slavemaster President*, 12, 202n4.

61 James L. Rogers II, "The Roorback Hoax: A Curious Incident in the Election of 1844," *Annotation* 30 (September 2002): 16; *Hawk-Eye* (Burlington, IA), 10 September 1844; *Albany (NY) Evening Journal*, 16 September 1844; *Centinel of Freedom* (Newark, NJ), 24 September 1844; *Constitution* (Middletown, CT), 25 September 1844; *Vermont Mercury* (Woodstock), 27 September 1844; *Richmond (VA) Whig*, 24 September 1844; "James K. Polk Going through Pennsylvania for the Tariff" (1844), Susan H. Douglas Political Americana Collection, #2214, Division of Rare and Manuscript Collections, Cornell University Library, https://digital.library.cornell.edu/catalog/ss:10637506. A search of online newspaper databases yielded the following sample of the national discussion of the Roorback hoax: Deep South—*Huntsville (AL) Democrat*, 9 October 1844; *Mississippi Free Trader* (Natchez), 11 October 1844. Upper South—*Richmond (VA) Enquirer*, 27 September 1844; *Louisville (KY) Daily Journal*, 2 October 1844; *Clarksville (TN) Weekly Chronicle*, 22 October 1844. West—*Council Grove (KS) Republican*, 28 September 1844; *Southport (WI) Telegraph*, 1 October 1844; *Cadiz (OH) Sentinel*, 9 October 1844; *Indiana State Sentinel* (Indianapolis), 10 October 1844. Mid-Atlantic—*Buffalo Commercial Advertiser*, 18 September 1844; *Lancaster (PA) Intelligencer and Journal*, 1 October 1844. New England—*Pittsfield (MA) Sun*, 3 October 1844; *Bangor (ME) Daily Whig and Courier*, 5 October 1844.

62 Rogers, "Roorback Hoax," 16; Rothman, *The Ledger and the Chain*, 229–236; *Boston Statesman*, 12 October 1844; *Albany (NY) Evening Journal*, 21, 26, 27, and 30 September 1844; George M. Dallas to James K. Polk, ca. 20 September 1844; William E. Cramer to James K. Polk, 4 October 1844; and James K. Polk to Charles J. Ingersoll, 4 October 1844, in *CJKP*, 8:95, 149, 151.

63 Peter Adams to James K. Polk, 22 August 1844, James K. Polk Papers, DLC; *The South in Danger* (Washington, DC: Democratic Association, 1844), 1–6; Robert J. Walker to the editors of the *Globe*, 2 October 1844, in *Washington (DC) Daily Globe*, 3 October 1844.

64 Sellers, *James K. Polk*, 2:150–151; Jeremiah George Harris to James K. Polk, 17 October 1844, and William E. Cramer to James K. Polk, 4 October 1844, in *CJKP*, 8:197–198, 148; Robert Armstrong to James K. Polk, 14 October 1844, James K. Polk Papers, DLC.

65 *Nashville (TN) Union*, 4 June 1844; West H. Humphreys to James K. Polk, 12 March 1844, Samuel H. Laughlin to James K. Polk, 24 April 1844, 7 June 1844, 19 September 1844, and Robert Armstrong to James K. Polk, 27 July 1844, in *CJKP*, 7:86, 107, 206, 405, 8:92; *The Spirit of Democracy* (Woodsfield, OH), 28 June 1844; *Richmond (VA) Enquirer*, 23 July 1844; *Tri-Weekly Nashville (TN) Union*, 24 August 1844, 29 October 1844; *Mississippi Free Trader* (Natchez), 5 September 1844; *Democratic Signal* (Raleigh, NC), 6 September 1844; John Sloane to Henry Clay, 9 May 1844, Henry Clay to John Sloane, 21 May 1844, and Robert P. Letcher to Henry Clay, 6 July 1844, in *PHC*, 10:56–57, 62, 81–82; "John Sloane," in *BDUSC*; Robert P. Letcher to James Buchanan, 20 June 1844, 7 and 19 July 1844, and James Buchanan to Robert P. Letcher, 27 June 1844, 27 July 1844, in Moore, ed., *Works of James Buchanan*, 6:59n2, 63n2, 63–64n2, 59–60, 63–65. "Carrying the war into Africa" was a commonly used phrase at the time that meant attacking an enemy's base of operations, thereby forcing them to switch from offense to defense, as Roman general Scipio had against his Carthaginian counterpart Hannibal during the Second Punic War; see Thomas Salmon, *A New Geographical and Historical Grammar* . . . (Edinburgh: Sands, Murray, and Cochran, 1767), 93; Kazlitt Arvine, *The Cyclopaedia of Anecdotes of Literature and the Fine Arts* . . . (Boston: Gould and Lincoln, 1852), 695; *Mariposa (CA) Gazette*, 24 September 1861.

66 Jeff Meyer, "Henry Clay's Legacy to Horse Breeding and Racing," *Register of the Kentucky Historical Society* 100 (Autumn 2002): 473–496; Henry Clay, Speech, 1 October 1842, in *PHC*, 9:781; *Nashville (TN) Tri-Weekly Union*, 13 August 1844; Cox, "White, Black and Indian Families of Richard Mentor Johnson," 123–124; L. Smith to Burton W. Smith, 25 May 1844, Filson Historical Society, Louisville, KY.

67 H. Edward Richardson, *Cassius Marcellus Clay: Firebrand of Freedom* (Lexington: University Press of Kentucky, 1976), 40; Cassius M. Clay to J. J Speed, 10 July 1844, in *New-York Daily Tribune*, 13 August 1844; Henry Clay to Daniel C. Wickliffe, 2 September 1844, in *PHC*, 10:108–109; Sellers, *James K. Polk*, 2:147; *Niles' National Register* 67 (12 October 1844): 83; *New York Evening Post*, 1 October 1844; Heidler and Heidler, *Henry Clay*, 391.

68 *Emancipator and Weekly Chronicle* (Boston), 18 September 1844, 9 October 1844; Fladeland, *James Gillespie Birney*, 234–235, 238–239; Joshua Leavitt to James G. Birney, 11 September 1844, Robert H. Folger to James G. Birney, 12 July 1844, and James G. Birney to Robert H. Folger, 24 July 1844, in *LJGB*, 2:840, 818–819, 822–827.

69 Fladeland, *James Gillespie Birney*, 241–251; James G. Birney to the editor of the *New-York Tribune*, 8 October 1844, in *Emancipator and Weekly Republican* (Boston), 16 October 1844; James G. Birney to the Liberty Party, 15 October 1844, in

New-York Daily Tribune, 21 October 1844. An example publication of the fake letter can be found in *Cleveland Herald*, 30 October 1844.

70 Fladeland, *James Gillespie Birney*, 233; Joseph G. Gazzam to James G. Birney, 27 December 1843, Reese C. Fleeson to James G. Birney, 10 January 1844, and James G. Birney to Reese C. Fleeson, 20 January 1844, in *Birney Letters*, 2:765–766, 773, 774–776; Davis, "Some Themes of Counter-Subversion," 205–224; *Green-Mountain Freeman* (Montpelier, VT), 16 August 1844.

71 *Cecil Whig* (Elkton, MD), 7 September 1844; George Mifflin Dallas to James K. Polk, 1 November 1844; John W. P. McGimsey to James K. Polk, 1 November 1844; Gansevoort Melville to James K. Polk, 1–2 November 1844; John McKeon to James K. Polk, 2, 4, and 6 November 1844; David T. Disney to James K. Polk, 3 November 1844; James Buchanan to James K. Polk, 4 November 1844; John K. Kane to James K. Polk, 4 November 1844; Fernando Wood to James K. Polk, 4 and 5 November 1844; Andrew Jackson to James K. Polk, 5 November 1844; Alexander Jones to James K. Polk, 6 November 1844; James D. Wasson to James K. Polk, 6 November 1844; Henderson K. Yoakum to James K. Polk, 6 November 1844; John P. Chester to James K. Polk, 7 November 1844; and Alexander Jones to James K. Polk, 21 November 1844, in *CJKP*, 8:253, 254, 255–256, 259–260, 261, 263, 266, 267, 273, 274, 277–278, 279, 283, 283–284, 285, 342–343; Richard Franklin Bensel, *The American Ballot Box in the Mid-Nineteenth Century* (New York: Cambridge University Press, 2004), 138–186; Gregory A. Borchard, "The *New York Tribune* and the 1844 Election: Horace Greeley, Gangs, and the Wise Men of Gotham," *Journalism History* 33 (Spring 2007): 53–56; John M. Sacher, *A Perfect War of Politics: Parties, Politicians, and Democracy in Louisiana, 1824–1861* (Baton Rouge: Louisiana State University Press, 2003), 124–125.

72 Cheathem, *Coming of Democracy*, 6–7; Scott C. James, "Timing and Sequence in Congressional Elections: Interstate Contagion and America's Nineteenth-Century Scheduling Regime," *Studies in American Political Development* 21 (September 2007): 19; Grinspan, *Virgin Vote*, 61–66; Bensel, *American Ballot Box*, x–xi, 1–85; Alexander Best to James K. Polk, 2 November 1844, in *CJKP*, 8:256.

73 Sylvester S. Southworth to James K. Polk, 2 November 1844; Alexander Jones to James K. Polk, 2 November 1844; Joel B. Sutherland to James K. Polk, 9 November 1844; Andrew Jackson Donelson to James K. Polk, 6 November 1844; James K. Polk to James Hamilton Jr., 31 October 1844; and Robert Armstrong to James K. Polk, 10 November 1844, in *CJKP*, 8:260, 258, 297, 276–277, 249, 298; Cheathem, *Old Hickory's Nephew*, 170–172.

74 John M. Morehead to Henry Clay, 29 October 1844; Henry Clay to William B. Campbell, 26 October 1844; Henry Clay to John Quincy Adams, 26 October 1844; and Henry Clay to Epes Sargent, 29 October 1844, in *PHC*, 10:139, 138, 137, 139.

75 Robert Armstrong to James K. Polk, 15 November 1844 (2 letters), in *CJKP*, 8:320, 321; Anson Nelson and Fanny Nelson, *Memorials of Sarah Childress Polk, Wife of the Eleventh President of the United States* (New York: Anson D. F. Ran-

dolph, 1892), 76–77; *Nashville (TN) Tri-Weekly Union*, 9, 12, 14, 16, 19 November 1844.

76 Grinspan, *Virgin Vote*, 163; Thomas B. Alexander, "The Dimensions of Voter Partisan Constancy in Presidential Elections from 1840 to 1860," in *Essays on American Antebellum Politics, 1840–1860*, ed. Stephen E. Maizlish and John J. Kushma (College Station: Texas A&M Press, 1982), 70–121; Lee Benson, *The Concept of Jacksonian Democracy: New York as a Test Case* (Princeton, NJ: Princeton University Press, 1961), 124; McBride, *Joseph Smith for President*, 202, 259n13. Unless noted otherwise, all voting data from this point forward come from Dubin, *United States Presidential Elections*, 72–96.

77 Robert Armstrong to James K. Polk, 15 November 1844 (2 letters), in *CJKP*, 8:320, 321; Andrew Jackson to James K. Polk, 18 November 1844, in *CAJ*, 6:329–330; Greenberg, *Lady First*, xx; Nelson and Nelson, *Memorials of Sarah Childress Polk*, vi, 77–79.

78 "Daguerreotype of James K. Polk and His Cabinet," 1846, James K. Polk Presidential Museum, Columbia, TN; "MANHATTAN" to the editors of the *New York Journal of Commerce*, 16 October 1844, in *New York Journal of Commerce*, 29 October 1844; Courtney E. Thompson, "A Propensity to Murder: Phrenology in Antebellum Medico-Legal Theory and Practice," *Journal of the History of Medicine & Allied Sciences* 74 (October 2019): 424–425.

CHAPTER 6. "THE REPUBLIC IS SAFE"

1 Samuel Medary to James K. Polk, 10 November 1844; James S. McFarlane to James K. Polk, 11 November 1844; William C. Bouck to James K. Polk, 15 November 1844; and Adam Huntsman to James K. Polk, 17 November 1844, in *CJKP*, 8:301, 306, 321, 328; William H. Seward to Henry Clay, 7 November 1844, in *PHC*, 10:142; I. C. Ray to Henry Clay, 16 November 1844, in *The Liberator* (Boston), 11 April 1845; Barbara Ann White, *A Line in the Sand: The Battle to Integrate Nantucket Public Schools, 1825–1847* (New Bedford, MA: Spinner, 2009), 37–38; *New York Tribune*, 21 November 1844; Leslie Combs to John M. Clayton, 20 November 1844, John M. Clayton Papers, DLC. A tomtit was a type of small bird, but it also meant "an insignificant person" (see "tomtit, n.," *OED Online*).

2 Sellers, *James K. Polk*, 2:157–161; Holt, *Rise and Fall*, 200; Lex Renda, "Retrospective Voting and the Presidential Election of 1844: The Texas Issue Revisited," *Presidential Studies Quarterly* 24 (Fall 1994): 837–841; Sean Wilentz, "The Bombshell of 1844," in *America at the Ballot Box: Elections and Political History*, ed. Gareth Davies and Julian E. Zelizer (University of Pennsylvania Press, 2015), 53–56; Laura Ellyn Smith, "Through the Eyes of the Enemy: Why Henry Clay Lost the Presidential Election of 1844 through the Lens of *The Daily Argus* of Portland, Maine," *Maine History* 50 (January 2016): 58–78.

3 Vernon L. Volpe, "The Liberty Party and Polk's Election, 1844," *The Historian* 53 (Summer 1991): 697; William E. Cramer to James K. Polk, 13 November 1844, and Joel B. Sutherland to James K. Polk, 7 November 1844, in *CJKP*, 8:317, 287; Brooks, *Liberty Power*, 40–42, 86–90, 94–103; Johnson, *Liberty Party*, 47;

Sellers, *James K. Polk*, 2:158–159; Holt, *Rise and Fall*, 195–198; Alexander, "Dimensions of Voter Partisan Constancy, 70–121; Volpe, "Liberty Party," 691–710; Renda, "Retrospective Voting," 837–841; Wilentz, "The Bombshell of 1844," 53–56; Benson, *Concept of Jacksonian Democracy*, 135, table 5; Ellis, *Old Tip vs. the Sly Fox*, 410n81.

4   Holt, *Rise and Fall*, 188–193; Leslie Combs to John M. Clayton, 20 November 1844, John M. Clayton Papers, DLC; Volpe, "Liberty Party," 701–703; Snyder, *Jacksonian Heritage*, 177–179, 184–186; Feldberg, *Philadelphia Riots*, 164–169; "Muhlenberg, Henry Augustus Philip," in *BDUSC*; "Governor Francis Rawn Shunk," Pennsylvania Historical and Museum Commission, http://www .phmc.state.pa.us/portal/communities/governors/1790-1876/francis-shunk .html.

5   *Niles' National Register* 66 (13 April 1844): 161; *New York Evening Post*, 22 November 1843; Louis Dow Scisco, *Political Nativism in New York State* (New York: Columbia University Press, 1901), 47–50; Michael Trapani, "A Deal Gone Sour: How a Henry Clay-Nativist Alliance Nearly Stopped the Civil War," *New York History Review* 12, no. 1 (2018): 27–47; John M. Read to James K. Polk, 4 November 1844, in *CJKP*, 8:269; Holt, *Rise and Fall*, 203–206; Volpe, "Liberty Party," 703; Benson, *Concept of Jacksonian Democracy*, 185; Sellers, *James K. Polk*, 2:153–154.

6   Edward A. Hagan et al., *William C. Bouck: New York's Farmer Governor* (Berwyn Heights, MD: Heritage Books, 2007), 29, 51; Garraty, *Silas Wright*, 309–329; Nicholas Carroll to Willie P. Mangum, 8 September 1844, in *Papers of Willie Person Mangum*, 4:180–183; Sellers, *James K. Polk*, 2:130–131; Holt, *Rise and Fall*, 203; Benjamin F. Butler to James K. Polk, 12 November 1844, in *CJKP*, 8:311–312; Henry D. Gilpin to Martin Van Buren, 15 October 1844, PMVB (mvb04074).

7   Grinspan, *Virgin Vote*, 6, 11, 29–32, 47, 68–69, 80–81, 114; Cheatham, *Coming of Democracy*, 2–3; *Historical Statistics of the United States, Colonial Times to 1970: Bicentennial Edition* (Washington, DC: Bureau of the Census, 1975), 1072. The minimum age for voting in 1844 was twenty-one.

8   Sellers, *James K. Polk*, 2:160.

9   US House, "Party Divisions of the House of Representatives, 1789 to Present," https://history.house.gov/Institution/Party-Divisions/Party-Divisions/; US Senate, "Party Divisions," https://www.senate.gov/pagelayout/history/one_item_and _teasers/partydiv.htm; Klunder, *Lewis Cass*, 143–144; Haley, *Sam Houston*, 294; McGrane, *William Allen*, 100–101; Belohlavek, *George Mifflin Dallas*, 108; Rakestraw, *Daniel Webster*, 108. The Oregon boundary dispute between the United States and Great Britain was settled via treaty in 1846, but at the 49th parallel, not the 54th; see, Pletcher, *Diplomacy of Annexation*, 413–417.

10   Michael J. Dubin, *United States Gubernatorial Elections, 1776–1860* (Jefferson, NC: McFarland, 2003), xxxv, 9–10, 23, 27, 76, 91, 97, 114–115, 139–140, 155, 158, 172–173, 184, 203–204, 224–225, 235, 277–278. One of the Whig gubernatorial gains was in Rhode Island, where incumbent James Fenner retained his seat with 96.39 percent of the vote. (The remaining votes were scattered.) He rep-

resented the Law and Order Party, a conglomeration of Whigs and conservative Democrats that had formed as a result of the Dorr War; see Erik J. Chaput, "Proslavery and Antislavery Politics in Rhode Island's 1842 Dorr Rebellion," *New England Quarterly* 85 (December 2012): 673.

EPILOGUE

1   John McKeon to James K. Polk, 8 November 1844, in *CJKP*, 8:293; Cheathem, "Ruptured Relationship," 124–129; Leahy, *President without a Party*, 340–342.

2   Sellers, *James K. Polk*, 2:20–209; Cole, *A Jackson Man*, 243; Joint Congressional Committee on Inaugural Ceremonies, "Inaugural Address," https://www.inaugural.senate.gov/inaugural-address/; Polk, Inaugural address, 4 March 1845, in Richardson, *Messages and Papers*, 4:373–382.

3   On the Mexican-American War, see Timothy J. Henderson, *A Glorious Defeat: Mexico and Its War with the United States* (New York: Hill and Wang, 2007); Amy S. Greenberg, *A Wicked War: Polk, Clay, Lincoln, and the 1846 U.S. Invasion of Mexico* (New York: Knopf, 2012); Peter Guardino, *The Dead March: A History of the Mexican-American War* (Cambridge, MA: Harvard University Press, 2017).

4   Joel H. Silbey, *Party over Section: The Rough and Ready Presidential Election of 1848* (Lawrence: University Press of Kansas, 2009), 145; Bolt, *Tariff Wars*, 173–208; Mark R. Cheathem, "'I Shall Persevere in the Cause of Truth': Andrew Jackson Donelson and the Election of 1856," *Tennessee Historical Quarterly* 62 (Fall 2003): 218–237.

5   Mark W. Summers, *The Plundering Generation: Corruption and the Crisis of the Union, 1848–1861* (New York: Oxford University Press, 1987), xiii; Bensel, *American Ballot Box*, 138–186; Joshua A. Lynn, *Preserving the White Man's Republic: Jacksonian Democracy, Race, and the Transformation of American Conservatism* (Charlottesville: University of Virginia Press, 2019), 34–67; Richards, *Slave Power*, 190–215; Brooks, *Liberty Power*, 218–221. On congressional violence, see Freeman, *Field of Blood*, and Williamjames Hull Hoffer, *The Caning of Charles Sumner: Honor, Idealism, and the Origins of the Civil War* (Baltimore: Johns Hopkins University Press, 2010).

6   Grinspan, *Virgin Vote*, 152–153, 163; Silbey, *Party over Section*, 133–136.

APPENDIX

1   James K. Polk, Inaugural Address, 4 March 1845, in Richardson, *Messages and Papers*, 4:373–382.

BIBLIOGRAPHIC ESSAY

Any scholar willing to write the history of a US presidential election understandably regards their subject as critical to understanding the period when it took place. Such is the case here. Not only do I consider the 1844 election indispensable to comprehending the transition from the Jacksonian period to the Civil War era, but it is also surprising to me that before now no one has written a full scholarly account of the contest. The only book-length treatment of the election is by journalist John Bicknell, *America 1844: Religious Fervor, Westward Expansion, and the Presidential Election That Transformed the Nation* (Chicago: Chicago Review Press, 2014), which highlights the competing political, religious, and economic visions that Americans had for the nation's future. Charles G. Sellers Jr.'s essay "Election of 1844" in *History of American Presidential Elections*, ed. Arthur M. Schlesinger and Fred L. Israel (New York: Chelsea House, 1971), 1:747–861, provides a good summary of the election, but it is simply a condensed version of the excellent coverage provided in his biography, Sellers, *James K. Polk*, 2 vols. (Princeton, NJ: Princeton University Press, 1957–1966).

Aspects of the 1844 election are covered in Thomas B. Alexander, "The Dimensions of Voter Partisan Constancy in Presidential Elections from 1840 to 1860," in *Essays on American Antebellum Politics, 1840–1860*, ed. Stephen E. Maizlish and John J. Kushma (College Station: Texas A&M Press, 1982), 70–121; Lee Benson, *The Concept of Jacksonian Democracy: New York as a Test Case* (Princeton, NJ: Princeton University Press, 1961); Gregory A. Borchard, "The *New York Tribune* and the 1844 Election," *Journalism History* 33 (Spring 2007): 51–59; Jayne Crumpler DeFiore, "'Come, and Bring the Ladies': Tennessee Women and the Politics of Opportunity during the Presidential Campaigns of 1840 and 1844," *Tennessee Historical Quarterly* 51 (December 1992): 197–212; John S. D. Eisenhower, "The Election of James K. Polk, 1844," *Tennessee Historical Quarterly* 53 (June 1994): 74–87; Robert B. Everett, "James K. Polk and the Election of 1844 in Tennessee," *West Tennessee Historical Society Papers* 16 (1962): 5–28; Worthington Chauncey, "The Campaign of 1844," *Proceedings of the American Antiquarian Society* 20 (October 1909): 106–126; Erika Pribanic-Smith, "Partisan News and the Third-Party Candidate: Press Coverage of James G. Birney's 1844 Presidential Campaign," *Journalism History* 39 (Fall 2013): 168–178; Pribanic-Smith, "Partisanship in the Antislavery Press during the 1844 Run of an Abolition Candidate for President," *American Journalism* 31 (Spring 2014): 186–212; Pribanic-Smith, "Southern Values and the 1844 Election in South Carolina Newspapers," *Journalism History* 41 (Winter 2016): 200–210; Lex Renda,

"Retrospective Voting and the Presidential Election of 1844: The Texas Issue Revisited," *Presidential Studies Quarterly* 24 (Fall 1994): 837–854; George W. Roach, "The Presidential Campaign of 1844 in New York State," *New York History* 19 (April 1938): 153–172; Laura Ellyn Smith, "Through the Eyes of the Enemy: Why Henry Clay Lost the Presidential Election of 1844 through the Lens of *The Daily Argus* of Portland, Maine," *Maine History* 50 (January 2016): 58–78; Michael Trapani, "A Deal Gone Sour: How a Henry Clay–Nativist Alliance Nearly Stopped the Civil War," *New York History Review* 12, no. 1 (2018): 27–47; Vernon L. Volpe, "The Liberty Party and Polk's Election, 1844," *The Historian* 53 (Summer 1991): 691–710; Clara Bracken Washburn, "Some Aspects of the 1844 Presidential Campaign in Tennessee," *Tennessee Historical Quarterly* 4 (March 1945): 58–74; Sean Wilentz, "The Bombshell of 1844," in *America at the Ballot Box: Elections and Political History*, ed. Gareth Davies and Julian E. Zelizer (Philadelphia: University of Pennsylvania Press, 2015), 36–58; and David Zarefsky, "Henry Clay and the Election of 1844: The Limits of a Rhetoric of Compromise," *Rhetoric & Public Affairs* 6 (Spring 2003): 79–96.

Four of the five major presidential candidates from 1844 have received significant biographical attention. Even though Charles Sellers never finished the third volume of his biography of Polk, it remains the gold standard on Young Hickory six decades after its publication. More recent treatments of Polk include Sam W. Haynes, *James K. Polk and the Expansionist Impulse* (New York: Longman, 1997); Thomas M. Leonard, *James K. Polk: A Clear and Unquestionable Destiny* (Wilmington, DE: Scholarly Resources, 2001); Walter F. Borneman, *Polk: The Man Who Transformed the Presidency and America* (New York: Random House, 2008); and Robert W. Merry, *A Country of Vast Designs: James K. Polk, the Mexican War and the Conquest of the American Continent* (New York: Simon & Schuster, 2009). The following articles provide insight into how Polk put himself in a position to run for president: Powell Moore, "James K. Polk and Tennessee Politics, 1839–1841," *East Tennessee Historical Society's Publications* 9 (1937): 31–52; Joseph M. Pukl, "James K. Polk's Congressional Campaigns, 1829–1833," *Tennessee Historical Quarterly* 40 (Winter 1981): 348–365; Pukl, "James K. Polk's Early Congressional Campaigns of 1825 and 1827," *Tennessee Historical Quarterly* 39 (Winter 1980): 440–58; and Charles G. Sellers, "James K. Polk's Political Apprenticeship," *East Tennessee Historical Society's Publications* 25 (1953): 37–53. For the political landscape of Polk's home state of Tennessee, see Jonathan M. Atkins, *Parties, Politics and the Sectional Conflict in Tennessee, 1832–1861* (Knoxville: University of Tennessee Press, 1997). Given Sarah Polk's intimate involvement in advancing her husband's political career, Amy S. Greenberg, *Lady First: The World of First Lady Sarah Polk* (New York: Alfred A. Knopf, 2019), is an essential read. William Dusinberre, *Slavemaster President: The Double Career of James Polk* (New York: Oxford University Press, 2003), provides a model for examining a president's identity as an enslaver.

Henry Clay was one of the unluckiest presidential candidates, but he has several fine biographies. David Heidler and Jeanne Heidler, *Henry Clay: The Essential American* (New York: Random House, 2010), is by far the best, but it should be supplemented by Robert V. Remini, *Henry Clay: Statesman for the Union* (New York: W. W. Norton, 1991). Another recent scholarly biography is James C. Klotter, *Henry Clay:*

The Man Who Would Be President (New York: Oxford University Press, 2018). Like Polk, Clay was an enslaver, a topic examined in Lonnie E. Maness, "Henry Clay and the Problem of Slavery" (PhD diss., Memphis State University, 1980).

John Tyler has received a surprising amount of attention in recent years. Dan Monroe, *The Republican Vision of John Tyler* (College Station: Texas A&M University Press, 2003), and Edward J. Crapol, *John Tyler: The Accidental President* (Chapel Hill: University of North Carolina Press, 2006), are solid studies of the Virginia president, but they are exceeded by the excellent Christopher J. Leahy, *President without a Party: The Life of John Tyler* (Baton Rouge: Louisiana State University Press, 2020). On James G. Birney, see Betty Fladeland, *James Gillespie Birney: Slaveholder to Abolitionist* (Ithaca, NY: Cornell University Press, 1955). The abolitionist presidential candidate deserves a better updated treatment than D. Laurence Rogers, *Apostles of Equality: The Birneys, the Republicans and the Civil War* (Lansing: Michigan State University Press, 2011).

Historians of Mormonism continue to expand our understanding of the most important religious movement of the Jacksonian period. Richard L. Bushman, *Joseph Smith: Rough Stone Rolling* (New York: Alfred A. Knopf, 2005), is the most authoritative biography of the Prophet. Spencer W. McBride, *Joseph Smith for President: The Prophet, the Assassins, and the Fight for American Religious Freedom* (New York: Oxford University Press, 2021), is a well-written and much-needed look at Smith's vision for his 1844 presidential campaign. Benjamin E. Park, *Kingdom of Nauvoo: The Rise and Fall of a Religious Empire on the American Frontier* (New York: Liveright, 2020), provides an engaging history of the Nauvoo community leading up to Smith's murder.

Of the four vice presidential candidates, George M. Dallas has benefited the most from scholarly analysis, as found in John Belohlavek, *George Mifflin Dallas: Jacksonian Patrician* (University Park: Pennsylvania State University Press, 1977). Robert J. Eells, *Forgotten Saint: The Life of Theodore Frelinghuysen: A Case Study of Christian Leadership* (New York: University Press of America, 1987), is idiosyncratic and unhelpful. Richard S. Van Wagoner, *Sidney Rigdon: A Portrait of Religious Excess* (Salt Lake City: Signature Books, 2006), is full of information but lacks critical analysis. Although Thomas Morris of the Liberty Party was one of the most significant abolitionist politicians of the era, no one has seen fit to provide him with a biography.

The three serious competitors with Clay for the Whig presidential nomination—John McLean, Winfield Scott, and Daniel Webster—have received mixed scholarly attention. Francis P. Weisenburger, *The Life of John McLean: A Politician on the United States Supreme Court* (Columbus: Ohio State University Press, 1937), is serviceable, but McLean's life could use a fresh look. Timothy D. Johnson, *Winfield Scott: The Quest for Military Glory* (Lawrence.: University Press of Kansas, 1998), provides insight into Scott's personality that clarifies his failure to challenge Clay for the 1844 nomination. John S. D. Eisenhower, *Agent of Destiny: The Life and Times of General Winfield Scott* (New York: Free Press, 1997), and Allan Peskin, *Winfield Scott and the Profession of Arms* (Kent, OH: Kent State University Press, 2003), are also useful. On Webster, the voluminous Robert V. Remini, *Daniel Webster: The Man and His Time* (New York: W. W. Norton, 1997), should be supplemented with the more recent Donald Rakestraw, *Daniel Webster: Defender of Peace* (Lanham, MD: Rowman & Littlefield, 2018), especially for Webster's diplomatic efforts as Tyler's secretary of state.

The men who competed with Frelinghuysen for the Whig vice presidential nomination have no substantives biographies. Constructing even a summary of the lives of John Davis and John Sergeant is difficult. Considering his political influence in New York, his brief presidency, and his role in the nativist Know-Nothing Party, Millard Fillmore has been woefully understudied and even less understood. The new Correspondence of Zachary Taylor and Millard Fillmore documentary editing project at American University, directed by Michael David Cohen, should spur more research on him. Until then, Robert J. Rayback, *Millard Fillmore: Biography of a President* (Buffalo: H. Stewart, 1959), is the only suitable biography to consult.

Potential Democratic presidential candidates in 1844 have received uneven scholarly attention. For a man credited with creating the Democratic Party, biographical studies of Martin Van Buren have been sparse, with Robert V. Remini, *Martin Van Buren and the Making of the Democratic Party* (New York: Columbia University Press, 1959), John Niven, *Martin Van Buren: The Romantic Age of American Politics* (New York: Oxford University Press, 1983), and Donald Cole, *Martin Van Buren and the American Political System* (Princeton, NJ: Princeton University Press, 1984), the only ones of note. They should be supplemented with Jerome Mushkat and Joseph G. Rayback, *Martin Van Buren: Law, Politics, and the Shaping of Republican Ideology* (DeKalb: Northern Illinois University Press, 1997), and Gerald Leonard and Saul Cornell, *The Partisan Republic: Democracy, Exclusion, and the Fall of the Founders' Constitution, 1780s–1830s* (Cambridge: Cambridge University Press, 2019).

John Niven, *John C. Calhoun and the Price of Union: A Biography* (Baton Rouge: Louisiana State University Press, 1988), was the standard biography of the South Carolinian for more than three decades, but Robert Elder, *Calhoun: American Heretic* (New York: Basic Books, 2021), has surpassed it in insight and narrative verve. Also useful for understanding Calhoun are Charles M. Wiltse, *John C. Calhoun*, 3 vols. (Indianapolis: Bobbs-Merrill, 1944–51), and Margaret Coit, *John C. Calhoun: American Portrait* (Boston: Houghton Mifflin, 1950). Surprisingly, Richard M. Johnson has not attracted a biographer. Christina Snyder's *Great Crossings: Indians, Settlers, and Slaves in the Age of Jackson* (New York: Oxford University Press, 2017), provides the best analysis of Johnson's personal life. Those looking for studies of Johnson's public career should consult two dissertations: Jonathan Milnor Jones, "The Making of a Vice President: The National Political Career of Richard M. Johnson of Kentucky" (PhD diss., University of Memphis, 1998), and Nicholas P. Cox, "The White, Black and Indian Families of Richard Mentor Johnson" (PhD diss., University of Houston, 2012). Willard Carl Klunder, *Lewis Cass and the Politics of Moderation* (Kent: Kent State University Press, 1996), does justice to the man who seemed poised to snatch the Democratic nomination from Van Buren. The useful John Arthur Garraty, *Silas Wright* (New York: Columbia University Press, 1949), should not be the only scholarly biography of one of the most significant politicians of the Jacksonian era and the man who plausibly would have defeated Clay by a larger margin than Polk if he had acquiesced to the will of the Democratic delegates in Baltimore.

The lesser contenders for the Democratic nomination have received disappointingly little attention. Despite James Buchanan's controversial presidency, often considered one of the worst, the only comprehensive biography of the Pennsylvanian is Philip S. Klein, *President James Buchanan: A Biography* (University Park: Pennsylvania State University Press, 1962). It should be supplemented with Thomas J. Balcerski, *Bosom Friends: The Intimate World of James Buchanan and William Rufus King* (New York: Oxford University Press, 2019). Largely forgotten today, Charles Stewart lived a fascinating life, and he merits a better biography than Claude G. Berube and John A. Rodgaard, *A Call to the Sea: Captain Charles Stewart of the USS Constitution* (Washington, DC: Potomac Books, 2005). Levi Woodbury also deserves more notice for his varied career, if not for the 1844 Democratic contest. Until then, Vincent Capowski, "The Making of a Jacksonian Democrat: Levi Woodbury, 1789–1851" (PhD diss., Fordham University, 1966), will have to suffice. Likewise, the two losing Democratic vice presidential contenders who were not also considered for the presidency have not fared well. John Fairfield's career has largely been ignored. William L. Marcy's only published biography—Ivor D. Spencer, *The Victor and the Spoils: A Life of William L. Marcy* (Providence, RI: Brown University Press, 1959)—is dated.

In addition to Van Buren and Tyler, two of the three former presidents of the era have been studied extensively. John Quincy Adams particularly has experienced a renaissance of interest lately. Of the recent biographies, William J. Cooper, *The Lost Founding Father: John Quincy Adams and the Transformation of American Politics* (New York: Liveright, 2017), is the best. Andrew Jackson has never lacked interest from historians. Robert V. Remini, *Andrew Jackson*, 3 vols. (New York: W. W. Norton, 1977–1984), has yet to be surpassed in its research breadth and narrative vigor. Mark R. Cheathem, *Andrew Jackson, Southerner* (Baton Rouge: Louisiana State University Press, 2013), examines Old Hickory's southern identity, a key component for the era's pursuit of Manifest Destiny. A much-needed study is one that addresses Jackson's postpresidential retirement, when he acted as the Democratic Party's statesman in directing attention to issues such as Texas annexation. William Henry Harrison has not attracted the same attention as the other two. Freeman Cleaves, *Old Tippecanoe: William Henry Harrison and His Time* (New York: Scribner's, 1939), is the best of a limited number of older, inferior biographies. Robert M. Owens, *Mr. Jefferson's Hammer: William Henry Harrison and the Origins of American Indian Policy* (Norman: University of Oklahoma Press, 2007), is an excellent study of Harrison's early life and military career, but it does not extend to his later political career.

Biographies exist of most of the critical political figures of the era, but some need serious updating. Among the best are Reginald C. McGrane, *William Allen: A Study in Western Democracy* (Columbus: Ohio State Archeological and Historical Society, 1925); Russel B. Nye, *George Bancroft: Brahmin Rebel* (New York: Knopf, 1944); Ken S. Mueller, *Senator Benton and the People: Master Race Democracy on the Early American Frontier* (DeKalb: Northern Illinois University Press, 2014); Elbert B. Smith, *Magnificent Missourian: The Life of Thomas Hart Benton* (Philadelphia: J. B. Lippincott, 1958); Smith, *Francis Preston Blair* (New York: Free Press, 1980); H. Edward Robinson, *Cassius Marcellus Clay: Firebrand of Freedom* (Lexington: University Press of Kentucky, 1976); Mark R. Cheathem, *Old Hickory's Nephew: The*

Political and Private Struggles of Andrew Jackson Donelson (Baton Rouge: Louisiana State University Press, 2007); Richard Douglas Spence, *Andrew Jackson Donelson: Jacksonian and Unionist* (Nashville: Vanderbilt University Press, 2017); W. Stephen Belko, *The Invincible Duff Green: Whig of the West* (Columbia: University of Missouri Press, 2006); James L. Haley, *Sam Houston* (Norman: University of Oklahoma Press, 2002); Clement L. Grant, "The Public Career of Cave Johnson" (PhD diss., Vanderbilt University, 1951); Donald B. Cole, *A Jackson Man: Amos Kendall and the Rise of American Democracy* (Baton Rouge: Louisiana State University Press, 2004); Louis R. Harlan, "Public Career of William Berkeley Lewis," *Tennessee Historical Quarterly* 7 (March 1948): 3–37, and 7 (June 1948): 118–51; John B. Edmunds Jr., *Francis W. Pickens and the Politics of Destruction* (Chapel Hill: University of North Carolina Press, 1986); Nathaniel Cheairs Hughes and Roy P. Stonesifer, *The Life and Wars of Gideon J. Pillow* (Chapel Hill: University of North Carolina Press, 1993); Dallas C. Dickey, *Seargent S. Prentiss, Whig Orator of the Old South* (Baton Rouge: Louisiana State University Press, 1945); William C. Davis, *Rhett: The Turbulent Life and Times of a Fire-Eater* (Columbia: University of South Carolina Press, 2001); Charles H. Ambler, *Thomas Ritchie: A Study in Virginia Politics* (Richmond, VA: Bell Book & Stationery, 1913); Claude H. Hall, *Abel Parker Upshur: Conservative Virginian, 1790–1844* (Madison: State Historical Society of Wisconsin, 1964); and James P. Shenton, *Robert John Walker: A Politician from Jackson to Lincoln* (New York: Columbia University Press, 1961).

With two exceptions, presidential elections between 1824 and 1848 have been expertly covered by entries in the University Press of Kansas's American Presidency Series: Donald J. Ratcliffe, *The One-Party Presidential Contest: Adams, Jackson, and 1824's Five-Horse Race* (Lawrence: University Press of Kansas, 2015); Donald B. Cole, *Vindicating Andrew Jackson: The 1828 Election and the Rise of the Two-Party System* (Lawrence: University Press of Kansas, 2009); Richard J. Ellis, *Old Tip vs. the Sly Fox: The 1840 Election and the Making of a Partisan Nation* (Lawrence: University Press of Kansas, 2020); and Joel H. Silbey, *Party over Section: The Rough and Ready Presidential Election of 1848* (Lawrence: University Press of Kansas, 2009). Historians looking at the 1832 and 1836 elections, both of which currently lack definitive treatments, should consult Samuel Rhea Gammon Jr., *The Presidential Campaign of 1832* (Baltimore: Johns Hopkins University Press, 1922), and Robert V. Remini, "Election of 1832," and Joel H. Silbey, "Election of 1836," the latter two in *History of American Presidential Elections, 1789–1968*, Vol. 1, ed. Schlesinger and Israel. Other more narrowly focused, but still important, studies of these two elections include Derek L. A. Hackett, "The Days of This Republic Will Be Numbered: Abolition, Slavery, and the Presidential Election of 1836," *Louisiana Studies* 15 (March 1976): 131–160; Richard P. McCormick, "Was There a 'Whig Strategy' in 1836?," *Journal of the Early Republic* 4 (Spring 1984): 47–70; Jonathan M. Atkins, "The Presidential Candidacy of Hugh Lawson White in Tennessee, 1832–1836," *Journal of Southern History* 58 (February 1992): 27–56; William G. Shade, "'The Most Delicate and Exciting Topics': Martin Van Buren, Slavery and the Election of 1836," *Journal of the Early Republic* 18 (Fall 1998): 459–84; and Laura Ellyn Smith, "Anti-Jacksonian Democratization: The First National Political Party Conventions," *American Nine-*

teenth Century History 21 (August 2020): 149–169. James S. Chase, *Emergence of the Presidential Nominating Convention, 1789–1832* (Urbana: University of Illinois Press, 1973), chaps. 7–8, provides a good foundation for understanding the way in which the national nominating conventions initially operated.

On the presidential administrations of Adams, Jackson, Van Buren, Harrison, and Tyler, consult the following volumes in the University Press of Kansas's American Presidency Series: Mary W. M. Hargreaves, *The Presidency of John Quincy Adams* (Lawrence: University Press of Kansas, 1985); Donald B. Cole, *The Presidency of Andrew Jackson* (Lawrence: University Press of Kansas, 1993); Major L. Wilson, *The Presidency of Martin Van Buren* (Lawrence: University Press of Kansas, 1984); and Norma Lois Peterson, *The Presidencies of William Henry Harrison and John Tyler* (Lawrence: University Press of Kansas, 1989). Polk's presidency is covered in the same series by Paul H. Bergeron, *The Presidency of James K. Polk* (Lawrence: University Press of Kansas, 1987).

The scholarship on the political parties of the Jacksonian era is uneven in its treatment. The Whigs have fared well, with Daniel Walker Howe, *The Political Culture of the American Whigs* (Chicago: University of Chicago Press, 1979), and Michael F. Holt, *The Rise and Fall of the American Whig Party: Jacksonian Politics and the Onset of the Civil War* (New York: Oxford University Press, 1999), providing comprehensive overviews of the party's origins, development, and demise. Also important to consult are Glyndon G. Van Deusen, "The Whig Party," in *History of U.S. Political Parties*, ed. Arthur M. Schlesinger Jr. (New York: Chelsea House, 1973), 1:333–493, and Thomas Brown, *Politics and Statesmanship: Essays on the American Whig Party* (New York: Columbia University Press, 1985). Democrats have not benefited from the same attention. Part of the scholarly deficiency proceeds from the centering of the party's politics on Jackson, as seen in Mark R. Cheathem, *Andrew Jackson and the Rise of the Democratic Party* (Knoxville: University of Tennessee Press, 2018). Old Hickory certainly cannot be ignored, but historians would do well to spend more time considering the ways in which those around Jackson developed the party machinery that made the Democrats successful. For a broader perspective of the Democratic Party's history, see Robert A. Rutland, *The Democrats: From Jefferson to Clinton* (Columbia: University of Missouri Press, 1995); Peter B. Kovler, ed., *Democrats and the American Idea: A Bicentennial Appraisal* (Washington, DC: Center for National Policy, 1992); and Michael Kazin, *What It Took to Win: A History of the Democratic Party* (New York: Farrar, Straus and Giroux, 2022).

The Anti-Masonic Party was brief in existence, but it demonstrated how third parties could influence, and be co-opted by, the major parties. Essential studies of this party include Michael F. Holt, "The Antimasonic and Know Nothing Parties," in *History of U.S. Political Parties*, ed. Schlesinger, 1:575–620; Kathleen Smith Kutolowski, "Antimasonry Reexamined: Social Bases of the Grass Roots Party," *Journal of American History* 71 (September 1984): 269–93; Paul Goodman, *Towards a Christian Republic: Antimasonry and the Great Transition in New England, 1826–1836* (New York: Oxford University Press, 1988); Donald J. Ratcliffe, "Antimasonry and Partisanship in Greater New England, 1826–1836," *Journal of the Early Republic* 15 (Summer 1995): 199–239; Steven C. Bullock, *Revolutionary Brotherhood: Freema-*

sonry and the Transformation of the American Social Order, 1730–1840 (Chapel Hill: University of North Carolina Press, 1996); and William Preston Vaughan, *The Anti-Masonic Party in the United States, 1826–1843* (Lexington: University Press of Kentucky, 1983). Reinhard O. Johnson, *The Liberty Party, 1840–1848: Antislavery Third-Party Politics in the United States* (Baton Rouge: Louisiana State University Press, 2009), provides an encyclopedic knowledge of the Liberty Party. Corey M. Brooks, *Liberty Power: Antislavery Third Parties and the Transformation of American Politics* (Chicago: University of Chicago Press, 2016), offers a persuasive argument about the party's importance to advancing the abolitionist cause. Still helpful is Aileen Kraditor, "The Liberty and Free Soil Parties," in ed. Schlesinger, ed., *History of U.S. Political Parties*, 1:741–63. Missing from the scholarship on political parties is a study of the National Republicans, the pro-Adams contingent that existed from approximately 1828 to 1834.

The political struggle between the Democrats and the Whigs has elicited significant study, even as the term often used for it—the "second American party system"—has been contested. Whatever its name, that rivalry—and the role of third parties such as the Anti-Masons and the Libertyites in relation to it—should include consulting the following works: Glenn C. Altschuler and Stuart M. Blumin, "Limits of Political Engagement in Antebellum America: A New Look at the Golden Age of Participatory Democracy," *Journal of American History* 84 (December 1997): 855–885; Paula Baker, "The Midlife Crisis of the New Political History," *Journal of American History* 86 (June 1999): 158–166; Todd Estes, "Beyond Whigs and Democrats: Historians, Historiography, and the Paths toward a New Synthesis for the Jacksonian Era," *American Nineteenth Century History* 21 (September 2020): 255–281; Ronald P. Formisano, "The 'Party Period' Revisited," *Journal of American History* 86 (June 1999): 93–120; Reeve Huston, "Rethinking the Origins of Partisan Democracy in the United States, 1795–1840," and Graham A. Peck, "Was There a Second Party System? Illinois as a Case Study in Antebellum Politics," in *Practicing Democracy: Popular Politics in the United States from the Constitution to the Civil War*, ed. Daniel Peart and Adam I. P. Smith (Charlottesville: University of Virginia Press, 2015), 46–71, 145–169; Mark Voss-Hubbard, "The 'Third-Party Tradition' Reconsidered: Third Parties and American Public Life, 1830–1900," *Journal of American History* 86 (June 1999): 121–150; and Harry L. Watson, "Humbug? Bah! Altschuler and Blumin and the Riddle of the Antebellum Electorate," *Journal of American History* 84 (December 1997): 886–893.

The concept of Manifest Destiny has produced a bevy of historical studies over the decades, including Frederick Merk and Lois Bannister Merk, *Manifest Destiny and Mission in American History: A Reinterpretation* (New York: Alfred A. Knopf, 1963); Reginald Horsman, *Race and Manifest Destiny: The Origins of American Racial Anglo-Saxonism* (Cambridge, MA: Harvard University Press, 1981); Anders Stephanson, *Manifest Destiny: American Expansionism and the Empire of Right* (New York: Hill and Wang, 1995); Amy S. Greenberg, *Manifest Manhood and the Antebellum American Empire* (New York: Cambridge University Press, 2005); and Laurel Clark Shire, *The Threshold of Manifest Destiny: Gender and National Expansion in Florida* (Philadelphia: University of Pennsylvania Press, 2016). The period leading up to Texas annexation has likewise drawn scholarly attention. Many of the studies are older, but they are still invaluable. These include Frederick Merk and Lois Bannister Merk, *Fruits of Propaganda in the Tyler Administration* (Cambridge, MA: Harvard University Press, 1971); David M. Pletcher, *The Diplomacy of Annexation: Texas, Oregon and the Mexican War* (Columbia: University of Missouri Press, 1973); Thomas R. Hietala, *Manifest Design: Anxious Aggrandizement in Late Jacksonian America* (Ithaca, NY: Cornell University Press, 1985); Sam W. Haynes and Christopher Morris, eds., *Manifest Destiny and Empire: American Antebellum Expansionism* (College Station: Texas A&M University Press, 1997); Michael A. Morrison, *Slavery and the American West: The Eclipse of Manifest Destiny and the Coming of the Civil War* (Chapel Hill: University of North Carolina Press, 1997); Richard Bruce Winders, *Crisis in the Southwest: The United States, Mexico, and the Struggle over Texas* (Wilmington, DE: Scholarly Resources, 2002); and Steven E. Woodworth, *Manifest Destinies: American's Westward Expansion and the Road to the Civil War* (New York: Knopf, 2010). On US–British relations during the era, see Howard Jones, *To the Webster–Ashburton Treaty: A Study in Anglo–American Relations, 1783–1843* (Chapel Hill: University of North Carolina Press, 1977); Howard Jones and Donald A. Rakestraw, *Prologue to Manifest Destiny: Anglo–American Relations in the 1840s* (Wilmington, DE: Scholarly Resources, 1997); and Sam W. Haynes, *Unfinished Revolution: The Early American Republic in a British World* (Charlottesville: University of Virginia Press, 2010). Several essays in Maxime Dagenais and Julien Mauduit, eds., *Revolutions across Borders: Jacksonian American and the Canadian Rebellion* (Montreal and Kingston: McGill-Queen's University Press, 2019), help explain the US–British conflict along the Canadian border. On Oregon, see Frederick Merk, *The Oregon Question: Essays in Anglo–American Diplomacy and Politics* (Cambridge, MA: Harvard University Press, 1967); Pletcher, *Diplomacy of Annexation*; and Thomas Richards Jr., *Breakaway Americas: The Unmanifest Future of the Jacksonian United States* (Baltimore: Johns Hopkins University Press, 2020).

The consequences of Jacksonian territorial expansion on Native Americans have been ably examined in a number of studies. Useful works include Ronald N. Satz, *American Indian Policy in the Jacksonian Era* (Lincoln: University of Nebraska Press, 1975); Tim Alan Garrison, *The Legal Ideology of Removal: The Southern Judiciary and the Sovereignty of Native American Nations* (Athens: University of Georgia Press, 2002); Jason Edward Black, *American Indians and the Rhetoric of Removal and Allotment* (Jackson: University Press of Mississippi, 2015); John Bowes, *Land Too Good for Indians: Northern Indian Removal* (Norman: University of Oklahoma Press, 2016); Jeffrey Ostler, *Surviving Genocide: Native Nations and the United States from the American Revolution to Bleeding Kansas* (New Haven, CT: Yale University Press, 2019); Claudio Saunt, *Unworthy Republic: The Dispossession of Native Americans and the Road to Indian Territory* (New York: W. W. Norton, 2020); and Christina Snyder, "Many Removals: Re-evaluating the Arc of Indigenous Dispossession," *Journal of the Early Republic* 41 (Winter 2021): 623–650. On Cherokee removal, see Ethan Davis, "An Administrative Trail of Tears: Indian Removal," *American Journal of Legal History* 50 (2008–2010): 49–100; Adam J. Pratt, *Toward Cherokee Removal: Land, Violence, and the White Man's Chance* (Athens: University of Georgia Press,

2020); Daniel Blake Smith, *An American Betrayal: Cherokee Patriots and the Trail of Tears* (New York: Henry Holt, 2011). For the Seminole, consult William S. Belko, ed., *America's Hundred Years' War: U.S. Expansion to the Gulf Coast and the Fate of the Seminole, 1763–1858* (Gainesville: University Press of Florida, 2011), and C. S. Monaco, *The Second Seminole War and the Limits of American Aggression* (Baltimore: Johns Hopkins University Press, 2018).

The definitions of personal character and political corruption in chapter 1 are narrow, but even those limited definitions encompass a plethora of scholarly studies. Especially useful are Norma Basch, "Marriage, Morals, and Politics in the Election of 1828," *Journal of American History* 80 (December 1993): 890–918; Thomas Brown, "The Miscegenation of Richard Mentor Johnson as an Issue in the National Election Campaign of 1835–1836," *Civil War History* 39 (March 1993): 5–30; Kenneth S. Greenberg, *Honor & Slavery: Lies, Duels, Noses, Masks, Dressing as a Woman, Gifts, Strangers, Humanitarianism, Death, Slave Rebellions, the Proslavery Argument, Baseball, Hunting, and Gambling in the Old South* (Princeton, NJ: Princeton University Press, 1996); John F. Marszalek, *The Petticoat Affair: Manners, Mutiny, and Sex in Andrew Jackson's White House* (New York: The Free Press, 1997); Bryan C. Rindfleisch, "'What It Means to Be a Man': Contested Masculinity in the Early Republic and Antebellum America," *History Compass* 10 (November 2012): 852–865; Craig Bruce Smith, *American Honor: The Creation of the Nation's Ideals during the Revolutionary Era* (Chapel Hill: University of North Carolina Press, 2018); Andrew S. Trees, *The Founding Fathers and the Politics of Character* (Princeton, NJ: Princeton University Press, 2004); Kirsten E. Wood, "'One Woman So Dangerous to Public Morals': Gender and Power in the Eaton Affair," *Journal of the Early Republic* 17 (1997): 237–75; Leonard D. White, *The Jacksonians: A Study in Administrative History, 1829–1861* (New York: Macmillan, 1954); and Bertram Wyatt-Brown, *Southern Honor: Ethics and Behavior in the Old South* (New York: Oxford University Press, 1982).

The economic issues of the Jacksonian period have received considerable attention over the decades. On the Bank War and its consequences for the nation's economy into the 1840s, see Stephen W. Campbell, *The Bank War and the Partisan Press: Newspapers, Financial Institutions, and the Post Office in Jacksonian America* (Lawrence: University Press of Kansas, 2019). Jessica Lepler, *The Many Panics of 1837: People, Politics, and the Creation of a Transatlantic Financial Crisis* (Cambridge: Cambridge University Press, 2013), expertly argues that the economic depression that doomed Van Buren's presidency was not a singular event. Sharon Ann Murphy, *Other People's Money: How Banking Worked in the Early American Republic* (Baltimore: Johns Hopkins University, 2017), is an effective summary of an often difficult topic. Much like the Second Bank of the United States, the tariff loomed large throughout the Jacksonian period, as seen in William K. Bolt, *Tariff Wars and the Politics of Jacksonian America* (Nashville: Vanderbilt University Press, 2017), and Daniel Peart, *Lobbyists and the Making of U.S. Tariff Policy, 1816–1861* (Baltimore: Johns Hopkins University Press, 2018).

The scholarship on Jacksonian-era slavery continues to add to our understanding of how the repressive system of unfree labor not only affected the enslaved but also how it permeated the era's politics. Recent overviews of the slave system to consult include Lacy K. Ford Jr., *Deliver Us from Evil: The Slavery Question in the Old South* (Oxford: Oxford University Press, 2009); Edward Baptist, *The Half Has Never Been Told: Slavery and the Making of American Capitalism* (New York: Basic Books, 2014); and Walter Johnson, *River of Dark Dreams: Slavery and Empire in the Cotton Kingdom* (Cambridge, MA: Harvard University Press, 2013). The domestic slave trade has been ably treated by Michael Tadman, *Speculators and Slaves: Masters, Traders and Slaves in the Old South* (Madison: University of Wisconsin Press, 1989); Walter Johnson, *Soul by Soul: Life inside the Antebellum Slave Market* (Cambridge, MA: Harvard University Press, 1999); Steven Deyle, *Carry Me Back: The Domestic Slave Trade in American Life* (Oxford: Oxford University Press, 2005); and Joshua D. Rothman, *The Ledger and the Chain: How Domestic Slave Traders Shaped America* (Basic Books, 2021).

As with the study of slavery, the struggle between abolitionism and the Slave Power has generated voluminous scholarship. Beth A. Salerno, *Sister Societies: Women's Antislavery Organizations in Antebellum America* (DeKalb: Northern Illinois University Press, 2005); Caleb McDaniel, *The Problem of Democracy in the Age of Slavery: Garrisonian Abolitionism and Transatlantic Reform* (Baton Rouge: Louisiana State University Press, 2013); and Kellie Carter Jackson, *Force and Freedom: Black Abolitionists and the Politics of Violence* (Philadelphia: University of Pennsylvania Press, 2019), are among some of the best recent additions to the field. David Brion Davis, *The Slave Power Conspiracy and the Paranoid Style* (Baton Rouge: Louisiana State University Press, 1969), and Leonard L. Richards, *The Slave Power: The Free North and Southern Domination, 1780–1860* (Baton Rouge: Louisiana State University Press, 2000), are the best works on the Slave Power. Works that address anti-abolitionist protests include Leonard L. Richards, *"Gentlemen of Property and Standing": Anti-Abolition Mobs in Jacksonian America* (New York: Oxford University Press, 1970); Michael Feldberg, *The Turbulent Era: Riot and Disorder in Jacksonian America* (New York: Oxford University Press, 1980); and David Grimsted, *American Mobbing, 1828–1861: Toward Civil War* (New York: Oxford University Press, 1998). The use of the "gag rule" to limit congressional discussion of slavery has been covered in Daniel Wirls, "'The Only Mode of Avoiding Everlasting Debate': The Overlooked Senate Gag Rule for Antislavery Petitions," *Journal of the Early Republic* 27 (Spring 2007): 115–138, and Corey Brooks, *Liberty Power*.

Three standard studies of Jacksonian-era nativism are older but solid: Ray A. Billington, *The Protestant Crusade, 1800–1860: A Study of the Origins of American Nativism* (New York: Macmillan, 1938); David Brion Davis, "Some Themes of Counter-Subversion: An Analysis of Anti-Masonic, Anti-Catholic, and Anti-Mormon Literature," *Mississippi Valley Historical Review* 47 (September 1960): 205–24; and Michael Feldberg, *The Philadelphia Riots of 1844: A Study of Ethnic Conflict* (Westport, CT: Greenwood Press, 1975). Three valuable, and more recent, studies of the topic are Jenny Franchot, *Roads to Rome: The Antebellum Protestant Encounter with Catholicism* (Berkeley: University of California Press, 1994); Angela F. Murphy, *American Slavery, Irish Freedom: Abolition, Immigrant Citizenship, and the Transatlantic Movement for Irish Repeal* (Baton Rouge: Louisiana State University Press,

2010); and Cassandra Yacovazzi, *Escaped Nuns: True Womanhood and the Campaign against Convents in Antebellum America* (New York: Oxford University Press, 2018). Tyler Anbinder, *Nativism and Slavery: The Northern Know Nothings and the Politics of the 1850s* (New York: Oxford University Press, 1992), primarily focuses on the 1850s, but it is also helpful in understanding the origins of Jacksonian nativism. Zachary M. Schrag, *The Fires of Philadelphia: Citizen-Soldiers, Nativists, and the 1844 Riots over the Soul of a Nation* (New York: Pegasus, 2021), provides a recent look at the 1844 Philadelphia riots.

Cultural politics remains a fertile field for Jacksonian historians to pursue. An essential collection to consult is Jeffrey Pasley, Andrew Robertson, and David Waldstreicher, eds., *Beyond the Founders: New Approaches to the Political History of the Early American Republic* (Chapel Hill: University of North Carolina Press, 2004). Mark R. Cheathem, *The Coming of Democracy: Presidential Campaigning in the Age of Jackson* (Baltimore: Johns Hopkins University Press, 2018), provides specific categories of cultural politics that grew in importance during the period between 1824 and 1840. M. J. Heale, *The Presidential Quest: Candidates and Images in American Political Culture, 1787–1852* (New York: Longman, 1982), is an underappreciated masterpiece of understanding the ways in which cultural politics interacted with traditional political culture. A sample of essential work on cultural politics includes Nancy R. Davison, "E. W. Clay and the American Political Caricature Business," in *Prints and Printmakers of New York State, 1825–1940*, ed. David Tatham (Syracuse: Syracuse University Press, 1986), 91–110; Roger A. Fischer, *Tippecanoe and Trinkets Too: The Material Culture of American Presidential Campaigns, 1828–1984* (Urbana: University of Illinois Press, 1988); Elizabeth R. Varon, *We Mean to Be Counted: White Women and Politics in Antebellum Virginia* (Chapel Hill: University of North Carolina Press, 1998); Richard J. Ellis, *Presidential Travel: The Journey from George Washington to George W. Bush* (Lawrence: University Press of Kansas, 2008); Kenneth Cohen, "'Sport for Grown Children': American Political Cartoons, 1790–1850," *International Journal of the History of Sport* 28 (May-June 2011): 1301–1318; Erika Piola, "The Rise of Early Lithography and Antebellum Visual Culture," *Winterthur Portfolio* 48 (Summer/Autumn 2014): 125–138; Kirsten E. Wood, "'Join with Heart and Soul and Voice': Music, Harmony, and Politics in the Early American Republic," *American Historical Review* 119 (October 2014): 1083–1116; Jon Grinspan, *The Virgin Vote: How Young Americans Made Democracy Social, Politics Personal, and Voting Popular in the Nineteenth Century* (Chapel Hill: University of North Carolina Press, 2016); Sean Scalmer, *On the Stump: Campaign Oratory and Democracy in the United States, Britain, and Australia* (Philadelphia: Temple University Press, 2017); Emily J. Arendt "'Two Dollars a Day, And Roast Beef': Whig Culinary Partisanship and the Election of 1840," *Journal of the Early Republic* 40 (Spring 2020): 83–115; Billy Coleman, *Harnessing Harmony: Music, Power, and Politics in the United States, 1788–1865* (Chapel Hill: University of North Carolina Press, 2020); and Teresa A. Goddu, *Selling Antislavery: Abolition and Mass Media in Antebellum America* (Philadelphia: University of Pennsylvania Press, 2020).

Scholarly overviews of the Jacksonian era include Sean Wilentz, *The Rise of American Democracy: Jefferson to Lincoln* (New York: W. W. Norton, 2005); Harry Watson,

Liberty and Power: The Politics of Jacksonian America, 2nd ed. (New York: Hill and Wang, 2006); Daniel Walker Howe, *What Hath God Wrought: The Transformation of America, 1815–1848* (New York: Oxford University Press, 2007); and Alan Taylor, *American Republics: A Continental History of the United States, 1783–1850* (New York: W. W. Norton, 2021).

Studies of the Jacksonian period owe a great debt to the work of the documentary editing teams that have made much of the source material of the era accessible in print and/or digital formats. Completed projects include *The Papers of John C. Calhoun*, 28 vols. (Columbia: University of South Carolina Press, 1959–2003); *The Papers of Henry Clay*, 11 vols. (Lexington: University Press of Kentucky, 1959–1992); *Correspondence of James K. Polk*, 14 vols. (Knoxville: University of Tennessee Press, 1969–2021); and *The Papers of Daniel Webster*, 15 vols. (Hanover, NH: University Press of New England, 1974–1989). Ongoing projects include *The Papers of Andrew Jackson*, 11 vols. to date (Knoxville: University of Tennessee Press, 1980–); The Joseph Smith Papers (digital edition), Church History Department of The Church of Jesus Christ of Latter-day Saints, https://www.josephsmithpapers.org/; and Papers of Martin Van Buren (digital edition) (Cumberland University), http://vanburen papers.org/. Many of the completed documentary editions listed above began as print editions and have now been added in digital form to the University of Virginia Press's Rotunda platform; the Smith and Van Buren projects are pursuing both print and digital editions simultaneously. Older collections of edited documents crucial to this study were *Letters of James Gillespie Birney, 1831–1857*, 2 vols., ed. Dwight L. Dumond (New York: D. Appleton-Century, 1938), and *Correspondence of Andrew Jackson*, 7 vols., ed. John Spencer Bassett and J. Franklin Jameson (Washington, DC: Carnegie Institute of Washington, 1926–35). Users should be aware, however, that these two collections were not completed to the same exacting editorial standards as modern projects.

INDEX

Aberdeen, Lord (George Hamilton-Gordon), 51

abolitionism, 301, 306, 309; and 1844 Democratic Party platform, 123; as alleged British plot against US, 40, 45, 51, 176, 209; and the *Amistad* case, 16; and anti-southern conspiracy, 34; and Birney, 161–163, 170, 206, 207; British support for, 51–52; and Calhoun, 88; and Cassius Clay, 206; and compensated emancipation, 7, 57, 137; and Elijah Lovejoy, 162; and Frances Wright, 182; and Frelinghuysen, 72; and Henry Clay, 58–59, 63, 163; and I. C. Clay, 214; influence on 1844 election results, 215, 217;and Lewis Tappan, 91; material mailed in support of, 15, 97; and moral suasion, 14, 171; in New York, 175, 201, 217; and northern voters, 202; in Ohio, 204; perceived as a threat to the US, 38, 53, 86, 123, 222; and political violence, 14; and Polk, 95; publications, 169; and slave narratives, 21; and the Slave Power conspiracy, 43–44, 52, 164–165, 166, 167, 168, 178, 199, 223, 224; and the Whigs, 185; and William Lloyd Garrison, 162. *See also* American Anti-Slavery Society (AAS); antislavery

Adams, Charles Francis, 144

Adams, John, 20, 141

Adams, John Quincy, 70, 71, 144, 174, 303, 305, 306; and 1824 election, 1; and 1828 election, 4, 7; and 1833 Massachusetts gubernatorial election, 69; and 1835 Massachusetts Senate election, 69; and 1840 election, 29; and Adams-Onís Treaty, 101; and *Amistad* case, 16; argues against "gag rule," 35; assessment of Caleb Cushing, 41; assessment of Harrison, 29; assessment of Tyler, 32; background, 2; Birney's criticism of, 168; and corrupt bargain, 1–2, 63, 84, 118, 187, 205; joins Whig Party, 6; and National Republicans, 5–6; opinion on Tyler's succession to presidency, 31; as possible 1844 Liberty presidential candidate, 167; as president, 2–4, 11, 97; suspects Slave Power conspiracy, 43–44; and Texas annexation, 43, 45, 66, 97, 164, 209; tries to stop Tyler's impeachment, 154–155; work on Treaty of Ghent, 2–3

alcohol, 24–25, 36, 39, 67, 74, 76, 94, 160, 170, 172, 183, 189, 195, 224

Alexander, Samuel, 182

Alien and Sedition Acts (1798), 19

Allen, William, 99, 220

Almonte, Juan M., 48

American Anti-Slavery Society (AAS), 14, 162, 163, 164

Barry, William T., 9
Battle of New Orleans, 193
Battle of the Thames, 13, 92
Bell, John, 188
Bennet, James Arlington, 141–143
Bennett, James Gordon, 145
Benton, Thomas Hart: accusations of corruption, 117–118; ally of Buchanan's, 84; consulted about Hammett letter, 99; criticism of Richard M. Johnson, 90; endorses Van Buren as 1844 Democratic presidential nominee, 81; Jackson's criticism of, 157–158, 174; opposes Texas annexation, 53, 105, 174; as potential 1844 Democratic presidential nominee, 77; and USS *Princeton* explosion, 48
Berrien, John M., 62, 65
Biddle, Nicholas, 7, 8, 35, 44, 48, 195
Birney, Agatha MacDowell, 160
Birney, Dion, 198
Birney, James, Jr., 198
Birney, James, Sr., 160
Birney, James G., 301; and 1840 election, 26–28, 163–165; and 1844 campaign, x, xii, 130, 159, 168–171, 172, 175–176, 178–179, 198–199, 206–208, 215; and 1844 campaign speaking tour, 168, 169–171; and 1844 Liberty presidential nomination, 165–168; as abolitionist publisher, 162–163; background, 159–165; campaign biographies of, 169; embrace of abolitionism, 161–163; as enslaver, 160, 206; and Freemasonry, 160–161, 207–208; and the Garland forgery, 207; influence on 1844 election results, 215; as mayor of Huntsville, Alabama, 160; move to Michigan, 167; and nativism, 198–199; and political corruption, 207; political songs about, 169; relationship with Henry Clay, 163; relationship

with Theodore Weld, 161; religious conversion, 160; and slavery, 159–165, 167–168, 171; supports colonization, 160–161; supports gradual emancipation, 161; supports temperance, 160; and the tariff, 178–179; and Texas annexation, 175–176; threatened with proslavery violence, 162; trip to the World Anti-Slavery Convention, 164–165; work for the American Anti-Slavery Society, 162–163; work for the American Colonization Society, 161
Birney, Margaret, 160
Birney, William, 169
Blair, Francis P., 80, 101, 120, 155; assists 1844 Democratic campaign, 173; criticism of Tyler, 32; publishes Jackson's pro–Texas annexation letter, 97; role in Tyler's withdrawal from 1844 campaign, 156–158; targeted for replacement as *Globe* editor, 186
Boggs, Lilburn, 131, 143
Botts, John Minor, 39
Bouck, William C., 214, 217
Boyd, Linn, 187
Brown, Aaron V., 85, 97, 109
Brown, William Saunders, 218
Buchanan, James, 303; and 1844 Democratic national convention, 111, 114–115, 117–118, 124; alleged same-sex relationship with William R. King, 85; campaign biographies of, 84; controversial involvement in 1824 election, 84, 205; declines attending 1844 Democratic Nashville mass meeting, 186; as minister to Russia, 84; and personal character, 84–85, 205; and political corruption, 84, 205; as possible 1844 Democratic presidential nominee, xi, 76, 83–85, 104; prediction about Van Buren's presidency, 6–7; as president, 223; and slavery, 84; and territorial

Buchanan, James, *continued*
    expansion, 53, 84; wins 1856
    election, 85
Butler, Benjamin F., 124; advises Van
    Buren on Texas annexation, 98;
    argues against two-thirds rule at
    Democratic national convention,
    112–113; attempts to nominate Silas
    Wright as Democratic presidential
    candidate, 117–118; credits Silas
    Wright with Democratic victories
    in 1844 elections, 217; encourages
    Jackson to support Van Buren's 1844
    presidential nomination, 101, 105;
    instructed by Van Buren to nominate
    Silas Wright for 1844 Democratic
    ticket, 116; reports party platform to
    convention delegates, 122; rumored
    as possible US Supreme Court
    nominee, 150; visits Jackson at the
    Hermitage, 98, 101; votes for Polk at
    1844 Democratic convention, 119

Calhoun, John C., 44, 49, 83, 92, 113,
    154, 186, 302; and 1824 election,
    1; and 1832 election, 4; and 1844
    Democratic national convention,
    114–117, 119, 124, 175; and slavery,
    15, 51–53, 85–86, 87; and banking,
    85–86; correspondence with
    Mormons, 133–134; correspondence
    with Richard Pakenham, 51–53;
    courts Polk as running mate,
    95; and the Eaton affair, 4–5;
    as nationalist, 4, 5; and the
    nullification crisis, 7, 87; opposes
    Dorr War, 86; political cartoons
    about, 61, 87, 94, 157, 192; as
    possible 1844 presidential nominee,
    xi, 53, 57, 61, 76–77, 81, 85–88, 94,
    95, 101, 104, 107, 114–117, 133–134,
    153, 157; as secretary of state, 50–53,
    151; as secretary of war, 1, 3; supports
    Jackson, 3; supports later 1844
    Democratic national convention

date, 81, 88; supports nullification,
    5, 7; supports Whig Party, 6; and
    the tariff, 7, 86, 87, 88; and Texas
    annexation, 50–53, 98, 100, 151, 185;
    as vice president, 4; withdraws as
    1844 presidential contender, 88
Calhoun, Patrick, 49
Canadian Rebellion, 18, 56
Carroll, Nicholas, 217
Cass, Lewis, 153, 302; and 1844
    Democratic national convention,
    109, 113–115, 117–118, 120, 124–125,
    175; and 1848 election, 223, 224;
    background, 88–89; and banking,
    89; campaign biographies of, 90;
    correspondence with Mormons,
    133–134; elected as Michigan
    senator, 220; and Freemasonry, 89;
    as minister to France, xi, 88–89,
    90; political cartoons about, 94;
    as possible 1844 Democratic
    presidential nominee, xi, 62, 76,
    88–90, 94, 96, 104, 106, 107, 109,
    113–115, 117–118, 120, 133–134; as
    possible 1844 Democratic vice-
    presidential nominee, 124–125;
    public correspondence with Mahlon
    Dickerson, 89; as secretary of war,
    xi, 88, 90; solicits Jackson's support
    for 1844 Democratic presidential
    nomination, 89–90; speaks at 1844
    Nashville mass meeting, 187, 190;
    supports later 1844 Democratic
    national convention date, 89;
    and the tariff, 89; and territorial
    expansion, 89, 107; as territorial
    governor of Michigan, 88;
Catholicism, 19–21, 71, 196–200, 207,
    215–217
Catron, John, 179
Catron, Matilda, 179
character, personal, xii, 6, 7, 8, 156, 172,
    223–224, 308; Birney's, 160, 167,
    169, 207–208; Buchanan's, 84–85,
    205; Charles Stewart's, 82; Clay's,

2–3, 12, 54, 73, 74, 163, 179; Dallas's, 128, 129; Frelinghuysen's, 71–74, 180, 193, 200; Jackson's, 12; Joseph Smith's, 133; Polk's, 128, 179–180, 213; Richard M. Johnson's, 13–14, 23–24, 62, 90, 92, 93; Thomas Morris's, 169; Tyler's, 32; Van Buren's 12–13, 81; Webster's, 12

Chase, Salmon P., 101, 169
Cheatham, Leonard P., 181, 183
Cheatham, Sarah, 181
Childress, William G., 127
Chinn, Dinah, 23, 245n54
Chinn, Julia, 13, 23
Chinn, Parthena, 13, 23
Church of Jesus Christ of Latter-Day Saints. *See* Mormons
Cicognani, Felix, 20
Cilley, Jonathan, 289n36
Civil War, xii, 224, 237n1, 237n2, 299
Clay, Cassius M., 190, 205–206
Clay, Henry, 46, 79–80, 106, 110, 300–302; and 1824 election, 1–2, 63, 84, 118, 187; and 1832 election, ix, 5, 62; and 1840 election, 22, 56; and 1844 campaign, 33, 122, 127, 128, 156, 157, 158, 159, 171, 172–175, 176, 179, 181–184, 187, 189, 190, 191–196, 198, 199, 200, 201, 204–207, 209–213, 214, 215, 217, 218, 219, 291n46; and 1844 Whig national convention, 71, 73–74; and banking, 2, 34–35, 60, 63, 73; campaign biographies of, 172–173, 209; and Freemasonry, 6; as the "Great Compromiser," xii, 2, 7, 63, 164; and National Republicans, 5–6; and nativism, 199, 217; one-term pledge of, 74; and personal character, 2–3, 12, 54, 73, 74, 179; political cartoons about, 61, 87, 94, 128, 157, 191–194, 201, 213; and political corruption, 2, 9, 62, 84, 187, 200, 204–205; political songs about, 194–196, 291n46; as possible 1844 Whig presidential

nominee, 122, 127, 128, 156, 157, 158, 159, 171–176, 179, 181–184, 187, 189–195, 198–201, 204–207, 209–215, 217–219, 291n46; and public letters about Texas annexation, 65–66, 100–101, 151, 154, 174–175; relationship with John Tyler, 33, 34–35, 39, 54, 57–58, 60; as secretary of state, 1, 4; and slavery, 54, 58–59, 66, 88, 163, 174, 204–206, 214, 215; and Texas annexation, 46, 64–65, 100–101, 151, 154, 174–175, 192, 214, 267n49; and the tariff, 2, 7, 59, 60, 63, 64, 88, 176; as US senator, 6, 7, 8, 9, 32, 33, 34–35, 37, 38, 39, 85, 87, 163, 289n36; work on the Treaty of Ghent, 2–3
Clay, Lucretia, 60, 205
Clay, Porter, 37
Clay, Thomas, 60
Clayton, John M., 62, 68–69
colonization, antislavery, 7, 58, 72, 161, 162; Virginia Colonization Society, 31. *See also* American Colonization Society (ACS)
conspiracy theories, 9, 53, 105, 118, 205, 214; abolitionist, 34, 44–45, 51, 185; Anglophobic, 40, 43, 44, 45, 51, 84, 92, 101, 187; Freemasonic, 5; money power, 7–8, 164–165; nativist, 19–21, 200; Slave Power, 43–44, 52, 164–165, 166, 167, 168, 178, 199, 223, 224, 309
Copeland, Solomon, 142–143
corporal's guard, 37
"corrupt bargain," 2, 9, 62, 84, 187, 205
corruption, political, allegations of, xii, 12, 172, 308; against the 1844 Democratic national convention, 111, 113, 118; against Henry Clay, 2, 3, 9, 62, 84, 187, 204–206; against Birney, 207–208; against the Democratic Party, 201, 223; against Jackson, 9–11, 63; against John Quincy Adams, 2,

corruption, political, allegations of, *continued*
3, 9, 62, 84, 187, 205; against Polk, 200–204; against the Second Bank of the US, 7–8, 124; against the Slave Power, 168, 224; against Tyler, 69; against the US government, 33, 132, 149, 200, 222, 223; against Van Buren, 11, 23; against the Whig Party, 28, 39, 196, 223

Cramer, William E., 204

Crawford, George W., 63

Crawford, William H., 1, 3, 31, 63, 84

Crittenden, John J., 39, 58, 59, 64, 65

Cruse, Isaac, 67

cultural politics, xii, 21–22, 24–25, 28, 63, 90, 122, 171, 172, 208, 310; influence on 1844 election results, 217–218, 219, 224. *See also* auxiliary organizations; material culture; music, political; print culture; public correspondence; public events; public speeches; visual culture; women's political activity

Currin, David M., 188

Cushing, Caleb, 37, 41

Daily National Intelligencer (Washington, DC), 32, 65, 100, 173

Dallas, Alexander J., 159–160

Dallas, George M., 123, 159–160, 301; advises Polk, 185, 200, 203, 208; background, 89, 124–125, 159–160; and banking, 125, 195; campaign biographies of, 173; contender for 1844 Democratic vice-presidential nomination, 124–125; estrangement from Van Buren, 125–126; material culture about, 189, 190; and nativism, 200; notified of 1844 Democratic vice-presidential nomination, 126–127; notified of electoral victory, 209; and personal character, 128, 129; political cartoons about, 192,

194; and political corruption, 208; political songs about, 184, 195–196; role in Tyler's withdrawal from 1844 campaign, 156, 158; and slavery, 185, 203; supports Cass for 1844 Democratic presidential nomination, 89, 124; supports place on Democratic ticket, 127–128, 173, 175, 186, 187; supports Van Buren for 1844 Democratic presidential nomination, 124; and the tariff, 125; and territorial expansion, 124, 125, 127, 189, 192, 220; as vice president, 220; vice-presidential nomination criticized, 129; wins 1844 Democratic vice-presidential nomination, 125

dark horse, x, xi, 237n3

Davis, John, 62, 69, 302

Democratic Party, 4–6, 8, 9, 11, 12, 13, 16, 17, 19, 31, 32, 33, 37, 39, 41, 42, 46, 47, 50, 51, 52, 53, 54, 56, 58, 59, 60, 62, 63–64, 67, 69, 70, 73, 74, 132, 134, 136, 137, 140, 142, 143, 144, 148, 149, 150, 153, 154, 155, 157, 158, 159, 164, 166, 168, 222–223, 238n9, 284n5, 291n46, 298n10, 302–303, 305, 306; and 1840 election, 22–28; and 1840 national convention, 24; and 1844 campaign, xi, xii, 172–196, 200–213; and 1844 election results, 211–221; and 1844 national convention, xi, 110–129, 145–146, 151, 152, 156, 172; Jacksonians, 4–5; Locofocos, 5, 87, 118, 192, 200, 238n9; and potential 1844 presidential nominees, xi, 76–93, 97–109; and potential 1844 vice-presidential nominees, 93–97

Democratic-Republican Party. *See* Republican Party (1790s–1830s)

Derry, Edmund S., 153

Dickerson, Mahlon, 89

Dickinson, Daniel S., 112

distribution of land revenue, 8, 31, 33,

New Orleans fine, 84, 92; political cartoons about, 9–11, 105, 157, 192, 193, 194, 201; political songs about, 195; as president, 4–5, 6, 7–11, 15–18, 19–21, 23, 28, 31, 35, 37, 39, 54, 63, 64, 71, 84, 85, 88, 91, 136, 200, 201; role in Tyler's withdrawal from 1844 campaign, 155, 157–159; and support for Texas annexation, 47–48, 66, 97–98, 100–101, 104, 105, 268n51; support of Polk on 1844 Democratic ticket, 94, 96, 101–102

Jackson, Rachel, 12
Jay, John, 166
Jay, William, 166, 167
Jefferson, Thomas, 2, 23, 32, 40, 56, 71, 85, 89, 141, 163, 181
Jeffersonian Republicans. *See* Republicans (Jeffersonian)
Johnson, Adaline, 13–14
Johnson, Andrew, 126
Johnson, Cave: advises Polk on the tariff, 177; analyzes Democratic reaction to Hammett letter, 101; appointed to Polk's cabinet, 121; assesses Polk's prospects for 1844 Democratic presidential nomination, 101–102; believes Democratic delegates will vote for Silas Wright, 113, 116; credited with Polk's nomination, 121; proposes plan to gain Polk Democratic vice-presidential nomination, 109; tasked with delegate organization, 102–104; work at Democratic national convention, 109, 110–111, 116
Johnson, Imogene, 13–14
Johnson, James, 91
Johnson, Richard M., 302; and 1836 election, 13–14; and 1840 election, 23–24, 92, 164; and banking, 91; background, 13, 23–24, 62, 90–93, 164; campaign biographies of, 13, 92; and the Eaton affair, 91; and

interracial relationships, 13–14, 23–24, 92, 93, 205; meets Van Buren on 1842 electioneering tour, 79–80; and personal character, 13–14, 23–24, 62, 90, 92, 93; political cartoons about, 94, 192; and political corruption, 62, 90, 91; as possible nominee on the 1844 Democratic ticket, xi, 62, 76–77, 80, 90–93, 94, 106, 114–115, 117, 121, 124–125, 133–134; predicts Polk as 1844 Democratic vice-presidential nominee, 96; and slavery, 13–14, 23–24, 91, 92, 93, 205; supporters oppose Van Buren at 1844 Democratic national convention, 113; and the tariff, 91; and territorial expansion, 91, 92, 192; as vice president, 91; as war hero, 13, 90, 92
Johnston, John, 66
Jones, James C., 93–94, 95–96, 188

Kane, John K., 177–178, 183
Kendall, Amos: advises Van Buren on Texas annexation, 106; assists Polk in writing inaugural address, 222; denounces Richard M. Johnson's interracial relationships, 24; dismissed as Polk biographer, 173; limits circulation of abolitionist material, 15; reassures Van Buren about 1844 Democratic presidential nomination, 80
Kennedy, Andrew, 126
Kennedy, John F., 1
Kennon, Beverley, 48–50
Kettlewell, John, 119
King, Leicester, 169
King, Preston, 122, 124
King, William R.: alleged same-sex relationship with James Buchanan, 85; as possible 1844 Democratic vice-presidential nominee, 93
Kitchen Cabinet, 37
Knore, Joseph, 292n54

Know-Nothing Party, 223, 302
Kreider, M. Z., 153

Lamar, Mirabeau B., 42
Larrabee, Benjamin, 161
Laughlin, Samuel H., 74, 173, 183, 189
Law and Order Party, 219, 298n10
Lawrence, Abbott, 69–70
Leavitt, Joshua, 164, 169, 206
Legaré, Hugh S., 38
Leigh, Benjamin W., 65, 68
LeMoyne, Francis J., 163
Letcher, Robert P., 58, 128, 205
Lewis, Dixon H., 37
Lewis, William B., 47, 52, 89–90, 158
Liberty Party: xii, 159, 301, 306; and
    1840 election, 28, 164–165; and
    1840 presidential nomination of
    Birney, 164; and 1841 national
    convention, 165–166; and 1841
    presidential nomination of Birney,
    166; and 1842 Massachusetts
    elections, 70, 166; and 1843
    affirmation of Birney's presidential
    nomination, 168; and 1843 national
    convention, 167–168; and 1844
    campaign, 168–171, 179, 182, 198,
    206–208; adopts official name,
    166; considers replacing Birney as
    1844 presidential nominee, 167; and
    controversy over Thomas Morris's
    vice-presidential nomination,
    168–169; debates ideological versus
    pragmatic approach to slavery,
    167; establishes party newspapers,
    166–167; influence on 1844 election
    results, 214, 215–216, 217, 219;
    invokes Slave Power conspiracy
    theory, 164–165, 166, 168; organizes
    for 1844 election, 166, 168; and
    shift from religious to political and
    economic antislavery arguments,
    166
Lincoln, Abraham, 188
Linn, Lewis F., 41, 84

Lovejoy, Elijah, 162
Lyman, Amasa M., 141

Madison, Dolley, 48, 149, 179
Madison, James, 2, 32, 40, 159, 160, 163
The Madisonian, 45, 66, 152
Magenis, Arthur L., 126, 273n98
Mallory, Francis, 34
Mangum, Willie P.: criticizes Clay's
    personal character, 3; describes
    reaction to Polk's presidential
    nomination, 128–129, 154; relays
    information about Texas annexation,
    65
Manifest Destiny. *See* expansion,
    territorial
Marcy, William L., 124–125, 150,
    240n22, 303
Margaret (Charles Stewart's partner),
    82
Marshall, John, 187
Marshall, John J., 206
Marshall, Thomas F., 187
Martin, Mary D., 180
masculinity, 12–13
Mason, John Thomson, 150
Mason, John Y., 50, 158
material culture, 22, 25, 67, 122,
    189–190; ash/Clay pole, 189, 218;
    badge/button/ribbon, 22, 67, 152;
    ball, 24–25, 189; banner/flag, 36,
    63, 96, 127, 152, 180–182, 184,
    188–190, 218; cedar tree, 169; effigy,
    36, 95; hard cider, 24–25, 36, 39,
    76, 94, 172, 189, 195, 224; hickory
    pole/twig, 63, 64, 189–190; liberty
    pole, 187; log cabin, 24–25, 36, 63,
    66, 76, 77, 94, 172, 189, 195, 224;
    Polk stalk, 189–190, 289–90n41;
    raccoon, 24–25, 36, 63, 67, 74, 76,
    77, 126, 173, 189–190, 191–192, 193,
    195, 196, 213, 218; rooster, 190, 192;
    transparency, 189, 190–191
Maxcy, Virgil, 48–49
McDuffie, George, 174

McKeon, John, 208
McLean, John, 54–57, 61–62, 69, 301
Medary, Samuel, 108, 115, 214
Melville, Gansevoort, 183, 184
Melville, Herman, 183
Mendenhall, Hiram, 58–59
Miller, John K., 114
Miller, Washington D., 48
Missouri Crisis, xii, 2, 63, 164
Monk, Maria, 20
Monroe, James, 2, 3, 23, 40, 54, 163
Mormons, x, xii, 19, 131–148, 167, 207,
    213, 275n11, 301; and 1844 national
    convention, 140; Council of Fifty,
    138–141, 143–145; electioneering
    missionaries, 140–141, 145; First
    Presidency, 138, 139, 161, 275n11;
    plural marriage (polygamy), 133,
    143, 147; question leading 1844
    presidential contenders, 133–134;
    Quorum of the Twelve Apostles, 135,
    136, 138, 141, 145, 148, 275n11
Morris, Thomas, 207, 301; receives
    1844 Liberty Party vice-presidential
    nomination, 166, 168; vice-
    presidential nomination criticized,
    168–169
Morse, Samuel F. B., 20, 120
Morton, Marcus, 109, 117, 124
Muhlenberg, Henry A. P., 216
Murphy, William S., 45, 46
music, political, ix, 22, 155, 208, 224;
    anti-Tyler, 36; "The Dying Coon,"
    195; "The Farmer of Ashland," 196;
    "Get Out of the Way Ole Kentucky,"
    127, 194–195; "Home Sweet Home,"
    48; "Jimmy Polk of Tennessee," 195;
    "New Yankee Doodle," 195; "Old Dan
    Tucker," 195; "The Rogue's March,"
    36; "A Song for the Man," 195; "A
    Song of the Hickories," 196; "The
    True-Hearted Statesman," 196; used
    by Democratic Party, 184, 195–196,
    213, 291n46; used by Liberty Party,
    169; used by Tylerites, 152; used by

Whig Party, 23, 63, 66, 67, 93, 107,
    110, 188, 190, 194–195, 291n46

Nashville Union, 102, 104, 117, 127, 187
Native Americans, 3, 11, 13, 15, 17–18,
    31, 41, 66, 71, 91, 137, 138, 167, 214,
    223, 233, 307; Cherokee, 17–18,
    56, 63; Chickasaw, 17; Choctaw, 11,
    17; Creek, 17; Seminole, 17, 308;
    Shawnee, 13
nativism, 172, 223, 302, 309–310; in
    the 1844 campaign, x, xii, xiv, 71,
    74, 197–198, 208, 215–218; and the
    1844 election results, 215–219, 220;
    origins of, 19–21; and violence, 19.
    See also American Republican Party;
    Catholicism; conspiracy theories
Naturalization Act of 1802, 292n54
Nauvoo, 131–134, 136–138, 140,
    142–148; Legion, 133, 142, 146, 147;
    University of, 142
newspapers, 22, 46, 47, 52, 54, 56, 58,
    67, 74, 82, 83, 85, 114, 115, 137, 141,
    142, 148, 151, 152, 189, 210, 237n3,
    246n3, 260n3, 293n61; abolitionist,
    14; anti-Catholic, 21; anti-Jackson, 11,
    13–14; and Cass's lack of newspaper
    network, 90; Democratic, 24, 66,
    74, 86, 102, 104, 110, 111, 61, 175,
    180, 183, 185, 190–192, 202, 203,
    205, 206; growth in 1840s, 173–174;
    Liberty, 166–167, 169, 207–208;
    Mormon, 136, 144–145, 147;
    northern, 18, 69, 147, 179, 181, 184;
    pro-Calhoun, 44; pro-Tyler, 31–32,
    45, 66, 148–149; pro–Van Buren,
    86; and publication of Hammett
    letter, 99–100; and publication
    of Raleigh letter, 65; and Richard
    M. Johnson's lack of newspaper
    network, 92; southern, 86, 101, 176,
    184, 185, 188; Whig, 18, 20, 57, 65,
    66, 69, 73, 175, 180, 188, 190, 191,
    198, 202–203, 207. See also specific
    newspapers

in Tyler's withdrawal from 1844 campaign, 156–159; and slavery, 188, 200–205, 214, 222, 224; and the tariff, 176–178, 214, 222; and Texas annexation/territorial expansion, 101, 102, 154, 174–175, 176, 186, 189, 192–193, 196, 214, 215, 222–223, 224;

Polk, Josiah F., 161

Polk, Sarah Childress, 300; assists husband's 1841 gubernatorial campaign, 94; assists husband's 1844 presidential campaign, 179–180; reaction to James Polk's victory, 213; and rumors about Buchanan-King relationship, 85; and slavery, 202

Polk, William H., 286n17

Porter, James M., 47

Pratt, Orson, 145

Prentiss, Sergeant S., 182–183, 188

presidential election: of 1824, ix, xii, 1–3, 4, 6, 9, 22, 31, 62, 63, 84, 118, 156, 179, 187, 205, 224, 304; of 1828, 3–4, 7, 22, 23, 54, 179; of 1832, ix, 4, 5, 11, 12, 22, 62, 71, 304; of 1836, 6, 11, 12, 13, 14, 20, 22, 23, 62, 191, 304; of 1840, ix, xi, xii, 11, 22–28, 29, 31, 36, 56, 62, 63, 69, 71, 74, 75, 76, 80, 82, 83, 88, 90, 92, 93, 94, 95, 107, 111, 112, 113, 132, 153, 154, 159, 163, 165, 172, 173, 179, 180, 181, 182, 183, 187, 189, 190, 193, 208, 209–213, 215, 216, 218, 224; of 1848, 70, 156, 175, 223, 224, 304; of 1856, 223, 224; of 1860, 187, 224; of 1932, 1; of 1960, 1; of 1980, 1; of 2008, 1

print culture, 22, 110, 122, 124, 143, 146, 163, 166, 168, 169, 172, 173, 183; 1844 Democratic Nashville mass meeting address, 186; abolitionist pamphlets, 15; abolitionist petitions, 15, 58, 91; anti-British articles, 44–45; anti-Catholic books, 20–21; anti-Clay pamphlet,

205; anti-Texas annexation petitions, 16; anti-Tyler Whig address, 38; campaign biographies, 12, 13, 22, 81–82, 84, 90, 92, 116, 126, 169, 172–173, 209; Mormon memorials, 145; Mormon petitions, 131–132; Mormon publications, 144; pro-Oregon petitions, 41; proposed Jackson memoirs, 90; pro-Webster circulars, 57; Robert J. Walker's pro-Texas annexation pamphlet, 47; Shockoe Hill (VA) Democratic Association resolutions, 107; Whig songsters, 67, 291. *See also* newspapers; *specific publications*

Protestant Reformation Society, 20–21

public correspondence, 22; and 1840 campaign, 25; by Andrew Jackson, 97, 102, 104, 157–158; by Cassius Clay, 206; by Daniel O'Connell, 165; Garland forgery, 295n69; by Henry Clay, 64–66, 67, 68, 100–101, 134, 151, 154, 174–175, 206; invitations to 1844 Democratic Nashville mass meeting, 185–186; by James Buchanan, 85; by James G. Birney, 161–162, 164, 167, 178–179, 198–199, 207–208; by James G. Birney's sons, 198; by James K. Polk, 101, 177; by John C. Calhoun, 88, 134; by John M. Clayton, 68–69; by John McLean, 55–56, 69; by John Tyler, 158–159; by Lewis Cass, 89, 90, 134; by Mahlon Dickerson, 89; by Martin Van Buren, 20, 98–104, 106, 107, 120, 128, 151; by Massachusetts Democrats, 204; by New York Democrats, 175; by Ohio voters, 198; by Silas Wright, 116, 122, 124; by the Liberty Party, 165; by the Mormons, 133–134; by Thomas Gilmer, 43, 97; by Thomas Hart Benton, 105

public events, 21–22, 224; in 1840 campaign, 25, 94, 107; 1844 Democratic events, 126–127,

successor, 148; as member of
the First Presidency, 139, 143; as
Mormons' vice-presidential choice,
143–144, 146; as potential 1844
Mormon presidential candidate,
147–148; tension with Joseph Smith,
143–144
Ritchie, Thomas, 66, 86, 107
Rives, William C., 89
Roane, William H., 107
Roberts, Eliza, 181
Roberts, Jonathan, 181
Robinson, Orville, 122, 124
Romney, George, 148
Roorback hoax, 202–204, 293n61
Roosevelt, Franklin D., 1
Rusk, Thomas J., 220

Sabbatarianism, 180
Salt River, 193
Sargent, Epes, 172–173, 209
Sargent, John O., 173
Sargent, Nathan, 173
Saunders, Romulus M., 111–112
Scott, Mrs., 99
Scott, Winfield, 301; background,
56; as contender for 1840 Whig
presidential nomination, 56; as
potential 1844 Whig presidential
candidate, 54, 56–57; as potential
1844 Whig vice-presidential
candidate, 62; as Tyler's classmate;
23
Sergeant, John, 302; as Clay's 1832
running mate, 5, 62, 71; as potential
1844 Whig vice-presidential
candidate, 62, 69, 70–71, 72–73
Seward, William H., 167, 196, 214
Sherman, William Tecumseh, 199
Shields, Ebenezer J., 188
Shunk, Francis R., 216
Six Months in a Convent (Reed), 20
slavery: ix, xii, 50, 143, 224, 300–301,
308–309; in 1844 campaign, 172,
174–176, 178, 188, 199, 200–206,

208, 214; and 1844 election results,
214, 215; at 1844 Democratic
national convention, 113, 123;
and the Amistad case, 16; among
Virginia Cabal members, 38, 43; and
Anglophobia, 40, 43, 44–45, 97,
209; and Birney, 159–168, 171, 176,
178, 199, 206, 208; and Buchanan,
84; and Butler, 98; and Calhoun,
15, 51–52, 85–86, 87, 88, 94; and
Cassius Clay, 205–206; and the
Chinn family, 13–14; defenses of,
14–15, 52; and domestic slave trade,
15, 42, 160–161, 166; and economic
profitability, 15; and Frelinghuysen,
72, 73, 74; and gambling, 208; and
Green, 44–45; growth of, 15; and
Harrison, 164; and Henry Clay, 54,
58–59, 63, 66, 163, 174–175, 204–
206; and implications for Whig
ticket, 62, 70, 72, 73; and Jackson,
7, 14–15, 97; and Joseph Smith, 137,
145; and Massachusetts Democrats,
204; and Mexican-American War,
223; and Michigan Whigs, 202; and
Missouri Crisis, 2; and New York
Democrats, 175, 201, 204; and New
York Whigs, 178, 201; and Ohio
Democrats, 201–202, 204; and Ohio
Whigs, 202; and Oregon, 41–42;
and Polk, 188, 200–204, 205; and
Republican Party, 223; and Richard
M. Johnson, 13–14, 91, 164, 205;
and Robert J. Walker, 47, 204; and
Roorback hoax, 202–204; and Scott,
56–57; and southern Democrats, 5;
and Texas annexation, 16, 40, 42,
43, 44–45, 46, 47, 51–52, 64, 66, 97,
98, 99, 107, 174–175, 214; and Texas
independence, 16; and Tyler, 31–32,
40, 42, 45, 51–52, 164, 166; and
Upshur, 44, 45; and Van Buren, 7,
15–16, 99, 164; violence of, 15; and
Virginia Democrats, 107. See also
abolitionism

of Guadalupe Hidalgo, 223; of New Echota, 63; Oregon, 297n9; Texas annexation, 42, 46, 47–48, 50–53, 65, 74, 98, 116, 174; of Washington (Webster-Ashburton), 41

Tucker, Beverley, 34

Turner, Nat, 14

Tyler, John, 47, 48, 66, 106, 301, 302, 303; and 1836 election, 23; and 1840 election, 23, 54, 63, 163, 164, 209; and 1841 special session, 35, 38; and 1842 protest message, 39; and 1844 campaign, 42, 44, 130, 144, 148–159, 171; as 1844 compromise candidate for Democrats, 101, 104, 125, 150–151, 152–153; and 1844 Tylerite national convention, 53, 151–154; attempts to eliminate 1844 challengers, 150–151; and August 1841 veto message, 36; and banking, 32, 34–40, 157; cabinet breakup, 37–38, 42; courtship of, and marriage to, Julia Gardiner, 48–50, 155; and estrangement from Whig Party, 33–40, 42, 54, 60, 148, 149, 150, 154–155; first annual message of, 40, 42; and immigration, 200; impeachment efforts against, 39, 40, 154–155; inaugural address of, 32; nicknames, 31, 149; opposes Jackson, 23, 31; and Oregon, 41–42; political cartoons about, 61, 87, 94, 157, 192, 194; and political corruption, 33, 39, 40, 44, 69, 74, 150, 156–157, 200; as president, 30–54, 56, 67, 68, 69, 76, 83, 85, 86, 100, 119, 124, 136, 137, 148, 166, 174, 222–223, 305; protests against, 36–37, 95; questions about presidential succession, 30–31, 73, 149; and relationship with Clay, 33, 34–35, 39, 54, 57–58, 60; and relationship with Webster, 33, 37–38, 42, 44, 57, 70, 149–150; reliance on Virginia Cabal, 34, 36, 37, 42, 50,

86; and slavery, 31, 32, 40, 42–43, 45, 51, 164; songs mentioning, 195; supports Jackson, 23, 31; supports territorial expansion, 38, 40; and the tariff, 185; and Texas annexation, ix, 40, 42–53, 64, 97, 151–152, 154, 157, 158, 159, 174, 222–223; and third annual message, 46, 64; and withdrawal from 1844 campaign, 154–159, 200; vetoes of, 35–36, 37, 39, 60; as vice president, 30

Tyler, Julia Gardiner, 48–50, 155, 156, 159

Tyler, Letitia Christian, 149, 155

Tyler, Priscilla Cooper, 149

Tyler, Robert, 100, 149, 150, 153, 156; political cartoons about, 192

Upshur, Abel P.: death in USS *Princeton* explosion, 48–50, 51, 151; as member of Virginia Cabal, 34, 86; negotiates Texas annexation treaty, 46–47, 50, 51, 174; as secretary of state, 44–50; as secretary of the navy, 38; supports territorial expansion, 38, 44–47, 86, 151, 174

USS *Princeton*, 48–50, 51, 151, 155, 174

Van Buren, Abraham, 99

Van Buren, Angelica Singleton, 79

Van Buren, Martin, 85, 90, 125, 129, 149, 174, 184, 192, 194, 195, 203, 222, 240n24, 260n3, 273n103, 302, 303, 305, 308; and 1824 election, 3; and 1832 election, 4, 5, 11, 71, 108; and 1836 election, 6, 11, 12–13, 14, 20–21; and 1839 electioneering tour, 78–79; and 1840 election, 11–12, 22–28, 29, 33, 75, 76, 80, 93, 132, 164, 179; and 1842 electioneering tour, 78–80, 261–262n7, 267n49; and 1844 Democratic national convention, 83, 106–122, 124, 126, 127, 156, 217; campaign biographies

Washington, George, 2, 23, 48, 66, 91, 141, 163, 181

Washington (DC) *Globe,* 32, 97, 99–100, 106, 112, 156, 173, 186

Webster, Daniel; 301–302; as 1836 presidential candidate, 6; assesses Whig Party's weakness during Tyler's presidency, 40; criticizes Calhoun, 52; criticizes Tyler, 44, 149–150; estrangement from John Davis, 70; feud with Abbott Lawrence, 69; helps organize Whig Party, 6; and personal character, 12; as possible 1844 Whig presidential nominee, xii, 53, 54, 57, 61; as possible 1844 Whig vice-presidential nominee, 68; as secretary of state, 33, 36, 37, 38, 41, 42, 43–44, 45; and slavery, 209; and territorial expansion, 41, 42, 43–44, 52;

Weed, Thurlow, 70, 73, 202–203

Weld, Theodore, 161, 163

Whig Party, 11, 12, 18, 19, 31, 32, 41, 77, 80, 89, 94, 95, 96, 98, 100, 102, 105, 110, 113, 118, 122, 126, 127, 129, 136, 137, 140, 144, 146, 154, 159, 164, 166, 301, 302, 305, 306; and 1836 election, 6, 14, 20, 22, 23; and 1840 election, 22–28, 56, 63, 76, 82, 83, 93, 132, 153, 163, 181, 182, 189, 208, 245n56; and 1844 campaign, xi, xii, 128, 172–196, 200–213, 291n46; and 1844 election results, 211–221, 297–98n10; and 1844 national convention, 53, 66–73, 145, 184; and estrangement from Tyler, 33–40, 42, 54, 60, 148, 149, 150, 155; origins of, 6, 10; and potential 1844 presidential nominees, xi-xii, 54–68; and potential 1844 vice-presidential nominees, 68–73

White, Captain, 136

White, Hugh Lawson, 6

White, Joel W., 153

Wilkins, William, 47

Wise, Henry A.: brawl with Edward Stanly, 35; gives pro-Texas annexation House speech, 42–43; influences Tyler to name Calhoun secretary of state, 50; as member of Virginia Cabal, 34, 42

women's political activity, 22, 149, 208, 218; and 1836 campaign, 13–14; and 1840 campaign, 25; and 1844 Whig national convention, 67; antislavery, 58, 91; Democratic, 127, 180–181, 182; and the Eaton affair, 4; Whig, 25, 58, 180, 181–182, 188. *See also* Polk, Sarah Childress

Woodbury, Levi, 303; and 1844 Democratic national convention, 114, 121, 124–125; as member of Jackson's cabinet, 93; as member of Van Buren's cabinet, 93; as possible 1844 Democratic vice-presidential nominee, 93, 121, 124–125; receives votes for 1844 Democratic presidential nomination, 114; supports Texas annexation, 53

Woodruff, Wilford, 143

Wright, Clarissa, 99

Wright, Elizur, Jr., 169, 170

Wright, Frances, 182

Wright, Hendrick B., 111, 113, 119, 126

Wright, John Seward, 169

Wright, Silas, Jr., 178, 302; as 1844 New York gubernatorial candidate, 128, 217, 219; ally of Buchanan, 84; attempted manipulation by Tyler, 150–151; blamed as obstacle to Calhoun's possible nomination, 87; considers Polk as possible replacement presidential nominee for Van Buren, 101–102; and the Hammett letter, 99–100; and influence on 1844 election results, 217, 219; offered Supreme Court appointment, 150–151; as possible 1844 Democratic presidential nominee, 101, 109, 113, 116, 117,

Printed in the USA
CPSIA information can be obtained
at www.ICGtesting.com
CBHW021400060724
11216CB00011B/128/J

9 780700 635733